Secret Scrolls

Secret Scrolls

Revelations from the Lost Gospel Novels

Robert M. Price

WIPF & STOCK · Eugene, Oregon

SECRET SCROLLS
Revelations from the Lost Gospel Novels

Copyright © 2011 Robert M. Price. All rights reserved. Except for brief quotations in critical publications or reviews, no part of this book may be reproduced in any manner without prior written permission from the publisher. Write: Permissions, Wipf and Stock Publishers, 199 W. 8th Ave., Suite 3, Eugene, OR 97401.

Unless indicated otherwise, scripture quotations taken from the New American Standard Bible®, Copyright © 1960, 1962, 1963, 1968, 1971, 1972, 1973, 1975, 1977, 1995 by The Lockman Foundation. Used by permission. (www.Lockman.org)

Wipf & Stock
An Imprint of Wipf and Stock Publishers
199 W. 8th Ave., Suite 3
Eugene, OR 97401

www.wipfandstock.com

ISBN 13: 978-1-61097-075-4

Manufactured in the U.S.A.

To Steven M. Stiles,
a plastered cistern that loseth not a drop.

Contents

Introduction: The Romance of Imaginary New Testament Scholarship | 1

1. Higher Critical Hoax | 7
2. Raiders of the Lost Gospel | 14
3. Mystery in the Monastery | 19
4. The Q Connection | 34
5. Strangers in a Cave | 43
6. Harpooning the Fish | 47
7. Evangel and Espionage | 63
8. The Gospel of Cain and Abel | 78
9. Pontius is my Co-Pilate | 85
10. Remembrance of Lives Past | 93
11. The Real (Strange) Bible | 104
12. Dem Dry Bones | 108
13. Bad News Oracle | 114
14. It's in the Vault | 117
15. Frisky Father Folan | 123
16. Looking for Luke | 129
17. Under the Lid | 135
18. But I'm Not Dead Yet! | 143
19. The Q Contender | 149
20. Profane Pilgrim | 157
21. The Hidden and the Revealed | 176

| 22 | Book of Betrayal | 183
| 23 | Messiah's Memoir | 194
| 24 | The Mother Lode | 206
| 25 | Sexy Swashbuckler | 213
| 26 | Elementary, My Dear Mary! | 218
| 27 | Nancy Drew versus Simon Magus | 222
| 28 | James M. Robinson in Strange Company | 226
| 29 | John's Gospel: The Sequel | 234
| 30 | Discovering Faith and Flesh | 239
| 31 | The Q Conundrum | 246
| 32 | The Q Conspiracy | 258
| 33 | The Merovingian | 267
| 34 | Skeleton Lock and Key | 276
| 35 | The Loosely-Conceived Gospel | 287
| 36 | Mary Maudlin | 293
| 37 | Ecumenical Revelation | 300
| 38 | Is it I, Lord? | 309
| 39 | The Ultimate Relic | 316
| 40 | Constantine's Conspiracy | 322
| 41 | Copts and Robbers | 328

Conclusion: Don't Look Now... | 334

Bibliography | 339

Introduction
The Romance of Imaginary New Testament Scholarship

> It is a fatal drawback that no historical judgment, however certain it may appear, ever attains anything more than probability. But what sort of a religion would that be which accepted a basis for its convictions with the consciousness that it was only probably safe? . . . It is a fatal error to attempt to establish the basis of faith by means of historical investigation. The basis of faith must be something fixed; the results of historical study are continually changing.
>
> —Wilhelm Herrmann, *The Communion of the Christian with God*

> The attachment of the certainty of Christian conviction to the unpredictable results of historical research [is] a stumbling block . . . I have become increasingly certain that my Christian faith cannot have a causal connection with the "authenticity" of the Gospels.
>
> —Martin Kähler, *The So-called Historical Jesus and the Historic Biblical Christ*

I AM ABOUT TO be your guide on a tour of a very specific literary genre, a sub-genre of the mystery adventure. We are embarking on an examination of some forty books in which someone discovers either a new, hitherto-unknown gospel or the body of Jesus Christ, or both. Sometimes the discovery will turn out to be a hoax, in which case we will eagerly wait to see if it is debunked before it can gain publicity and work its mischief. At other times, the artifact will prove quite real. Then we will be left wondering whether the intrepid discoverers can bring it to light, or whether corrupt church officials can manage to prevent it. Those villains won't care if the newly discovered gospel is theologically harmless; they just don't want to rock the boat: "Our present New Testament is fine, thank you! We don't need any more books added to it!"

But in some of our adventures, the new find will not be merely a reiteration of what we already had; it will threaten to "blow the lid off" Christianity! Sometimes the pious villains succeed in suppressing the discovery in the name of the sacred status quo. In other cases, it will be the discoverers themselves who suppress or destroy it, fearing the wide-scale chaos that might otherwise ensue. And occasionally we will encounter an author who has enough imagination to depict what might happen should the new gospel (or, in one case, news of the Jesus corpse) become publicly known. And then we are in for a wild ride!

In this literary tour, I will devote some space—usually not a great deal—to summarizing the basic plot of each work, using most of my pages to evaluate what the author has to say about historical Jesus scholarship or New Testament research in general. Some of those authors have done their homework, and they manage to give the reader a bit of an education while spinning their yarns. Other ones don't bother, and they wind up dishing up Sunday School platitudes, followed up with crazy rewrites of history and outlandish theories. What they finally produce is the laughable equivalent of a science fiction story positing breathable atmosphere on the moon, like Robert Bloch's *Flowers from the Moon*.

But in my opinion as both a writer and an editor of fiction, virtually every one of these books is well written and genuinely imaginative. All are fun to read, and most are real page turners. They are meant to entertain, not to educate, though some of their authors apparently realize that there is no drawback in doing both at the same time. I realize that the scholarly angle is not uppermost to the writers of these novels or to most of their readers. But I have to admit as well that my own interest in these books (kindled first by the 1972 publication of Irving Wallace's *The Word*) stemmed from my preoccupation (even as a college freshman) with Christian apologetics and New Testament research. I already loved science fiction and fantasy novels, and here came a sub-genre that combined speculative adventure fiction with biblical studies! It was a literary love affair that has continued to this day, with an ever-flowing stream of these books. It is about time someone analyzed the genre, and I am happy to be the one to do it.

Introduction 3

DIGGING UP THE SUBTEXT

Beneath the glittering excitement and adventure on the surface of these novels, the reader must suspect there is a subtext, one dealing with abiding and uncomfortable issues of religious faith. This subtext is not buried very deeply, though. Virtually every one of the Lost Gospel novels, for example, features a desperate band of churchmen (usually the Roman Catholic hierarchy, some Black Ops group within it, or some quasi-heretical zealots secretly parasitic upon it) who oppose the newly discovered text. They try their best to prevent, suppress, or destroy the Lost Gospel in order to protect the status quo and the authority of the Church.

Their anxiety is quite real, and that is where the epigraphic quotations at the head of this chapter from Wilhelm Herrmann and Martin Kähler come in. The attempts to suppress newly discovered gospels cannot be dismissed as the mere reflexes of hierarchies and bureaucracies who want to squelch new discoveries, like those nefarious Big Corporations that have allegedly bought up and hidden energy-saving inventions to protect their profits—a parallel drawn in Irving Wallace's *The Word*. No, every intellectually alert believer struggles with the same fears, even without some new discovery setting off the alarm. As soon as you become aware of the utility of biblical apologetics (the discipline of refuting skeptical objections to the Bible and its miracles), you have stepped onto the unstable, marshy ground of probabilistic arguments, an entirely different epistemology (way of "knowing") that automatically replaces the simple faith in whose name it was first invoked.

The would-be defender of the faith, unless he is absolutely cynical, has embraced what Tillich called "methodological doubt"[1] as soon as he sees the need to scrutinize arguments before he brings them to bear in debate, lest he sound like a fool, speaking inanities he knows he cannot defend. And so he comes to hold his religious convictions more rationally, and thus more tentatively, having become genuinely vulnerable to new evidence and better ways of understanding the evidence. He may not remain a believer for long.

Having already passed from real faith to more-or-less confident opinions, he may yet graduate to "merely" juggling possibilities, paradigms, and rival theories, like a sort of butterfly collector. Each step

---

1. Tillich, *Dynamics of Faith*, 19.

along this journey to genuine intellectual honesty is an attempt to rid oneself of what Sartre called "bad faith" (*mauvaise foi*),[2] the opposite of sincere conviction. One begins with satisfaction at the wonderful verities in which one believes. Then the thought occurs: "But what if something should come up to unbalance the equation?" Then one's faith is dangerously predicated on the dubious assurance that nothing new *will* come up, that no new discovery will send one back to the drawing board.

Actually, all historical apologetics rests on such a questionable basis. When the exponent of a historical, bodily resurrection shoots down (as he supposes) every proposed naturalistic explanation for the empty tomb, and then proclaims as the winner his own belief (stemming from Sunday School catechism) that God raised Jesus from the dead, he is betting that no other alternative will ever present itself. Every real historian, by contrast, knows good and well that new data may always pop up from some unexpected quarter. It is miserable obscurantism to tell oneself and others to be confident that no further information will be forthcoming, and to be glad about it! If new data did come to light, is it far-fetched to imagine such an uneasy believer trying to suppress or to minimize it? And that's what the pious villains in our novels are doing, and that's why.

"I believe that Jesus is risen! Er, at least as long as no new evidence or argument shows otherwise... Er, ah. Hallelujah..." That, as Herrmann and Kähler recognized, is no real faith. But neither is the foolishness of betting one's soul on the prospect that all the results are already in.

Our Lost Gospel novels are, on one level, narrative dramatizations of this dilemma. Sometimes, as anthropologist Claude Levi-Strauss showed,[3] a problem not susceptible to rational solution may instead be "mediated" by being narratized as a myth. Maybe that is what is really happening here.

WOULD YOU BETRAY THE SON OF MAN WITH A SPADE?

But also lurking an inch or so beneath the surface of these novels, I suspect, is the vitriol of the disappointed believer. People disappointed by religion, whether abused by jack-booted nuns or loud-mouthed preachers—or by sophisticated medicine show apologists—may relish the prospect of seeing their old enemy taken down by some new discov-

---

2. Sartre, *Being and Nothingness*, 86–116.
3. Levi-Strauss, *Structural Anthropology*, 212.

ery that debunks the authority of their old slave-masters. Some scholars see Morton Smith's likely fabrication of his Secret Gospel of Mark as stemming from such motivation. (Again, Irving Wallace synthesizes such venom better than anyone else, as we shall see.) Writing novels in which this actually happens is good therapy as well as good art, if one is fortunate. I certainly don't mean to complain!

I think it is quite interesting, as we survey the Lost Gospel novels, to assess what each author imagines it would take to derail and debunk Christianity, since that is usually what is at stake. How mighty a blow must be dealt before the religion would fall dead on the mat? Some authors, like Dan Brown with his cherished notion that a married Jesus would debunk the Nicene Creed, seem to have a pretty superficial picture of Christianity as a glass-jawed champion who will go down for the count in the first round.

But this sword cuts both ways. Our novels frequently do a wonderful job of depicting a rancid faith, one that has degenerated into a mere party-line position paper, rote repetition of the talking points. This is a "faith" that is merely blind obedience to the Grand Inquisitor, a faith which need not concern itself with facts at all, lest one lose one's berth on the heaven-bound choo-choo.

So the Lost Gospel novels pose a challenge to faith by the simple trick of depicting the challenge to faith posed by shocking gospel discoveries. We are missing a crucial opportunity to test, and to grow, our faith if we read these books for mere entertainment's sake (as entertaining as they certainly are!). And this fact necessitates my two-pronged approach. This is going to be a unique and (and I hope) quite powerful book. It will weave history in with a review of fiction in a way I doubt you have seen done before. I want to teach you, my readers, about real scriptural discoveries as well as astonishing developments in biblical scholarship while also introducing you to a smorgasbord of (mostly) interesting fictional works.

Wilbert Francis Howard once argued in his brief and fascinating history of New Testament research[4] that there is a genuine "romance of New Testament scholarship." Those of us who enjoy that adventure, who regard F. C. Baur, Rudolf Bultmann, David Friedrich Strauss, and Albert Schweitzer as so many Indiana Joneses, are always delighted to have the adventure continue, even if only in the speculative imaginations of

---

4. Howard, *The Romance of New Testament Scholarship*.

Irving Wallace, Robert Ludlum, Barbara Rogers, and other capable novelists. Let's strap on our backpacks and get going, shall we?

Robert M. Price
March 29, 2010

1 | Higher Critical Hoax

Guy Thorne, *When It Was Dark:*
The Story of a Great Conspiracy

CHISELER AT THE TOMB

THE EARLIEST MEMBER OF the literary species we are considering in this book is a 1904 novel by Guy Thorne, *When It Was Dark*. No extensive text worthy of the tag "gospel" is discovered. The ruckus fictively chronicled here is rather more on the order of the recent hubbub over the discovery of the "Jesus Family Tomb" in Talpiot, Israel. The world of the late nineteenth century is turned upside down by the report of the discovery of a new candidate for the last resting place of the remains of Jesus Christ. Located outside the Damascus Gate of Jerusalem, the newly uncovered tomb bears the inscription "I, Joseph of Arimathea, took the body of Jesus, the Nazarene, from the tomb where it was first laid and hid it in this place" (p. 197). Some organic residue is scraped up, but we never hear of a verdict on whose it was. It's a moot point, though, because the whole thing turns out to be a hoax. We are not only not surprised; we couldn't be surprised if we wanted to be because the beans get spilled early on. The goal is not to string the reader along, as we might expect in a mystery. It is rather to chart the course—as the novel's subtitle says—of a master plan, its disastrous fruits, and its eventual collapse.

The faking of the tomb inscription is the brainchild of one Constantine Shuabe, a prominent British (and Jewish) philanthropist and leader of English secularism. He is in cahoots with Professor Robert Llwellyn, the leading British exponent of the Higher Criticism of scripture. That affiliation spells trouble right up front, since the author of this novel is an Evangelical Anglican. "Higher Critic of scripture" likely—no, definitely—equals "villain." It seems the professor has been borrowing large sums from the Jewish secularist for the upkeep of his mistress,

Gertrude Hunt, a musical comedy actress. Once Llwellyn has got in deep enough, Shuabe blackmails him into applying his antiquarian skills to archaeological fraud. The ordinary course of debate and polemic is apparently not effective enough to suit Shuabe; he wishes to expedite the passing of orthodox Christianity into the dustbin of history. And definitive proof that Jesus did not rise physically from the tomb ought to do the trick! Indeed, it does! Or very nearly so. One Church of England clergyman describes the situation:

> The recent "discovery" in Palestine, which appears to do away with the Resurrection of Christ, is in my opinion entirely responsible for the increase of crime ... Now that the Incarnation is on all hands said to be a myth, the greatest restraint upon human passion is removed. (p. 304)

Not only is there a great increase in violent street crime in Britain, but America is subject to constant rioting, even on the verge of civil war. The British Empire is fragmenting as the Christian glue somehow holding it together gives way. Muslims massacre Christians in the Ottoman Empire. Slavery returns. Attendance in the traditional churches, both the Church of England and Dissenting sects (Baptists, Congregationalists, Methodists, etc.) shrinks, their former members either gleefully throwing off former restraints to go a-wenching and blaspheming to their hearts' content, or swelling the ranks of Unitarian congregations. But among Protestants, as well as the "C of E," one can find without too much difficulty pietist conventicles gathered in faithful prayer, undisturbed by the so-called discoveries of the scholarly elite. Roman Catholics and Greek Orthodox hierarchies have declared the discovery a fraud and forbidden their flocks to think about it or even to speak of it among themselves. Their docile sheep survive unthinking but unscathed.

Two bombs are exploding side by side. On the one hand, Guy Thorne seems to imagine the Christian faith as a metaphysical force of good, preventing the utter moral chaos that should otherwise ensue. He makes it tantamount to the Reformed doctrine of Common Grace, a divinely imposed brake on the otherwise inevitable results of Original Sin. When Christianity seems to collapse under proof that the tomb of Jesus was not empty, except by natural decay, it is as if "there is one restraining it right now till it is taken out of the way" (2 Thess 2:7),[1] and then,

---

1. Price, *The Pre-Nicene New Testament*, 436.

like a table cloth yanked out from under the dinnerware by an inept stage magician, the restrainer *is* taken away: everything goes flying. And crashing. Even the financial system, for some reason. It is obvious, then, that our author has no great confidence in the moral power of Judaism, Unitarianism, Islam, Hinduism, or plain old secularism.

Second—and this makes a bit more sense—Thorne depicts the vengeful hatred of the disappointed faithful. "Surely in vain I have kept my heart pure, and washed my hands in innocence; for I have been stricken all day long, and chastened every morning.... When my heart was embittered, and I was pierced within, then I was senseless and ignorant; I was like a beast before Thee" (Ps 73:13–14, 21–22 KJV). However, one may question whether even such disillusionment as Thorne describes could have such drastic effects. I am reminded of one of Jack T. Chick's most (unwittingly) hilarious *Crusaders* comic books, *Sabotage?* In it, a wide-eyed Bible College student is affronted (to say the least) to learn that his professor does not believe that the 1611 King James Version is based on manuscripts verbatim identical with the original Greek autographs of the first century. This shocking revelation shatters both the lad's faith and, seemingly, his very sanity, as he leaps over the classroom desks and attempts to stuff his Bible down the throat of the "modernist" professor (who only believes what Benjamin B. Warfield believed!), then is apprehended trying to set the school on fire! It's a bit much. And it is disturbing to see someone depict his own religion as essentially so fanatical that a true believer, despoiled of his faith, would become a maniac.

WHERE IS THE THREAT?

Thorne has a character raise a very good point: would most people, Christian or not, ever reckon with either the fact of the discovery or its implications? Personally, I doubt it. I suspect it would remain of concern only to debaters, skeptics, apologists, and clergy. But even if it were but a teapot tempest, what exactly would the shouting be about? There are two points of theological confusion. First, Thorne's characters appear to believe the problem would be that the discovery of Jesus' tomb, from which his resuscitated flesh-body failed to emerge, would debunk the Godhood of Jesus Christ. For Thorne, Christian faith in Jesus is simply this: "You know that Christ is God!" (p. 47). One priest advises another: "In all your teaching and preaching hammer away at the great central fact of the

Incarnation . . . Preach the Incarnation day in day out" (p. 114). But this begs a great many questions that remained to vex Christian thinkers for three centuries after the first Easter. It is not clear, to me at least, that the resurrection of Jesus, even if it happened, would imply Trinitarianism. The two doctrines (the deity of Christ and the resurrection of Christ) have little to do with one another, even if both are true.

Second, Thorne appears to believe that Christianity is done for, cooked, if the gospels' resurrection narratives (Matt 28, Mark 13; Luke 24, and John 20–21) turn out not to have been accurate. What, after all, does the Joseph of Arimathea inscription appear to debunk? It contradicts, very specifically, the notion that the absence of Jesus' corpse—from the tomb in which Joseph buried it immediately after the crucifixion—was due to Jesus having risen from the dead. It would mean that the resurrection was a hasty and gratuitous inference by Mary Magdalene et. al. The tomb was empty because the body had already been moved elsewhere for permanent burial (John 20:15), and it was that second burial place which had now ostensibly been found. But is the resurrection preaching of the early church simply to be identified with the empty tomb narratives?

It is striking that the empty tomb is never mentioned in any epistle or in the Acts of the Apostles. First Corinthians Chapter 15 is by far the most extensive discussion of the resurrection, explicitly of believers united with Christ, implicitly of Christ himself. Yet it makes no mention of a tomb found unoccupied or attended by angels or of the witness of pious women. In fact, it seems to argue for a resurrection of a "spiritual body" or "pneumatic body" that leaves the dead flesh-husk behind like the discarded seed shell once the flower emerges. If Christians believed in such a resurrection as this, they would not bother inquiring to see if the burial place of Jesus were empty or occupied. If it were tenanted, what would they care?

It is not as if Guy Thorne was unaware of this alternative version of resurrection faith. The "spiritual body" interpretation (p. 226) is sneered at as "this flimsy pretense of reconciling of statements, which, if true, made Christianity a thing of nought, to a novel and trumped-up system of adherence to it" (p. 229). But this is to mischaracterize what is an exegetically solid reading of the key New Testament text on the character of the resurrection body. The spiritual resurrection idea is not some cheap jury-rigged substitute for the *real* doctrine of resurrection. What is so offensive about it that, if it should prevail as the Christian resurrection doctrine, all would be lost for Christianity? I think the answer is that the Joseph inscription, debunking the gospel Easter stories, would threaten not the doctrine of Jesus' resurrection, which could still stand solidly as the teaching of 1 Corinthians 15, but rather *the doctrine of biblical inerrancy*. And this would be fatal for faith because the whole enterprise is built upon the will to believe that whatever seemingly improbable thing the Bible tells us must be true. Otherwise, how to establish even the existence of Jesus? His virginal conception? Any single miracle or teaching ascribed to him?

Once one realizes that some biblical statements might be true while others are false, one must resort to something other than pure fideism to decide which is which, and then one is assuming the role of an historian, weighing and rejecting sources. One is no longer recognizing *any* text, much less *all*, as an authority binding one to belief. And then we are left to measure our heads for wearing two very different hats simultaneously. The historian makes only provisional and tentative judgment calls, because he knows new evidence may show up and cast a new light on everything. But the believer feels he cannot be satisfied with such "double-mindedness." He must make a faith decision now and stick to it, come hell or high water.

Those two attitudes are like fire and water, utterly incompatible. Some claim they can maintain them both, but they inevitably wind up cheating. Christian apologists who pretend to offer "the scientific and historical evidences for the truth of the Resurrection ... the overwhelming and stupendous evidences for the truth of the Gospel narratives" (p. 122) begin and end in a pathetic attempt to rationalize, by any trick in the book, a belief based not on evidence but on the sheer will to believe. In the end, many such apologists' consciences get the best of them, and they switch sides, becoming genuine "Higher Critics" like those whom Thorne ruthlessly caricatures in this book. It is a wrenching struggle both of intellect and of conscience, an issue that has been the subject of much searching inquiry for a couple of centuries now.

AN EPISTEMOLOGY OF SENTIMENT

There is a great danger implied in both the fundamentalist repudiation of historical criticism on the one hand and the liberal quest for the historical Jesus on the other. Both approaches in the last analysis tend to make the believer's faith in Jesus dependent on the probabilities of historical research. Fundamentalists find themselves defending the most precarious and improbable apologetical arguments in order to safeguard the gospel-portrait of Jesus as historically inerrant. Liberals' reconstructions of Jesus and his teachings are so tenuous and arbitrary that no two liberals come up with the same reconstruction! In both cases, not only is it true that faith is being trivialized to the level of holding more or less probable opinions, but the believer is deprived of any real security of faith. His confidence is either suspended on a thin apologetical thread ready to snap at any moment, or it is blown about by every wind of changing historical theory. Surely faith must rest on a more certain foundation, immune from the uncertainties of historical scholarship.

Guy Thorne puts the same insight well when one of his characters describes the perpetual plight of the would-be believer who, e.g., fears or cheers the latest vote tallies of the Jesus Seminar. They "sit anxiously waiting to know the precise value which this or that Gospel may possess, as its worth fluctuates like shares in the money market, with the last quotation!" (p. 208).

Thorne's favorite characters share what we might call a "faith *über alles*" stance. Their Christian experience of their personal savior Jesus renders them invulnerable to any doubts produced by the discovery of the Joseph inscription that destroyed the faith of so many others:

> I have seen the paper and read of this so-called discovery, too. Of course such a thing harmonises exactly with the opinions of those who want to believe it. But go and tell a devoted son of the Church that he has been fed with sacraments which are no sacraments, and all that he has done has been at best the honest mistake of a deceived man, he will laugh in your face, as I do! There are memories far back in his life of confirmation, when his whole being was quickened and braced, which refuse to be explained as the hallucinations of a well-meaning but deceived man. There are memories when Christ drew near to his soul and helped him ...You are incapable of understanding the heart to which experience has made it clear that Jesus was indeed the very Christ ... But if we *know* Him, if we can look back over a life richer and fuller because we *have* known Him ... then your explorers may discover anything and we shall not believe. (p. 208–9)

All over England the serene triumph of the Gospel, deep, deep down in the hearts of quiet people, gave the eternal lie to Shuabe and his followers. Never could they overcome the Risen Lord in the human heart. (p. 263)

I sat down and cried, to think that there would never be any Jesus any more to save poor girls ... And as I sat there I saw that it *couldn't* be true that Jesus was just a good man, and not God ... If the paper was right then why was it I was so happy, happier than ever before in my life ...? Why was it that I could see Jesus in my walks, hear the wind praying—feel that everything was speaking of Him? (p. 283)

ALL TOLD

In the end, plotwise, the two conspirators come to bad ends when (thanks to the detective work performed by hardy Anglican priests and a Christian newspaper editor) the hoax is exposed. While the Christians live happily ever after, biblical critic Llwellyn receives a visit from an angry mob, presumably of outraged Christians (!) who proceed to lynch him. Constantine Shuabe goes insane and is incarcerated in a loony bin, where, with other sideshow freaks, he is on exhibit to visiting gawkers who do little to hide their contempt for the fallen villain. What becomes evident after reading Guy Thorne's work is that he means to tell us that all biblical criticism, Higher Criticism, is essentially a great hoax intended to upset the faith of the pious, whether or not it involves gross imposture like the faking of ossuaries, inscriptions, or gospels.

2 | Raiders of the Lost Gospel
Arthur Train, *The Lost Gospel*

PULP THEOLOGY

Arthur Train's *The Lost Gospel* first appeared in the pages of *The Saturday Evening Post* (June 7, 1924) and was reprinted as a separate book by Charles Scribner's Sons in 1925.[1] Though published in one of the high-class "slicks," it has a decidedly pulp magazine feel to it and would have been at home in *Magic Carpet* or *Oriental Stories*. It is in fact highly reminiscent, if one knows about it, of Robert E. Howard's tale, "The Fire of Asshurbanipal." Such fictions have lately become all the rage once again in the wake of 1980's *Raiders of the Lost Ark* and its sequels (and imitators). Only, whereas most of these stories involve the search for holy relics believed to possess occult power or great monetary value, Arthur Train makes a gospel text the object of search. It is not the physical manuscript so much as the long-lost knowledge that is about to be rediscovered. And thus does he create a new sub-genre of mystery-adventure.

The Lost Gospel opens with a lazy sunset gathering of the idle rich on the Nile in British colonial Egypt. With the kind of providential prescience one expects only in fiction, the party is discussing the present doldrums into which the Christian religion has fallen, with the suggestion that, if some fresh new gospel containing unknown and newly relevant sayings of Jesus were to come to light, that might be just the spark needed to ignite Christian revitalization. There has even been rumored, one of them mentions, the existence of a Lost Gospel or Fifth Gospel hidden away in the lost, sand-buried city of Kurafra. Then another bored Westerner, Hugh Calthrop, joins the circle, displaying a letter he has just received from an old acquaintance, a fellow Egyptologist named Paul

---

1. All page references are to the book version.

Trent, dead some ten years. It has taken this long for a letter from Trent, once passed along through some Arab trader, to make it to Calthrop. The letter tantalizes with the report of a great, even earth-shaking discovery Trent has made on an expedition in the company of the great scholar-adventurer Max Harnach-Hulsen. (It is hard not to think this name a combination of tongue-in-cheek references to Max Müller, Orientalist and founder of the Sacred Books of the East series, and the prolific New Testament and Early Christianity scholar Adolf von Harnack.) No such discovery was ever reported; what could it have been? On the spot, Calthrop resolves, having nothing better to do, to make his way to Bukhara, whence the letter stemmed, and to try to retrace the late Trent's mysterious steps.

This he manages to do, enduring pretty much the same scorching desert sun and winds and fickle loyalties of superstitious native guides that Trent had suffered. He finds lost Kurafra which seems to appear and reappear from time to time, like Brigadoon, because of the shifting of the sands that can drown it for decades at a time. Once there, it is without too much additional difficulty that he finds a small pyramid and a metal box in which the Lost Gospel (for of course that was the great discovery of Trent) had once been deposited. Only it is absent. The box still does contain some letters, one from Kaiser Wilhelm who financed the expedition, and whom the explorer Harnach-Hulsen idolized as the very incarnation of Germany's noble warlike spirit. Another, which suspiciously stops in mid-sentence, is a sequel to the earlier one from Trent, explaining the discovery, the announcement of which Trent then thought imminent. These old papers accompany an ornate Roman gladius, or short sword, which Trent had found with the papyrus. It seems both had belonged to a young Roman officer named Gaius Marcus Claudius Silenus, who had interviewed the captive Jesus while the latter awaited trial before Pilate.

This Silenus prepared a report to Emperor Tiberius. He began the report, containing many "new" teachings of Jesus on peacemaking and the relations of nations (among other things), in Jerusalem but must needs take it to his next posting, on a hunt for Kurafra. There he met death at the hands of robbers who stored their loot in the pyramid that Trent and Harnach-Hulsen discovered. While Calthrop sits there amid a sandstorm, half-sensing disembodied voices of the past, he falls into a vision in which he finds himself witnessing the whole of history as if rapidly moving back through it, a scene not unlike that undergone by

Halpin Chalmers in Frank Belknap Long's "The Hounds of Tindalos." The function of the vision is to reinforce the actantial identity between the earlier Trent and the later Calthrop as two instantiations of the same narrative function. As he slides along the thrusting blade of time's advance and retreat, Calthrop in effect becomes what the structure of the narrative has already revealed him to be: Trent at another stage of the plot, revealing to the reader what "he" had earlier come to the edge of revealing in his first letter.

So what happened to the Lost Gospel? With the help of an Arab guide who had been along for the original expedition, Caltrop determines that poor Trent's letter, the one contained in the metal box, was cut short. Why? Because his senior partner, Dr. Harnach-Hulsen, having read the gospel text and seen the damage it could cause to Imperial German militarism, resolved that it should not see the light of day: he incinerated the papyrus after stabbing Trent with the ancient sword of Silenus! The Arab servitors feared they should inherit the blame for the murder, so they killed the eminent Harnach-Hulsen and presumably placed the letters and the sword in the metal casket for the sand to devour.

The symbolism of the Roman sword being found without the gospel that threatened to blunt its edge is powerful. So is the resonance with other biblical motifs, such as that of the persecution of the newborn prophet-messiah by the wicked rulers of this world, whether Pharaoh or Herod the Great. Only this time they succeeded in strangling the Fifth Gospel in its metal cradle before it had a chance to move out into the world and to redeem it. In this way, Arthur Train laments a world so addicted to war that it has proven itself unworthy of redemption. We must think of the Wisdom tradition (Prov 8:22–36; 1 Enoch 42:1–3) according to which Divine Wisdom appeared on earth to invite mortals to seek a higher way, only to be rebuffed and to return to heaven in disgust.

Of course, the pessimism of the story may be illusory, the reason for the destruction of the gospel due to a different consideration altogether. Perhaps Train felt it would open his modest literary exercise way too wide if he were to "end" it with the propagation of the new gospel and the resultant renovation of human affairs. To hint at such a thing without delivering on it might have seemed too much of a cheat. In the same way, when asked why he did not end his horror tale "The Dunwich Horror"[2] with the anticipated invasion of the interdimensional Old Ones to wipe

---

2. *Weird Tales*, April 1929, 481–508.

our planet clean of human life, H. P. Lovecraft admitted that such an ending would have involved far too wide a scope and much more of an epic than he had in mind to write. It was far more economical to clamp the artery. And this in any case is what Arthur Train wound up doing. We will see several more Lost Gospel novelists making the same decision, though occasionally one will go the whole way, as we shall see in Chapter 6 with Irving Wallace's *The Word*, perhaps the best of all these books.

Why does Train implicate Adolf Harnack in the villainy of the murdering fanatic Harnach-Hulsen? Perhaps he did not mean to. It may be that it was only the aspect of the character's being a scholar of ancient discoveries that led Train to borrow Harnack's name for him. But there may be more to it. When young Swiss pastor Karl Barth was stunned one day to find in the newspaper an endorsement of Kaiser Wilhelm's militarism signed by his old seminary professors,[3] it so shook him that he had to step back and evaluate his whole theology. His elite and erudite mentors had all subscribed to "Kulturprotestantismus," the Hegelian conviction that the will of God could be discerned as the guiding force of German culture and the German state. If such a belief could lead to a baptism of bloodthirsty militarism, Barth realized the whole approach had been reduced to absurdity. To replace it, he created the Bible-centered approach of Neo-Orthodoxy. Guess whose name was prominent in black and white endorsing German imperialism? There was Herr Professor Harnach, er, Harnack. Arthur Train's name game winds up as a piece of penetrating satire, whether or not he so intended it.

In a post script to *The Lost Gospel*, Train relates a weird episode that might have gone nicely into the book had he found a place for it. He tells how in early 1924 he entered the library of the University Club in New York City, planning to begin his narrative. He had done his research and planned the whole thing out. Now he found a single book left on the table: William Schuyler's 1906 novel *Under Pontius Pilate*. This book was ostensibly derived from the Latin letters of a young Roman officer named Caius Claudius Proclus, who paralleled Train's own character Gaius Marcus Claudius Silenus in astonishing detail, not the least of which was that both were imagined as cousin to Procula, Pilate's wife. Both had been traveling from Armenia and Cappadocia to Egypt and as witnessing various gospel scenes on the way. The odd thing is: Train had never heard of either Schuyler or his book! And now how came it to be resting, as if lying in wait to mock him, in such strange circumstances?

---

3. Rumscheidt, *Revelation and Theology*, 202–3, n. 54.

SERMON FODDER

Methodist preacher Robert F. Luccock borrowed the title of this story for a sermon he preached about it, and the sermon became the title piece of a 1948 collection: *The Lost Gospel*. Much in the spirit of Luke 16:29, 31 ("They have Moses and the Prophets; let them heed the scriptures . . . Look, if they are deaf to Moses and the Prophets, they'd find a way to discount someone rising from the dead, too!"),[4] Luccock deflates the popular dream of a lost gospel document whose discovery would renew Christianity.

> But there is a lost gospel! Not lost in the obvious sense of being buried in the sands of a desert, but lost in the sands of neglect and indifference. The *real* lost gospel is in Matthew, Mark, Luke and John . . . The essence of the gospels is scarcely on the page, and when those who can creatively interpret it and reveal it are gone, the gospel is lost. The discovery of ten more gospels would not change anything in the world. Their essence must be reborn in every age in the lives of those who live it.[5]

There is a Buddhist analogy to the Christian hope for the discovery of a lost gospel, and that is the expectation of Maitreya Buddha. The hope is that a new Buddha's eventual advent will usher in a golden age in which it will become easy for people to renounce ego and craving and to commit themselves without reserve to the Buddhist dharma. Obviously, such a doctrine has despaired of any hope for religious revival in the present, in the mundane world. This may be the result either of a period of genuine decadence and backsliding or of unrealistic measurement of the Buddhist community against the picture of a mythic "time of beginnings," as when Acts 2:41 imagines Peter converting three thousand souls with a single sermon on the day of Pentecost.[6] What an insult to the dharma that Buddhists already possess; to think it is not powerful enough to suffice for every burdened soul! And likewise, Luccock protests, the hope of an invigorating gospel discovery is to shortchange the gospels we already possess and to damn them with faint praise.

---

4. Price, *The Pre-Nicene New Testament*, 543.
5. Luccock, *The Lost Gospel*, 2–3.
6. Wilken, *The Myth of Christian Beginnings*.

3 | Mystery in the Monastery
J. H. Hunter, *The Mystery of Mar Saba*

MUSCULAR ANTI-CHRISTIANITY

THIS OFT-REPRINTED 1940 NOVEL partakes of both adventure and evangelistic genres. I suspect the author's aim was to write a page-turner that an evangelical Christian reader could enjoy and pass on to an unconverted friend who might be affected by the not-so-subtle pitch for conversion repeated periodically throughout the story. Such a hybrid aim might be thought a sure recipe for literary disaster (like certain other efforts at born-again propaganda one might mention). But J. H. Hunter manages to pull it off. His is an advertisement for "muscular Christianity"—a term, often used in connection with baseball player evangelist Billy Sunday, that Hunter actually has a character use only half-ironically. That becomes almost cartoonishly clear as we keep meeting muscular Christians—young, virile, white men who do not hesitate to punch out Arab assassins and German plotters, and whose minds are pure of corrupting doctrines like evolution (pp. 67, 216) or limited inerrancy. By my count, there are three nearly identical protagonists who have been thus cloned mainly to spread out that literary role's availability to simultaneously cover several points in the developing action. Joining them in the action are a small group of interchangeable Nazi subversionists, a handful of hard-to-distinguish Arab allies, a pair of beautiful, blonde Christian fiancées, a pair of biblical scholars (one seeking the answer the other provides), and a set of "managers" of the gospel crisis. They include the evangelical editor of *The Times*, the head of Scotland Yard and the Archbishop of Canterbury, plus his opposite number, the impotent, blithering (and Unitarian!) Prime Minister.

The novel partakes of a certain Victorian and post-Victorian British stiff-upper-lip seriousness, back-lit by a sentimentality that, to this day, remains powerful enough to convince educated audiences when logic runs short. (I once remarked, during a friendly debate with the great English evangelical apologist Michael Green, that I might as well give up at the start because Green's delivery was so winsome it was more convincing than anything I might say!) The cultural and rhetorical cards are stacked against the unbeliever in a narrative universe set in the British Empire between the wars. The "plausibility structure" implied in and underlying the story is that of a Christian England and her hegemony over the swarthy peoples of the East and Near East. In fact, Hunter makes it explicit that Christian doctrine is the marrow and mortar of British imperialism:

> Has it ever struck you, sir, what a testimony this is to the spiritual basis on which our nation rests? Who would have believed that the greatness of the Empire was rooted and grounded in spiritual things, and that the resurrection of our Lord was the foundation stone on which it rests? (p. 400)

> The empty tomb still remains the symbol of the Christian faith and hope of the people of Britain. It is no dead Christ on a crucifix that we worship as a Protestant nation, but a living, loving, reigning Saviour. It is faith in this Living One that has made this people great, and extended the boundaries of our Empire to the uttermost parts of the earth. (p. 408)

THE ULTRA SECRET GOSPEL

Nazi Germany is the enemy in this novel. While that might well be natural for a British author writing at the onset of World War II, it is ironic to recall how the conservative Neo-Orthodoxy of Karl Barth was sparked as a reaction to exactly such "culture Protestantism" as *The Mystery of Mar Saba* gladly ascribes to Britain: the spirit and goals of Britain and Jesus Christ are one and the same—except insofar as pesky Marxists, Unitarians, theological Modernists, and Higher Critics of scripture seek to lead the British faithful astray. Barth repudiated German Protestant endorsement of the Kaiser's imperialism as a false idol; Hunter roots for the British version as the hand of God in history.

But in this book the nefarious Nazis do not seek to clothe their expansionism in the saintly robes of Christianity. Far from it: their scheme is to debilitate Britain, on the eve of a planned invasion, by shattering her people's faith in the resurrection of Jesus. To this end their fiendish agents have blackmailed the world's greatest ancient manuscript scholar, one Peter Yphantis, into fabricating *The Shred of Nicodemus*, a parchment strip containing the admission of Nicodemus that, in order to keep the corpse of Jesus out of profane hands, they had removed it from Joseph's garden tomb and reinterred it beneath Absalom's Pillar in the Kidron Valley. Why record their act, then, providing a map for any grave defilers who might read it? They had heard of the spreading resurrection belief, a gross mistake as they were in a unique position to know, and they hoped to nip it in the bud. Their motive was simply to correct a mistake (pp. 398–99). They wouldn't have been trying to bring down a great world religion. Christianity had not reached such proportions yet. But it had in the twentieth century, and Hitler's minions were trying to bring it down—around the pious ears of the English.

The diabolical scheme succeeds immediately, once the discovery is dutifully reported by Sir William Bracebridge (a fictional counterpart to apologist/archaeologist Sir William Ramsay, unless I miss my guess), who, to his credit, feels a duty to make the facts known, no matter what their result. (Another character echoes the sentiment: "I have the inward assurance, the witness within my heart that Christ lives, but that does not absolve us from our duty as scientists in giving this ancient manuscript to the world. We would be recreant to the faith we profess did we do otherwise," p. 296.)

All manner of moral decay and financial ruin proceed apace in both Britain and America:

> In the United States, fierce riots that broke out in Chicago, Pittsburgh and Los Angeles had left scores of dead. Communism was increasing so fast that the police were unable to cope with the demonstrations taking place, and tens of thousands of police had been added . . . In India the Nationalist party was clamoring for the expulsion of all Christian missionaries, since they said Christianity was founded on a fraud. (p. 314)

The reader might well ask why the lords of Germany did not fear such "moral disintegration" among their own populace? The answer: Hunter implies they were already much farther down the same road. What had effectively killed Christianity in Germany? The erosion of the people's faith in the scriptures by means, not of an elaborate practical joke, but through the insidious influence of the Higher Criticism, i.e., the historical-critical method. Scientific criticism since the days of pioneering scholars F. C. Baur, Julius Wellhausen, Abraham Kuenen, and D. F. Strauss[1] had indeed blown biblical literalism out of the water. British biblical scholars assimilated many of the results of the Higher Criticism, as it was called, but only with great difficulty, including heresy trials for pioneers like Bishop Colenso[2] of the Church of England and James Robertson Smith[3] in the Church of Scotland.

British moderates accepted from the new learning what they could manage to squeeze into the categories of inspiration and orthodoxy, but conservatives totally repudiated the German criticism and regarded English moderates as bearing the infectious taint.[4] Author J. H. Roberts fears the results if the Higher Criticism should prevail in England: the Empire should be lost! All men would become rapists, all women slatterns. It quickly becomes evident that Hunter means the fictitious *Shred of Nicodemus* to stand for the very real "threat" of German biblical criticism. If this were not clear enough in broad outline, the matter is clinched when we read that the mastermind of the scheme is "Professor Heimworth, noted German Higher Critic" (p. 11). His unwilling compatriot, the reluctant forger Yphantis (whose beautiful sister the fiendish Professor holds hostage and demands to marry), rebukes him:

> It is the inward faith of her people that you must first destroy, and that is rooted in the veracity of the Bible ... That faith has been weakened as you, Herr Professor, know, through the permeation of her colleges with the destructive teaching of Higher Criticism, and the use of your own textbooks in particular. (p. 15)

Would that the careful scholarship of the giants of the Higher Criticism might be as easily debunked as the *Shred of Nicodemus* (eventually) is! Once rescued from the clawed hands of Nazi Higher Critics, poor Yphantis is glad to confess his forgery performed, as it was, under great duress. Fundamentalists like to fantasize such recantations; they circulate false tales of Darwin, Voltaire, and Marx repudiating their doctrines in the hour of their death, as if that would settle anything anyway. The poor fundamentalist imagines that it would, because he is used to believing

---

1. Hodgson, *The Formation of Historical Theology*; Harris, *The Tübingen School*; Harris, *David Friedrich Strauss*; Rogerson, *Old Testament Criticism in the Nineteenth Century*.

2. Guy, *The Heretic*.

3. Rogerson, *The Bible and Criticism in Victorian Britain*.

4. Glover, Jr., *Evangelical Nonconformists and Higher Criticism*.

what he believes on the simple basis of citing authority, and he imagines that evolutionists likewise merely have faith in Darwin, Modernists in Strauss, etc. No, it is the scholarly evidence and arguments these men mounted that have convinced their readers, and those our fundamentalists are ill-equipped to meet. Nothing would change if some great "unbeliever" did recant his theories without also providing a genuine, scholarly self-refutation. It is safe to say that no one learning of Antony Flew's late and confused conversion to Theism is much moved by the simple fact of his turning coat. He would have to convince his estranged fans of his Theism as he once convinced them of his atheism. The same is true with Eta Linnemann, a one-time Bultmann protégé and critical scholar who embraced fundamentalism in her latter years. And the advice of Socrates was to "care little for Socrates but much more for the truth."[5] It has ultimately never mattered who originally propagated an idea; the idea itself was what mattered. Likewise, it hardly matters who repudiates a doctrine, even the author of it. It is the truth of the matter—insofar as we can determine it—that counts, and nothing else.

FAITH IN MID-AIR

The Mystery of Mar Saba does not rest, at least not overtly, on pure faith. If fundamentalists like its author did not suffer from failure of nerve, they would indeed rely upon pure—that is to say, arbitrary—faith, as deep down they really do. Note the amazing degree to which one of the Christian heroes is oblivious of the irony of his position. Police Chief Alderson is asked, "Why are you so sure that Jesus Christ rose from the dead?" He smiles and replies, "Because I talked with Him this morning. Because I live with Him, and Christ liveth in me. That, my friend, is why I am so sure" (p. 162). And yet listen to the same smug evangelical poohpooh the alleged subjectivism of the hated Modernist:

> The keystone of the Christian faith is the bodily resurrection of the Lord Jesus Christ. Take that away and everything goes. Your Modernist speaks of it as a psychical experience or a spiritual resurrection in which Christ lives in the lives of His followers by His spirit, and in doing so vitiates the whole plan of salvation and leaves mankind still in their sins. (p. 162)

---

5. Plato, *Phaedo*, trans. E. M. Cope, 63.

What, one may ask, is the difference between his own evangelical "walk with Jesus," self-authenticating as it appears to be to Alderson, and the despised Modernist "alternative"? How does any bodily resurrection make a difference to this scenario one way or the other? Either way, one's belief in the risen Jesus amounts to the subjective experience that one chooses to call "Christ living inside his followers by his spirit," does it not?

I say evangelicals base their faith squarely on their faith. But they pretend (to themselves) that the facts support them. For instance, though it could not be plainer that the imagined British faith in the resurrection is held by force of sheer willpower, we read the same stale apologetics we have heard for generations, and still hear, from defenders of this faith:

> What about the testimony of all who saw the Lord, who spoke to Him and ate with Him in Jerusalem [Acts 1:4; Luke 24:41–42?]; and Galilee [John 21:9–10?], and of the vast company of upwards of five hundred men and women [1 Cor. 15:6] "to whom He showed Himself alive after His passion by many infallible proofs" [Acts 1:3]? The testimony of His disciples is not lightly to be set aside. They talked with Him; they walked with Him [Luke 24:13–27], and they were present with Him at the last when on the slopes of Olivet He ascended into heaven [Luke 24:51 in some mss.; Acts 1:9]. (p. 399)

These are no arguments, for we simply do not have any such testimony of Jesus' disciples. What we have is an appendix to an anonymous gospel ("John" 21), another anonymous gospel ("Luke"), and some bits from a long narrative about the apostles whose authorship and date are completely up for grabs. But no such considerations are in the mind of Hunter or his character. Inspector Maxwell is simply quoting the Bible, which is supposedly authoritative because it is the Bible, God's Word, Holy Scripture. It is all a vicious circle, faith resting "solidly" upon faith. It is as if we were being asked to believe Dorothy Gale really arrived in Oz because we have the testimony of her companions, the Tin Woodsman and the Scarecrow in Frank Baum's *The Wizard of Oz*.

With each Lost Gospel novel we ask, what is at stake? What is the danger posed by its possible release to the public? The answer tells us much about the author and the point he seeks to make. It tells how important, positively or negatively, the Christian faith is, as well as how brittle, how vulnerable, it is, what it would take to debunk it—if anything. Well, for J. H. Roberts, the stakes are high indeed, as we have already seen from his descriptions of the social, moral, and even economic chaos ensuing on the publication of the *Shred of Nicodemus*. Here it is in sum:

> But think, man, what it means. Christianity is predicated on the truth of that story, on the fact that the tomb of the Saviour was found empty on the third day. If that were proved untrue it would mean the destruction of civilization as we know it. (p. 294)

> Gentlemen, this world cannot go on without Christianity. If it should go, everything would go—all that makes life worth living, love, kindliness, brotherhood, our hopes for this life and that which is to come. Without the Christian hope and faith, the world will revert to a paganism and barbarism, aided by all the scientific devilishness of demon-inspired men that will eventuate in a struggle and carnage the like of which has never been seen since man appeared upon the earth. (p. 319)

To any sane person, all this might seem an exaggerated, even a paranoid, fear. Was the world so bad when it had only Judaism to look to for a shining beacon? Would it be so bad now? Are the morals of the other great religions really so dismal? And Hunter too quickly forgets the pagan origins of the very jurisprudence that civilizes the West (not the Levitical one, thank God). And talk about logocentrism! He is imagining a scenario in which a particular religious doctrine has the power to civilize and sanctify, a doctrine whose sudden loss would plunge the world into the Hobbesian War of All against All. What is supposed to sanctify Christians, after all? A doctrine? Or the power of Christ's Spirit? If the discovery of the *Shred of Nicodemus* were to give the lie to the resurrection, it would mean either that there was upbuilding power in a piece of belief about paranormal events—surely a strange and implausible notion—or that it had never been that doctrine's power, but the general moral culture of the churches, that had sanctified Christian character. Hunter seems to picture the situation like a Roadrunner cartoon in which Wile E. Coyote runs to, then off, the edge of a mesa and remains suspended in mid-air till he notices he is not standing on any solid ground. The joke is that gravity affects you only so long as you remember it. Even so, Hunter's disillusioned Christians seem to be poor fools who had been growing spiritually standing in mid-air with nothing holding them up until they realized there was nothing sanctifying them after all.

HIGHER CRITICISM TO THE RESCUE

One wonders why the heroes of *The Mystery of Mar Saba* did not at once test the authenticity of *The Shred of Nicodemus* by grabbing their spades and delving beneath the still-standing Pillar of Absalom to see if there were any trace of Jesus' mortal remains. Why wouldn't they? It's not as if anyone in past ages would have had reason to rob the tomb. Who knew there *was* a tomb till the *Shred* came to light? It is like the old apologetic argument for the resurrection: why didn't they produce the body? The absence of Jesus' corpse would have gone a long way, not towards proving the resurrection of Jesus, but towards exploding the *Shred* hoax. Yet nobody looks.

Even more ironically, the novel does not consider whether there would have remained any defense for the resurrection of Jesus even in the face of the *Shred*'s authenticity. Modernists are ridiculed for selling out the Christian faith when they suggest that the resurrection was spiritual, not physical. But that is not the only alternative. Amazingly, the avenue of rescue had already been paved by none other than the hated Higher Critics. For, with a liberty made possible by stripping away the straightjacket of inerrantism, critics had stratified the Easter materials in the New Testament. They had taken the list of resurrection appearances in 1 Corinthians 15:3–11 to be the earliest resurrection tradition.[6] The gospel stories of the empty tomb and the ensuing appearances, critics judge, are subsequent embellishments of the tradition which had originally pictured Jesus rising from the dead (in whatever form) and ascending directly to heaven. Essentially the resurrection was the ascension, and nobody saw it.

A critic who shared this estimate of the evidence would at once declare *The Shred of Nicodemus* a fraud, albeit an ancient one seeking to debunk an already embellished and therefore unhistorical version of the events of Easter morning. The discovery would in no way impugn the resurrection itself. It would be the exact equivalent of Matthew's note that evil Jews had spread abroad the rumor that the disciples had stolen the body of Jesus despite the presence of Roman guards (Matt 28:11–15). Mark mentioned no guards, so where did Matthew get them? Tradition and polemic were already embroidering the story in an almost antiphonal, back-and-forth manner. First, Mark said the tomb was found empty.

---

6. Most still do, though I don't. See my "Apocryphal Apparitions: 1 Corinthians 15:3–11 as a Post-Pauline Interpolation."

Non-believers replied: "Well, if it was, then the answer is simple: his disciples came and stole the body." Matthew's answer to this: "Fat chance, since the body was guarded by a detachment of Roman soldiers! Yeah, that's the ticket!" And so on. Now, to peel away these apocryphal layers in no way implies Jesus did not rise. In fact, it clears away an obstacle to accepting the resurrection by removing a silly version of it. *The Shred of Nicodemus* would be more of the same: an ancient but fictive anti-Christian counterblast to Christian claims embodied in the empty tomb. And we can recognize this if we exercise the glorious freedom of the sons of Baur and Strauss.

Then again, who's to say that Jesus didn't rise from beneath the Pillar of Absalom?

Why do these possibilities not occur to the characters in the novel, or to their author, J. H. Hunter? Simply because the price tag would be way too high: it would entail sacrificing biblical inerrancy, "believing the Bible" at face value. The critical outlook requires the admission that evidence must be sifted, not automatically credited as the Bible believer rejoices to do. It is more important to the evangelical to maintain the belief (actually an illusion) of an infallible Bible. The loss of it would easily be equally disastrous as forfeiture of the resurrection: the evangelical edifice would crumble. And that not because any solid basis for it would have been taken away but rather because the illusion of standing in mid-air would have been dispelled. It would become obvious that the whole thing had never rested upon anything but the will to believe. Believe what, exactly? Well, whatever is in the Bible. This is made all the more clear in a passage that would at first sight seem to repudiate such bibliolatry:

> "An intellectual belief in the truth of God's Word will no more save a soul than will a belief in the historical accuracy of Thucydides' 'Peloponnesian War.'" . . . Alderson looked at him for a moment before replying. "It is not belief in a Book that saves, but in a Person . . . It is Christ crucified and risen from the dead who saves." (p. 161)

Colonel Alderson is making absolute belief in the Bible into a necessary, just not a sufficient, condition for salvation. And that is because the Savior in whom one is to believe is a character in the Bible. If you didn't start by an arbitrary act of belief in the Bible, you would not even know whether there was a Jesus or that there was any point in putting your faith in him.

I suspect that all meaning is a matter of imposing a fictive narrative onto an inherently meaningless stream of raw events. It is not that events *should* carry meaning with them and have somehow lost it. No, rather meaning must be, in the nature of the case, in the eye of the beholder. How could it be anywhere else? Evangelical Christians are desperate to take a mythic epic contained in the Bible and insert themselves into it, as its ongoing sequel. It is not too different from a *Star Trek* fan so loving his favorite show that he wishes it were real and that he could join Starfleet. Trekkies pretend they have done just that when they attend conventions dressed as Vulcans, speaking Klingon, toting phasers, etc. Evangelicals do it by going to church.

FROM *THE MYSTERY OF MAR SABA* TO A REAL LIVE HOAX

Few now remember Hunter's *The Mystery of Mar Saba*, but that doesn't mean its influence is over. Indeed, some of us think it was this novel that gave Morton Smith the idea for a real live "lost gospel" hoax of his own, the promotion of the so-called *Secret Gospel of Mark*. We will conclude this chapter and our discussion of Hunter's fiction by turning to Smith's obstensible fact. In 1973 Morton Smith issued twin volumes, *Clement of Alexandria and a Secret Gospel of Mark* and *The Secret Gospel: The Discovery and Interpretation of the Secret Gospel According to Mark*. From the beginning, a number of Smith's colleagues and critics charged him with forging the document as a hoax, which is exactly what happens in Hunter's old novel. Some said Smith, once an Episcopal priest, had a poisonous hatred for the Christian religion, especially for its historic homophobia, and that Smith's *The Secret Gospel* was an attempt to even the score.

What Smith presented was actually a fragmentary quotation from this hitherto-unknown gospel, contained in an ostensible letter from Clement of Alexandria. It made brief but suggestive reference to the possibility that Jesus practiced a libertine ritual of homosexual initiation with his disciples. Clement warns his correspondent Theodore, who had written him with questions about an esoteric gospel used by the churches in Clement's orbit as well as by the Carpocratian Gnostics in the vicinity. One passage in particular seems to trouble Theodore. Clement reassures Theodore that the specific passage in question was a heretical interpolation by the trouble-making Carpocratians. As Smith knew, such a statement would mean only that Clement would have found such a passage objectionable though he liked the rest of the text. Classifying a bad passage as secondary was an old trick: Jeremiah had already used it in Jeremiah 7:22; 8:8. So did the Ebionites, who believed Jesus had come to identify false pericopes in the Torah so the faithful could henceforth disregard them.[7] Smith himself professed to think both the Clementine letter and the underlying Markan apocryphon authentic, and thus as sources unlocking the mysteries of Christian origins.

Smith ventured that Jesus was a kind of antinomian Gnostic who led his disciples into a trance ecstasy, experiencing the Kingdom of God on earth, much as Irenaeus tells us that Markos the Magician used to teach wealthy New-Age matrons how to speak in tongues and prophesy. Smith said that, yes, this initiation included homosexuality as a rite of liminality, betokening the transcendence of this world by the holy-minded transgression of its categories and its laws. Such notions are common to Tantric Hinduism and Buddhism, though for Smith to claim Jesus and the first Christians indulged in such adventurous pieties is rather like John Allegro's theory that the early Christians were a mushroom cult like the Brahmin priests with their sacred Soma.[8] Both theories are possible, however offensive they may strike us. But what good is a Christianity that does not offend somebody? The relevant question is whether there is sufficient evidence for one's proposals.

Smith has, to one degree or another, managed to persuade writers as diverse as the anonymous author of the July 4, 1973, *Advocate* article "Jesus Christ . . . Supergay?"[9] and John Dominic Crossan.[10] Others still harbor doubts, not necessarily because they balk at full-fledged acceptance of the Gay Jesus hypothesis, since one is certainly free to accept Smith's case at any of three different levels. One might buy the whole store, Gay Jesus and all. Or one might simply accept the genuineness of the Clementine letter, in which case *Secret Mark* must be accepted as a genuine ancient document, whether authentic or pseudepigraphical. Again, one might accept *Secret Mark* as genuinely Markan but follow Clement in excising the juicier portions.

---

7. Schoeps, *Jewish Christianity*, 94–98.
8. Allegro, *The Sacred Mushroom and the Cross*.
9. Enroth and Jamison, *The Gay Church*, 58.
10. Crossan, *The Historical Jesus*, 330.

THE LITTLE MANUSCRIPT THAT WASN'T THERE

No, the doubts stem from the elusive character of the original manuscript which Smith claimed he discovered written onto the end pages of a bound book in the library of the Mar Saba monastery near Jerusalem in 1958. Edgar J. Goodspeed had long ago warned that in the absence of supposed originals, one must always suspect any new gospel discovery claim (of which there have been very many) to be imposture. For instance, Nicolas Notovitch's *Unknown Life of Jesus Christ*, allegedly based on an old Tibetan codex, foundered on such an embarrassment.[11] Quentin Quesnell charged that Smith's "discovery" failed this test, too.

But Goodspeed did allow that facsimile photographs might be good enough, and as it happens, Smith had indeed provided photographs of the text. He explained, however, that he did not and could not bear away the originals. Subsequent attempts by other researchers to gain access to them have proved fruitless, with a single exception. As Charles W. Hedrick explains,[12] in 1977 the Archimandrite Kallistos Dourvas, a monastery librarian, made a set of color photographs of the manuscript pages, which had been removed from the printed book. The pages themselves have since been mislaid. Perhaps they will one day come to light. In the meantime, Hedrick argues persuasively that certain matching stain marks shared by the last page of the printed book and the (photographed) pages of the Clement manuscript prove beyond reasonable doubt that the pages all originated in the same bound book, just as Smith claimed.

Is that the end of the story? I must confess that I remain unconvinced. Unlike love, I do not believe all things. It occurs to me that there is still a forgery scenario that remains untouched by Hedrick's research. Suppose Smith found some blank pages at the end of that library book, and they spoke eloquently to him nonetheless, whispering to him of an opportunity for a rich joke. And then perhaps he got to work composing the Clement piece with its implied homosexual evangel. If so, he would have been following the precise strategy employed by the scheming forgers of the *Shred of Nicodemus* in *The Mystery of Mar Saba*, the Q document in James Hall Roberts's novel of that title (which we will encounter in the next chapter), and the *Gospel of James* in Irving Wallace's *The*

---

11. Goodspeed, *Famous Biblical Hoaxes*, 11.
12. Hedrick with Olympiou, "Secret Mark: New Photographs, New Witnesses."

Word, whose forger used pages from genuine ancient manuscripts which he then filled with spurious but ancient-seeming writing about Jesus. To be sure that Smith had not done the same, though leaving the pages in the bound volume he found them in, we would need to examine what we do not have: the manuscript leaves themselves. We would need to test the ink. The paleographers, on the other hand, could save themselves the trouble: if anyone could mimic the handwriting style of a desired period, it would be the erudite Smith.

SPEAKING IN TONGUES IN CHEEKS

If Smith had forged the text, a few items would make additional sense. For one, it would be a bit less surprising to see that Smith presumed to print his name on one of the previous printed pages! "Smith" along with the manuscript number he assigned it, 65, is plainly visible in the photographs. Was he signing his own work?

And I confess that I wonder, with all the warnings of Clement to his reader to beware of Gnostic forgeries, whether Smith is not winking to his readers to beware of his own hoax! This almost qualifies as a form-critical feature of gospel hoaxes. I call it "the wink statement." Sometimes it is an instance of "protesting too much." For example, *The Gospel of the Holy Twelve* (1923) opens in a way that seems to anticipate skepticism: "It is a faithless and perverse generation, as of old, that asks for a sign, and there shall no sign be given; for if the very writers of the Aramaic original were raised from the dead, and testified to their authorship, unbelieving critics would still ask for a sign; and the more signs they were given, the more they would ask for in the hardness of their hearts."[13] Others come very near to admitting the true, recent, authorship, as in the Foreword to *The Love Letters of Saint John* (1917): "it may be that the letters were written by some unknown hand, or under the influence of some teacher long forgotten. What does it matter?"[14] In my inscribed copy of *The Long-Lost Second Book of Acts* (1904), "discoverer" Kenneth Sylvan Guthrie has written, "If every word of ours were inspired, would we not be prophets? Having prayer, whose fault is it if we are not?"[15] Using Clement's elbow, is Smith similarly poking us in the ribs?

---

13. Udny, "Introduction" to Ouseley, *The Gospel of the Holy Twelve*, xiii.
14. Kennerley, *The Love Letters of St. John*, 9.
15. Guthrie, *The Long-Lost Second Book of Acts*, flyleaf inscription by the author.

In 1985 I asked Morton Smith how he responded to charges of forgery, recently renewed in Per Beskow's excellent book *Strange Tales about Jesus*.[16] He told me the now-familiar story of the custodians of the manuscript secreting it away out of embarrassment at the notoriety Smith's book *The Secret Gospel* had brought them, henceforth wanting to suppress the evidence. He asked, furthermore, what business Beskow had in condemning all the more recent New Age gospels as spurious: if they embodied someone's faith, weren't they authentic gospels, no matter who wrote them or when? Later I wondered if his words did not apply equally, even especially, to his own *Secret Mark*!

But why would Smith, if he created the whole thing, not have written up something more overtly spectacular? Why settle for what appears to be a simpler version of Lazarus' resurrection, the only episode related in the "quoted" text? He knew the psychology of critics: the new text would be especially attractive to many, not least conservatives, if it seemed to draw John closer to the Synoptics, in this case seeming to supply a missing link between them. Many reject the Johannine Lazarus story (John 11), pointing out that such a public spectacle, if real, could not have escaped mention by the other evangelists who must have known and reported it. But if one accepted the *Secret Gospel*, one might retain the credibility of John, and to some that might not seem too high a price to pay.

Then why would Smith have had Clement reject as an interpolation the homosexual element, which must have been the real barb of his hoax, if that is what it was? Simple: it is a teaser, a distancing device, not unlike the initial skepticism of the onlookers in a gospel miracle story. Smith thus places the thinnest of veils over the shocking vision, as if to disguise the fact that his main goal is to show it off.

If *Secret Mark* is Morton Smith's own creation, where might he have derived the idea for it? This question brings me at last to a chance discovery of my own, the event that caused me to reassess the whole question after I thought Professor Hedrick had laid it to rest. Some years ago, I was in Detroit on a speaking tour and chanced to be poring over the shelves of a large but lackluster second-hand bookstore. My eye fell upon the title of one worn-looking volume, *The Mystery of Mar Saba*. Thinking instantly of Morton Smith's fateful visit to Mar Saba, I picked up the book with mild curiosity, thinking, "What if it turns out to be one of those 'lost gospel' novels?" Well, as we have seen in this chapter, it certainly did!

16. Beskow, *Strange Tales about Jesus*, 96–104.

INFINITE REGRESS?

One cannot deny that a whole slew of parallels may be drawn not only between *The Mystery of Mar Saba* and Morton Smith's *Secret Gospel* hoax, but equally between the novel and its predecessor *When It Was Dark* of chapter 1. Consider a few of them. First, the dangerous discovery turns out to be a hoax, a confession that Joseph of Arimathea (plus Nicodemus in *Mar Saba*) reburied the corpse of Jesus. The hoax is engineered by a wicked enemy of Christianity. In one novel, it is a Nazi-leaning Higher Critic who forces a young and idealistic scholar to forge the text. In the other, the bad guy is a secularist who forces a famous biblical critic to forge the inscription. In both cases, the mastermind blackmails the scholar-forger by means of a woman dear to the scholar—in one case his sister, in the other his mistress. In both cases the world is plunged into socioeconomic and religious chaos as a result of the publication of the "news," though in the end the truth prevails. Is it likely that J. H. Hunter was inspired by Guy Thorne's earlier novel, as I have suggested Morton Smith was inspired by Hunter's? It certainly remains possible, though none of it seems too close for coincidence.

4 | The Q Connection
John Hall Roberts (Robert L. Duncan), *The Q Document*

EXPATRIATE EXPIATION

MYSTERY WRITER ROBERT L. Duncan wrote his fascinating 1964 novel *The Q Document*[1] under the pen name John Hall Roberts, so in what follows I shall refer to him as "Roberts." The novel centers about a man known only as Cooper, still technically on staff as an historian of early Christianity and manuscript expert at a small college. But he has been on leave, has finished it, and has been playing hooky in Japan. His self-exile there, we soon learn, was an attempted refuge from personal tragedy. While he was away presenting a paper, his home burned down, killing both his eleven-year-old daughter and his unfaithful wife, though the man she was sleeping with at the time managed to escape. The whole thing left Cooper so shell-shocked that all emotion as well as concern for anything and anybody drained out of him, apparently never to return. When we meet him, he has come under the employ of one Victor Hawkins, a trader in vice and manuscripts, both operating a gourmet brothel and selling rare papyri (or forgeries, he doesn't much care which, as long as they look real enough). It is a strange pair of pots to have one's pudgy, bejeweled hands in, and one suspects the peculiar combination is a shortcut for facilitating the plot, creating a set of pincers in which to hold fast the hero for a hundred or more pages to come.

We also meet two more expatriate Americans in Japan. One is a Catholic priest, Father O'Connor, attached to a seminary. The other is an over-the-hill, hard-drinking reporter named Willa Cummings. O'Connor is something of a surrogate for Cooper's department chairman Stevenson back stateside, and the two have friendly debates over tea

---

1. All page references are to the Morrow hardcover edition.

every week. Cummings is a place-holder for Cooper's lost wife. Cooper sleeps with her and cares about her, but he isn't sure—his emotions being so black and blue—that he can feel real love for her or anyone else. For her part, Cummings is looking for a big break, a new height to climb to regain the glory she once had when she won a Pulitzer for her reporting from the front lines of the Korean War. She is willing to use any contacts, and even to use the man she loves, to recapture the fame and fortune of the past.

TURNCOAT TALMUDIST

What stirs the ingredients in this pot is a new and unique assignment for Cooper. Victor Hawkins announces he has come into possession of a long-lost and much-rumored cache of manuscripts called the Baum-Brenner Collection. They represent the legacy of a most peculiar figure: Rabbi Martin Baum, leader of Jewish resistance in Poland who one day went and changed his name to Martin Brenner and joined the Nazi Party. He worked on a translation project for his new masters for two years, using his privileged status to gain medical attention for his daughter and finally permission for her to escape to Switzerland. After this he fell from favor and was sent to his doom in Auschwitz.

Compared to the enigma of his double treason, any secret lurking in Baum's extant papers must seem anticlimactic. The collection was smuggled out of the Peoples' Republic of China during the rescue of an old priest held prisoner there, and now the Chinese want it back. Victor wants Cooper to translate and to authenticate the ancient texts. He discovers that the papyri contain anything but an anticlimax; they are a set of interrelated documents dating, to all appearances, to the first century CE.

One of the documents is a Latin letter from Roman officer Lucretius Septimus requesting of his superior Tigellinus the transfer of several condemned prisoners for assignment to the Roman arena. The list includes the name of one Gaius Claudius Paulus, better known as Paul the Apostle! His crime: neither sedition nor blasphemy, but *murder*. The second document, this one in Greek, is in effect a fourth Pastoral Epistle with stylistic and biographical links to 1 and 2 Timothy and Titus. Of special note is 2 Timothy, which treats of Paul's coming capital trial. It refers, a bit circuitously, to unjust accusations made against Paul and of the guilt of Alexander the silversmith (Acts 19:24; 2 Tim 4:14), who could have revealed the truth if he had wanted to do so. A third text, also in Greek, is an account by none other than Luke the evangelist of the martyrdom of Paul. A fourth document, in Aramaic, is a letter written by Joseph of Arimathea to his son John, upbraiding him for betraying the memory of Jesus by seeking to foment revolutionary violence in his name. Any of these finds, if genuine, would be earth-shattering to the world of early Christian studies.

But a fifth document in Baum's collection makes the rest seem like crumpled Bojangles wrappers by contrast: it is a summary account of Jesus' teaching—written in Jesus' own hand! Though much of this gospel-like material is quite familiar, there is a repeated edge of militaristic fanaticism, as by a fanatical Jihadist convinced of his divine mandate. Fully expecting his own imminent death and resurrection, and planning to appeal to this miracle as proof of God's summons to a Boxer Rebellion against Rome, Jesus was disappointed, as history shows. Any way an apologist might like to cut it, the document certainly leaves no possibility of any public, triumphant return of Jesus to earthly life, where he might have been able to just take up where he left off and oust Rome from power. Old Joseph of Arimathea stressed this very fact to try to dampen his son's renewed revolutionary fervor.

PAUL APALLS

As Cooper reconstructs the ancient scenario from the puzzle pieces provided by these documents, he realizes that Paul had been arrested for murdering John of Arimathea, who had come to him for help raising a new messianic army. Paul was by this time invested in the spiritualized messianism familiar to us today as Christianity, and he wanted nothing to do with this return to Zealot-like agitation. John threatened to make known what he knew of the original intentions of Jesus and his failed resurrection if Paul did not cooperate, leaving the apostle no choice but to kill him.

Here is the danger to faith as Cooper (and presumably author Roberts) conceives it: "It's pretty easy to kill a religion if you can demote a god to the status of a mortal. It doesn't make any difference if you can prove he was a fine mortal and a good man, just so long as you can prove he's not a god" (p. 219). This is the danger in Dan Brown's later novel *The Da Vinci Code*, too: if it could be shown Jesus was married and had children, that would supposedly debunk the Nicene Creed. The error of Brown and his characters was the notion that Christian orthodoxy taught Jesus was divine *and therefore not human*. The official position was, rather, that Jesus had been both fully divine and fully human. You may judge for yourself whether that makes any sense, but it certainly in no way excludes the possibility of Jesus having fathered offspring. But to see Jesus as a failed insurgent, well, that's a more bitter pill. It ascribes to him the willingness to use revolutionary violence, as well as anticipating a triumphant struggle—which he lost! One might point out that the crucifixion appears to be no great triumph either, yet Christians rejoice in it as an act of redemption; could they not have so regarded a military defeat of Jesus?

Remember, the gospels depict Jesus walking toward his destiny with eyes wide open, lest he seem to have been taken by surprise. It is stretching things too much to posit a true messiah who was grossly in error as to his purpose and mission. Or so most Christians would think, and that is why the Liberation Theology portrait of Jesus as a peoples' revolutionist cut from Zealot cloth has never caught on. Hermann Samuel Reimarus[2] understood all this very well, which is why he left his manuscript "On the Intention of Jesus and his Disciples" unpublished when he died, leaving it for someone after him to unearth. Lessing did just that, publishing portions of Reimarus's work as *The Wölfenbüttel Fragments*.

Roberts actually has his character Farther O'Connor mention *Fragments* by name as a previous "attempt to fictionalize the life of Christ" (p. 162). Indeed, Reimarus had seriously argued that Jesus preached a gospel of anti-Roman political messianism, and that, when it inevitably failed, his bereaved apostles decided to turn a failed revolution into a money-making opportunity. Reimarus knew that his contemporaries could never brook such an understanding of "gentle Jesus meek and mild." Lessing was a bit less timid, but when he published excerpts, he diplomatically pretended to side with orthodoxy against Reimarus' blasphemies, hoping meantime for the seeds he had sown to bear fruit thirty, sixty, or a hundred-fold.

QUESTIONING ONE'S DOUBTS

In our novel, when Cooper first shares what he is working on with his friend O'Connor, the poor priest pretends not to be phased in the least:

---

2. Talbert, *Reimarus: Fragments*.

he knows these documents must be forgeries. Cooper is almost completely persuaded otherwise, though to him there is no existential issue. From within his defensive shell he cares not what may happen to the faith of millions. It is easy for him to say that it is better that the truth be known than for people to take comfort in a lie. Nonetheless, he eventually begins to entertain doubts of his own. Yes, the carbon-dating and the paleography check out: the papyri all seem genuinely, sufficiently ancient. Nor are there anachronisms protruding like sore thumbs. But isn't it just a wee bit odd that the quartet of documents reinforce and interpret one another in such a way as to suggest they were composed for precisely that effect?[3] And is it not worrisome that when, where, or how the documents were discovered are unknown (a consideration besetting recent biblical hoaxes like the supposed Ossuary of James), or that no one can imagine a scenario in which the five texts would have been recovered, collected, and passed down from antiquity? Why preserve them? Who would have wanted to?

Cooper finally learns that Baum-Brenner's daughter, now a successful interior decorator, can be reached. And from her he discovers that, as he suspected, the old man had entrusted to his fleeing daughter a sheaf of seemingly random papyrus scraps and fragments, which he said were the "key" to his project. At the last minute, Cooper pieces together what must really have happened. Since all his sons and brothers had been wiped out in the Nazi persecutions, Rabbi Baum feared his line would be extinguished (a concern made explicit in the old man's letters). He then abandoned his opposition to the Third Reich and offered to collaborate if it meant he could protect his daughter, his last chance to keep his family going. His special scholarly talents meant he could offer the Nazis an unparalleled propaganda weapon. He offered to forge a set of documents that would seem to discredit Christianity in the eyes of the German people, softening them up to replace Jesus with Hitler, a step Hitler is well known not to have dared, since he knew it would be pushing his people too far. But this might do the trick! And so the Nazis gave the old scholar a new identity and set him to work. He gathered various old papyri discovered when the Nazis demolished old Polish monasteries, and he developed new techniques for bleaching the writing from them in a manner no one could discover. Then he set about composing.

---

3. That is also one of the reasons for suspecting that the so-called Ignatian Epistles are forgeries.

So he had not translated anything but freely invented everything. Yet he did not want to be responsible for wrecking a faith cherished by millions, even if not his own, so he left behind a key to the mystery.

It was this key that Cooper finally recognized among the tatters. He recognized them as the samples Baum-Brenner had cut from the papyrus sheets to test in his ink-removal experiments. Others were cut from the same sheets without removing the writing. The result was that, if one took the trouble to compare the "ancient" documents with the snippets, one would discover that the larger sheets had once borne completely different writing. With this explanation revealed, both the Vatican and the Red Chinese put their check books away with twin sighs of relief.

A QUEER Q

Where, the theologically astute reader may ask, in all this is the Q document? When he first mentions it, Roberts does seem to know what it is. An abbreviation for the German *Quelle* ("source"), Q is a theoretical source document for the gospels of Matthew and Luke. From the great degree of verbatim overlap, it is clear that Matthew and Luke have each independently used Mark's earlier gospel. But there is a great deal more text that Matthew and Luke share, which we know they did not borrow from Mark for the simple reason that Mark does not contain it. So where did Matthew and Luke get it? Presumably from a second common source document, but one which does not survive independently, unlike Mark. One may ask, if the church saved Mark—though most of it was preserved in the two longer gospels—why did they not keep making copies of Q as well? A plausible answer is that Matthew and Luke may have used up Q almost completely, whereas both later evangelists leave out at least a bit of Markan material. If they used up the whole of Q between them, scribes might have thought it completely pointless to keep copying Q.

Roberts correctly summarizes the situation:

> The Q document is a hypothetical document invented by German biblical historians in the 1800s to explain a gap in our knowledge of the early Christian Era. The four gospels in the New Testament are repetitious and there was obviously a good bit of conscious duplication. For instance. Both Matthew and Luke undoubtedly made use of the book written by Mark. Luke, as a matter of fact, lifted out large sections from Mark's work and inserted them

> into his own gospel. [So did Matthew.] But some historians think there was another source common to both Luke and Matthew, a manuscript which contained most of the sayings of Jesus. In reconstructing this hypothetical source, the Germans theorized that it must have been an account which was set down by somebody who had traveled with Jesus. For want of a better name, they called this document the *quelle* or "source" document. Later this was shortened to "Q." (p. 33)

Actually, it is only conservative apologists[4] who contend that Q might have been compiled by an eyewitness, reinterpreting the famous report of Papias, second-century bishop of Hierapolis, to the effect that "Matthew copied down the sayings of the Lord." Before the advent of source criticism and its delineation of Q as a pre-gospel source, Papias had been understood as referring to the complete Gospel of Matthew. If he *had* been referring to Q, eventually taken up and incorporated by the anonymous evangelist we call Matthew (as distinct from the disciple Matthew), that would furnish a pretty direct link between the historical Jesus and the Gospel of Matthew even if one were forced to admit that we don't know who the author of the whole, final-edition gospel was. Given this, it is surprising to hear Father O'Connor's exceedingly negative estimate of Q: "Foolishness. The Q document doesn't exist at all . . . I think it borders on heresy to believe that it *could* exist. The belief itself is a denial of basic faith in the divine inspiration of the scriptures" (p. 74).

But Aquinas knew better. He didn't know about Q, but he did know that Old Testament chroniclers often made references to pre-canonical documents by name. Aquinas readily admitted that canonical authors could and did make use of noncanonical ones. And there was nothing in that the least bit threatening to the doctrine of inspiration. One need only draw the distinction (by no means contrived) between inspiration on the one hand and revelation on the other. When John of Patmos declares that he heard these words from a heavenly voice resounding like a trumpet, that is revelation. When the Holy Spirit guides the editorial and artistic skills of a biblical redactor, that is inspiration. One may certainly believe in the inspiration of the gospels without commitment to the belief that the Holy Spirit dictated the documents verbatim to the authors.

4. Bruce, *The New Testament Documents*, 39.

Cooper accepts the document ostensibly written by Jesus himself as the long-lost Q source. But surely there is nothing new in Q if it is simply the non-Markan material common to Mathew and Luke? What could this document contain that would discredit and debunk Christianity? We already know: grandiose claims to be God's messiah who should shortly die, rise for all to see, and then march against the Romans. But we read nothing of that in the passages common to Matthew and Luke—nor anywhere else in the New Testament. So has author Roberts just cast aside the proper denotation of Q for the sake of a good story? Well, quite possibly, but one must hypothesize that he means this: it must be that Matthew and Luke skipped and suppressed what they did not like in Q. The "hot stuff" was what they left on the cutting room floor. New Testament specialists would be thrilled if someone discovered a Q document closely matching what we have reconstructed as the source of Matthew's and Luke's common non-Markan sayings, because then we'd be able to see how closely we had approximated the original wording. But no one else would have much cause to get excited. No, it would be front page news only if the original now proved to have been much different, and if the church had censored it. And that, I judge, is the implicit point of Roberts's Q seeming so different from Matthew and Luke and at the same time being their common source.

We have no business hypothesizing (which Roberts is not doing; he is writing fiction, after all) that the original Q was all that different from the Q material Matthew and Luke preserved, for the simple reason that no evidence now suggests it. (Nor is Roberts saying there is: in his story, remember, it is a big surprise to everyone.) But as to the broader idea that Jesus had been the figurehead of a (failed) political movement—that is neither new nor unreasonable. To my mind, strong (though hardly irrefutable) cases have been made for this notion by S. G. F. Brandon,[5] whose books suggest that the extant gospel tradition as a whole seeks to whitewash an earlier, anti-Roman messianic movement—just as Reimarus held.

Roberts's biblical text pastiches are quite good. He takes few liberties with the Jesus material he "quotes." Most of it is a matter of slight refocusing of familiar sayings. Roberts leaves the wilder stuff that would make Jesus seem like Osama bin Laden in the form of allusion and sum-

---

5. Brandon, *The Fall of Jerusalem and the Christian Church*; Brandon, *Jesus and the Zealots*; Brandon, *The Trial of Jesus of Nazareth*.

mary. He does a good job emulating the "Paul" of the Pastoral Epistles, who, however, reads a good bit differently from the Paul of the other letters. The stylistic (and other) differences have long ago convinced most critics that these three letters (1 and 2 Timothy and Titus) are of more recent vintage, written to refute the appeal to Paul made by Marcionites, Encratites and Gnostics, all targets of the Catholic Church. In fact, the first sign of the manuscripts' inauthenticity should have been this similarity to the Pastorals. And as Roberts should have known, that should have made Cooper suspicious right off the bat.

5 | Strangers in a Cave
Elizabeth Peters, *The Dead Sea Cipher*

THIS SOMEWHAT FORMULAIC ROMANTIC espionage mystery[1] involves our themes, all right, but, the discovery of a lost gospel appears almost marginal compared to the triumph of love among the spies. Even though the discovery of forbidden scrolls forms the climax of the action, it appears to be more of an excuse for the romance and intrigue rather than of interest in its own right.

GRAND OLE SOAP OPERA

The heroine is a young opera singer, the daughter of a retired minister and amateur Bible scholar who has sent her on a tour of the Middle East, where his age and illness prevent him from venturing. In colorful Beirut she happens to hear the sounds of a struggle in the hotel room next door and to witness the last words of a dying man. Much later we learn that he was an out-of-work archaeologist, an alcoholic, disputing with a smuggler, and that his last utterance was "Wadi Qumran." It seems he had, after many years, vindicated his theory that there were yet more caches of Dead Sea Scrolls hidden away among the cliffs. And beyond this he had left but a tourist brochure with a list of abbreviated titles of these "new" scrolls, forming an acrostic clue to the cave where they might yet be found.

Dinah, our heroine, becomes the center of attention for various spies already assigned to locate the rumored discovery. They think that, having heard the last words of the dying archaeologist, she may know more than she is saying; she might be able to lead them to the hiding place of the scrolls. As the action progresses, we ride with Dinah and a busload of fellow tourists through the bazaars and ruins of Lebanon, Syria, and Israel, pretty much waiting for something substantial to

---

1. All page references are to the Dell paperback edition.

happen. Dinah is shadowed by two attractive men, one of whom turns out to be another archaeologist, an old friend of the murdered discoverer, while the other is a cad and a spy for the Bad Guys. Which will woo her? Not surprisingly, she winds up with the right one, and the two of them find their way to the hiding place of the scrolls. The other potential boyfriend, the spy, follows and confronts them, intending to seize the scrolls for whomever is paying him. But the happy couple is at the last moment rescued by nearly all of the other tourists, who also turn out to have been spies all along, each representing different governments or other unnamed interests.

What is in those scrolls? That is always the chief question. We may not be treated to any full texts in these novels, as that would ruin the mystery and inevitably disappoint the reader (just as H. P. Lovecraft refused all fan requests that he write the whole *Necronomicon*, an ultra-secret magic book of his own creation, since it would have to prove anticlimactic).[2] But we need at least to be tantalized! Give us a glimpse! A scrap! Something! Believe me, in a popular novel, the big revelation had better be juicier than a new manuscript of the Qumran *Manual of Discipline*, as much as such a find might occasion rejoicing among scholars. In *The Dead Sea Cipher*, there are six intact scrolls plus other, less promising detritus. Not even their discoverer was able to read the complete text of any of them, since, as long as they were left where they were found (albeit in containers designed to stave off further deterioration), he dared not attempt to open the fragile writings far enough to be able to read more than the first couple of lines. And neither does anybody else in the novel.

But while the protagonists are merely speculating as to the scrolls' contents, they float the possibility that they might contain the Q source, here left unexplained, possibly a tip of the hat to Roberts's *The Q Document*. Once they pore over the dead man's cryptic list of titles, they realize there are copies of Matthew, Mark, Luke, and John—in Qumran Aramaic and dating before the year 70 (necessarily, given the destruction of the Qumran monastery in the Jewish War with Rome ca. 73 CE). Such a discovery would indeed revolutionize New Testament scholarship, giving bragging rights to apologists who would be able to make a better case

---

2. Letter to James Blish and William Miller, May 13, 1936: "If anyone were to try to write the Necronomicon, it would disappoint all those who have shuddered at cryptic references to it."

that the canonical gospels are much closer to the historical Jesus than most critics today theorize. A few distinguished scholars (Charles Cutler Torrey, Matthew Black, George M. Lamsa)[3] have argued for an Aramaic original of the canonical gospels, while George Howard[4] makes a good case for a Hebrew Matthew written by the same author as the Greek Matthew but for a different audience.

Peters also puts two other scrolls in her story, *The Book of the Virgin* and *The Life of Jesus*. We get nary a look at either, but it is particularly difficult to picture a Mariological work stemming so early from the Jewish Christians of Jerusalem. Veneration of Mary seems to be a second-century phenomenon, attested in works such as the *Gospel of James* (aka *Protevangelium of James*) and the *Gospel of the Nativity of Mary*, both pretty late. Our heroes speculate that the *Life of Jesus* might tell us what Jesus was up to during the "lost years" between his visit to Jerusalem at age twelve and his Jordan baptism at age thirty. Also, maybe the text would be kind enough to vindicate the theory of William E. Phipps, then recently published, that speculated Jesus was a married man.[5] But we never find out.

EASY COME, EASY GO

What would be at stake if these new texts were to see the light of day? Again, the characters speculate:

> Even the possibility of a thing like marriage ... is recorded in one of the scrolls? Imagine the impact that would have on one of the most basic tenets of the Church of Rome—especially now, with the ferment among the young liberals in the priesthood. Can't you just see the lights burning late in the Vatican palace, and agitated prelates rushing up and down the corridors? (p. 159)

The Vatican must have been pretty worried about that possible threat to priestly celibacy, because it turns out that Father Benedetto, one of the faux tourists, was a spy, presumably for the Church, and as soon as the scrolls are rescued from the clutches of the bad spies, the good padre grabs the box containing the Life of Jesus and throws it over the cliff,

---

3. Torrey, *Our Translated Gospels*; Black, *An Aramaic Approach to the Gospels and Acts*; Lamsa, *New Testament Origin*.

4. Howard, *Hebrew Gospel of Matthew*.

5. Phipps, *Was Jesus Married?*

where an avalanche buries it. "'A pity,' he said, in the voice that had been trained to move crowds. 'But necessary'" (p. 216).

Our archaeologist hero, who has risked so much, retorts,

> And that's good, isn't it. Good for you, good for all the skulking, cautious cowards you represent. When you don't know for sure—destroy. When something might be dangerous—get rid of it. (Ibid.)

It is almost perfunctory, a capsule protest by the intellectual conscience when the plot calls for it. The whole novel partakes of this truncated, unsurprising, unimaginative quality, despite the author's apparent ease with narrative and dialogue. But that is not really our business here, except to indicate how underplayed the lost gospel theme is, and that is a shame since the choice of such a theme implies great questions will be posed, if not answered. Not this time.

6 | Harpooning the Fish
Irving Wallace, *The Word*

YOU GAVE ME THE WORD, I FINALLY HEARD

Until its successor *The Da Vinci Code* by Dan Brown, surely the most commercially successful of the Lost Gospel books was Irving Wallace's fat novel *The Word* (1972).[1] Aside from being a well-written page-turner (much like *The Da Vinci Code*), it had the advantage of educating the reader in recondite matters of biblical criticism. Dan Brown's book is likewise stuffed with scholarly tidbits, but they all happen to be grossly in error, while Wallace took the trouble to get it right. In fact one suspects *The Word* constituted the greatest single vehicle for popularizing critical New Testament scholarship before or since. How ironic, then, to see how the blocks of scholarly exposition alternate with juicy passages of darn-near pornography! For the book is first and foremost a piece of entertainment, espionage, mystery, and intrigue. It sets the characters and the action in a profane world the better to contrast the dawning light of hope ignited by a newly discovered gospel.

Though it is nowadays almost hard to remember it, the early Sixties witnessed both celebrations and lamentations over the decline of traditional religion and the seemingly irresistible tide of secularity threatening (or promising) to engulf America. Mainstream Protestantism (Lutherans, Presbyterians, Episcopalians, Congregationalists) saw a drastic decline in attendance, while Evangelicals and Fundamentalists labored under the belief that they were marginalized, ignored, and powerless. Both camps sought relevance, the former by veering leftward into political activism, the latter by increasingly garish evangelistic commercialism, with Christian rock music and "Things Go Better with Christ" posters. Many mainstream Protestant laity were disgusted and enraged

---

1. All page references are to the paperback edition.

by the positions taken by their denominational hierarchies. For a moment it looked as if America was about to catch up with Western Europe, where church attendance was way, way down and the masses—as well as culture in general—seemed to have abandoned traditional religion. As is now well known, the requiems for God and religion in America were premature, and the patient sprang up from the deathbed. New religions and spiritualities suddenly flourished as the youthful enthusiasm of the New Left sublimated itself into TM, the Jesus Movement, and the Divine Light Mission. Traditional and pop evangelism succeeded spectacularly until in the 1980s it was already evident that Evangelicals formed the new mainstream.

Irving Wallace wrote *The Word* just before the sea change. His characters all dread the erosion of faith they see all around them, among liberals as well as conservatives. The time is right for some unpredictable event to occur that will change the game board and make faith not only plausible but exciting again. That event turns out to be the discovery and publication of the *Gospel According to James*. On the eve of it, Wallace lets us overhear the musings of the Reverend Tom Carey:

> Our churchmen have failed to reinterpret, modernize, make useful a faith born in an ancient time. They've taken too little cognizance of social upheaval, a world of instant communication, a world teetering on a hydrogen bomb, a world that has sent men to the stars. In this new world where the cosmos becomes a fact seen on television, where death becomes a biological certainty, it is hard to keep one's faith in an amorphous heaven. Too many adults are too educated to reality ... to accept a creed that demands belief in Messiahs and miracles and a hereafter. Most of the young are too independent, knowledgeable, doubting, to look with respect on a religion that seems mythic, old-fashioned, a mere opiate. (p. 53)

A voice crying in this wilderness is the Dominee (i.e., Reverend) Maertin de Vroome, a controversial Dutch Reformed theologian, much like Bishop John Shelby Spong in our own day, but possibly inspired by the equally incendiary Bishop James Pike a generation earlier. The conservative but increasingly desperate Rev. Carey is tempted by his message of an avowed secular gospel and underground church: "He feels this Jesus [the supernatural Christ], as well as the superstitions about miracles and the Ascension, the events after the Resurrection, destroy the effectiveness of the New Testament and limit the church in its activity" (p. 54).

Later on, George L. Wheeler, a major Bible publisher with much invested in the publication of a new Bible containing the new hush-hush gospel, shares a very different estimate of de Vroome:

> De Vroome is a heretic, a student of form criticism, influenced by that other heretic, Rudolf Bultmann, the German theologian. De Vroome is skeptical about the events presented by the gospel writers. He believes the New Testament must be demythologized, shorn of miracles—turning water into wine, feeding the multitudes, raising Lazarus from the dead, the Resurrection, the Ascension,—before it can have meaning to modern scientific man. He believes that nothing can be known of the Jesus of history, he downgrades the existence of Jesus, he even suggests that Jesus may have been invented as a prop for Christianity's new message, and that the only thing worthwhile is the message itself when made relevant and rational for modern man ... De Vroome would see instantly that our revelation would reinforce the church hierarchy and orthodoxy, and turn wavering clergymen and congregations away from religious radicalism and back to the solidity of the old church. (pp. 111–12)

Wallace has done his research here. He appears to have based Wheeler's diatribe against the Dominee on various sensational passages from Rudolf Bultmann's seminal essay, "New Testament and Mythology":

> Can Christian preaching expect modern man *to accept the mythical view of the world as true?* To do so would be both senseless and impossible. It would be senseless because there is nothing specifically Christian in the mythical view of the world as such. It is simply the cosmology of a pre-scientific age ... For all our thinking to-day is shaped irrevocably by modern science. A blind acceptance of the New Testament mythology would be arbitrary, and to press for its acceptance as an article of faith would be to reduce faith to works ... The only honest way of reciting the creeds is to strip the mythological framework from the truth they enshrine ... No one who is old enough to think for himself supposes that God lives in a local heaven. There is no longer any heaven in the traditional sense of the word. The same applies to hell in the sense of a mythical underworld beneath our feet. And if this is so, the story of Christ's descent into hell and of his Ascension into heaven is done with. We can no longer look

for the return of the Son of Man on the clouds of heaven ... It is impossible to use electric light and the wireless and to avail ourselves of modern medical and surgical discoveries, and at the same time to believe in the New Testament world of spirits and miracles ... Again, the biblical doctrine that *death is the punishment of sin* is equally abhorrent to naturalism and idealism, since they both regard death as a simple and necessary process of nature ... what a primitive mythology it is, that a divine Being should become incarnate, and atone for the sins of men through his own blood![2]

De Vroome's theology would be embodied in a radically democratic, anti-hierarchical, feminist, ecological, pro-abortion community completely dedicated to transforming this world into the Kingdom of heaven on earth (pp. 349–52). His vision for such a church resembles Don Cupitt's proposals in *Radicals and the Future of the Church*,[3] though they cannot have been derived from this later work. But when Wallace wrote, Protestant presses were churning out titles like *The Secular Congregation*, *The Underground Church*, *Quotations from Chairman Jesus*, and *The Secular Meaning of Prayer*.

Traditionalists, though equally concerned that Christianity not ossify, viewed this sort of "reform" as a cure worse than the disease. As things unfold, we realize that the new *Gospel According to James* has become a football kicked around between these two Christian factions: the status quo, hoping to jump-start traditional faith by unveiling a new and fresh Jesus, now proven to be more than myth, and the radicals who declare good riddance to a Jesus who has become an obstacle to the realization of his own transformative vision. Smack dab in the middle stands our hero, Steve Randall, a top-tier promotion man engaged by the Bible cartel to prepare the way of the Lord, leading up to the unveiling of the *Gospel According to James* and orchestrating its media aftermath. The *Gospel's* very existence, much less its contents, must at all cost be kept secret until the big day when television will spread this evangel through the whole world at one blow. On a more modest scale, we have actually witnessed something much like this a few years ago when the National Geographic Society arranged for the authentication and translation of the *Gospel according to Judas*. Zero Hour witnessed TV specials and documentaries galore, interviews with Bible wonks of various persua-

---

2. Bultmann, "New Testament and Mythology," 3–7.
3. Cupitt, *Radicals and the Future of the Church*.

sions, publication of more than one edition of the text,[4] ensuing debates (still going on) over the proper translation of crucial passages,[5] etc.

RESURRECTION TWO

Ultimately, however, the real-life promotion of the Judas Gospel paled in comparison to the fictional world-shaking advent of the James evangel because Judas was a piece of esoterica mainly of interest to specialists in early Christian history and heresiology. The Church Fathers had listed a heretical "*Gospel according to Judas*," but no copy seemed to have survived. When it did, scholars rejoiced, but there was no real effect on Christianity or the life of the churches. With James's gospel in Wallace's novel, however, the impact would score high on the Richter Scale. Why? Two things.

First, the text was supposed to be a set of biographical reminiscences of Jesus by his brother, James the Just, head of the Jerusalem church, martyred in 62 CE. It would therefore be a very early source, earlier than Mark even by the earliest reasonable scholarly estimates. James would have been relying on his own memories of what Jesus had done and said, so we would not have to wonder if we were on the far end of a game of Telephone, the message having become irreparably garbled in transmission. Our doubts would be satisfied: we would finally be in touch with the real historical Jesus.

Second: *James* conveyed new teachings in addition to many familiar from the four canonical gospels. And of these teachings some seemed especially relevant to the twentieth century. For example, James' brother prophesied the eventual conquest of space as mortals learned to visit the other planets. This is a bit hard to imagine, since the ancients did not reckon with planets as, so to speak, other earths. They were rather lights or fires or living, glowing entities not far from us and not very large. There was only one world: ours. At any rate, this Jesus also spoke of an eventual league of nations where the kingdoms could sort out their differences peacefully. James' Jesus has a decidedly progressive social agenda and actually sounds more like Baha'ullah, the nineteenth-century founder of the Baha'i Faith.

---

4. Kasser, et al., *The Gospel of Judas from Codex Tchacos*; Kasser et al., *The Gospel of Judas, Together with the Letter from Peter to Philip, James, and a Book of Allogenes.*

5. De Conick, *The Thirteenth Apostle.*

The real shocker, however, is the report of James' gospel that Jesus survived the cross, only to resume his ministry until, many years later, he was immolated on another cross in Rome—and only then did he actually rise from the dead and ascend into heaven!

> James the Just found out that his brother had not expired on the Cross, that Jesus was alive and breathing.... He could only say Jesus recovered, and clandestinely continued His ministry in Palestine, in other provinces, finally appearing and preaching in Rome—*in Rome*—in the ninth year of the reign of Claudius Caesar, in 49 A.D., a time when Jesus would have been fifty-four years of age. And it was not until then that the real Resurrection and ascension occurred. (pp. 79–80)

As this passage tells us, there is a second discovery—or rather, a second item was discovered alongside the first, the report of Petronius the Centurion, in the name of Pontius Pilate, to Tiberius Caesar—documenting the arrest and crucifixion of Jesus. It is "an unprejudiced pagan source" (p. 103). Why should this matter? For more than two centuries, radical critics have alleged that Jesus Christ cannot have been an historical figure since he does not appear in any contemporary non-Christian writing, unlike other analogous figures (such as Apollonius of Tyana or Proteus Peregrinus) whom a handful of extant ancient writers mention they had met or seen. Granted, ancient evidence is fragmentary, and such mentions of a Rabbi Jesus might have existed but perished. But an absence of evidence is still evidence of a sort, and one may wonder how a miracle-working superman such as Jesus is depicted in the gospels would not have found a toehold in contemporary writings. Christian apologists like to protest that Jesus *is* mentioned by ancient writers, but none of these need be more than mere reflections of the fact that Christians in their time believed there had been a historical Jesus. None of these writers claims to have seen him or to know anyone who had. Much is made of the two mentions of Jesus in Josephus' *Antiquities of the Jews*, but almost all scholars agree that the main passage, the so-called *Testimonium Flavianum* ("Testimony of Flavius Josephus") has either been doctored or fabricated wholesale. Wallace's character Wheeler puts it better than many scholarly discussions do:

> Several [scholars] are convinced that Josephus did refer to Jesus twice, but they also agree that what Josephus wrote was evidently uncomplimentary and some centuries later was touched up by a

pious Christian scribe who didn't like the passage . . . But they are only speculating, so it proves nothing. (p. 101)

Wallace shows himself keenly aware of this debate and what is at stake in it. He supplies the very piece of evidence—from a disinterested Roman source, an eyewitness of Jesus—that all parties agree would resolve the issue. He knows the parameters of the scholarly debate over the issue. Steve Randall, a layman, states the seemingly obvious: "Of course, for a start, it proves that Jesus actually existed," to which another character, a Dr. Evans from the National Council of Churches, replies, "Oh, it's not that . . . After all, only a small school of skeptics, mainly in Germany, ever denied there was such a person as Jesus" (p. 91). Most mainstream scholars possess Dr. Evans's blithe assurance, but there is another side to the debate, as we learn from Bible magnate George Wheeler: "despite what Dr. Evans told you . . . about the majority of biblical scholars always having believed in the existence of Jesus, there has been less confidence . . . among religious rationalists and secular historians [some of whom] insisted that He was a myth" (p. 98).

There is certainly a reasonable conservative explanation for the sparse state of the evidence for Jesus, and Wallace makes Dr. Evans an eloquent mouthpiece for this view. "His followers felt no need to record history because to them history was about to end. They were not interested in how Jesus looked, but in what He did and said. . . . But . . . [t]o people of our time . . . Jesus has become unreal, the fictional figure of a folktale, like Hercules or Paul Bunyan" (p. 92). Yes, that would explain it. It *would*, that is, if we knew that was an accurate description of the case. And that is precisely what we do not know, lacking the convenience of a time machine enabling us to go and check it out. But one fact remains: as the fictive Dr. Evans says, doubt about there ever having been an historical Jesus Christ is probably more widespread among the non-specialist public than scholars tend to think. And it may not be because the public is "an accursed multitude that knoweth not the law" (John 7:49 KJV). The Christ Myth theory does not arise from amateurish ignorance. Rather, the blithe assurance of the scholarly guild may arise from the mutual reinforcement of a peer group, what Peter Berger and Thomas Luckmann[6] call a "plausibility structure" of the like-minded, in this case, a professional clique whose assumptions may be predetermined more

---

6. Berger and Luckman, *The Social Construction of Reality*, 154–56.

than they'd like to think by their church backgrounds, whether they continue to embrace them or not. The outsider may, just may, possess the advantage of the clear-eyed child who pointed out the emperor's lack of clothes.

I recall how my daughter Victoria, when only six years old, stopped my wife Carol in the middle of a bedtime Bible story about Jesus. Something Carol said implied Jesus was a real person, and Victoria protested: he couldn't have been, because no real person is that "popular." She seemed to mean that "Jesus" was more like a media fabrication or a fairy tale character, not someone like a sports star or the president. She hadn't heard such heresy from me, I can tell you. Not that she was right, mind you; I'm just suggesting that Wallace correctly portrays common sense making common people question whether such a figure ever existed, any more than Superman exists in the real world. Thus the importance of "the Ostia Antica discovery establishing for the first time the irrefutable historicity of Christ" (p. 86).

Not only would the discovery settle questions about the bare existence of Jesus; the supernatural element would be reinforced all the more strongly via the astonishing story of the second crucifixion and genuine resurrection of Jesus in Rome. This is brilliant: Wallace's *Gospel of James* first seems to vindicate the old Rationalistic hypothesis of Bahrdt and Venturini that Jesus merely swooned on the cross, was taken down prematurely and nursed back to health: "An Essene may well have healed Jesus. That was the contention of Karl F. Bahrdt and Karl H. Venturini, [each of] who[m] wrote a life of Jesus in the late 1700s.[7] They theorized that the Essenes had staged Christ's miracles, staged the Resurrection, and that He was removed from the Cross not dead but merely unconscious, and was revived by an Essene healer or physician" (p. 548). Wallace seems to think that the two men collaborated on a single book, but in fact they wrote separately. Bahrdt's *Ausführung des Plans und Zwecks Jesu. In Briefen an Wahrheit suchende Leser*, appeared in 1972, comprised of eleven volumes, over 3,000 pages. Venturini's *Natürliche Geschichte des grossen Propheten von Nazareth* appeared in four volumes, for a total of 2,700 pages, from 1800 to 1802. (Later on, Wallace tips his hat to one of these Rationalist theologians and their theory of an Essene healer when he names Augusto Monti's psychiatrist "Dr. Venturi.")

---

7. Schweitzer, *The Quest of the Historical Jesus*, 38–57.

So it first appears that the miraculous element of the life of Jesus has been exploded by James's gospel—until we read that he did in fact die and rise later on, in full view of witnesses! This is a sucker punch, making the supernatural climax all the more dramatic for following the seeming anticlimax of the survived crucifixion. The legendary embellishments of the familiar gospels are absent in James's gospel, which would vindicate Bultmann and the form critics in their view that the canonical stories grew in the telling. But—whammo!—*James* ends with a solid miracle after all, one worth all the others put together! And it is this element of *James*, together with the fresh teachings and immediate portraiture of Jesus, that accounts for the rebirth of Christian faith the text is supposed to ignite.

If Wallace derived the notion of Jesus surviving the cross and pursuing his ministry in parts unknown from Bahrdt and Venturini, where did he come by the further development of Jesus winding up in Rome? This much comes from another work Wallace makes sure to mention in a slightly contrived manner: he has the forger Le Brun refer to "That challenging but iconoclastic work, *The Nazarene Gospel Restored*[8] by Graves and Podro" (p. 547). Wallace owes more than that to this once-controversial book, which is now generally ignored, as we shall see. But the business about Jesus' post-Golgotha travels bringing him to Rome comes from a smaller work by Graves and Podro, *Jesus in Rome*,[9] which they call an appendix to their earlier tome. Wallace winks an acknowledgment to this little book when he has Randall muse: "I still find that hard to believe. Jesus in Rome. It's incredible" (p. 107). The ingenious argument of Graves and Podro (rehabilitated today by Barbara Thiering)[10] asks us to suppose that the "resurrection appearances" and visions of the early church were actual, physical encounters with the still-living Jesus. When his disciples went about preaching their gospel, they sometimes ran into their Lord who they mistakenly supposed had died on Calvary years before. When Saul of Tarsus saw Jesus on the road to Damascus, he really saw Jesus. When Paul maintained that Jesus was still alive despite general belief in his execution (Acts 25:19) he means Jesus escaped death, averted it.

---

8. Graves and Podro, *The Nazarene Gospel Restored*.
9. Graves and Podro, *Jesus in Rome*.
10. Thiering, *Jesus and the Riddle of the Dead Sea Scrolls*.

This argument is consonant with a story in the apocryphal *Acts of Peter* where Peter, fleeing Nero's persecution, hurries away from Rome and suddenly meets Jesus heading into the city. He is stunned and asks, "Where are you going, Lord?" Jesus answers, "To Rome, to be crucified again." Peter is stricken with shame for trying to evade his ordained martyrdom (John 21:18–19), and he pivots in his tracks, returning to Rome where his own cross awaits him. Of course we have always taken this appearance story to denote a vision of the ascended Christ that shames Peter into doing his duty, but Podro and Graves suggest that it is a record of a real historical encounter. Jesus still lived and was on his way into Rome to preach there. They pick on the otherwise-inexplicable notice in Suetonius that Claudius Caesar expelled Jews from Rome (in 49 CE) because of rioting instigated by one "Chrestus." But they infer Jesus could not have been executed for causing this conflict because we would surely have heard about it if he had.

After this point, Graves and Podro drift off the track and have Jesus go East, to Kashmir, an idea they derive from the Rationalistic nineteenth-century Ahmadiyya sect,[11] Muslims who believed Jesus was crucified but survived it and went on to preach in Central Asia, finally dying at a ripe old age and interred in Srinagar. Irving Wallace ignores this continuation of the post-crucifixion ministry in favor of Irenaeus' statement (*Against Heresies* 2.22.4–5)[12] that Jesus died at (or around) age fifty *in the reign of Claudius*. One really feels it would have made far more sense for Graves and Podro to have gone this way. And of course, the second crucifixion, followed by a real, miraculous resurrection, is Wallace's own contribution. In view of the final fate of Jesus Christ according to the James gospel, the code name of the secret publication project, Resurrection Two, takes on a whole new meaning.

THE NEW GOSPEL

I have already mentioned some of the more extraordinary teachings attributed to Jesus in Wallace's *James*, teachings so extraordinary they verge on the anachronistic. Others quoted by Wallace are obvious versions of canonical sayings. Still others have a ring of familiarity about

---

11. Ahmad, *Jesus in India*; Schonfield, *The Essene Odyssey*; Pappas, *Jesus' Tomb in India*.

12. Grant, *Irenaeus of Lyons*, 33, 51, 114–15.

them even though we do not recall them from Matthew, Mark, Luke, or John. Here are three. First, "Any two who make peace with one another in this house, they shall say to the mountain, Be moved, and it shall be moved." This one comes from the Nag Hammadi *Gospel of Thomas*, saying 48: "Jesus says, 'If two make peace with each other in this one house, there is nothing they cannot do by joining their forces. They shall say to this mountain, "Be moved!" and it shall be moved.'"[13]

The second example also comes from Thomas: "Those who obey shall make the earth like the heaven, and they shall inherit and know the kingdom of God." This is a short version of *Thomas* 22:

> Jesus saw children being nursed. He says to his disciples, "These nursing children are like those who enter the kingdom." They say to him, "Are we, then, to become children in order to enter the kingdom?" Jesus says to them, "When you make the two sexes one, and when you make the inner reality as the outer appearance and the outer body as the inner spirit and the heaven above as the earth below, and when you make the male and the female into a single one, so that the male will no more be male nor the female be female; when you make eyes in the place of an eye, and a hand in the place of a hand and a foot in the place of a foot; an image in the place of an image, then you shall enter the kingdom."[14]

The third *James* saying is as follows: "Let not the kingdom of heaven wither, for the kingdom is like a palm branch whose fruits fall about it, and the fruits are goodness that must be salvaged and again planted." (All three occur on p. 227.) This one comes from another Nag Hammadi text, the *Secret Book of James*, a text Wallace mentions elsewhere in the novel. Here is the source text from the *Secret Book of James* (not to be confused with Wallace's fictional *James*):

> Do not let heaven's kingdom wither away. It is like a palm shoot whose dates dropped around it. It produced buds, and after they grew, its productivity dried up. This is also what happened with fruit that came from this single root. After it was harvested, fruit was obtained by many. It certainly would be good if you could produce new growth now. You would find it [i.e., the kingdom]. (4:10–12)

---

13. Price, *The Pre-Nicene New Testament*, 980.
14. Ibid., 977.

Wallace, then, hardly ignores the Nag Hammadi library. "The importance of this fifth gospel discovery exceeds by far the discovery of the Dead Sea Scrolls in Israel and the Nag Hammadi papyri in Egypt" (p. 91). "This find consisted of thirteen papyrus volumes . . . In these fourth-century writings were a hundred and fourteen sayings of Jesus, many never known before this Coptic library was revealed" (p. 131). But why is the *Gospel According to James* such a big deal if the *Gospel of Thomas* had already been unearthed and found to contain a trove of "new" Jesus sayings? Perhaps we have been minimizing the importance of Thomas and other gospel discoveries, not in favor of the fictional James gospel, but for the benefit of Matthew, Mark, Luke, and John.

JAMES AND Q

We have already discussed the theory of the Q Source or Q Document in our summary of John Hall Roberts's novel *The Q Document* in Chapter 4. It is, briefly, the hypothetical source of the sayings appearing in both Matthew and Luke which these two did not derive from Mark's prior gospel. Irving Wallace seems to want to identify his *Gospel According to James* with the Q Document.

> The papyri that were found—that we now possess—are the lost source for the Synoptic Gospels [Matthew, Mark, and Luke], the so-called Q document, the fifth but actually the first and original gospel—the Gospel According to James. (p. 79)

Wallace also liked Graves and Podro's work, and in *The Nazarene Gospel Restored* those scholars tried to reconstruct a hypothetical megagospel from which *all four* canonical gospels broke away like separate continents from primal Pangaea. But that is not Q, which has a much narrower range, covering only the overlaps between Matthew and Luke that do not appear in Mark. Wallace liked the Nazarene Gospel hypothesis, which accounts for his references to *James* as the origin of all four gospels.

> Throughout, James had recollected precepts, aphorisms, maxims, adages of Jesus that had been heretofore unknown, as well as some that obviously served as the original source material for the writers of the four traditional gospels and for the writers of the many apocryphal gospels. (p. 226)

They would like nothing more than to be proved right by the discovery of a lost gospel—one they had always believed had existed as the primary source for the four accepted gospels. (p. 549)

It gets worse when Wallace also tells us explicitly that the canonical gospel writers had never seen James's gospel (p. 232)! Those who knew about the whole story agreed to suppress it, and only three copies of the *Gospel According to James* were ever made. Two perished with Peter and Barnabas, the third hidden in Ostia Antica. In this case, it is simply impossible for James's gospel to be identified with either Q or the *Nazarene Gospel,* much less both. The canonical evangelists could never have seen James's text. Whence this glaring contradiction? I think it is the result of Wallace's attempt to combine three favorite sources that ultimately diverged. First, though I cannot prove it, I suspect there is more than coincidental similarity between Wallace's *The Word* and John Hall Roberts's *The Q Document* from a decade earlier, a novel which had probably not escaped Wallace's attention.

Consider some parallels. In both books, the lost gospel turns out to be a fake, a hoax engineered to discredit Christian faith (how *James* is supposed to do that, we will discuss presently). Both forgers simulated ancient ink and wrote their work upon genuine ancient parchment/papyrus, blank in Wallace's case, erased in Roberts's. Both schemers saved back fragments from the ancient parchments and papyri on which they inscribed their gospels, making it possible to prove the gospels were modern forgeries. In both cases, the protagonist learns of this evidence through cryptic clues left by the forger. Both protagonists sooner or later get more of the story from the grown daughter of the ostensible discoverer of the lost gospel. So I propose that Wallace simply borrowed the identification of the new gospel with Q from Roberts's earlier novel and the notion of the Nazarene über-gospel from the work of Podro and Graves. But once he decided to mix in the fascinating theory of Podro and Graves that Jesus had survived crucifixion, and ended up in Rome, he was stuck with the problem of why the canonical gospels know nothing about this denouement. So he said Matthew, Mark, Luke, and John had not been privy to this information, hence neither with James's gospel. It just doesn't work. He is trying to have his cake and eat it, too. And a doughnut besides.

WE HAD HOPED HIM THE ONE TO REDEEM ISRAEL

What was at stake in the *Gospel According to James* hoax? Remember, in *The Mystery of Mar Saba*, the forged document discredited the resurrection, and the disclosure of it came close to toppling Western (Christian) civilization. A tsunami of nihilism and anomie ensued before the imposture was exposed. In *The Q Document* the fear was that the forged document, should it be published, would debunk Christianity as nothing more than a whitewashed version of a failed political movement, as if someone were trying to make Abbie Hoffman into the Messiah. Again, faith would have been undermined but for the exposure of the fraud at the last moment.

In *The Word*, the prospect is a little different: Christianity seemed to be standing on the brink of decay and death, giving way to the progress of scientific secularism. The *James* hoax was meant to offer false hope of rejuvenation, and then to dash it when the originator of the hoax exposed it himself. People had quickly rejoiced that their old doubts as to the historical truth as well as the modern relevance of Christ had been overcome via the new gospel, almost a second coming of Christ in itself. How did we manage to get along before *James*? Once *James* was debunked, people would snap out of the dream of faith and awaken to a cold, gray morning of doubt, devoid once again of God. Better never to have hoped than to hope and have hope dashed! That was the strategy. But the joke turns out to be on the forger, Robert Le Brun, and his advocate, Steve Randall, for the forces of Big Church and Bible Publishing outsmart them, rubbing out Le Brun and silencing Randall. And the world welcomes the publication of the International New Testament with twenty-eight books, starring the new *Gospel According to James*, rejoicing in a new age of faith. Even Maertin de Vroom hops aboard the bandwagon, though, like Randall, he secretly knows better. But the publishers secure his cooperation by promising him the coveted leadership of the World Council of Churches, a position he plans to use to advance his radical plans. The new Jesus, granted, would tend to get many people focused heavenward, but on the other hand, in the new text Jesus does also teach social progressivism, so it seems a reasonable swap.

An aside: When I first read *The Word* I found it amusing, though hardly significant, that at the very time *The Word* appeared, the New York Bible Society International was unveiling their own new version of the New Testament called the *New International Bible*, now better known as the *New International Version*. It has since become the most popular translation among conservative Protestants. One day back then I found myself sitting in the church pew next to Edwin H. Palmer, Executive Secretary of the NIV's Committee on Bible Translation, the front man for the project. I couldn't resist asking him if he was aware of Irving Wallace's novel of the publication of a new Bible, containing a new gospel, and bearing very nearly the same name as his own new version. He had never heard of it. They had already changed the title from *The Holy Bible: A Contemporary Translation* to *The New International Version*, and I guess it was too late to change it yet again, to avoid confusion.

HAS IT HAPPENED?

I have already drawn a startling and uncomfortable parallel between the late Morton Smith, ostensible discoverer of the *Secret Gospel of Mark* (issued in the very same year as *The Word*) and the devilish hoaxer in *The Mystery of Mar Saba*. Indeed, I suggested that in Smith's case, life was imitating art. Well, we have a striking literary doppelganger for Smith in *The Word*'s Robert Le Brun. This bitter man, betrayed again and again by the Catholic Church, was determined to have his revenge against the religion that had once promised to redeem him (p. 499). In Smith's case, so the story goes, it was revenge against the homophobia of the conventional churches that prompted his fabrication of a "lost" gospel of a possibly homosexual Jesus, a "Jesus Christ Supergay." Le Brun's plotting even paralleled Smith's in detail: "To have secreted my handiwork in some cave in Israel or Jordan, or in some storage room in a monastery in Egypt, would have been easier, more logical" (p. 550). But Le Brun had determined to hitch his wagon onto the credibility of archaeologist Augusto Monti, and Monti had famously theorized one might discover some ancient gospel or gospel source amid the ruins of Rome's seaport, Ostia Antica. So it was there that Le Brun secreted his gospel, sealed up in the base of a statue, waiting for Monti's questing spade.

What ensued upon the announcement of Smith's *Secret Gospel* was a scholarly debate over its authenticity that continues today. The numerous theories based on the assumption of a genuinely ancient longer edition of Mark are venturesome and daring (though none so much as Smith's own), making Jesus into a magician and a sexual libertine not unlike seventeenth-century messianic pretender Jacob Frank. But it was a tempest in a scholarly teapot, a gust of wind about the top of the ivory tower, nothing like the hoopla that greets *James*'s publication in *The Word*.

Finally, one is tempted to ask what critics might make of the *Gospel of James* if it were not merely the product of Irving Wallace's imagination. My guess is that astute critics would take the claims that the gospel was seen by hardly anyone before its rediscovery to be just like the empty tomb story of Mark, a late add-on using secrecy as a cloak for recent origin. One can picture early Christians suddenly hearing these tales and saying, "Now wait just a minute, son. I've been a Christian for years, and I've never heard of this! Why not, if it's as true as you say?" "Oh, well, you see, the truth was hidden away for a long time because the women at the tomb forgot to tell the apostles about their visit and Jesus' plans to meet them in Galilee, so nobody showed up, and the story went no further—till now. Yeah—that's the ticket!" Same thing here. "Oh! Er, you see, James only made three copies. Martyrs lost two of them, and James' was hidden away—till now! Lucky you!" So even if *James* turned out to be a genuinely ancient writing, scholars might well still conclude it was a hoax, albeit an ancient one. And then what would the point have been? What would the forger have been trying to achieve? I suggest the James gospel would be viewed as an attempt to vindicate a hitherto-unknown Jesus-pretender such as Mark 13:6, 21–23; Matt 24:24–25; Luke 21:8 warns of: "Many will appear trading on my name, saying, 'It is I!'"[15]

Nor would biblical critics be the only ones to greet a new James gospel with suspicion. Wallace badly misreads fundamentalists when he pictures them as welcoming a new gospel that contradicts the conventional four. Despite the utility of the new text for securing belief in a historical, even a resurrected Jesus, fundamentalists would reluctantly refuse it for the sake of maintaining their dogmatic belief in the infallibility and inerrancy of scripture. Viewing Matthew, Mark, Luke, and John merely as historical sources about Jesus, open to the possibility of human error, would come as much too high a price tag for any benefits that a new, eyewitness gospel might offer. "And no one accustomed to vintage wine wants the new, for he thinks, 'The old is good!'" (Luke 5:39).[16]

---

15. Price, *The Pre-Nicene New Testament*, 552.
16. Ibid., 513.

7 | Evangel and Espionage
Peter Van Greenaway,
The Judas Gospel

ISCARIOT, INVICTUS

READING THIS FASCINATING NOVEL[1] by Peter Van Greenaway, penned before some of the works that have since made him more famous, one is hard-pressed not to think of two previous literary works that are in their own ways attempts at modern gospels. So let's begin by taking a closer look at those before we get to Van Greenaway's own work, starting with the parable of the Grand Inquisitor, a separable piece of Dostoyevsky's *The Brothers Karamazov*.

Dostoyevsky's parable is the imaginary tale of an unheralded second coming of Jesus, not in apocalyptic glory, but rather as an itinerant healer and friend of the poor, mingling with the medieval Spanish masses who recognize him immediately. It is something in the nature of a "second first coming." As soon as they get wind of this, the Holy Office (in other words, the Spanish Inquisition office) decides to take matters in hand. The Grand Inquisitor orders the Nazarene clapped in manacles in the local hoosegow. Finally he visits Jesus in his cell to report his sentence: the Church has ruled that he, the holy troublemaker, shall perish in flames on the morrow. It must be so for the wellbeing of the Catholic Church as well as for the poor, shivering flock that has mortgaged its conscience to this Institution which guarantees them a ticket to heaven and, better yet, takes the serious business of independent thinking, autonomous decision-making, out of their hands once and for all, a sacrifice they regard as a bargain indeed! Jesus was crucified in the first place for cruelly threatening to enslave people, chaining them to the wheel of freedom. No one wanted this! They were happy to be

---

1. All page references are to the paperback edition.

rid of such a Jesus and hounded him down the Via Dolorosa. And now, after all these centuries, here comes Jesus as if to raise his own ghost as a standard around which fools may rally until they realize the danger he poses to their timid souls and turn on him again. No, the Church will not let him open old wounds and entice and disturb the minds of men with his destructive Siren Song. The Inquisitor considers himself, not Jesus, the true friend of men's timid souls. But, at length, after this bitter tirade, he suffers a moment of sentiment, recalling the earlier years of his own idealism. And so he opens the cell door and tells Jesus to get out of town.

The second gospel-like text that springs to mind just as powerfully in connection with *The Judas Gospel* is Andrew Lloyd Weber and Tim Rice's *Jesus Christ Superstar*, in which Judas Iscariot serves as both a prophetic discerner of Jesus' fate (and its ironies) and as an unsuspecting dupe in that fate. It is Judas who worries at Jesus' petulance and seeming failure to take their danger seriously, who sees the faith of his followers already threatening to hoist Jesus' crucified form onto the prow of their own ship to sail it where he never dreamed of going. Ahead of time Judas can see Jesus carelessly leading his disciples and his whole nation into the hungry maw of Rome. After the fact, when an angel-winged Judas returns after hanging himself, to ponder the meaning of all that the characters have done, he christens the fate of Jesus an enigma that must be left for future ages to solve. Left with his ignorance, Judas is not sure anyone else will ever understand—any better than he himself did when he surrendered his life—the mystery of Jesus.

I suppose it is possible that Van Greenaway was influenced by either or both of these works, but it is the parallels themselves that are important for understanding his novel and what it means to communicate. Essentially, Van Greenaway has cast Judas in the role of the Grand Inquisitor, one with sympathy and even love for Jesus, yet baffled by him. But the novel's Judas is also granted prophetic powers—like the Judas of *Superstar* but even more important—so that his actions seem to envision future ages to which he ought not to be privy. For Van Greenaway, Judas knows good and well what will happen now that Jesus' other disciples have managed to copyright his name and likeness: Christianity will be born, or invented. And it will begin already as a confidence trick. Overnight, or should one say, after three days, it will turn into the Church of the Grand Inquisitor.

> I tell you the truth, son of Joseph. They will make of you the keys of their kingdom. They will cudgel men's minds with your bones. They will stifle their senses in the sickly folds of your winding-sheet; you will live again, wrapped in an odour of wormwood and sanctity. (p. 99)

And Van Greenaway has in mind specifically the Roman Catholic Church, though admittedly he uses them to represent all organized religion in general. Here's a typical tirade, from an unbeliever to a priest:

> Damnable cant. It's made your organisation the envy of the Devil himself. If destruction won't serve then you turn to instruction. Your doctrines are so riddled with fallacies you must needs employ the best artists—designers, architects, musicians, writers—to obscure, camouflage and explain them away. (p.192)

Not only does Judas have a keen view of his movement's future, but his will for the truth (what truth? Hang on!) to come out seems to create an ineluctable trajectory cutting through the millennia to an ultimate disclosure. His ancient will becomes virtually a necromantic providence tugging at the mind of an archaeologist to go and discover he knows not what, but which an instinct and a hunch tell him lurks somewhere in the area in which the Dead Sea Scrolls were earlier discovered. It finds a way to elude and evade every obstacle placed in the path of its final surface-breaking. And in the end Judas' gospel proves the truth of the verse, "what you hear whispered in your ear, proclaim from the housetops!" (Matt 10:27b). But at this point we must back up for at least a summary of the plot.

Our protagonist (it might be too much to dub him our hero) is a British professor of Semitic languages, one Mallory, whose jaded cynicism toward organized religion is increasingly colliding with his wife's sudden interest in converting to Roman Catholicism. He is surprised at the temporary escape from domestic tensions afforded him by an improbable invitation by Sir Max Lonsdale, an old friend and far more successful colleague, to accompany him on an expedition to the Judean desert. He is sure, for some reason, that there awaits him one more ancient scroll with staggering implications. ("One short passage, destroying for ever and ever the credibility of a theomaniac foisted on millions by successive elites with a special interest in perpetuating the authorized version," p. 85). He remains cagey in such a way as to imply he may know more than he says, whether from psychic intuition or some obscure clue in an ancient source. But Mallory never finds out which, since, shortly after their arrival in Israel, his party is attacked and massacred by a band of Jordanian guerillas. Only Mallory manages to survive by virtue of having wandered away from the camp in search of bathroom privacy. Hearing the trouble, he desperately seeks and finds a barely navigable cave mouth high up on a stone slope. Safely inside, he discovers a rolled parchment scroll.

Intercutting flashbacks have already told us that this scroll was planted by Judas Iscariot. Judas, having neither hanged himself as Matthew 27:5 tells us (a passage that in fact borrows the death of Ahithophel from 2 Sam 17:23) nor exploded in a shower of his own entrails as per Acts 1:18, lived to fight the Romans in the Jewish War of 66–73 CE. Fleeing to the Essene monastery at Qumran, he requested shelter and writing materials, then set about recording for posterity the facts already being smothered by the hierarchy of the Jesus movement.

THE TESTAMENT OF JUDAS

Essentially Judas' legacy is the recollection of a Jesus who failed to live up to the legends now surrounding him, or even to the public relations of his own day. Himself already a revolutionary leader, Judas saw great potential in Jesus but began to think him more of a risk than an asset. Jesus appeared to lack a certain note of gravitas, viewing his followers with a hint of cynical levity and, in his teachings, retreating behind rhetorical equivocations so that people might perceive him as saying whatever they wanted to hear. As Judas observed, Jesus too easily acquiesced in the flattery and false solicitude of a self-regarding oaf named Simon Peter. On the whole, the relationship drawn here between Judas and Jesus is again not unlike that in *Jesus Christ Superstar*, except that Webber and Rice impart to their Jesus some sense of his own destiny even though his understanding of it is rather limited, limited enough to make him chafe on occasion.

Eventually Van Greenaway's Jesus did take a stand and attempted to ignite an uprising against Rome, but it was quickly squashed: the Romans knew what Jesus' men would do in the temple before they even got there. And somehow friends and allies were prevented from knowing about the ambush, making it all the more effective. Judas surmises that it was Peter who sabotaged Jesus' uprising, then turned him in to the authorities. And as soon as the body was buried, Judas tells us, Peter began to take control of what remained of the community, which became a self-enriching sect.

What Judas describes is a scenario much like that posited by the seventeenth-century rationalist Samuel Hermann Reimarus. Like Judas in *The Judas Gospel*, Reimarus wrote his bombshell, *On the Intention of Jesus and his Disciples*,[2] and deferred it for posthumous publication. (That publication would be done by Lessing, as we saw in Chapter 4). Reimarus's was the first critical sketch of the historical Jesus, and he took Jesus for a failed rebel, his disciples as con men who set themselves up as heads of a first-century televangelism series built on their mythologized master.

So with Van Greenaway. Someone among Jesus' lieutenants had to take the fall, and Judas was drafted for the job. The blame for the death of Jesus came to rest on his shoulders, though in fact it had been the cowardly, blustering Simon Peter who sold him out for the first of several cash infusions he hoped to gain from Jesus, his new golden goose.

Forty years later, with Roman soldiers hot on his trail, Judas has just finished his account and finds an obscure cave in which to toss it, awaiting eventual rediscovery. Guess which cave? Across the centuries, the hillside vacuum called out to poor Mallory, offering him shelter, and more. Retrieving the mysterious scroll, he is electrified to have recovered what bills itself as *The Testament of Judas*. Israeli patrols rescue him and he is all over the news, but merely for surviving. He is in no mood to announce his discovery, not wanting to be deprived of it by the authorities, since legally it does belong to Israel. He seems to make a clean exit, scroll in his satchel, and returns to England and his wife's annoying pieties. Eager to shut her up, he slips and tells her about the scroll. She is sure it must be a fake but blabs about it to the priest who is coaching her for conversion.

In the meantime, Mallory gets together with an old friend, an ad man fallen on hard times for allowing his integrity to spoil his business. They confer on how best to deal with the discovery. Mallory, who owes his survival and his discovery to his insistent bladder, is no hero, and now he proves it. He decides not to make the text known, but rather to blackmail the Vatican for a million Pounds Sterling.

Imagine the heart-stopping surprise (literally) of the head of the Holy Office upon reading Mallory's letter with its photographs and

---

2. Talbert, *Reimarus: Fragments*.

translation of the *Testament of Judas*, together with an age-testable parchment fragment! His blithering assistant rushes from the chamber to report the Cardinal's death, and who should he run into but Giovanni della Paresi, commonly known as The Dominican, a sort of Black Ops priest combining the suavity of James Bond with the ruthlessness of Jack Bauer. He reads the letter and its dismaying contents, and realizes that the church must act immediately.

Receiving authority from the Pope to do whatever, *ahem*, is necessary, left in pretty vague terms, the Dominican departs for England where, via various intrigues, he winds up murdering Mallory, his wife, the ad man and his wife. He also absconds with *The Testament of Judas*. Unfortunately he had no way of knowing about the priest who heard Mrs. Mallory's revelations. And the priest eventually helps Scotland Yard put the pieces together. The Dominican manages to get his dirty deeds done and to fly back to Vatican City one step ahead of the Yard.

But the news is not good. The Pope is none too happy with him. It turns out that the Israeli authorities had snuck the scroll away from Mallory, photographed and translated it, and now they have published it in full in the daily papers! Plus, the British investigation has laid the murders at St. Peter's steps. The Pope now disavows all knowledge of the Dominican's dirty work, selling out his champion much as his patron St. Peter had long ago sold out Jesus. Nor is the Pope the only contestant for the role of betrayer; as we have seen, Mallory, despite his acid contempt for Catholicism, also preferred to make a few extra bucks over revealing Judas' irresistible truth. But they both failed and Judas' will is what prevailed in the end.

JUDAS AND OEDIPUS

Van Greenaway seems to have had Sophocles' *Oedipus the King* on his mind as he wrote. He mentions the Oedipus character in passing once, and in another passage uses wording clearly based on Sophocles' tale about King Oedipus and his quest to discern oracular signs of the cause for a plague besetting his city of Thebes. Oedipus gets rather closer to the truth than he might wish when he questions a shepherd as to the identity of an infant he had once rescued from exposure on the hillside. The infant turns out to have been Oedipus himself, whom his royal father had turned over to a servant to dispose of. A prophecy foretold that the infant son should unseat and kill the father, and this fate King Laius sought to avoid. But the servant could not bring himself to do the deed (as thoughtlessly common as such infanticides were in antiquity), so he committed the baby to the arms of a shepherd, who has now, years later, been found. And Oedipus is piecing the old story together. The shepherd sees where it is all headed, toward the implication of Oedipus as his father's unwitting murderer and the cause of the plague. And to the king's questionings he finally protests, "For the love of the gods, do not, master, do not ask anything more!"[3] Van Greenaway uses almost the same words when the Pope asks his agent if he thinks the newly discovered Judas text is real:

> "Do not ask me; for the love of God, do not ask." The Dominican whispered a beggar's command from the depths of his desperate soul. For he knew, they both knew, more than they dared to admit even to the atom of tortured freedom rotting in the darkest cells of their subconscious. (p. 162)

But I am thinking also of Rene Girard's musings on Oedipus, as he describes the process that led to the "recognition" of Oedipus as the root of the plague.

> The attribution of guilt that henceforth passes for "true" differs in no way from the attributions that will henceforth be regarded as "false," except that in the case of the "true" guilt no voice is raised to protest any aspect of the charge. A particular version of events succeeds in imposing itself; it loses its polemical nature in becoming the acknowledged basis of the myth, in becoming the myth itself . . . At the point where two, three, or hundreds of symmetrical accusations meet, one alone makes itself heard and the others fall silent.[4]

The chaos leading to and following the defeat and capture of Jesus, insofar as Van Greenaway describes it with vivid realism, invites us to speculate on the dynamics of the situation of which he depicts but the iceberg tip. It would have been, indeed must have been, such a matrix as Girard describes: the failed compatriots of Jesus, licking their wounds, must have sought to ease their collective conscience as a defeated party by narrowing the blame to the real or imagined subversion of a single villain. Perhaps because they had observed Judas previously taking a

---

3. Sophocles, "Oedipus the King," 143.
4. Girard, *Violence and the Sacred*, 78.

critical view of Jesus, refusing to flatter him, most inferred that Judas sold him out. Something must have led them to choose him, after all. Meanwhile, Judas merely surmises the guilt of Peter, also based on his previous disposition (ironically as a flatterer!). Judas' professed certainty attested in his *Testament* is never proven there. It is finally no clearer to the reader (or shouldn't be, at any rate) that any single figure, whether Judas or Peter, was responsible for Jesus' defeat. That is the way scapegoating works. Often no single person would have had the power to subvert a whole endeavor anyway. The choice of a scapegoat salves the collective conscience by the choice of a shared delusion.

What is at stake in the publication of *The Testament of Judas*? The case envisioned is much like what we saw in James Hall Roberts's *The Q Document* back in Chapter 4. It is not as if some supernatural secret is revealed, a counter-miracle to that believed in by Christians. No, the shock is of a different kind. The air will be completely let out of the tire.

> These, the actual words, written by Christ's greatest enemy on earth, these words, simply and effectively stripping the Saviour of all heavenly endowment, reducing him to a charlatan, a disillusioned rebel against authority—the father of all Catholics a simple protestant. (pp. 193–94)

Jesus as a failed freedom fighter? Well, one supposes he might still have been Messiah and Son of God, his crucifixion an inspiration like that of Spartacus. But Judas reveals Jesus as something of a mediocrity. Still, Christian faith tends to view the humanity of Jesus in an abstract way, concerned mainly to show that Jesus was a genuine human being, neither an angel or an alien. It was only early twentieth-century Liberal Modernist Protestantism that verged on a personality cult of Jesus, as witness Harry Emerson Fosdick's sermon *The Personality of Jesus—The Soul of Christianity*.[5] But on any traditional understanding of faith, why need we expect Jesus not to have been irritating or disturbing? How many people have had the good fortune to meet some artist or official they had idolized, only to be crushed by some slight or disgusted by some perceived flaw? The simple fact they had not expected it means such personal idiosyncrasies had formed no part of the greatness that was so admired, nor did they detract from that greatness. They are simply irrelevant.

5. Fosdick, *The Personality of Jesus*.

So how disappointed would we have to be in Jesus before we decided to write him off? Think of the portrayal of Mozart in the film *Amadaeus*. What a snotty little creep! But do we venerate Mozart as a paragon of emotional maturity, or as an inspired composer? Likewise, it might take a bit more than what disappointed Judas to do the trick. Bultmann says somewhere that, while we do not need, really, to know any specifics about Jesus' life, faith would be in danger if we were to discover that Jesus had been dragged kicking and screaming to the cross. Short of that, though, who cares?

But still I wonder. Remember how Miguel Servetus, condemned by Calvin to be burnt alive for his denials of the Trinity, did in fact have to be dragged sobbing and begging to the stake. Yet I for one cannot hold it against him that he could not maintain Stoic calm in such circumstances. Can you? He is a martyr for faith and free thought in any case, as even subsequent Calvinists recognized when they erected memorials to him in atonement for Calvin's mad cruelty. I think it would have been the same with Christian faith in the wake of Judas' gospel being made public. Still, Peter Van Greenaway's *The Judas Gospel* stands as a fine parable of how a religious institution elevates itself to a despicable, false idol as soon as it finds it necessary, in order to protect its interests, to silence the truth and those who know it.

THE REAL THING?

In Eastertide 2006, the media was all aflutter with news of the publication of the ancient *Gospel of Judas* by the National Geographic Society. Usually I find media coverage of scholarly religious issues so inept, so biased toward what the Nielsen Ratings say that people want to hear, that I cannot bear to view it. But this time they got the emphasis exactly right. They raised the question, what if we have to revise our centuries-old opinion of Judas Iscariot as the despicable betrayer of the greatest man who ever lived? It was a sensationalist approach. But it was the right approach.

Scholars had known of the existence of a *Gospel of Judas* for most of Christian history. Bishop Irenaeus of Lyons discussed and condemned the text back in 180 CE in his massive treatise *Against Heresies* (1.31). From his account we knew that the Cainite Gnostics circulated this text (and presumably wrote it), and that it set forth their belief that Jesus had conspired with Judas, *asking* him to turn him over to those who would crucify him. His death was a saving act, not least for Jesus himself, as it would extricate him from the imprisonment of the incarnation, setting his spirit free. Thus, Judas was being recruited for a holy, even a priestly, mission. If this depiction of Judas sounds familiar to you, it may be that you remember it from either the book or the film version of Nikos Kazantzakis's *The Last Temptation of Christ*. When you think about it, it is a little strange that Christians believe the crucifixion was a wonderful deed of salvation and yet vilify the chosen instrument of divine providence that brought it about: Judas Iscariot. Well, it turns out there were some Christians who were a little more consistent.

Irenaeus discussed various other "heretical" gospels and revelations that we couldn't read for ourselves—until 1945, when the Nag Hammadi library was discovered. Among the manuscripts were the *Gospel of Thomas*, the *Gospel of Truth*, and the *Secret Book of John*. The last of these Irenaeus had discussed at some length, and it was now seen that he had been very accurate. He mocked, but he did not caricature. And it would seem he was right on target with the *Gospel of Judas*, too. It was discovered thirty years after the Nag Hammadi texts, also in the sands of Egypt.

WHAT'S NEW, ISCARIOT?

The TV anchors posed the question: do we have new evidence about Judas? Well, no we don't. And on this point all the interviewed scholars rightly agreed. The great James M. Robinson, veteran expert on the Nag Hammadi texts (and strangely excluded from the *National Geographic*'s "dream team" of textual experts and archaeologists), when interviewed on TV, quipped that the portrait of Judas in the new gospel is "a product of second-century religious fantasy." As soon as he said it, I thought, "You mean—just like Matthew, Mark, Luke, and John?" The astonishing fact is that Irenaeus provides us not only our earliest mention of the *Gospel of Judas*. Irenaeus is also the first writer to list our conventional four gospels! He quotes an earlier bishop, Papias of Hierapolis (writing about 125 CE) as describing the origins of Matthew and Mark, but it is by no means clear that Papias was talking about our two gospels. Irenaeus is the first to mention Matthew, Mark, Luke, and John. So they, too, must have been written before 180 CE. But how much before? There are no clear quotations from them in earlier writers, much less citations by name. Personally, I favor a second-century date for all four canonical gospels. And what they tell us about Judas (and Jesus!) is liable to be just as fictive as the new Judas gospel.

At first, it seems that the story of Jesus' arrest and death did not feature a Judas character. It began with the simple assertion that Jesus was "delivered up" or "handed over" (Rom 8:32) for our sins. Who did this deed? God the Father, that's who! You see, the Greek word *paradidomai* can mean "yielded up" or "betrayed," depending on the context. In 1 Corinthians 11:23, Paul speaks of the Last Supper, which took place on "the night he was betrayed" or "delivered up." There is no way to know whether the intended agent is God or some malicious human being. Up to this point there seems to have been no detailed story of how and why Jesus died, or under what circumstances. The epistles speak of Jesus' death at the hands of invisible, angelic powers (1 Cor 2:8; Col 2:13–15), but have nothing to say about the involvement of the Jewish Sanhedrin, Herod Antipas, or Pontius Pilate. Mark was the first to try to tell a coherent story of the death of Jesus, and he cobbled together material from Psalm 22 to make his crucifixion account. So he had to ask himself, precisely how is Jesus going to go from the friendly surroundings of supporters and disciples to the clutches of enemies who will crucify him?

The easiest recourse was to incarnate the plot development as a single character existing only to "do the job."[6] He is what Tzvetan Todorov[7] calls a "narrative-man." Such "characters" are scarcely characters at all, more like narrative functions come to life. They are often given punning names to signal their sheer utility. In this case, the betrayer is "Judas," a Jew, or rather, *the* Jew. And he is named Iscariot, or "Man of Falsehood."[8]

That Judas is a single-use literary tool is evident from two facts. First, no narrative motivation is ascribed to him in Mark's account, where it is simply stated that he went to the Sanhedrin and offered them Jesus (Mark 14:10–11). Matthew thought this odd, so he rewrote the scene to suggest that Judas approached the council with money on his mind (Matt 26:13–15). John liked that and kept it, but he also picked up

---

6. Kermode, *The Genesis of Secrecy*, 84–85.

7. Todorov, *The Poetics of Prose*, 66–79.

8. Gärtner, *Iscariot*. Other such pun-names in the gospels include Nicodemus ("ruler of the people"), Martha ("lady of the house"), Bartimaeus ("son of poverty"), Jairus ("he will raise up"), and Zacchaeus ("almsgiving").

Luke's attempt to improve Mark, having Judas possessed by Satan to do the dirty deed (Luke 22:3-6; John 13:2).

Second, Judas does not fit into the narrative of any of the gospels. Why do the enemies of Jesus *need* Judas? He guides them to the Garden, but anyone could have shadowed a prominent group like Jesus' entourage. He tells the arresting party that he will point out the man they want. But they are there to seize him on account of his dangerous popularity! How could they not know which one he was? "Hey, which of you guys is Elvis?" Judas has been clumsily shoe-horned into the story. Why does he betray? Because he is the betrayer. How does he betray? By being on the scene.

JUDAS THOMAS

Before the surprise discovery of the ancient *Gospel of Judas*, one scholar[9] thought it more likely that the bishop of Lyons misunderstood a reference to the Nag Hammadi *Gospel of Thomas*, in which Thomas is actually called "Judas Thomas" (common in Syrian church tradition). Thus no separate "*Gospel of Judas*." Apparently he was wrong. But there may be an element of truth in his conjecture. Some think that there was after all a historical Judas, or rather that the apostle Judas Thomas was later vilified and caricatured as "Judas the Betrayer," perhaps for theological reasons. Gregory J. Riley[10] argues that Thomas was associated with numerous doctrines at which the Gospel of John takes aim, which is why John portrays Thomas as a doubter, a fatalist, etc. (Elaine Pagels warms over the same thesis in her *Beyond Belief: The Secret Gospel of Thomas*.) The *Gospel of Thomas* does indeed feature a scene much like one in the new *Gospel of Judas*. Here are the two compared:

> Jesus says to his disciples, "Compare me and tell me what I am like." Simon Peter says to him, "You are like a righteous angel." Matthew says to him, "You are like a philosopher possessed of understanding." Thomas says to him, "Master, my mouth can scarcely frame the words of what you are like!" Jesus says, "I am not your master, because you have drunk, you have become filled, from the bubbling spring which I have measured out." He took him aside privately and said three things to him. So when Thomas rejoined his companions, they pressed him, saying, "What did

---

9. Peason, *Gnosticism, Judaism, and Egyptian Christianity*, 106.
10. Riley, *Resurrection Reconsidered*.

> Jesus say to you?" Thomas said to them, "If I tell you even one of the things he said to me, you will pick up stones and hurl them at me—and fire will erupt from the stones and consume you!" (Gospel of Thomas, saying 13)[11]

> Knowing that Judas was reflecting upon something that was exalted, Jesus said to him, "Step away from the others, and I shall tell you the mysteries of the kingdom. It is possible for you to reach it, but you will grieve a great deal. For someone else will replace you, in order that the twelve disciples may again come to completion with their god."[12]

The scenes have much in common, suggesting that they might be two versions of the same original. In both, Judas/Thomas is singled out among the twelve and physically removed from them for Jesus to confide elite teachings. The eventual reaction of the eleven is excommunication. The *Gospel of Thomas* anticipates that the eleven would seek to execute Judas Thomas for heresy if they heard his doctrine, so shocking would they find it. The *Gospel of Judas* plainly predicts Judas Iscariot's expulsion and replacement (as in Acts 1:16–26) in the council of the Twelve. And in both cases the reason is the shocking nature of his teachings, an advanced course from Jesus the revealer. Such was his infamy: Orwellian "Thoughtcrime."

The secret that orthodox Christianity fears the most is the truth that would expose its dogmas as infantile. The Gnostics wanted to put away childish things, no matter what became of conventional belief as a result. As Nietzsche said, "faith is not wanting to know the truth,"[13] and Gnostics, who took Judas for their symbol, were glad to sacrifice faith to gain knowledge. Judas' "gospel" symbolizes whatever that higher knowledge is that discredits Christianity while allowing its knower to transcend it.

ANOTHER JUDAS GOSPEL

What would have been the point of composing a "*Gospel of Judas*"? Basically, it is the same as Friedrich Nietzsche writing his book called *The Antichrist*, starring himself. It signals an attempt to parry the truth

---

11. Price, *The Pre-Nicene New Testament*, 975.
12. Kasser et al., *The Gospel of Judas from Codex Tchacos*, 23.
13. Nietzsche, *The Anti-Christ*, 51.

claims of orthodox, "apostolic" Christianity. A Judas evangel is not intended as a parallel alternative to Christianity, like Buddhism or Islam, but rather a counterpoint *within the Christian tradition*. It is to announce a transvaluation of the values of traditional Christianity, seizing the higher moral ground to attack it. This is certainly the purpose of at least one twentieth-century fiction with a similar title in addition to Van Greenaway's *The Judas Gospel*, the remarkable book, *The Gospel according to Judas Iscariot* written by Ernest Sutherland Bates and published in 1929, the same year Peter Van Greenaway was born.

Bates's evangelist Judas disdains the Hebrew God Jehovah in a fashion quite reminiscent of Nag Hammadi Gnosticism, not to mention Nietzsche. But his alternative is simply to seek knowledge and to realize one's solidarity with all humanity. The life within us is the only "God" we need. In the *Gospel according to Judas Iscariot*, Jesus first allies himself with Judas and shares his enlightened views. Satan appears to Jesus, but he withstands his temptations. But he is not so stolid when *Jehovah* shows up to tempt him! To Judas' shock and disgust, Jesus accepts Jehovah's offer to sell out to him, becoming his Son and preaching his soul-destroying gospel of Christian priestcraft. The scene recalls the one in *It's a Wonderful Life* when Mr. Potter tries and nearly succeeds in buying off George Bailey, only Jesus does not see through it.

In contrast to both Bates's *Gospel according to Judas Iscariot* and Peter Van Greenaway's *The Judas Gospel*, the recently published *Gospel of Judas* has been promoted in the real world. But is it, as everyone seems to think, a real, a genuine ancient work (whether or not written by a historical Judas)? It may not be. Richard J. Arthur,[14] an expert in Coptic dialects and on the Nag Hammadi codices, argues that *National Geographic*'s text is a modern hoax. Why? Arthur notes three things. First, just as *Secret Mark* betrays an awareness of modern, not ancient, attitudes toward homosexuality, *The Gospel of Judas* seems to be editorializing on the priestly scandals of our time, as it depicts priests sleeping with women and "sacrificing" children, this last perhaps pointing to abortion or molestation. Second, part of this gospel has been copied from the *Secret Book of John*, but the impression one gets from reading it is of a patch transferred out of context, no longer making the sense it did in the original. While an inept ancient scribe might have done that, it seems more natural to understand it as a cheap expedient of a modern forger trying to lend

---

14. Arthur, "The Gospel of Judas: Is It a Hoax?"

his text some genuine Gnostic color. Third, the Judas text repeats a goof found in one of our Nag Hammadi copies (there are three) of the *Secret Book of John*, the improper use of an Achmimic form. This makes it look very much like someone has chosen a portion of the *Secret Book of John* that happened to feature an odd scribal error and preserved it into his new work. What are the odds of an ancient Gnostic scribe working from one of our copies of the *Secret Book* (Apocryphon) *of John*? Remember, the *Gospel of Judas* was not part of the Nag Hammadi collection. If it had been it would not be so strange to suggest it was copied from a Nag Hammadi copy of *The Secret Book of John*. But it is part of a different manuscript (unless, of course, it is a fake): the Tchacos Codex. Likewise, what are the chances that the scribe of Judas copied from another (i.e., non-Nag Hammadi) copy of *The Secret Book of John* that made the *very same goof in the very same spot*? Arthur pictures the hoaxer doing just what Beim-Brenner did in *The Q Document* and Robert Le Brun did in *The Word*, writing his new gospel on genuine ancient papyrus leaves.

In Peter Van Greenaway's *The Judas Gospel*, a genuine *Testament of Judas* is discovered and made public. He introduces his lost gospel in the world of fiction. But he, too, addresses the Gnostic motif that the greatest, most hated secret of Christianity is a truth that, if known, would debunk it. If Jesus was the Lamb of God, Judas was the Scapegoat.

8 | The Gospel of Cain and Abel
Robert Ludlum,
The Gemini Contenders

THE ALLURE OF A lost gospel continues to be attractive to mystery writers, including some of the best, like Robert Ludlum. Not for the first time, however, I get a distinct impression that one may read such a book mainly for the intrigue and action, with the gospel element merely negotiable window-dressing. It could have been anything else, the fox for the chase, and in Ludlum's other books, of course it *is* something else. On the other hand, one may read the novel eager for the speculation about gospel origins (surely fewer readers do), with the action, no matter how well written, being mainly filler. Thomas Ligotti once said that about writing horror novels: he preferred to stick to evocative short stories, because otherwise he would have to float the rare scenes of eerie effect on the vast sea of indifferent soap-operatic filler. I confess that *The Gemini Contenders*[1] struck me as being only half-heartedly interested in its theological premise, especially since that premise kept changing underfoot.

GEMINI CRACKPOTS

The novel's title refers to a pair of pairs of brothers, one pair opening the book, the other closing it. The initial two are Greeks, one a monk belonging to the fanatical Order of Xenope, the other his hapless brother, a rail engineer. It seems the Order possesses secret documents which, with the Nazi menace looming, they feel the need to transfer from Greece to north Italy. (Ah, *closer* to Germany?) Well, anyway, they do the job by night in an ultra-secret railroad operation overseen by the monk. Once the delivery is complete, the monk blows his brother's brains out, then his own, so as to more adequately protect the information trail.

---

1. All page references are to the Dell edition.

The Gospel of Cain and Abel

Few know much of anything about either the trove of documents or the operation to secret them. Italian aristocrat Savarone Fontini-Cristi, staunch opponent of the Fascists, takes receipt of the vault of documents and sees to its burial. But he neglects to pass the information on to his eldest son Vittorio before it is too late and a Nazi execution squad shows up, led by a fanatical Catholic Cardinal, to massacre the whole Fontini-Cristi clan. Vittorio alone escapes by virtue of being late to the party, but he sees and swears revenge. Rescued by British secret agents, he is given a rank in the British army and trained for espionage. When interrogated about the documents, he knows nothing, leaving everybody disappointed and some distrustful. But he proves an able ally in the war against the Ratzis. In the course of things he marries an old flame and begets a pair of sons.

The family relocates to America after the war. Decades pass and the boys, fraternal twins, grow further and further apart. The sixties and seventies witness one of them, Adrian, becoming a lawyer and New Left activist. The other, Andrew, becomes a stalwart army zealot involved in a plot to overthrow the corrupt leadership of the Pentagon. His plot is derailed by Old World forces (both Greek and Roman) who put out new feelers for the lost documents, trying to squeeze from the brothers and their father whatever they may know concerning the mystery. The brothers have become enemies, each seeking to undermine the other, and they do not manage to team up against common foes.

In the end, each pieces together the resting place of the secret papers, and Adrian kills Andrew just in time to save his own life. Whereas soldier Andrew hoped to marshal the deadly secrets of the texts to gain the power needed to purify the military and the government, Adrian only wanted to see the long-suppressed truth come to light. At the end of the book, we are left wondering whether he will publish them or if he will think the dangerous truth better suppressed again.

All right, what was the secret, and what was the danger? A Xenope monk explains a bit of it to the foredoomed monk who will see to the transportation: "We are the custodians of a vault, a sarcophagus, if you will, that has remained sealed in a tomb deep in the earth for over fifteen hundred years. Within that vault are documents that would rend the Christian world apart, so devastating are their writings" (pp. 15–16). The last thing the West needs in wartime is a new apple of discord to alienate the different Christian countries from one another. "Above everything, the documents in enemy hands would be an ideological weapon beyond anything imaginable" (p. 215).

AND FROM THE SON

Initially we learn that the forbidden documents are collectively dubbed "the Filioque denials," a file of data refuting the Western (Roman Catholic) Church's high-handed decision to unilaterally amend the fourth-century Nicene-Constantinopolitan Creed by adding the phrase *filioque* to it, just after the affirmation that the Holy Spirit "proceeds from the Father." Filioque means, simply, "and from the Son." What difference does that make, you ask? The Creed was designed to be ecumenical, that is, binding upon the whole Christian Church. For one group of churches to revise the Creed without a general debate and vote among all the bishops, East and West, was like having half the states ratify the Equal Rights Amendment to the U.S. Constitution without waiting, or even calling, for a general vote, and then going ahead to revise their copies of the Constitution accordingly! You can imagine the ire such a procedure would occasion, and that is exactly what happened between Eastern Orthodox and Roman Catholic Churches in the ninth century, leading, two centuries later, to a split that remains open and bleeding to this day.

But it was far from a merely procedural issue. The underlying question was one of the equality of divine Persons in the Trinity. Western thinkers noticed that the Creed posits the origin of the Spirit from the Father only, not from the Son. Admittedly one could not have the Spirit proceeding from the Spirit, but the same contradiction does not come up in the hypothetical case of the Spirit proceeding from the Son. That would involve no such self-contradiction. Why can't the Son also function as the source for the Spirit, that is, if the Son is truly the equal of the Father, which the Trinity doctrine says that he is? So we had better amend the Creed to correct this slight to the Son. If he is truly God, then the Spirit should have been emitted from the Son as well as the Father, right?

Wrong, said the Orthodox: though each member of the Trinity is equal in divine dignity and power, they differ as to function. No one would contend that the Spirit begets the Son; only the Father does that. That is what we mean by calling them "father and son." We wish to indicate a particular filial relation *which we do not posit as obtaining between Son and Spirit*. Only the Father begets the Son, the Spirit does not beget the Son. In the same way, the Spirit can proceed from the Father, but not from the Son. In this way, each person of the Trinity has his own relation to the other and his own job. So if we were to say the Son shares the duty and possibility of serving as an origination point of the Spirit, we would be positing a function and a power as common to the Son and the Father. And we would be denying that function and power to the Spirit, though to do otherwise would leave us with the admittedly odd-sounding proposition of the Spirit proceeding from the Spirit! But if the Spirit is truly God like the Father and the Son, one has no right to attribute a divine duty and function to two of the Trinitarian persons and not to the third.

One might object that nobody thinks to attribute an atoning death to the Spirit, and that is not taken as some slight or omission, but only as a legitimate division of roles. But that is different for it concerns what God does outside his inner life, in the course of history.

Granted, it is all a bit abstruse, though I think it makes sense (whether true or not). But Ludlum does not get it right. He has Agent Brevourt explain to Vittorio (and thus to the reader):

> The Filioque was a later addition [to the Nicene-Constantinopolitan Creed of 381 CE] that once and for all established the Christ figure as one substance with God. It's rejected by the Eastern Church as misleading. For the Eastern church, especially the sects that followed the scholar-priest Arius, Christ as the son of God was a teacher; his divinity was not equal to God's. (pp. 215–16)

This is all wrong, grossly wrong. First, that Christ shared the very nature of the Godhead was established at the Council of Nicea in 325 CE, summoned by Emperor Constantine, himself something of an amateur theologian. The goal was to settle the raging debate among Christian thinkers whether Jesus Christ, incarnation of the heavenly Logos, through whom the world was made, was actually God, sharing the nature of the Father/Creator, or a creature himself, the firstborn of creation. The latter was the opinion of Arius, Eusebius of Caesarea (not the famous church historian, also alive at this time), and Asterius. The former was the view of Athanasius of Alexandria. This debate, settled, as I say, at Nicea (325 CE), was over by the time of the Council of Constantinople (381 CE), when the role of the Spirit was elaborated a bit beyond the attention accorded him in the original Creed of Nicea. Now it said that the Spirit is "the Lord and giver of Life, who proceeds from the Father. He has spoken through the prophets," etc. But the *filioque* was a later addition still (late sixth century!), and the Arians had long ago slunk away in defeat. It was not Arians who protested the addition of the *filioque* but full-blooded Athanasians who had long believed in the full divinity of Jesus Christ. The "Eastern Church" Ludlum mentions had despised and anathematized Arius as a blasphemer and a heretic. Their objection to the *filioque* clause, "and from the Son," was instead an indication, as they regarded it, of an inconsistent view of the fully divine Son. If, as East and West firmly agreed, Jesus Christ was fully divine, it was merely a question of whether one might consistently imagine the Spirit emerging from both Father and Son. As I understand it, they were not accusing one another (as they had Arius) of being consistent non-Trinitarians, but rather only of being inconsistent Trinitarians.

Is there any sense in which the Western *filioque* might have been, as Ludlum seems to think, an advantage for Rome as opposed to the Eastern Orthodox Church? Only in that, if you let them get away with it, you would be strengthening their hand, admitting they had the right to unilaterally change the creeds of Christendom without consulting anybody else. But as for religiously based imperialism? It is possible to argue that a divine Christ gave the Christian hierarchy of East and West alike the excuse to conquer ever more widely,[2] but this happened long before the *filioque* debate and had not a thing to do with it. Constantine had experienced his vision of the Christian Chi-Rho (abbreviation of "Christos") in the sky, accompanied by the heavenly voice commanding him to "conquer by this." But that was before the battle of the Milvian Bridge which secured his rule as the single Caesar of the Empire.

It is just silly to suggest that any old documents attempting to refute the Western addition of the *filioque* clause to the Creed could cause the civilization-toppling unrest which Ludlum has the Order of Xenope and the British Secret Service dreading. After all, the debate remains open today without undue turbulence. I have never been able to explain the controversy to students without them either yawning or laughing at the whole thing. It almost seems, however, that Ludlum began to realize that "the Filioque denials" as he calls them, were insufficient for his purposes, so he upped the stakes. As Brevourt explains to Vittorio:

---

2. Cupitt, "The Christ of Christendom."

> In the Patriarchate's fervor to deny the Filioque, it sent out priests to the holy lands, met with the Aramaic[-speaking?] scholars, unearthed everything that ever existed relative to Jesus. They unearthed more than they were looking for. There were rumors of scrolls written during the years just preceding and after the mark of the first century. They traced them, discovered several, and brought them back to Constantine. It is said that one Aramaic scroll raises profound and very specific questions as to the man known as Jesus. He may never have existed at all. (p. 216)

Such a quest is ludicrous to imagine. And surely Ludlum means they returned not to Constantine (long dead by the time of the *filioque* controversy), but to Constantin*ople*, the capital named for him. And they discovered "several" manuscripts. And now we learn that one scroll somehow preserves a smoking gun proving that Jesus Christ was someone's invention. Now *that's* interesting! And it might hold enough dynamite to shake Christian civilization, that is, if believers were all objective historians to whom evidence really made any difference!

GEMINI CONFUSIONS

But it is all moot, for Ludlum discards that, too! Later it turns out that "Brevourt never knew the whole story," as another Xenope monk explains: "It was never the denials. Never the scroll. It [an additional text] was—*is*—a confession ... that predates all the other documents" (p. 254). It is the work of Simon Peter, trying to unburden his conscience on the eve of his crucifixion in Rome. It seems that, though Jesus was quite willing to sacrifice himself, Peter and others just could not let him do it. They seized him in his sleep, substituted another man for him, and snuck him away to safety. But Jesus was horrified at this miscarriage of God's plan and killed himself three days later (pp. 407–8).

Ludlum here flirts with the notion that Jesus was a political revolutionary, as if that would be a blow to conventional faith, the same notion we have found in Roberts's *The Q Document*, but that quickly pales in comparison to the news that Jesus had committed suicide instead of being crucified. Ludlum does not make as much of this as he might. It has long been suspected, even taught, by various Gnostic and Islamic "heresies" that Jesus was rescued from crucifixion and replaced on the cross by another, either an enemy or a volunteer. Such a scroll, such a confession of Peter, would corroborate those teachings. The impact of such a revelation would be shattering indeed. And for a disappointed would-be martyr Jesus to have instead slit his wrists or taken poison, well, that would pretty much mean he had bought himself a one-way ticket to Hell in Roman Catholic terms, suicide being a mortal sin.

But then Ludlum needlessly fudges the facts again, and to little purpose. "There is no record of Simon Peter's having gone to his death with the early Christian martyrs. Certainly it would be part of the legend, yet there's no mention of it in biblical studies" (p. 408). Well, that is the opposite of the truth. There are numerous accounts, albeit none very reliable, of Peter's death. And it is from such that Ludlum has derived the notion of Peter's ultimate crucifixion.

One has to say that *The Gemini Contenders* ends with the other shoe having not yet fallen. It is as if we were being led to anticipate a sequel, but none ever materialized.

9 | Pontius is my Co-Pilate
Warren Kiefer, *The Pontius Pilate Papers*

DEADLY DISCOVERY

THE COVER BLURB HYPES this book[1] as "a spellbinding thriller of power and passion unmatched since *The Passover Plot*," perhaps forgetting (and hoping the reader will forget) that Hugh J. Schonfield's shocking best-seller was a sober work of historical scholarship and not a novel. Well, what passion and power *The Pontius Pilate Papers* may possess do not come from any implied religious bombshell. True, a cache of archaeological treasures, stolen from their murdered discoverer, form the object of pursuit, but it might as well have been anything else—a list of CIA operatives, the Pink Panther diamond, you name it. For our purposes it is really immaterial to say much more concerning plot and characterization than this: author Kiefer is adept at crafting both. Exotic but plausible characters pop into existence every once in a while, and there is plenty of intrigue and chasing around, deals with blackmailers, requisite sex scenes irrelevant to the plot, etc. One cannot help noticing that the narrator hero is both a physician and an amateur archaeologist who has inherited great wealth, enough to provide the author with many convenient shortcuts. Anything can be paid for, favors can be called in from the high and mighty, and connections are made with much less trouble and effort than in real life. Thus is a potentially much longer (and possibly tedious) story rendered short.

What is the controversial element symbolized by the discovery of the Pilate documents? Actually, they are letters *to* Pilate from his brother-in-law, Gaius Longinus Procula, a fellow functionary of the Roman state assigned to Palestine and not liking it very much. The case and fate of Jesus are mentioned almost in passing, though in ample detail. The Jesus

---

1. Page references are to the HBJ paperback.

depicted there was a failed revolutionary king allied with the Zealots, a Jewish revolutionary movement claiming descent and inspiration from Judas the Gaulonite/Galilean who took up arms against annexation and taxation by the Roman Empire in 6 CE. Their guerrilla tactics continued throughout the New Testament period until the Jewish War with Rome, their handiwork, spelled their end in 73 CE. According to the letters, Pilate had called in Jewish witnesses of the crucifixion to make an example of him, but Jewish leaders did not initiate Roman proceedings against Jesus. It was Pilate's idea. Our narrator speculates that in the succeeding years Paul and other Gentile Christians must have minimized the Jewish character of earliest Christianity, expunging its original political character, and making it into a pro-Roman mystery cult and its revolutionist founder into a Hellenistic Son of God figure fit for Gentile worship.

In the novel, word of the Pilate connection leaks to the media, but not the precise nature of it. Characters actually minimize the envisioned impact, dismissing it as a tempest in a teapot except to a few "red-neck Baptists" and the like. The Vatican has sneering dismissals at the ready. In fact, I feel rather sure that Kiefer's estimate of the possible disclosure is sound. Probably nothing much would happen. Those already of a skeptical bent would say, "Told you so!" and wonder why believers would still refuse to budge.

We pick up a clue to another possible impact once it develops that the new "discoveries" are at least partial forgeries, mainly the juiciest one concerning Jesus' trial and crucifixion. The forger was archaeologist Victor Lanholtz, a Jew who escaped from Nazi Germany and devoted much of his scholarly career to studying anti-Semitism. It seems he wanted to "prove" the scholarly speculation that Rome had plenty of reason, from its point of view, to dispense with Jesus, and that Jews had no role in the matter. By this means Lanholtz thought to draw the venom of anti-Semitism for all time, removing the "blood libel" against the Jewish people as "Christ-killers." But, the reader may ask, why also bring in the business of Jesus being a Zealot revolutionist? Isn't that like aiming an elephant gun at a mouse? Wouldn't this seeming blasphemy turn off the very same people (traditionalist Catholics and conservative Protestants) whom the forgery sought to disabuse of their anti-Judaism? Yes, probably it would have, though it is hard to see why "Jesus the Freedom Fighter" would be so distasteful (as it does remain) to Christians who are patriotic Americans venerating devout military men like George Washington and Robert E. Lee. Jesus was the Son of David? David was a mighty man of war. At any rate, Kiefer understands that if Jesus were not the target of Jewish hostility as a mere heretic, he must have been sufficiently offensive to the Roman administration for them to kill him. Thus the Zealot Jesus. But, as I say, in the end, the Pontius Pilate Papers are discredited, so everyone is free to return to their default belief in Jesus as a first-century Norman Vincent Peale. By the way, the proof of their artificial character comes in the form of a missing piece, secreted away, of the original papyrus, known to be blank when discovered, but now filled with spurious Pilate text. If this seems familiar, we saw basically the same debunking device in *The Q Document* and *The Word*.

PILATE ERROR

The spurious Pilate-related documents in Kiefer's novel are fictional counterparts to a long and ancient series of real-life Pilate pseudepigrapha. Already in the second-century Gospel of Luke we find the beginnings of the Pilate apocrypha in the reconciliation of the previously feuding tyrants who have found new fellowship in their common alliance against the Son of God ("And Herod and Pilate became friends with each other that very day, for before this they had been at enmity with one another," Luke 23:12). How had the execution of Jesus settled whatever personal or political scores each had outstanding against the other? It is a legendary motif: the powers of darkness putting aside their differences in an emergency. A later pair of writings (attested only in fifth- to sixth-century copies), *The Letters of Pilate and Herod*, continue the same trajectory. Here the two villains commiserate on their subsequent sufferings, but Pilate also tells of a trip he and his wife Procla, along with the crucifixion-centurion Longinus, took to see the resurrected Jesus preaching to the 500 brethren in Galilee. In the course of the visit, Jesus laid hands on Pilate, saying, "All generations and families shall call you blessed, because in your days the Son of Man died and rose again."[2] Here we easily detect the ultimate product of the gospel tendency to whitewash the Roman Pilate while vilifying the Jews. Pilate, his place of honor in the Creeds assured, will go on actually to become a canonized saint in the Ethiopian churches!

2. Elliot, *The Apocryphal New Testament*, 223.

A similar version of events meets us in *The Delivering Up of Pilate*, which is based on traditions also underlying the *Acts of Pilate*, though the full text of the former is attested only later. In it Pilate is called to account by Caesar who is convinced, based on miracle reports he has heard, that Pilate foolishly crucified God's Jewish Messiah. Pilate and Procla are both condemned to death despite the former blaming the Jews for deceiving him. But an angel appears to catch Pilate's severed head. Seeing this, Procla dies in holy joy. This drama has grown from already-legendary developments on display in Matthew 27:19, "Now as he sat on the judgment seat, his wife sent word to him, saying, 'Have nothing to do with that righteous man, for today I suffered many things in a dream thanks to him!'"[3] Does she mean merely that she has tossed and turned because of a nightmare in which Jesus figured? Or does she mean she has experienced a prophetic dream in which she has become one of Jesus' female followers who wind up suffering martyrdom, like Thecla? I suspect Matthew already has something like the latter possibility in mind, but at least we can be sure someone subsequently took the verse that way and elaborated it into the sort of thing we see in the Pilate apocrypha.

Late in the second century someone circulated a fictitious *Report of Pilate* (or, *The Letter of Pilate to Claudius*), according to which Pilate tells the Emperor of his fatal error in condemning Jesus to death. He was, he avers, misled by the scheming Jews of the Sanhedrin into dismissing Jesus' miracles as the stunts of a magician, but came to believe differently once his tomb guards returned to him with the news that Jesus had risen from the dead. Seeing through the pathetic ruse that they had all fallen asleep (itself a capital offense!), Pilate converted to faith in Jesus Christ as the Son of God. Obviously this document is not free-standing but is hypertext on Matthew's gospel, where these elements appear. This text may be that referred to with such confidence by both Justin Martyr and Tertullian, who challenged their opponents to look it up in the Roman records for proof of the gospel. We find the *Report* incorporated into the longer work, *Acts of Peter and Paul*. Another fairly early work in much the same vein was *The Letter of Pilate to Tiberius*, only in this one, despite extravagant praise of Jesus and vilification of Jews, Pilate is depicted as a "noble pagan," avowing himself by Hercules and citing the oracles of the Sibyls.

3. Price, *The Pre-Nicene New Testament*, 173.

The most important ancient member of the Pilate genre was no doubt *The Acts of Pilate* (also called *The Gospel according to Nicodemus* as of the Middle Ages) and written between the fifth and sixth centuries, or in the opinion of others, already in the mid-fourth century. It is a composite work consisting of a Christian's imaginary reconstruction of a Roman post-crucifixion investigation of Jesus' case and a revelation of Christ's saving descent into Hell to rescue the ancient righteous held hostage by Satan and Beelzebub. Its point, naturally, is to show just how wrong Pilate was to have acceded to the crucifixion of Jesus, as well as to reveal for Christian curiosity's sake the unseen effects of that holy death. We are told that in the reign of the Emperor Maximin, the Romans published what they claimed were the authentic Acts of Pilate, the "smoking gun" disproving, as they thought, Christianity. The plan was much like those that Kiefer sets forth in our *The Pontius Pilate Papers*. Many have theorized that the extravagant *Acts of Pilate/Gospel of Nicodemus* was a much later replacement for the anti-Christian version put abroad by Roman polemicists, and that the pagan version was destroyed.

I am of the opinion that this late bit of Pilate apocrypha is the source for an oddity that has crept into the text of 1 Corinthians. One version of the *Acts of Pilate* tells us that the Roman guards stationed at the tomb of Jesus (Matt 27–28) numbered half a thousand, and that their privileged witnessing of the very resurrection of Jesus from the tomb eventually converted them to faith in Christ. Not long afterward these men all journeyed up into Galilee, where they witnessed the conclusion of the matter: the ascension of Jesus into heaven. Some scribe, recopying 1 Corinthians, did not recognize 1 Corinthians 15:5–8 as a list of apostolic credentials based on Easter visions, but instead took the pericope for a list of evidential witnesses to the fact of the resurrection. So he decided to fill in what he saw as a gap, adding to the list this appearance to over five hundred brethren. Did he get it directly from the text of our *Acts of Pilate*? It is a messier business than that, especially once we keep in mind the multiform state of the text of the *Acts of Pilate* and the additions to it. All I feel safe in saying, though I feel sure of it, is that the same developing tradition that eventually lodged in the *Acts of Pilate* concerning the believing tomb guards also found its way to 1 Corinthians 15:6, and at more or less the same time.

The death of Pilate forms the subject of still other works. Some see him as a villain pure and simple, as in the medieval *Death of Pilate* in which Tiberius Caesar is healed by Veronica's image-bearing veil, becomes a Christian believer, and has Pilate executed. Pilate's corpse is then weighted and sunk into the Tiber. But the demons infesting the river celebrate the burial by causing great lightning and hailstorms, whereupon the locals persuade the Roman troops to fish out the body and take it somewhere else. The same disturbances continue in the neighborhood of the Rhone once Pilate's stinking carcass is removed there, as well as in Lausanne when he is buried there, and in the vicinity of a mountain lake where he finally comes to rest. The (perhaps) eleventh-century *Letter of Tiberius to Pilate* closes with an added note summarizing how various Passion Narrative villains met their well-deserved ends, and Pilate is said to have been killed by an arrow Tiberius fired at a deer but which accidentally plunged through Pilate's window.

French playwright Joseph Mery (1798–1867) once happened to read a Latin manuscript concerning Pilate, probably one of the well-known apocrypha we have just surveyed. The old writing gave him the idea for a story ("Ponce Pilate a Vienne," *Revue de Paris*, 1837) in which the aging Pilate reminisced about the glory days. Somewhere along the line W. D. Mahan, a Missouri Presbyterian minister, came upon an 1942 English translation of the story (*Pontius Pilate's Account of the Condemnation of Jesus Christ and his own Mental Sufferings*) which omitted the author's name and presented the story as the verbatim contents of an old Latin manuscript. Apparently the anonymous translator had misunderstood Mery when the latter credited the broad inspiration for the story to an ancient text. Mahan liked what he read and pirated it,[4] claiming to have discovered the text in 1859, based on a report that such a book existed amid the musty vaults of the Vatican Library. This he published two decades later under the title, *A Correct Transcript of Pilate's Court*. The plagiarism was a great success, satisfying the hunger of all Bible fans to know *more*. So Mahan went back to the drawing board (or should one say, the tracing board) and padded out his original with a dozen more spurious texts, much of the contents taken word for word from Lew Wallace's *Ben-Hur*. The expanded work was called *The Archaeological and the Historical Writings of the Sanhedrim and Talmuds of the Jews*. It was later reprinted as *The Archko Library* and *The Archko Volume*. Given the wide readership of both *Ben-Hur* and *The Archko Volume*, it is amaz-

---

4. Beskow, "Pilate's Own Story," 51–56.

ing that no one caught on to the hoax until Edgar J. Goodspeed did in 1931.[5]

Walter Kiefer's *The Pontius Pilate Papers* fits into this trajectory, not of course as a new hoax, but rather as a novel about such hoaxes.

DID JESUS CARRY A SWORD BEFORE HE CARRIED THE CROSS?

It is really by no means an eccentric theory that Jesus was some sort of anti-Roman revolutionary. The founder of historical criticism of the gospels, Hermann Samuel Reimarus (*On the Intention of Jesus and his Disciples*, 1778) pointed out that, if even as late as the ascension the disciples expected Jesus' imminent kingdom to be a political regime on earth (Acts 1:6), then he cannot earlier have "corrected" such an opinion as a crass falsehood, as we usually assume. Rather, we must infer that, when he had sent out the same disciples on a preaching tour (Mark 6:7) announcing the soon coming of that kingdom, he must have checked and rechecked their understanding. If they had grossly misunderstood him, he would have set them straight at that time. But if Acts 1:6 can portray the disciples still cherishing nationalistic hopes ("Lord, will you at this time restore sovereignty to Israel?")[6] so late, then such must have been the remembered teaching of Jesus; he hadn't corrected them, and Jesus must then have been a (failed) revolutionary.

To this picture Robert Eisler (*The Messiah Jesus and John the Baptist*, 1931) sought to add substance by appeal to the neglected Slavonic version of Josephus' *Wars of the Jews*, which contained a long section about John the Baptist and Jesus as revolutionary leaders.

Perhaps the best statement of the case was that of S. G. F. Brandon in *The Fall of Jerusalem and the Christian Church* (1951), *Jesus and the Zealots* (1967), and *The Trial of Jesus of Nazareth* (1968). Owing little to Eisler, Brandon noted that Jesus' "cleansing of the temple" must have been a military assault if it took place at all. Mark has reduced the scope of the scene as if Jesus had merely thrown over some card tables in a church basement rummage sale. Why? Because this event was the direct cause of Roman intervention to destroy him, and such facts were dangerous at a time, post 70 CE, when Christians sought coexistence with the Romans

---

5. Goodspeed, "The Report of Pilate," 28–44.
6. Price, *The Pre-Nicene New Testament*, 564.

and hoped to bury the original revolutionary character of their founder and movement. And if Rome's favor were to be curried, blame had to be assigned to someone else: the Jews, from whose involvement in the recent war with Rome Christians sought to distance themselves.

But vestiges of the endeavor's revolutionist character survive, as significant loose ends, in our gospel traditions. Otherwise, why did Jesus urge his disciples, on the very night of his arrest, to sell their cloaks to buy swords even in that eleventh hour (Luke 22:35–38), swords which some of those disciples actually drew to defend Jesus against the arresting party (Mark 14:47)? Their defensive action was hitherto puzzling, but now becomes clear. And absent this revolutionism, why too would Jesus have a disciple nicknamed "the Zealot" (Mark 3:18), another named "the Siccariot" (the assassin's dagger, Mark 3:19), still another called *Baryona*, or "the Terrorist" (John 1:42)?

Then consider that Bar-Abbas, the criminal released in Jesus' place (Mark 15:15), had been arrested for murder in a very recent "insurrection" (Mark 15:7). Which one? Presumably the one Jesus ignited at the temple, which was after all, as large as three football fields and festooned with armed police! Jesus is depicted as occupying the whole extent of it since Mark slips and informs us that Jesus would not allow anyone to carry sacrificial vessels through the place (Mark 11:16), something he could do only had he controlled all the entrances.

The multiplications of loaves and fish for the mass of Jesus' followers are reminiscent of the Egyptian messiah mentioned by both Josephus (*Jewish War* 2:13.5; *Jewish Antiquities* 20:8:6) and Acts 21:38, who summoned his followers into the wilderness, promising them miracles betokening liberation from Rome. John's version (John 6:14–15) makes the link with popular kingship explicit. Apologists like to point out that Jesus is there shown as being so horrified at the notion that he immediately goes into hiding. But that is just what we would expect on Brandon's theory, Jesus' originally revolutionary connections being subsequently whitewashed.

It remains a strong theory. For my money, if we feel compelled to posit an actual historical existence of the Jesus character, as of course most do, then I should say Brandon wins the prize. It may be surprising to realize that what would have been an earth-shaking surprise had the Pilate papers hoax succeeded, according to Kiefer's novel, is already pretty close to the surface even in the familiar gospels, provided you know where to look.

10 | Remembrance of Lives Past
Barbara Wood, *The Magdalene Scrolls*

THIS BOOK[1] APPEARS TO be aimed at the women's romance novel market, though the love element actually winds up being pretty secondary. As we will shortly see, the hero alienates one lover (the requisite sexy fashion model type, like Steve Randall's girlfriend Darlene in the beginning of *The Word*) and attracts another (a scholarly researcher who appreciates the hero's work, like Angela Monti in *The Word*) as he undergoes increasing psychic dissociation. But the first lover fades out of the picture with less than the anticipated friction, and the two women never have a showdown. We have our own jilted expectations: when we pick up this novel we feel sure we will be reading of a virtually messianic Mary Magdalene (a la *The Da Vinci Code*), but we soon learn that the title comes rather from the place of discovery, Migdal/Magdala in Galilee. Mary Magdalene appears but very briefly as a character in the flashback sections, where she is also seemingly equated with Mary the mother of John Mark (Acts 12:12).

TEXTUAL TIME TRAVEL

A professor of Archaeology and Middle Eastern Languages, Dr. Ben Messer, is an Aryan-looking closet Jew who has long since renounced his faith because of childhood traumas connected with it. His mother, a concentration camp survivor, could (understandably!) never shut up about the horrors she and her husband had suffered there. He first accepted the role his mother assigned him as a junior defender of the Jewish faith against the Gentiles, but in order to know the foe better, inquisitive young Benjamin took to clandestinely reading the New Testament. This proved to be the last straw for his domineering mother. And this in turn broke the camel's back for him.

---

1. Page references are to the Avon paperback edition.

Thus his continuing interest in ancient Semitic history and culture swerved from the rabbinate and into secular scholarship. The new discovery in Migdal of a set of jars filled with first-century scrolls forces Ben to reexamine his faith, even his identity. He becomes absolutely obsessed with the scrolls and their author, one David ben-Jonah, an ancient counterpart who had recorded the highlights and, more importantly, the lowlights of his religious journey. First impressed with the fact of a self-conscious, autographical writer, something hitherto believed not to have existed before Augustine of Hippo penned his *Confessions* some four centuries later, Ben soon finds himself drawn back into the past more vividly with each new scroll photograph his friend and old mentor mails him from the site of discovery.

When a new installment comes, Ben plunges into it, losing all connection and concern with his job and his fiancée, Angie, who, needless to say, is not very happy about the neglect and eventually leaves the strangely apathetic scholar. Her place is soon taken by Judy Golden, a young, Jewish, and modestly pretty student of Ben's who is interested in his work. Affection between the two Jews, neither of them precisely Orthodox, grows slowly through shared work, but Judy, too, comes to fear losing Ben to total absorption in the delusion of the past. While translating the scrolls, Ben (and soon, with him, Judy) seems to get sucked back in time a la Rudolf Steiner, actually seeming to live the narrative he is reading, as if he himself had experienced it all in former days. (Judy, too, eventually identifies with an ancient character in the story, the beautiful Sarah, David's friend's wife for whom David cannot deny a romantic fixation.) Before long, Ben comes to believe that the ghost of David is haunting him; he can even see him standing in the room! Finally Ben decides that he and David are aspects of the same personality, "Ben" being mainly an amnesiac epiphenomenon who now at last recalls his earlier life in first-century Judea and Galilee.

There, as David ben-Jonah, he had studied Torah with Rabbi Eleazer until a chance meeting with some Greeks resulted in his enjoying an evening getting soused in a Jerusalem topless bar and, he thinks, being swindled out of his hard-earned savings by Salmonides, a Greek trader who convinced him to invest in a shipping proposition. Disgraced, David accepts expulsion from the Rabbi's house and ekes out a pittance working as a secretary for hire in the marketplace. Eventually he gets recruited by none other than Mary Magdalene to the new sect of the Poor, who await the imminent return of their Messiah, the recently crucified Jeshua.

Reconciled with his mentor Eleazer, who had hoped the younger man would succeed him as a doctor of the law, David feels unworthy of this honor. Also, he falls for his friend's wife and has a rendezvous with her. Never mentioning it again, he nonetheless carries the guilt, and such failure and disappointment become a pattern for the poor wretch. He is pious but cannot forgive himself for his lapses. The worst of these occurs in the midst of the terrible famine in the land during the Roman siege of Jerusalem, which he escapes by pretending to be a leper whom no one will dare accost. But before he leaves the besieged city, he attends a communion meal of the Poor and poisons the cup so to save them more hideous fates at the hands of the Romans or of their hungry countrymen. He is stricken with grief, not so much at having killed them, but at having cheated them of the chance of greeting the advent of Jesus, which might, after all, still have occurred in time for their Lord to have rescued them.

David is at length reunited with his old agent Salmonides (who, it turns out, had invested his money and not in fact cheated him) as well as with his secret love Sarah (her husband now having perished), as well as his godson, Sarah's son, Jonathan. Only it now turns out that Jonathan was really conceived during David's and Sarah's single afternoon of forbidden love. The kid's legal father, David's best friend, always knew about it but never mentioned it, and now the coast is clear. We learn that David, fearing never to see Jonathan again, scribed the whole dozen scrolls to tell him his true identity and the character and failures of his father, then hid the texts next to the fruit preserves jars in the basement of a house in Migdal, hoping the lad would discover them in the days to come. However, united with Sarah, Salmonides, and Jonathan, he tells Jonathan in person and leaves the scrolls for future Jews to find. David's ancient last words were that whoever now does find these writings, however many years or centuries it may take, can consider himself their proper addressee, "my son" in a spiritual sense. It seems that Ben Messer turned out to be that son.

But then should we conclude Ben and David were really transmigrational counterparts, type and antitype? One has to suppose so, since we are apparently not to believe that the several other translators working on the text back in Israel were all thus obsessed with David's autobiography, at least not to the point of becoming absorbed by the dead man's identity. But then what was the point? One must guess that Providence thus sought to return Ben to his Jewish faith. But that's shooting a mouse with an elephant gun. (And Leviticus prohibits that, doesn't it?)

The structure and premise of *The Magdalene Scrolls* is ingenious, closely reminiscent of one of H. P. Lovecraft's major works, *The Case of Charles Dexter Ward*, where obsessive research on an alchemist ancestor leads to the old wizard's return from the hoary past and his displacement of his latter-day counterpart's personality. Both novels are structured by juxtaposing the present with the past in the form of extensive historical flashbacks among episodes in the modern time, flashbacks that are shared by narrator, characters, and readers alike. But, though *The Magdalene Scrolls* is twice as long as *Charles Dexter Ward*, its present-day sequences serve mainly as mere filler between the juicier ancient episodes. Many things happen in the past; it is where the real story lies. In the present, all we see are Ben's confused musings and increasing panic as he desperately awaits the (inevitably delayed) delivery of each new scroll and goes a little bit crazier with each new one he reads.

NONFICTION FACTIONS

As always, these scrolls are "hot," filled with surprises that might upset the Christian applecart. Judy, though, is inclined to look on the bright side: "David's verified some of the sayings of Jesus, which ought to make everyone happy" (p. 193). There are a couple of parables, as well as missionary material from Matthew Chapter 10. But sharp-eyed readers may think it odd that David ben-Jonah's decidedly non-Christian rabbi Eleazer twice tells or refers to "the parable of the prodigal son." Is he supposed to be implicitly quoting Jesus? No one, character or narrator, ever explains this, but in fact there is no error. We do know of an at least roughly contemporary rabbinical parable of the prodigal son.[2] There is also a Buddhist version.[3] In the Jewish version, a king has a son traveling very far away. He sends word to him, calling him to return. The son replies that he is now too far away. (Never mind that the messengers seem to have had no difficulty covering the distance!) The king then replies that his son need journey back only as far as he can, and his father will be glad to meet him halfway.

Judy sees no problem with the discovery, and thinks Ben is being an alarmist: "These scrolls will fill in so much history, prove so many

---

2. Schechter, *Some Aspects of Rabbinic Theology*, 327; Price, *Deconstructing Jesus*, 255.

3. Lotus Sutra (*Saddharma Pundarika*), IV.

theories to be true, and refute others. They will clarify the dim beginnings of the Church. Think of the enlightenment, Ben, what's wrong with that?" (pp. 174–75). Ben counters: "It certainly isn't anything the Vatican will applaud—one of the original Jesus followers condemning the Rome Church" (p. 215).

As we see more and more of the David ben-Jonah narrative translated, we come to see that both Judy's optimistic and Ben's pessimistic estimates are in some measure correct. At issue are rival theories about Christian origins. Just as Judy says, the scrolls, as described, tend to favor the classic hypothesis of nineteenth-century New Testament scholar Ferdinand Christian Baur. Baur noticed a repeating pattern among major New Testament (and slightly later) documents. Some Christians seemed to believe that the Jewish Torah was binding on all Christians for the simple reason that Christianity (not their term for it) was the exclusive province of Jews. One faction opposed admitting Gentile, pagan converts at all (which, however, didn't mean they considered them damned).

> Jacob [James the Just] was a Nazarite, a man of the firmest convictions and of the strongest vows. At Simon's side, he helped in the leadership of the Poor.... Simon [Peter] and his followers went about the country preaching their new covenant... It would not be long before the prophecies of old would be fulfilled and Israel raised up to be the rightful ruler of the world... all Jews had to be prepared, and it was the task of Simon and Jacob to organize the missions and to see that all houses of Israel were reached [Matt 10:6]. (p. 186)

> Jacob [explained]: "We are to go into every city of Israel [Matt 10:23] and speak with every Jew there. We were instructed to avoid the way of the Gentiles and not enter the city of the Samaritans. [Matt 10:5] For the Kingdom is at hand for Jews alone." (Ibid.)

Another faction was willing to accept Gentiles but only if they embraced the Torah in its entirety: circumcision, sabbatarianism, kosher laws, etc. Christianity was state of the art Judaism, so converts had to become Jews as well as Christians.

> At this point there arose an argument... Saul of Tarsus... claimed to have spoken with the Master on the Damascus Road and... was given instruction to preach to the Gentiles.

> But Simon and Jacob, being the overseers of the Poor in all matters, counseled them strongly against going among the uncircumcised, for unless they became Jews as we were—that is, if they suffered the rite of circumcision—and promised to keep holy the Torah, the Gentiles might not enter the New Covenant. (Ibid.)

Still another faction (associated with the name of Saul or Paul of Tarsus) reasoned that biblical morality was binding upon Gentile converts to Christ, but none of the uniquely ritual boundary markers of Jewish culture. The Gospel of Matthew is the product of an evolving Jewish-Christian (or "Nazarene" or "the Poor," as Wood correctly calls them) community. The missionary instructions in Chapter 10 disqualify Gentiles and Samaritans from evangelistic outreach, but the so-called Great Commission of chapter 28 sends Christian missionaries off to all nations, with the proviso that they be taught to keep every commandment of Jesus who in this gospel (5:17–19) has pointedly stipulated that all his followers must keep every last Torah statute.

The Jewish wing of early Christianity was led by the Twelve apostles, supposedly companions of the historical Jesus but whose number probably denotes their being representative of New Covenant Israel, whether it was Jesus' idea or not. But the relatives of Jesus (the so-called "Heirs" or "Pillars") formed a rival group of figureheads.

> You know that Simon was the Master's best friend and his first disciple. You know also that Jacob was the Master's brother. Because of this, a small dissention arose. Simon and Jacob vied for absolute supremacy over the Poor. (p. 186)

The situation would have been exactly parallel to that prevailing in early Islam, where authority was divided (and disputed) between the Companions of the Prophet and the Pillars, Muhammad's relatives. There is some evidence that Peter took the most liberal view regarding the conversion of Gentiles and their subsequent freedom from the Law, but then allowed himself to be intimidated by James's authority and opposition, whereupon Peter, too, became a "Judaizer" of the Gentiles (Gal 2:11–14). Wood gets most of this right on target, though she allows herself to succumb to the Roman Catholic tradition that Peter and Paul worked as a team in founding the Roman Church. Baur saw such apocryphal accounts as trying to reinforce a much later ecumenical reconciliation, not between Peter and Paul themselves, but (generations later) between the churches who cherished the two apostles as figureheads.

For Wood, the two apostles did reconcile, but it was Peter who moved toward Paul and away from James. Formerly, "Simon and Jacob fought the idea of admitting Gentiles into the group," (p. 186) but Wood depicts him many years later coming round to Paul's view.

That probably did happen very early on, as witnessed by Galatians 2, but then Peter seems to have retreated to James' legalism during the Antioch fiasco. His liberalism was at an end.

Paul, on the other hand, not only championed Gentile freedom from the Torah (for both Jews and Gentiles), as per Baur's theory, but could even be called "the second founder of Christianity" (Wilhelm Wrede),[4] abandoning residual Jewish messianism. (What after all could any of that Jewish nationalism mean to Gentiles?) He replaced it with the theology and trappings of the Hellenistic Mystery Religions, with their secret sacraments of baptism and communion as means of appropriating the redemption wrought by the dying and rising savior god. Accordingly, Wood has Ben Messer reason, "All this mythology came much later, when the Gentiles joined" (p. 199).

A vision of a late reunion between David ben-Jonah and Simon Peter shows the former rebuking the latter, now an enthusiastic Paulinist (as the pseudepigraphical 1 and 2 Peter epistles depict him). "They . . . have simply changed the names of their own gods. . . . And in their hearts they will still be heathens" (p. 212).

Of course, this is not the only possibility. It is, for example, by no means far-fetched to suggest, with Gerardus J. P. J. Bolland,[5] that Christianity grew out of Gnosticism in Alexandria, Egypt, and clothed itself in Jewish trappings only when missionaries brought their messages to Israel and found eager hearers there. Those mystically inclined Jews would have found it easier to convert to the new faith if they could minimize the distance they would have to leap. So, just as David ben-Jonah suggests in *The Magdalene Scrolls* that pagans mixed their favorite elements of paganism with the Jewish gospel, so might newly Gnostic Jews have Judaized the gnosis to make it less of a wrenching transition.

---

4. Wrede, *Paul*, 179.

5. Bolland, *De Evangelische Jozua*. Rylands, *The Evolution of Christianity*; Rylands, *The Beginnings of Gnostic Christianity*; Zindler, *The Jesus the Jews Never Knew*, 340, and others similarly held that Christianity began variously among Hellenized Jewish settlements throughout the Diaspora, with allegorized Jewish elements being made almost unrecognizable by their intermingling with gnostic mythemes.

For example, the reinterpretation of the Lord's Supper as some kind of a new Passover Seder runs aground on the notion (unthinkable for pious Jews) of symbolically drinking blood in a sacrament. But that element is obviously very much at home in the Hellenistic Mystery Cults, from which the syncretistic Gnostics must have derived it. Likewise, for Egyptian Gnostics, "the Christ" must have denoted "the Risen One," referring to the anointing of Osiris' corpse with oil, whereby Isis brought Osiris back from the dead.[6] Once this faith was adapted to Jewish categories, "Messiah" was reinterpreted as denoting "Anointed, Davidic king," though anyone can see the lack of fit between the gospel Jesus and any Davidic Messiah model. The gross disparity has bequeathed us any number of desperate theories of how Jesus must have "believed himself to be" something which he went on to immediately redefine in every way—which pretty much means he did *not* believe himself to be it after all.

I say there are various possible reconstructions of Christian origins, but that Barbara Wood has, in the main, adhered to that of F. C. Baur. How would ancient scrolls that described the competing parties in the primitive church in this fashion have been "a fifty-megaton bomb"? Simply because it would completely debunk, as Baur realized, the propaganda theology of Orthodox/Catholic Christianity, which claims the exclusive copyright on Christian truth. The traditional view—often called the Eusebian or Hegesippian view, after the fourth- and second-century ecclesiastical historians who propounded it—holds that Jesus Christ, the God-man defined at the Councils of Nicea and Chalcedon, came to earth to reveal the saving truth to his disciples, who then taught it to the first bishops whom they appointed in churches all over the Mediterranean, who then passed it down to their own successors. Thus they maintained the pure doctrine of genuine Christianity. Then, just to make things interesting, Satan sent various teachers of heresy, men like Simon Magus, Marcion of Sinope, Montanus, and Arius to propagate false ideas and to corrupt the faith of anyone stupid and morally retrograde enough to listen to them. There had never been any legitimate diversity of opinion, nor any room for it. "Heresy," in fact, comes straight from the Greek word *hairesis*, "choice," implying the soul-destroying effrontery of daring to choose one's own beliefs instead of meekly accepting what the Church has spoon fed you.

6. Compare the related theory of Massey, *The Historical Jesus and the Mythical Christ*, 98–99.

But if Baur were correct, the nature and teaching of "true" Christianity had from the beginning been in the eye of the beholder, up for grabs amongst numerous sects and parties who interpreted Jesus differently, something they could have had occasion to do only if he had *not* set out definitive doctrines and practices for his believers to follow. This kind of thinking is dangerous to the party line, so the Party claims that such thinking, or indeed any independent thinking at all, is dangerous to one's eternal salvation. Thus the *Magdalene Scrolls* of David ben Jonah would indeed be a bombshell, but, to borrow Karl Barth's memorable metaphor, it would be a bomb lobbed into the midst of the theologians' playground. No one else would be in any particular danger since the ensuing crisis could hardly escape the confines of the ivory tower of religious intellectuals. It should not be this way; religious believers should take responsibility for examining the basis of their beliefs. But how many of them do so? Most would rather just "leave the driving to" their favorite religious leaders, despite the fact that those leaders are obviously going to engage in butt-covering spin doctoring. That is, after all, what institutional apologists are paid to do.[7] If we fail to see what they are doing, i.e., anything but engaging in impartial scholarship, we have only ourselves to blame.

ART IMITATING ETERNAL LIFE

It is tempting to get carried along with Wood's narrative and experience the feeling that Baur's theories have been confirmed, but this is a literary illusion. After all, we are only reading a novel. No wonder a particular theory appears to have been corroborated; the novelist has chosen one of the theories of scholars to use as the basis for her fiction, not the other way around. But Wood has made a solid point with genuine scholarly relevance. If new discoveries do suggest an unsuspected degree of early diversity in Christianity, the implications might indeed be revolutionary.

F. C. Baur's theories are not the only ones borrowed by Barbara Wood. In general she interprets Jesus and the origin of Christianity along the lines of the Essene hypothesis beloved of Rationalists of the eighteenth century (Bahrdt, Venturini, etc.), flirted with again after the discovery of the Dead Sea Scrolls in 1948, and recently revived and ably

---

7. Berger and Luckmann, *The Social Construction of Reality*, 87–88.

defended by Barbara Thiering. According to this scenario, not an implausible one by my reckoning, Jesus was an Essene or Essene heretic. His healings were the product of an advanced medical science. The resurrection was really the rescue of Jesus, drugged into a simulated death, from the cross by Essene confederates. The striking similarities between early Christianity in the Acts of the Apostles and the sect of the Dead Sea Scrolls (voluntary poverty and celibacy, baptism, apocalyptic expectation, a council of twelve with an inner circle of three, etc.) all suggest that the early Church *was* the community of the Scrolls. Both called themselves both "the Poor" and "the Way." It is no great shock to imagine Jesus having been an adherent of a strict baptizing sect, since the gospels explicitly have him initiated by John the Baptist in the Jordan. The theory is often dismissed as being "speculative," which as far as I can see is merely to default from the unfamiliar possibility to the familiar one.[8] The real problem for many is the Rationalist explaining away of the healings and the resurrection. That is true in Wood's novel, too: David ben-Jonah's old friend Saul (not Saul of Tarsus), does not share David's faith in Messiah Jesus, and he tries to set David straight.

> Their leader did not die on the tree, for he hung there for but a few hours. Everyone knows that death on the cross takes days. He was taken away by men in white robes, whom ignorant witnesses called angels, and was taken to their monastery by the Sea of Salt. You have seen the wonders they perform in healing, as they have done for a hundred years, and that their name Essene means healer. I do not doubt that their leader is alive today and in the desert. They are fanatics, David, ... clinging to a miracle that never took place. (pp. 169–70)

Remarkably, though this item by itself would be enough to cause real and widespread controversy, Wood just mentions it and moves on. Perhaps that is because even in the novel the Swoon Theory, as it is commonly called, is floated only as the surmise of an opponent of Christian faith, not as any kind of proof.

One last thought raised by this interesting novel: Wood shows the early Christians/Nazarenes eagerly expecting the imminent return of Jesus. That appears to be quite accurate. But what would have led these believers to posit so quick a Second Coming? Why not assume that it might be many hundreds of years away? A speedy second advent is not

---

8. Fish, *Is There a Text in this Class?*, 276–77.

an obvious or especially natural inference to draw, after all. Compare the analogous myth of the second advent of King Arthur: he should return to aid England in the hour of her greatest need, whenever that might be. There would seem to have been no reason to suppose it would be soon. But what if the inner circle of Jesus knew that he had been taken down alive from the cross, then nursed back to health? In that case, they would have known he was not far off in heaven where he might abide for unguessable ages. They would have known for solid reasons that the deadline for his victorious return must be the natural limit of his mortal life. Thus if he were ever to come again, it must be before his generation had passed from the scene, and him with it.

11 | The Real (Strange) Bible
Edward Whittemore, *The Sinai Tapestry*

THIS NOVEL,[1] THE FIRST installment in the author's "Jerusalem Quartet,"[2] stands alone quite well. One feels that adding the three sequels onto it would not clarify the controlled chaos of *The Sinai Tapestry*. The book is sufficient of itself to create an impression not unlike that achieved by Hermann Hesse in *Siddhartha*: a lapping sea, a flowing river of life and its seemingly random adventures. What perspective we may gain on our own experiences appears to be provided by their striking, again and again, a true note against the sounding board of the same events replayed throughout history as one plays one's own role and that of others, making one huge fugue. The novel is resilient muscle flesh having grown on the firm but outsize frame of five outlandish characters. The first of them is the twenty-ninth Duke of Dorset, Plantagenet Strongbow, a Victorian mutant of great height, powers, imagination, and intellect, not to mention appetites (of which, paradoxically, asceticism seems to be one). He is an explorer, astronomer, swordsman, and sexologist (author of a thirty-three volume study of sexual anthropology), a pilgrim, healer, prophet, and more.

THE *REAL* BIBLE

Strongbow comes to learn of an ostensible "original Bible," a compilation of wild tales often told and retold to travelers, for money, and as much for entertainment as for edification. It sounds much like *The Thousand and One Arabian Nights* and *The Book of Zohar*, to both of which it is eventually compared. The stories (some repeated, some homespun) are the dictation of a blind hermit, transcribed by an idiot savant (these

---

1. All page references are to the Avon edition.
2. *Sinai Tapestry*, 1977; *Jerusalem Poker*, 1978; *Nile Shadows*, 1983; *Jericho Music*, 1987.

characterizations suggesting the Gnostic Demiurge, a blind idiot Creator), both dwelling at the foot of Mount Sinai in the tenth century BCE. Once their work is finished, they bury it in a cistern for posterity. It is a strange and frightful scripture, violating all accepted chronology, making Isaiah a contemporary and colleague of Muhammad, both living centuries BCE, but fewer centuries before the actual birth of Christ, who turns up centuries before history places him. It is not that this "original Bible" would debunk the familiar scripture, threatening to turn biblical chronology topsy-turvy. No, the point is that the compilation serves as a window on the howling vortex of historical precedent and repetition, the usurpation of one "original" event by another, and the strange fugue of existence itself.

The same point is made with another of the main characters, an old Arab Jerusalem antiquities dealer called Haj Harun ("Aaron the Pilgrim"). He has encountered Strongbow as well as his son Stern, plus O'Sullivan Beare (a displaced Irish freedom fighter running guns for Stern who is trying to create a pan-Semitic republic in which all three Abrahamic faiths may live in perpetual peace), and Catherine (a man) Wallenstein, an Albanian noble who has given up his wealth to go in quest of the original *"Sinai Bible."* Haj Harun once abetted Strongbow in the writing of his set of sex volumes, providing room and board during the many years he worked on the project. As a token of gratitude, Strongbow had given his friend a rusty old crusader helmet. From that time on, Hal Harun had never been out from under the helmet, and it appears that he gained from it the borrowed memories of three thousand years of Jerusalem history. Throughout the book we are seemingly asked to believe that he has actually passed three thousand years in service to his beloved Holy City, but the hint is that the memories are those of three millennia of warriors (and others) who have loved Jerusalem and died for it. He comes to share them and, at the last, to believe himself to have been, all along, the undying Melchizedek, king of (Jeru)salem in Abraham's time.

Haj Harun had similarly given shelter to the crazed Wallenstein, who, having discovered the *Sinai Bible*, that wasp-nest of temporal paradox, determines to rebury it and to fabricate a substitute Bible in Greek upon ancient parchment. A linguistic genius like Strongbow, Wallenstein undergoes some fifteen years of preparation, gathers the necessary materials, and proceeds to forge an ancient-seeming Bible that conforms in most respects to the Greek into which the Septuagint translated the Old Testament and in which New Testament was itself written.

> Of course Wallenstein couldn't place his forgery in the tenth century BCE, when the imbecile had recorded the blind man's recitations. His Bible had to be a genuine work of revealed history, not a jumble of capricious tales assembled by two stray tramps. Thus it had to come from some time well after Christ, which meant writing it in Greek. But when? ... The great Saint Anthony had gone into the desert in the fourth century, so that would be the date of his forgery. Time enough after Christ for all the truths to have been gathered, yet still earlier than any complete Bible in existence. (p. 40)

FAKING THE REAL THING

To lend it an air of fourth-century antiquity, as from before the definition of the canon, he adds two more New Testament books, the *Shepherd of Hermas* and the *Epistle of Barnabas*. He arranges to stay overnight at the now-famous monastery of St. Catherine at Mount Sinai and hides the forgery there for someone to find, he hopes. Later Constantine Tischendorf (a real historical character) does find it, and dubs it "Codex Sinaiticus." New Testament textual criticism is revolutionized. (Actually, this wouldn't have made the difference Whittemore pretends, since there is another copy of the same edition, Codex Vaticanus, which by itself would be enough to secure readings of the same type as those which appear in Codex Sinaiticus.) And with this observation arise several other related questions, which author Whittemore seems not to have bothered to think out—not that we would expect him to be so pedantic, as he is writing a kind of wild, visionary epic of his own, much like the *Sinai Bible*.

For one, Wallenstein is not pictured as creating the content of a more respectable Bible, but only of back-dating the contents of the one in general use in his own day. It is not as if the eccentric *Sinai Bible* had been the Bible used in churches all this time. At some point it must already have been replaced with what we recognize as scripture. When does Whittemore mean us to suppose this had happened? And who did it the *first* time? That is, who substituted the new, more serious Bible for the crazy one written by the hermit and his idiot savant? Unless it was done very early, wouldn't the identity of such a person still be known?

And the persistent rumor is merely that there somewhere survives an original version of the Bible that is very different, entirely different, from the one we know, nothing more. And then why should anyone suppose that the crazy *Sinai Bible* is in any way related to the canonical Bible? In what sense is one a version of the other at all?

At any rate, poor Wallenstein at length retreats into blind madness (much like the pair responsible for the composition of the original *Sinai Bible*, and not coincidentally), ultimately arriving at the unshakable conviction that he himself is the Creator God. (Why not, if you wrote the Bible?) This is one of many grand visions possessed by or possessing the extravagant characters in *The Sinai Tapestry*. Some of those visions crash and burn and we call them delusions (like Stern's ecumenical pan-Semitic homeland), while others cannot be true in the nature of the case (Wallenstein's Godhood). Either way, Whittemore seems to suggest that the grandeur of grand schemes and of delusions of grandeur are both genuine measures of human greatness, human divinity. A delusion may be viewed as a reach that far outruns one's grasp—just like an ideal. The pursuit of it may color one's life with meaning whether it turns out to be attainable or not. What is it for which you spend your life? What is worth your allegiance? For it exists as a cause, as a value, whether or not it is some actual shore one day to be reached. Strongbow largely fulfills his dreams, save for locating the *Sinai Bible* (which the reader somehow knows would not affect his life anyway), while his son Stern pretty much fails to achieve his vision but fills his time with adventures anyway. In the end, they are all stories and nothing more, whatever they may be worth. And thus all these stories are the *Sinai Bible*, the result of random weaving by unseen Fates.

12 | Dem Dry Bones
Charles Templeton, *Act of God*

EX-EVANGEL

CHARLES BRADLEY TEMPLETON (1915–2001) was a polymath who in his time served as reporter, editorial cartoonist, newspaper editor, TV host, inventor, ad man, actor, and, perhaps most famously, evangelist. He was known as "the Canadian Billy Graham" and worked with his American counterpart, forcing the desegregation of one of their crusade meetings in the American South. Graham and Templeton together founded the still-thriving Youth for Christ para-church ministry. Dissatisfied with the rudimentary theology underlying the message he preached, Templeton sought to deepen it with a seminary education, but he graduated as an agnostic. He never entirely abandoned his interest in religion, though, expressing it in a non-fiction work, *Farewell to God* (1995), and in his 1977 novel, *Act of God*,[1] a major best seller in Canada which barely clung to the list in America.

This brisk and fast-paced novel nonetheless spends enough time detailing characters so that they strike the reader as more than they are: mere stage setting and filler to delay the unfolding of the fascinating plot. Our progress to the end is retarded by distraction toward these people and their doings, but we do not mind. We hardly notice, for we feel we are gaining insight into people who are persuasive simulations of real individuals whom we should never otherwise meet. Here is our chance to learn from and about them. In a novel of ideas it is particularly good to have some narrative sugar to help the medicine go down. We do not feel we are trapped in a lecture hall for hours when we would rather be asleep or out having fun. We may expect the exploration of ideas in the form of inter-character dialogues, and author Templeton excels in this

---

1. All page references are to the Bantam edition.

technique. One easily believes that Michael Maloney, Roman Catholic cardinal, and his old school chum Harris G. Gordon, archaeologist and secularist, would believe and espouse the positions Templeton feeds us through their mouths.

The narrative sparkles with striking descriptions, wise mini-insights on things glimpsed along the way, little jokes, and vivid descriptions. It is much better than it needs to be, a real treat to read. But down to business: Professor Gordon has discovered the very skeleton of Jesus, removed from the tomb of Joseph of Arimathea to be reentered in the family plot of Jesus' disciple Simon the Zealot. As Simon himself explains in a manuscript deposited with the bones, he hoped a trumped-up resurrection of Jesus would spark revolution among the Jewish masses, the perpetual goal of the fiery Zealots. So Simon and some co-conspirators absconded with the corpse of Jesus and placed it in Simon's family tomb. But the theft of the body became known, at least rumored, and the plan fell flat (pp. 62–63). Simon then removed the body on the eve of the fall of Jerusalem lest it be desecrated by Roman troops.

When the Cardinal and the archaeologist chance to meet after many years, Dr. Gordon has lost his teaching position, having pretty much abandoned that work when he became absorbed in his discovery, the nature of which he dared not then disclose. The Cardinal invites him to stay in a basement apartment in his own church residence for as long as he needs to finish his research. Once Gordon reveals his discovery to Maloney, the latter pretends (to his friend as well as to himself) that it cannot be true. The debates on this and other religious topics are, as I say, well drawn, never caricatured. But one cannot help feeling that Cardinal Maloney is at bottom a spin doctor. He is no longer at liberty to entertain hypotheses disqualified by his institutional superiors, and he must manipulate his own thinking to simulate the appearance that he just happens to echo Roman Catholic dogma on every point, in every case, and by his own unbiased, spontaneous judgment. This repressed identity as an *apparatchik* leads us to expect that he will eventually act decisively to suppress the truth in the name of the Church. It is all nicely subtle, and the debates between the two old friends, as well as Cardinal Maloney's overheard inner monologues, give us much to consider.

EASTER GHOST

When we considered another novel in which archaeologists had seemingly uncovered the bones of Jesus, Guy Thorne's *When It Was Dark*, I took issue, as many New Testament scholars do, with the hasty inference that such a discovery would debunk Christianity. To jump to such a conclusion, I said, would be to ignore the very real evidence (in 1 Cor 15:35–57 and 1 Pet 3:18) that at first Jesus was believed to have arisen spiritually, not physically. That would not have involved the absence of his fleshly corpse. Thus the empty tomb stories of the gospels must stem from a secondary, legendary stage of the gospel embellishment when even believers had begun to feel that "John Brown's body" demonstrably "a-molderin' in the grave" made the assertion of a "spiritual" resurrection seem an arbitrary, cooked-up evasion.

Ex-evangelist Templeton, having lost his own faith-commitment, draws the issue in a more compelling manner, as seen from the standpoint of one lacking the liberty to rethink his position: the erudite Cardinal Maloney. Faced with the discovery of Jesus' well-preserved dead body (no hoax this time), the Cardinal cannot allow himself to accept what his better judgment tells him must be true. He takes refuge in his superior intellect, comforting himself with the realization that, though the discovery leaves untouched the spiritual (hence unverifiable) character of the resurrection of Jesus, the common Catholic might be impatient with such distinctions. Their earnest attempts at faith might thus receive a crippling blow from which recovery would appear impossible.

> Even if one insisted that the resurrection was essentially a reviving of the *spirit* of Jesus the argument grew gruel-thin when you could visit a museum and see the bones—the very *bones!*—and know that he had not triumphed over death; that, as happens to all men, his heart had stopped, the impulses in his brain and nervous system had faltered and ended, and for all the myrrh and aloes and spikenard, for all the wrapping in a shroud impregnated with spices, the corruption of his flesh had taken place, and in the end there was nothing but the bones. (pp. 66–67)

Once you put it that way, it is indeed difficult to take the "spiritual resurrection" alternative any more seriously than pathetic evasions of the Jehovah's Witnesses' and Millerites after their failed prophecies about the imminent onset of Armageddon. Both sects had the hard-shelled courage to endure skepticism and ridicule as the clock ticked away. So deeply had they become invested in this claim, so far out on the limb had they built their nest, that when the deadline passed with no visible effect, they dared to explain that the Second Coming *did* happen; it *must* have happened (you guessed it) *invisibly, spiritually, in heaven, not upon earth*, and therefore visible only to the eye of faith. In the same way, such "virtue of necessity" talk of a "spiritual resurrection" sounds like a fall-back position. Perhaps Jesus had predicted he would rise; perhaps his first followers merely inferred that he would and later ascribed such predictions to him. But then, like modern cultists who keep vigil around their guru's increasingly ripe corpse till the neighbors summon the police, they gave up hope for a *real*, fleshly resurrection and manufactured a "spiritual resurrection." Such a resurrection required faith instead of establishing faith. And no one could prove it happened, admittedly, but, more importantly, no one could *dis*prove it either. It is the kind of bold yet patently contrived claim that no one would buy who did not require a plank from the shattered ship to hang onto and avoid drowning.

Some describe faith as proceeding along a path marked out by the evidence as it far as it goes, then daring to keep walking in the same direction when visible clues end (as in Aquinas's arguments for the existence of God). But such faith as this seeks to marshal the superhuman strength to overthrow the weight of a building that has collapsed atop one, pinning one to the ground. You can't really blame anyone for not having it. It would be quite a surprise if anyone does. And if they do, you may find you have some real estate in the Everglades to sell them. In other words, such reality-denying faith may seem like less of a good idea, even to the religious person, than it did at first. It is laid bare as sheer obduracy, fueled by nothing but a stubborn will to believe, an attitude that tends not to commend, but to render suspicious, any belief served by it.

FAITH WITHOUT FACTS IS DEAD

The good Cardinal had no idea that, when he extended his hospitality to his old friend, the man would claim to have discovered the bones of Jesus. But once he learns the secret, he realizes he has created a world of trouble, and not least for himself. For it turns out that the reigning Pope Gregory is close to death and that he, Michael Maloney the Pope's protégé, is the papal favorite as the successor. Now, how is it going to look if it comes out that this candidate for the Throne of Peter was offering comfort and shelter to the man who was putting the finishing touches on a work that destroyed the world's belief in the resurrection? The Cardinal comes to believe that his friend Dr. Gordon is mistaken, *must* be mistaken, or else is mounting a Morton Smith-style hoax.[2] In neither case can he allow him to proceed. So Cardinal Maloney determines that, for the good of the faith of the Church, he must nip the whole thing in the bud. Like someone who knew, or should have known, what Hitler would do should he come to power, the Cardinal feels it is his duty to prevent the villainy—by killing the villain before it is too late. To try to keep his motives unselfish, he takes himself out of Papal consideration. On the day before Dr. Gordon plans to take his finished manuscript to his publisher, the Cardinal contrives to dine his guest into diabetic shock, then to inject him with CO_2 rather than the glucagons he needs. But unable to go through with it, he races to find the proper injection, alas too late. He proceeds with his scheme and removes all evidence of the scroll, the skeleton, and his dead friend's manuscript. Then he turns his attention to the campaign for the papacy. Who better to take the office than one so confident, like Kierkegaard's Abraham, that the call of God to the individual Knight of Faith justified his transcendence of the moral absolute: Thou shalt do no murder.

The only trouble is that, a month later, the Israeli Antiquities Authority files a complaint against the late Dr. Gordon. We already knew the old rascal had managed to smuggle the scroll and skeleton out of the Holy Land, but it seemed he had succeeded in evading the Israeli authorities. Apparently not. His misdeed comes to the attention of Copeland Jackson, police detective and fiancé of the Cardinal's niece. The detective's search eventually alienates his fiancé, her uncle, and Copeland's own superiors, but he persists in climbing a lonely mountain, lifting himself by clues that are so subtle, like tiny irregularities in the rock face, that they allow him progress only with slow difficulty.

He finally reaches the top and realizes what the Cardinal has done. Detective Copeland even locates the sacred skeleton, the scroll, and the manuscript. He leaves a letter for the Cardinal demanding he come clean, but it falls into the hands of his daughter, Copeland's estranged fiancé, and she commits suicide. Cardinal Maloney fails to gain the votes needed for the papacy, and he embarks on a period of monastic asceticism, while the bones (what about the scroll of Simon Zelotes and the

---

2. See chapter 3 for a discussion of my suspicions (as yet unproved) about Smith's *Secret Gospel of Mark*.

manuscript of Harris Gordon?) are turned over to the Vatican's agency for authenticating the miracles of nominated saints.

In short, the novel does not furnish much of a glimpse of the change the world or the Church might undergo if such discoveries were to be made public. That is disappointing to theological nerds like me, but the reason for it is plain enough. The archaeological discovery motif is the premise for the various mysteries linking the characters together, and the threat posed by the discovery provides the resolution of the mysteries with the needed urgency. After that the job is done. The curtain falls on the lives (in this case, ruined ones) of the main characters. The drama has not been about the larger world, but about them and the discovery's effects on them alone.

13 | Bad News Oracle
Barbara Rogers, *The Doomsday Scroll*

DAMIEN LITE

THIS FAST-PACED ESPIONAGE NOVEL[1] is strongest in those areas that really do not concern us here, namely plot, intrigue, characterization—all the important stuff! At least those are the important factors from the standpoint of conventional literary analysis. But we are more interested in the imaginary scholarship and the pseudo-theology posited by these authors, as they present us with a series of interesting thought experiments. Barbara Rogers's *The Doomsday Scroll* at first sight appears to hold great promise in two pop literature subgenres: both the Lost Gospel type and the Antichrist novel (the subject of my *The Paperback Apocalypse*). Rogers's book looks especially interesting in that it combines both genres. Sadly, it largely fails to deliver as either a Lost Gospel novel or an Antichrist fiction, much less as an amalgam of the two. There is too much left at the stage of preparation, as if it were all preparing the groundwork for a sequel—which, as far as I can determine, the talented Barbara Rogers never wrote.

Her Antichrist character has a lot of potential: he is an adolescent boy named Dov Weissmann, the son of an Israeli physicist who has discovered a potent fuel based on simple water. Naturally, such a discovery, yet to be announced but known to spies, holds equally great promise and danger. Arab oil producers will not relish seeing their universally coveted export reduced to worthlessness. But others are afraid that Israel, once in command of such a new resource, will blackmail the world. Improbable alliances form, and schemers attempt in various labyrinthine ways to steal the formula, destroy the samples, etc. All this loosely recalls the circumstances of Revelation chapter 13 in which we see the Beast gain

---

1. All page references are to the Dell edition.

control of the world by doling out food rations only to his loyal minions during a universal famine. Certain Arab interests contrive to kidnap the inventor's son to hold him hostage for the hydrofuel formula. But it is evident at once that the boy is working with them. He believes himself to be the new prophet, the Son of Light or Son of the East whose imminent advent has been revealed by an ancient scroll unearthed at Masada, the ancient palace of Herod Antipas where nine hundred Jews committed suicide rather than surrender to Roman besiegers in CE 73. And his Arab confederates believe it, too.

Here is the major departure of *The Doomsday Scroll* from the Lost Gospel genre: the manuscript discovery is not a gospel but rather an apocalypse: a poetic prediction of the events of the End Times: not a record of the first advent of Christ, but an anticipation of the second.

Like the infamous Grigori Rasputin, the young Weissmann had once been at death's door, having caught a fever and lapsed into a coma. He returned to apparent normalcy, but he was a changed person. Of course the implication is that the innocent Dov died and was replaced by an infernal spirit. He has the same sort of mind-reading and mind-controlling powers Rasputin is said to have possessed, as well as a generous dose of the same depraved appetites. And he recognizes himself and his mission in the newly-discovered scroll.

It predicts the coming of one to be hailed as Israel's Messiah, but one who would soon reveal his true colors as the Antichrist. If you are thinking that it would be mighty peculiar for anyone to claim the role of arch-villain while hoping to attain prominence or even world dominion, you are right. Part of the intrigue of the novel derives from the attempts of the boy and his Arab henchmen to secure the ancient scroll itself as well as a few circulating photocopies. They need to grab the text before it becomes widely known, because they want to bring in a biblical scholar to replace the last paragraph and remove the revelation that the Son of Light will be revealed as the False Messiah.

We have seen how Lost Gospel novels tend to fall into two categories. In some the new gospel is a hoax. In the rest, it is genuine (at least in the fictional setting of each novel). We have also seen how the novels differ as to whether their gospel (true or false) manages to see the light of day. In some, genuine discoveries are prevented from becoming widely known, even destroyed. In others, whether hoaxes or the real thing, the gospel makes it to public attention. We might even divide these further according to whether the public revelation winds up making any real difference. So where does *The Doomsday Scroll* fall? Its scroll is genuine but becomes falsified when its conclusion is rewritten. So it starts out being the story of a genuine ancient document, then becomes the tale of a hoax. The scholar forced into forging the conclusion, however, manages at the last minute to hide the scroll, taking advantage of gunfire and general confusion to wrap up a pair of sandals in the cloth that was to contain the text. So the plans of the young Antichrist are unclear. Will he find some other way to gain his ends?

Finally, the anomaly of the rediscovered pseudo-biblical text being a future-telling apocalypse (like Revelation) rather than a past-telling gospel (like Matthew) produces a very striking comparison. In the case of hoax-gospels as in Irving Wallace's *The Word* or James Hall Roberts's *The Q Document*, the danger of public acceptance of the spurious gospel, destructive to true Christianity, would amount to the replacement of a true Christ with a false one, an Antichrist, albeit not a living individual. A newly prevailing false character-portrait or heretical estimate of Jesus Christ taking the place of the familiar one would amount to the supplanting of Christ by Antichrist, would it not? Indeed it would, even if both spoke only from the flat page.

14 | It's in the Vault
Barnaby Conrad and Nico Mastorakis, *Keepers of the Secret*

JESUS CHRIST'S SMARTER SISTER

THE BASIC PREMISE THIS time out is that a hidden gospel reveals that Jesus was only the adoptive son of Joseph and Mary, that their God-possessed child was a female, and that she backed Jesus up during his ministry, enabling him to teach wisdom and perform miracles on her tab. This was needful because ancient Judea was so chauvinistic that a female messiah would have gotten exactly nowhere. Well, one immediately objects, why didn't the Almighty simply manipulate a chromosome and have a male child born? The answer is simple: if he had, we wouldn't have much reason for this novel. But here is an abridgment of the text:

> I, John, bear witness that I was with Jesus in the garden when he went out to suffer. And I fled to the Mount of Olives and wept. Now each day I suffer anew, not only for the suffering of Jesus, but for the untruths that abound. I say to you now, Jesus was not the Messiah. Jesus was the Son of God, as we all are, but he was not the one chosen by the Father to save all mankind. (pp. 9–10)

The bit about John leaving the Garden of Gethsemane and making a bee-line for the Mount of Olives comes, with some garbling, from the apocryphal *Acts of John*, specifically the section in it called The Preaching of John. There, John is summoned from Golgotha to a cave in the Mount of Olives by the spiritual, divine Christ, who hastens to inform him that the crucified figure is not the real Jesus, though successive generations will believe so. And therefore Christ requires faithful John to get and keep the record straight, which of course is just what he is depicted as doing in The Preaching of John. Same here: though the revelation is quite different, the scenery is the same.

Going back to the beginning, the Nativity section of the novel's gospel tells us that Mary and Joseph did not skip town before Herod's hit squad reached Bethlehem, but that the holy couple were safe—when it turned out their new infant was a female! (pp. 12–13). Obviously the shocker here is that the Christ child turns out to be female. More about this below. For the present, it is good enough to note that this ostensibly Johannine version of the Nativity (something of which the Gospel of John tells absolutely nothing) combines elements of the Nativity stories of Matthew and Luke. It is mainly Matthean, with statements about this or that scripture being fulfilled, the persecution of Herod, and the flight into Egypt. From Luke comes the notion that the baby was born in a ramshackle stable; in contrast, Matthew assumes that Mary and Joseph lived in Bethlehem, Jesus was born at home, and the Magi visited two years later. To this our novel adds the assistance of an informal midwife, which comes from the apocryphal *Infancy Gospel of James* (also called *The Protevangelium*, or *Proto-Gospel of James*).

Mary and Joseph name the baby Mary Lael, the latter denoting "the chosen of God." They go to Alexandria, Egypt, just in case Herod becomes an equal-opportunity persecutor and starts sniffing around for their daughter. Then things get pretty weird: "her eyes never blinked and . . . when she walked, she left no footprints in the sand" (pp. 13–15). These details (which, in real life, would surely make Lael's parents hasten to question their own sanity) are borrowed, again, from The Preaching of John, where the apostle recalls how he never saw any footprints laid down by Jesus in the sand, nor his eyes blinking. Of course these details are "marks of the superman," signaling that their possessor is no creature of genuine mortal flesh but only projects that image.

In Egypt, Mary Lael and her parents add to their family unit an orphaned boy named—you guessed it—Jesus. It soon becomes clear she is the real Daughter of God, but she will share her gifts with her new foster brother.

But Mother Mary is not quite on her wavelength.

> And Mary [her mother] did not understand her words. "I do not always understand your meaning, but you speak as a girl-woman who knows the All."

The beatitude on Mary, "you speak as a girl-woman who knows the All," comes right out of the Nag Hammadi text *The Dialogue of the*

Savior, "She spoke this way because she was a woman who knew the All" (139:11–12). Mary Lael herself gives forth this cryptical oracle: "If you bring forth what is within you, what you bring forth will save you. If you do not bring forth what is in you, what you do not bring forth will destroy you." There our authors are drawing upon the *Gospel of Thomas* saying 70: "If you bring out what is inside you, what you have will save you. If you do not have it inside you, what you lack will be the death of you." But Lael, like our authors, has derived what she knows of the Gnostic sayings tradition from Elaine Pagels, for the version given of this saying follows Pagels's highly dubious translation of it. (I once asked Professor Pagels about this, and she answered that this was the best sense she could make of it.)

BEHIND EVERY GREAT MAN

The general drift of the gospel posited in *Keepers of the Secret* is a sort of Affirmative Action treatment of Mary Magdalene, giving her equal importance with Jesus. Though no ancient text went so far, it is certainly true that second- and third-century Gnostic texts depicted Mary Magdalene as the equal of the blustering male disciples, or even as their superior. But it's all for nothing in the long run, since later on we find that Lael was *not* in fact the same person as Mary Magdalene, but was only mistaken for her! (pp. 108–9). She was just some dumb whore, and she has acquired a saintly reputation by this confusion with the righteous Lael.

PARTING IS SUCH SWEET SORROW

She went to Jesus and put her face near his, and there were tears on her cheeks and I could hear her as she spoke to him, saying, "Now the hour has come. Be strong, my brother, my love, my very life. I am you and you are me forever, from this day forward. Whatever is done to you, so shall it be done to me." And then did she drop to her knees and kiss his hand.

And Jesus spoke to her, saying, "I shall be strong, do not fear, for it is you who make me strong."

And Jesus was dragged away from Lael, but he looked back to her, and in his eyes were shining tears, yet on his lips was a smile. (pp. 19–22)

SPLICE 'N DICE

Well, one must say that all this is comical, unwittingly hilarious. What we see is a modern feminist version of the same strategy undertaken by the ancient Priestly editor of the Pentateuch, who, in order to usurp for his colleagues an equal share of Moses' glory, systematically inserted alongside Moses the priestly Aaron character as a second Moses, again and again, so that it is Aaron who wields the miracle-working rod and brings down the plagues on Egypt, Aaron who speaks Moses' words, etc. In the gospel of Lael, the Jesus character is rudely shoved aside in favor of the fictive Lael, the *real* (and *female!*) Messiah. She is Cyrano lurking in the background while poor Jesus is on stage vainly trying to raise Lazarus from the dead! It is she who steps in to tack Malchus's severed ear back on, through Jesus, of course. The authors' agenda could scarcely be less blatant, less blunderingly overt, less crude and grotesque!

And it is Lael who reinforces Jesus' quivering backbone when the time comes for him to go to the cross. The sickening gooiness of the sentiment shared between Jesus and his adoptive twin sister is enough to make the reader check back to the title page to see if the authors are actually males. The result is something like a *Mists of Avalon* version of the gospels, where women are the real heroes, the real powers, the real movers and shakers in history, for some reason allowing frail, childlike males to assume the spotlight. Lael is pretty much an apostolic Yoko Ono.

Things proceed to the Hill of the Skull, where eventually Jesus cries out, not quite what we expect, but rather: "Lael, Lael, *lama sabachthani!*" (pp. 85–86). So, let me get this straight: Jesus was asking, bitterly and rhetorically, "Lael, Lael, why did you forsake me"? Because that's what it would have meant.

One might compare this fictive gospel with the American release of the Toho Studios movie *Godzilla the King of the Monsters*. American audiences enjoyed seeing the familiar face of actor Raymond Burr, later famous as TV's Perry Mason. Burr played Steve Martin, intrepid American reporter covering the apocalyptic destruction wrought upon Japan by the awakened dino-monster Godzilla. In its original Japanese language release, *Godzilla* featured no such character, nor was he important to the plot even in the English language version. Rudely inserting the American character into the story, alongside the original characters (some of whom were brought back to share "filler" scenes with Burr), was simply a gimmick intended to enable American audiences to feel more at home with a film otherwise filled with alien landscapes and cultural references. We have the same character duplication and scene-interpolation in *Keepers of the Secret*.

With John's help, Lael took down Jesus' body, hung it over a donkey's back, and absconded with it to parts unknown. Naturally everyone else jumped to the conclusion that the slain rabbi had risen from the dead. You know the rest (pp. 229–30). Uh, let's see: who are the deceivers in the name of Jesus? Naturally, the implication is that these deceivers are the founding Guardians to whose ancient order the blood-scheming cardinals in this book belong, the eponymous "Keepers of the Secret." But doesn't the narrative itself say that Lael was the first hoaxer, removing the body for no other apparent purpose than to facilitate the erroneous inference of the disciples that Jesus had risen from the grave?

THAT BAD?

As in various of the Lost Gospel novels, the unknown text poses such dangers to the faithful that their self-appointed protectors are willing to rub out whomever threatens to expose the secret. The same, predictably, is true here. An unofficial cadre of Vatican zealots, including some cardinals, shed most of the blood in the book. What exactly are they afraid would happen if the Lael gospel were to become known?

But I wonder if your curiosity may not end up simply jeopardizing the faith of many, many people . . .

You mean the global repercussions, the domino principle, the lowering of the power of the Vatican, the social and political implications?

True or not, it could cause chaos—a moral A-bomb. (p. 90)

But what, exactly, would render this new gospel such a bitter pill? Our intrepid investigator sums it up: "really heretical. Crazy stuff, the Messiah being a woman" (p. 116). Pardon me, but in my opinion, the gender issue would be a minor bump in the road compared to the Christological train wreck that must result from the story we have read in the scroll so far. For one thing, both Jesus and Lael would have to be understood not as incarnations of the divine Logos, hence persons of the Trinity, but rather as having been adopted as God's children, and this in two different ways. Lael, like the Valentinian Jesus, would have been the fleshly host or channeler for the heavenly Christ spirit that would finally leave her while she was still alive in the flesh. Jesus would have been adopted God's son in a purely honorific fashion, just as some ancient Jewish Christians seemed to understand him. Another thing: it is hard to see how either Jesus or Lael could be considered a savior in any traditional terms. Lael at least had something of divinity in her, but she did not die on the cross. Lael is eventually reported (though not in the gospel text) to have perished through the intrigues of the Guardians, who had the Apostle John whacked for good measure. Jesus did die on the cross, but he was not essentially divine, and according to Catholic and Orthodox thought, that means he would not have had it in his power to transfer to us, through his death, a divine immortality that, it now seems, he did not possess. He certainly could not function as the trigger ("the first fruits") of the general resurrection of believers—since he did not rise from the dead!

I am not saying no new doctrine of salvation might be constructed on the basis of the Lael gospel. It is just that the very necessity of doing it must mean traditional Christianity is headed for the scrap heap. It is no minor modification we are talking about. The authors, presumably speaking through their hero, reporter Jason van Cleve, utterly fail to grasp the true nature of things: "But you have read them. Are they so blasphemous? Just because they tell the same story, the same philosophy in a different way?" (p. 231).

PITCHING IT

Finally, after all the risks taken and blood shed in order to secure the precious gospel of Lael, the novel ends—absolutely inexplicably—with reporter Jason van Cleve cramming the photos and translations of the gospel into a trash can and setting it all afire! One speculates whether Conrad and Mastorakis might have done us a favor to treat their own manuscript the same way.

15 | Frisky Father Folan
Richard Ben Sapir, *The Body*

DESTROYER OF FAITH?

ONE MIGHT GO INTO this novel[1] expecting a good mystery, a strong plot, and brisk writing from the author/creator of the Destroyer series of pulp novels, and one would by no means be disappointed. We are neither lost in the necessary scientific detail nor sickened by too much romance, though both are major and necessary components of *The Body*. The hero is a young Jesuit priest, Jim Folan, former Marine and CIA operative, now a part-time teacher of Roman history and dean of students. To his profound surprise, he finds himself summoned, along with a number of others, for consideration for a special mission in Jerusalem. Despite his almost complete lack of archaeological experience or expertise, he is awarded the undesired position and commissioned by the pope himself, who assures his young champion that he has what it takes for his assigned mission. And that is? Well, our other major character, renowned archaeologist Dr. Sharon Golban, has stumbled upon what appears to be a forgotten tomb at a construction site in Jerusalem, and all evidence points to it being the tomb, and the skeleton, of Jesus Christ. The Israeli government hastens to call in the Vatican and to place the archaeological dig under their control, because if the dead man does turn out to be the distinctly *un*risen founder of Christianity, Israel does not want to risk appearing to have torpedoed the Christian faith, inviting a new wave of anti-Semitism.

Father Folan is a handsome young man, while Dr. Golban is stunningly beautiful and voluptuous, and you can guess the direction things are headed. Their first meetings are filled with her thunderous hatred of all religious orthodoxy: she is quite sure the Jesuit has been sent to neu-

---

1. All page references are to the Pinnacle edition.

tralize the discoveries of science to cover the exposed posterior of faith. The priest protests: while, as a matter of faith, he feels sure the remains cannot be those of Jesus, on the other hand, the last thing he wants is any appearance of scholarly impropriety, which would of course cast onto the Church the very suspicions that it is trying to avoid. The game must be played according to the rules, and to everyone's satisfaction, if the Church is to have any chance of winning it. Let the chips fall where they may. Sharon need not worry that Jim's faith will skew the outcome; by contrast, it is his faith that frees him from the need to attempt anything untoward. If it does turn out he is wrong, well that's a hypothetical he need not worry about in the meantime.

CAN'T BE

So Folan employs his intelligence-gathering skills, honed in the military, to eliminate any possibility of a fraud or hoax mounted by interested parties. From there on in, pure archaeology, Sharon's department, can proceed. Soon into the investigation, Jim thinks he has found proof that the body cannot be that of his Lord and Savior for the too-simple reason that the man was not tall enough. That is, compared with the man whose image appears on the Shroud of Turin. Author Sapir indulges in a bit of fictional padding at this point, positing for the sake of the novel that the Vatican had already performed Carbon 14 dating tests on the fabric and found it to stem from the first century CE, concluding that it must be the genuine image of the crucified Jesus and that he was unusually tall, if only by scant inches. (Of course, the Turin Shroud has since been analyzed in much the same way Sapir posited, and the results were not happy: the cloth goes back only to the fourteenth century.)

Alas, Father Folan shortly comes to realize his error. Sharon bids him peruse the familiar gospels again, and see what he notices. Finally it dawns on him that nowhere did it note a superior height for Jesus (as 1 Sam 10:23 did for King Saul). That would at least mean that there was insufficient reason to think Jesus had been a towering man, and then the slightly shorter skeleton might as well have represented him. There was no name on the Shroud, after all. It was a toss-up.

But didn't the new evidence squarely contradict the gospels on the central point: the emptiness of the tomb? Here Sapir demonstrates an imagination to match that of the eighteenth-century Rationalists, whose trademark was defending the details of the gospels as absolutely historical while providing far-fetched naturalistic explanations. The bones, now seemingly those of Jesus, were discovered behind an inner wall of clay bricks hastily erected after interment to hide and protect the body. But so closely did such mud-bricks resemble a natural clay wall that anyone gazing into the tomb would think it empty. Beyond that? Well, visions of a departed loved one are by no means uncommon and do not prove much of anything.

LET THE DEAD BURY THE DEAD

One of the more interesting sequences in the novel concerns the clash between the archaeologists and a sect of ultra-Orthodox Jews who do not want to see the burial place of any Jew, ancient or modern, violated. They ambush Jim and Sharon, seizing Jim's brief case in the melee. They do not know it contains a related artifact, the *titulus* or inscribed stone disk suspended from Jesus' neck, declaring him to have been executed as a royal pretender: "King of the Jews" in Aramaic. Sharon successfully sends their attackers flying by ripping open her shirt and exposing her ripe breasts, horrifying the ultra-pious ascetics. Pursuing them to the dwelling of their Rebbe, Jim enters into a three-hour pow-wow in which he displays a surprising grasp of Talmudic logic, something he had picked up in a special seminar in school. Finally all agree that the sectarians have an interest in the tomb only if the body can be proven that of a Jew, which Jim says can in fact be proven by their methods. If a Jewish identity can be established, there will be no attempt to remove the bones. From that point on, the Hasidim assist the scientists, providing watchmen for the dig.

All the while, we can see Jim and Sharon, their initial sparring over (a typical feature of romantic comedies), finding one another increasingly irresistible until Jim's vows of celibacy are cast aside along with his Roman collar at the foot of Sharon's bed. Henceforth Father Folan is plagued both by the now-seemingly certain identification of the bones as Jesus' and his betrayal of Jesus in bed with Sharon. At one point he bitterly reproaches himself for momentarily thinking it would be good if the resurrection were debunked, because then his vows would mean nothing, and he could have sex without guilt.

The Catholic authorities, including the unnamed pope, listen to the reports and are compelled to admit that the bones appear to be those of Jesus. The pope explains to Jim, whose confessed infidelities he seems willing to take in stride, that he and the Church are not prepared to admit that the bones are those of Jesus, only that it could blame no one for thinking they were. Their discovery was a total surprise, and who knew but that the future might yield another find, equally unsuspected, that would put a whole new light on the matter? Here the pope (with Sapir) seems acutely aware of the history-faith dilemma as Martin Kähler, Wilhelm Herrmann, and Paul Tillich[2] discussed it (though of course he need not have derived his thinking from them): can any faith remain stable as long as it remains at the mercy of whatever new scrolls or relics might be unearthed tomorrow? And does honest faith simply refuse to admit that the future might disclose such revelations?

> "You saw bones and you saw reports. James, I do not know science other than today's facts are not tomorrow's. I will not put faith in such a thing when I know He is risen. And this is where you know," said His Holiness, putting a finger on Jim's chest. (p. 344)

So the official plan is for the Mossad to spirit away the evidence and bring it safely to Rome, the Vatican buying the silence of the Israeli government by granting official recognition, after all these years, to the State of Israel. The Vatican had never before recognized Israel because they didn't want to alienate numerous Arab states, much less to invite persecution for the substantial Arab Catholic minorities in some of these countries whose loyalty was already considered suspect by their Muslim overlords.

But the discovery and its probable significance had not gone unnoticed by the Soviet government (still in power when Sapir wrote), who sent an Arab lackey to Israel to find out what he could. This man, Warris Abouf, had eventually come to fear for his life, caught in the crossfire (figuratively and literally) between pro-Soviet Syrian and PLO factions. He is a Communist atheist but fears for his Christian family's safety should the Vatican recognize Israel. He contacts Father Folan, now sunk into depression at the loss of his cherished Easter faith, and the two hatch a scheme to seize the bones and smuggle them to some place where they can be destroyed, in one stroke rescuing Catholicism and the vulnerable Arab Christians. Dodging surveillance as well as bullets all the way, the

---

2. Kähler, *The So-Called Historical Jesus and the Historic, Biblical Christ*; Herrmann, *The Communion of the Christian with God*; Tillich, *Systematic Theology II*, 101–17; Harvey, *The Historian and the Believer*.

pair is finally captured by one of Abouf's enemies, who smashes and burns the remains.

Or does he? A chastened Jim Folan returns to Rome, freely and tearfully confessing his sins, and requests a dispensation to set aside his vows and to marry Sharon. But his superiors inform him that Sharon was slain when she attempted to follow him. The pope tells him he has another special task for him: he must serve in Rome as custodian of the bones. The Vatican and Israeli authorities had feared an attempt to steal and destroy them, so they had quickly replaced them with fakes. In his grief and near-hermit solitude, Jim keeps his vigil for decades, mourning the loss of his one true love. He does not suspect that Sharon is still alive and has been similarly lied to: Jim is dead at the hands of Arab radicals. And, most surprising of all, an Afterword takes us two thousand years into the past, where we learn that the bones in that tomb were in fact *not* those of Jesus but rather of an unknown contemporary. The pope was right: no matter how convincing the evidence, it could still be wrong—and it was.

OMNIPOTENT AUTHOR

What an ending! And yet what lesson are we to take away from this? Should the reader resolve his or her own doubts by the same expedient? No, for we must keep in mind that Richard Ben Sapir is not only the omniscient author, knowing what is happening and who is thinking what. He is also the *omnipotent* author who creates a fictive world with all its "realities" as he chooses them. He has created a narrative universe here in which, apparently, Jesus did rise from the dead but with the evidence seeming to point in the opposite direction. And that might parallel the way things are in our actual world of history. But there is no way to know. Sapir only "knows" because he made up the story. For us to maintain the same sort of "superior knowledge" our author ascribes to the pope in *The Body*, we, too, should require some knowledge, independent of extant evidence. And we don't have it. Within the story, though, does the pope not possess it? No: he "lucks out," but his psychological certitude is purely subjective. It is the sheer will to believe, and that settles nothing, at least not in any rational or legitimate way. It is rather the certitude of the coffee-mug slogan: "My mind's made up. Don't confuse me with the facts."

And why do believers so shield their faith? One Soviet bureaucrat in the novel sums up the sad truth:

> It will not be the end of the Catholic Church, nor will it be the end of Christianity. Religion is not based on a rational system of proofs. It survives because of needs. If we offer proof that Christ has not risen, then those who believe will not believe us. Some will fall away, but Christianity will remain because it fills too much in the human personality. (p. 316)

16 | Looking for Luke
Donald C. King, *The Manuscript*

THIS LIVELY NOVELLA (it is so much shorter than most of these books that I hesitate, with no criticism implied, to call it a real novel) is written in an engaging style, but the smooth flow of the narrative renders it almost superficial. Not enough happens. There are visible remnants, an underlying pattern, of the typical Lost Gospel novel, but they are treated peremptorily, cursorily. An adventurous photographer, jaded with human violence, lets himself be drawn into a project headed by a pious but witty biblical archaeology professor—and his beautiful daughter. They are negotiating with an ornery Arab who has stumbled upon what looks to be the original autograph manuscript of Luke's gospel. Before they can settle the deal, a bunch of thugs steal the scroll. The police catch up to them, but the thieves have also stolen some dynamite, hoping to sell it to terrorists. During the police siege, the explosives go off, and it seems the precious scroll is no more. Then we learn that one of the bad guys managed to sneak it out just before the explosion, and that he tossed it into a nearby creek bed. Then another old scavenger took notice and picked it up, hoping eventually to be able to sell it along with his other valuables, such as shoe laces, knives, and string. Meanwhile, as one might surmise from this book being published by Tyndale House, the photographer reads Luke from a modern Bible—and gets converted, Hallelujah! Apparently, for an evangelical author, there is more joy in heaven over one sinner who repents than over the possible discovery of a priceless biblical manuscript.

The Manuscript follows a pretty clever blueprint. One chapter depicts modern-day events, leaving us hanging while the next chapter takes us back to the ancient world and the circumstances of Luke writing his gospel, attending Paul, etc. The historical gap is gradually closed as we jump ahead into the time of Emperor Justinian who caused the

Lukan autograph to be packed away to Saint Catherine's monastery, then on to text-critical pioneer Constantine Tischendorf, who discovered the famous fourth-century Codex Sinaiticus in that monastery but just missed the (fictive) Luke scroll. It's imaginative. It's good. It should have been a lot longer.

King's narratizations of Luke, his gospel, and his attendance upon the journeying Paul, proceed from and embody the standard Bible College literalism for which Tyndale House stands. We have, of course, the Gospel of Luke actually being penned by the Luke mentioned in Colossians 4:14 and 2 Timothy 4:11 as Paul's personal physician. He is writing his gospel while Paul is held captive in Caesarea Philippi in the later 50s CE. This date is, I consider (in company with a great many scholars) ridiculously early, maybe by as much as a whole century. And to ascribe the book to anyone named "Luke," much less Paul's Dr. Luke, is purely a matter of tradition, since no name is contained in the text.

Donald King knows well that many scholars rule out so early a date for the gospel, but he thinks this a biased, hare-brained speculation of the insidious Tübingen School (it *was* their hypothesis), aimed at denigrating faith in an inerrant scripture. This is like calling germ theory a fiendish scheme to undermine people's faith in evil humors and spirits as the cause of illness. King summarizes (pp. 100–103) the arguments of the apologist and archaeologist William Ramsay, who thought to have vindicated Luke's accuracy by demonstrating the accuracy of the references in Acts (Luke's second volume) to particular Roman geography, government offices, and historical figures. Given that much of that information would have been known just as well to a writer of the second century (as well as the high likelihood that Luke used Josephus as a source),[1] such accuracy is not particularly surprising and proves nothing against the second-century date to which various genre conventions and comparative vocabulary strongly point. Plus, Luke commits egregious howlers in both his gospel and Acts, e.g., placing the birth of Jesus in the reign of Quirinius, some dozen years later than Luke's own references to Herod the Great would require. His notion of a Roman census requiring subjects to register not where they lived and could be found by the tax collector, but rather where their remote ancestors had dwelt a full millennium before, marks him as a novelist who used correct details only

---

1. Mason, *Josephus and the New Testament*.

to create a general backdrop of verisimilitude against which to place his own fictive departures from well-known events.[2]

We have seen how, in one after another of the Lost Gospel novels, the prospect of a new gospel discovery (or the equivalent) would, it was feared, blow the Christian religion sky high. Much is at stake, as gauged by the efforts spent by some factions to destroy or suppress the manuscript and others to publish it. In the specimens of the genre we have examined that were written by evangelicals, there has not yet been a genuine gospel discovery, but only a deadly hoax threatening to destroy Christian faith. The Christian heroes manage to expose the trick and restore faith to the world's populace. Now, in *The Manuscript*, we finally see the promise of a refreshing change. This time there really is a lost gospel. But even here things begin to slope down to an anticlimax. We hear time and again how the loss of the Lukan original, while "tragic," would not really be so bad.

> Jim asked, "Tell me, professor, if you recover this scroll, do you think the Bible will have to be updated?"
> "You mean, do I think I will find something in the manuscript that differs from the Gospel of Luke as we know it? No, I don't think so." (p. 97)

> "First of all, though the scroll was never recovered, Dr. Crawford has said that no real damage has been done."
> "That's right," Jim replied. "He said that there is virtually no question that the Gospel of Luke as we know it today is the same as it was when Luke wrote it—sometime before A.D. 60." (p. 200)

Then why all the hubbub? Was the original Luke just some kind of collector's item, a first edition? No, there is a deeper issue that accounts for the deflationary ending. Obviously fundamentalists are not going to countenance a tale, even a fictive one, in which a discovered text debunks Christianity in any measure. Such a thing would be impossible since we already—they believe—have an inerrant Bible that tells the true account of Jesus and Christian origins. So any subversive document discovery *must* be a hoax, as it turned out to be in *When It Was Dark* and *The Mystery of Mar Saba*, which we encountered in chapters 1 and 3, respectively. But neither can they brook the opposite possibility, i.e., a discovery that would prove an article of faith, say, that the resurrection

---

2. Pervo, *Profit with Delight*; Pervo, *Dating Acts*.

of Jesus really happened. Not even a new gospel adding significant new teachings of Jesus to the ones we already had would be accepted. Why? Because such discoveries would imply that what biblicists have now is not perfect in its sufficiency. No, God wouldn't do that to us. Or, closer to the truth, we cannot afford to entertain the possibility that we possess only part of the truth. If we had to admit that the future might surprise us with some disclosure that would change the look of things, we would be forced to confront the implication that we are not right in having absolute faith in what we've already got. And evangelical Christianity is all about believing you know the truth, the whole truth, and nothing but the truth about Jesus, creation, the second advent, etc. That of course is the exact opposite of the scientific method embraced by scholars, who entertain all hypotheses only tentatively and provisionally, not fearing that new evidence might raise its head but actually hoping that it will.

This is why the lost gospel in question is merely the original of one of the canonical four. There can be no question of a new gospel entering the canon. No, that might confuse things! But even the possibility, which one would think exciting, of a recovered Lukan autograph manuscript settling all manner of text-critical debates, cannot be allowed, since that would imply we are stuck in an undesirable place with the way things actually are. That would mean God had left us with ambiguity, something incompatible with stalwart Bible-thumping. Should we retain "Father forgive them; they know not what they do" (Luke 23:34)? Some copies of Luke lack it. Should we snip out "Ye know not what spirit ye are of. For the son of man came to save men's lives, not to destroy them" (Luke 9:55 KJV)? Is the longer version of the Lord's Supper's words of institution (Luke 22:19b–20) right, or the shorter? Are the "Western non-interpolations" (as Westcott and Hort[3] called them: Luke 24:12, 40, 51b) really absent from the original text of Luke? If so, Luke has no ascension. It seems to me that a Lukan original would come in mighty handy. But the evangelical, ever an apologetical spin-doctor, cannot allow himself to admit there is a problem. No, it's fine the way it is, which means God must *want* it this way. And we don't want to be heard complaining, no sir!

I recall once hearing a prominent evangelical textual critic say in a lecture how all the autograph originals of the Bible perished—"Thank God!" The seminary students laughed, knowing he couldn't really mean

---

3. Metzger, *The Text of the New Testament*, 134.

it! A textual critic, dedicated to determining the original manuscript readings—glad that such a solution would never be possible? Was this scholar like the rumored doctor or pharmaceutical manufacturer, suppressing a remedy for cancer because it would make his business unnecessary? That would actually be better, for I am afraid what we witness in the professor's words, and in the sheepish reassurances of his fictional counterpart, Dr. Crawford, is instead a contemptible pious obsequiousness. If God, who demands literal belief and obedience to the letter of scripture, has nonetheless prevented us from knowing the exact readings of the original "inspired" text, then we must pretend to thank him for cheating us. We become like the son in Matthew 7:9 who asks his father for bread but is given a stone instead. The situation would be reminiscent of the *Twilight Zone* episode[4] in which the world is terrorized by a brat with omnipotent psychokinetic powers. Anything he decrees will come to pass. So those relatives and neighbors who survive must kowtow to him at every point, pretending to affirm every blow he sends crashing: "Uh, it's *good* you sent the hail that destroyed the crops, Anthony! That was *fine!*" It's either that or end up "in the cornfield," turned into a hideous living jack-in-the-box. We must make virtue of necessity and swallow the Catch 22s God assigns us. "Professor So-and so, wouldn't you love to have a definitive text of Luke to solve the mysteries?" "Uh, *no*, no, I *wouldn't* because, ah, the version we've got is already just *fine*! Yessir, it's just fine!"

I would go farther in my theological analysis of the underpinnings of *The Manuscript*. It turns out to be a narrative allegory of the peculiar apologetic of the famous Benjamin B. Warfield, chief proponent of the modern fundamentalist doctrine of biblical inerrancy. Warfield[5] denied that any factual error might occur in a divinely inspired book, and yet he had to admit there were occasional (rather an understatement!) apparent errors and contradictions. He inferred that, even with no manuscript evidence in hand, we could declare that said errors had not occurred in the original document but were all the result of careless or mischievous copying by ancient scribes. Scripture was inerrant—a belief necessary to the trust evangelicals want to place in the Bible—but technically it was inerrant only as originally written, in the original authorial holographs. And, uh, we don't have any of *them*. And, remember, Warfield did not

---

4. Rod Serling based on Jerome Bixby, "It's a Good Life."
5. Hodge and Warfield, *Inspiration*, 36.

require any manuscript evidence to make such judgments! This means that, for all we know, *any* passage of any gospel or epistle might have been sabotaged somewhere along the line and we would never know it! He did not seem to realize what he had done to the supposedly inerrant Bible he wanted to believe in—at a single stroke turning the "solid rock" of biblical authority into a marshy bog where no step was certain. Oblivious of these implications, Warfield and his minions have from that day to this rehearsed his argument to reassure themselves that the Bible is without error. At least the *real* Bible, the *original* Bible that we can never consult. The error-riddled copies we read and cherish? Good enough, one supposes, though the poor Catholic priests will have to wait for Judgment Day to discover, as the joke has it, that the original text said "celebrate," not "celibate." All of this is artistically symbolized for us in *The Manuscript*. The presumably inerrant and infallible original autograph of Luke's gospel exists, albeit forever unavailable to us. It functions like a Platonic Idea floating above our paper copies, at the same time guaranteeing their accuracy and undermining it.

17 | Under the Lid
Peter Hernon, *Earthly Remains*

THIS MYSTERY NOVEL,[1] WRITTEN in something approaching a hard-boiled *Noir* style, transports us back in time to 1948 when the discovery of the Dead Sea Scrolls was trickling into the awareness of both scholars and the public. It is an occasion whose actual history is well worth addressing before and during our review of the fictional story that Hernon builds upon it.

The discovery was made by a shepherd boy, Muhammad the Wolf, during his search for a runaway goat (cf. 1 Sam 9:30ff.). He spotted a high-up cave in a mountain face where he thought the fugitive might be hiding. Rather than repeat the difficult ascent himself, he unerringly pitched a rock into the cavity, hoping to scare his quarry into quitting the place. The goat was not there, but something else was: a clay jar, smashed by the thrown rock, containing one of several ancient scrolls. These were the Dead Sea Scrolls, named for that strange body of water near Khirbet Qumran where they were found.

Numerous caves in the area were eventually explored and either looted or excavated, depending on who got there first. Such antiquities still form a lucrative market, and for that reason the unscrupulous like to forge their own editions to exploit well-paying collectors. At first some thought the old Hebrew and Aramaic scrolls of Khirbet Qumran were fakes, too, while others dated them to medieval times. But they turned out to be an invaluable authentic find, portions of an ancient Jewish library.

FOSSILS OF SCRIPTURE

The texts, many reconstructed later from postage-stamp fragments, consisted of multiple copies of every Protestant Old Testament book except

---

1. I am working from a bound proof.

the dubiously canonical Esther (unpopular in some quarters for failing to mention God!). This by itself would have made the discovery enormously important since the scrolls dated to the first centuries BCE and CE, far earlier than any other extant copies of these scriptures. The previous age record, not very impressive, was held by the medieval Massoretic Text (copied by a monkish order called the Massoretes) whose manuscripts dated only back to about 900 CE. That is of course quite far removed from any proposed date of original composition. There was also the Samaritan Pentateuch, which contained somewhat different readings at certain points, though these were commonly dismissed as sectarian alterations to beef up Samaritan claims. Finally, there was also the Greek translation of the Old Testament, called the Septuagint ("the Seventy," named for the legend of that many scholars being convened to work on the project), which had oddly different readings from the Massoretic text. Since the Septuagint (LXX) had been copied from much older Hebrew manuscripts than those the Massoretes bequeathed us, there seemed a good chance the LXX preserved earlier Hebrew readings.

The Dead Sea Scrolls texts surprised everyone. They were not uniform, for one thing. Some had the same readings, in this or that verse, as the Samaritan Pentateuch. Other texts attested readings that matched the Hebrew texts from which the LXX was translated. All these types of texts, then, went way back into ancient times. And to everyone's considerable relief, there was no huge disparity between the ancient Qumran texts and the more recent ones. There were interesting differences, to be sure, even significant ones in some ways, but nothing earth-shaking. One example is that Goliath turned out to be only six and a half feet tall (consistent with the LXX), not the exaggerated nine and a half feet height of the Massoretic text. Another is that a couple of verses, the like of which scholars had long thought must have been accidentally omitted before the beginning of 1 Samuel 11, obligingly popped up.

More controversial was the discovery of a number of sectarian documents. Some of these were already known, including the *Book of Enoch* (*1 Enoch*), the *Book of Jubilees*, and the *Testaments of the Twelve Patriarchs* (this one, however, in a very different, albeit fragmentary version). These are quasi-biblical documents, the same sort of thing we find in the Bible, but dated a bit later, some of them expanded rewrites of biblical books. But another group appear to have been the products of a Jewish sect like the Essenes described by Josephus, Philo, and Pliny the Elder. In fact, most think these writings were the actual library of the Essenes, though others have nominated the Zealots[2] or the Ebionite Christians.[3] There were charter documents such as *The Community Rule* (or *Manual of Discipline*) and the *Damascus Covenant* (or *Damascus Document*), the *Messianic Rule* (which contains a kind of Eucharistic liturgy), the *War of the Sons of Light against the Sons of Darkness* (a detailed battle plan for Armageddon), the *Habakkuk Pesher* (Commentary), and the *Hymns of the Just*, which are a collection of psalms that commemorate the founding of the community by the unnamed Teacher of Righteousness (or Righteous Teacher).

There are ruins near the caves where these scrolls were discovered, which most scholars have pegged as the ruins of a monastery where they would have been produced, later taken over and used as a Roman fortress. However, some scholars like Norman Golb[4] insist that the caves were merely one hiding place for the manuscript library of the Jerusalem temple, swiftly removed from the city when the Roman siege was imminent. But the core Dead Sea Scrolls would, as even Golb admits, have been the documents of an Essene or Essene-like sect, whether they dwelt in Qumran or elsewhere.

In his novel *Earthly Remains*, Hernon sets forth the possible ramifications of the scrolls with their striking hints and intriguing equivocations. He gets the story right because it had already happened in real life by the time he wrote: "Your scroll could compel the Christian churches to reevaluate their common history. It could be of revolutionary importance. There is no other way to describe it. I cannot begin to imagine the confusion this will cause—the anguish" (p. 225). That's what happened, all right. Researchers were quick to point out striking similarities between the order described in the writings and the early Christian church as described in the Acts of the Apostles, such as the common ownership of property, an organization with a council of twelve and an inner circle of three. There was also the sacred meal, water baptism and religious language featuring such familiar New Testament terms as "sons of light," "Beliar" (the Antichrist), the Way, the New Covenant, and an end-time baptism of both spirit and fire. As Hernon has one character put it, "You

2. Roth, *The Dead Sea Scrolls*.

3. Jacob L. Teicher wrote a number of articles on this theme in the *Journal of Jewish Studies*. See the list in my *Deconstructing Jesus*, p. 72.

4. Golb, *Who Wrote the Dead Sea Scrolls?*

have a sacred meal celebrated in common with bread and wine," he said. "You have the doctrine of love of neighbor and the practice of baptism by water . . . Does any of that sound familiar? . . . Christianity before Christ" (p. 227).

We know from their *Damascus Document* that the sectarians, like John the Baptist, ate locusts! It will not surprise you to read that many scholars have argued that John the Baptist must have been, at least for a time, a member of the Dead Sea Scrolls sect. He was in the right place (the Judean Desert) at the right time. He spoke in their terms and followed their ascetical diet. And, of course—he baptized! At least the Dead Sea Scrolls show that the kind of Judaism John practiced was at home in the Holy Land at the time.

Even before the Qumran discoveries, some scholars had posited that Christianity had evolved from Essenism, based on the broad similarities between the two movements discernible from reading the ancient historians who describe the Essenes. Jesus would then have been more of a reformer than a founder. As Hernon's character Sara says, "Doesn't this suggest that the birth of Christianity was the result of an evolutionary process? The seeds may have been planted long before Jesus of Nazareth came on the scene" (p. 227). This would not constitute any bombshell, since on any traditional reading that was precisely the relation between Jesus and Judaism as a whole. Nobody (except Marcionites!) said he started the whole thing *de novo*.

ESSENE ESSENCE?

What fostered more venturesome speculation was the role of the Teacher of Righteousness, for the scrolls said he had been ambushed and martyred by the Wicked Priest and his minions. There was even some indication that the men of the sect expected their martyred master to rise up at the end of days and take vengeance upon his slayers. Some scholars therefore speculated that the Teacher was a kind of "Christ before Jesus" who had provided the pattern for Christian belief in Jesus as a slain messiah soon to come again in judgment. That would tend to undermine the cherished notion of Christian uniqueness and might even imply that the Christian story had been borrowed from that of a contemporary sect. Again Hernon addresses the issue through his characters' puppet mouths: "This scroll could challenge the uniqueness of Christ"; "A lot of Christians won't be happy to hear news like that" (p. 228).

Others wondered whether the Teacher of Righteousness might have been Jesus himself,[5] which would explain the otherwise strange parallels between the two figures. Similar theories, still current today, nominate John the Baptist[6] or James the Just ("brother of the Lord")[7] as the Teacher of Righteousness. While it is impossible to prove any of these theories, none is absurd, especially in view of the plain fact that the cipher language of the scrolls seems to be referring to *someone* of major importance in that historical period, someone we should have otherwise heard of. Then the question is, who is the best candidate? There is a threat posed for many conventional believers by all of these theories, a threat that may be indexed by the knee-jerk scorn and ridicule heaped upon theorists like Robert Eisenman and Barbara Thiering who promote them.

Earthly Remains mentions real historical characters who have some connection to the Dead Sea Scrolls, e.g., Eliezer Sukenik, Israeli archaeologist, but it tells a tale of a group of adventurers who buy a scroll or two from an unscrupulous dealer, then discover another. Any reader who knows anything about the scrolls and the actual events surrounding their discovery will scratch his or her head, asking, "But, wait a minute! Didn't real people like John M. Allegro and Roland DeVaux do this research? Who are these characters?" Well, such liberties are to be expected and excused in a historical novel, but the stickler might keep in mind that the Qumran finds yielded multiple copies of both biblical and sectarian manuscripts. Hernon's archaeologists come into possession of Qumran copies of the Book of Kings (1 and 2 Kings) and of the *Manual of Discipline*. We need only suppose that their copies (lost in the course of the novel) were otherwise unknown duplicates. But this argument will not work when we come to the unique *Copper Scroll*, which Hernon's characters discover on site and begin to study some four years (1948) before it was really discovered. *The Copper Scroll* is a set of directions to the hiding places of various treasures removed from either the Qumran monastery or the Jerusalem temple for safe-keeping. (None of it has ever been found, as far as we know.)

---

5. Teicher, "Jesus in the Habakkuk Scroll."
6. Thiering, *Jesus and the Riddle of the Dead Sea Scrolls*.
7. Eisenman, *James the Brother of Jesus*.

THE USUAL SUSPECTS

Nor is this all our heroes discover. Their version of the *Copper Scroll* provides directions, locally, for a burial place of some unnamed saint or prophet, then another. First discovered is a headless skeleton buried with a metal bowl. The next is the mummified body of a crucifixion victim. It is not difficult to guess that the first carcass is that of John the Baptist and the second that of Jesus Christ, manifestly *not* risen from the dead. Hernon has his characters, Roman Catholic clergy and archaeologists alike, dispute those identities, and we never see either one confirmed. But the chances seem great enough that some zealots in the Vatican's Curia (who are, as in *The Da Vinci Code*, more Catholic than the pope) first attempt to buy the scrolls and the bodies from our intrepid investigators, and then, when they won't sell, assassinate them one by one. Eventually one of the heroes conceals the mummy from these Romanist Black Ops guys and is beaten to death under interrogation. The secret of the reburied body of the maybe-Jesus thus perishes with him.

Well, the two bodies never see the light of day, but the scrolls do, though this happens off stage. When the first scrolls were published (not just in the novel, but also in real life), they unleashed an epidemic, at least among scholars, of what was dubbed "Qumran fever," as specialists explored every possible Dead Sea Scroll-New Testament link. In the popular press, the "Christ before Jesus" theory stirred up some sensationalism, but the most controversial claim was that the *real* smoking gun to debunk Christianity had yet to be revealed, that the Roman Catholic hierarchy was preventing the release of one fourth of the scrolls that only the (almost exclusively Catholic) Dead Sea Scrolls team had ever laid eyes on. Why were they sitting on them so long? The real reason, we finally learned, was much more mundane: scholarly one-upsmanship. These elite professors were determined to keep the manuscripts to themselves for as long as possible, just so they could say the last word about them before anyone else got the chance to say their first! They were just hogging all the action. Eventually, thanks to Robert Eisenman and a few others, the University of California at Huntington published their library of photographic facsimiles of the scrolls for everybody to scrutinize. And it turned out there was no smoking gun after all.

So that urban legend was exploded via full disclosure. The Scrolls remain controversial and full of potential to rock the boat of early Christian studies, but it is all a matter of interpretation of these intentionally cryptic texts. As already anticipated, it would make all the difference in the world, both as to understanding the texts and as to reconstructing Christian origins, if we knew who the Teacher of Righteousness was supposed to be: Jesus? John? James the Just?

YOU DON'T HAVE TO BE THE EASTER BUNNY TO JUMP TO CONCLUSIONS

Finally, though Hernon makes nothing in particular of this history, there is a subtle echo in *Earthly Remains* of one of the theories about the empty tomb on Easter morning. Narrator Paul Davoren comes looking for his friend and co-conspirator Tom Lawrence with whom he had earlier stashed away the body of the crucified man in an old cemetery in Mississippi. Davoren stops by the secret burial place.

> Using the flashlight, I saw that the boards had been pried off the top of the marble sarcophagus, which resembled a low altar. Swallowing, I looked inside. The metal casket was still there; but the lid was ajar. The inner casket that contained the body was missing. Lawrence must have taken it, I thought. But why? (p. 293)

It turns out that his friend had removed the body once he got wind of the fact that the Catholic goons were on its trail—and his. He managed to hide it from them and would not yield his secret even under torture. As we saw, he died at their unholy hands, taking the secret with him. In all this, do we not have striking parallels with the gospels' Easter stories? Davoren is like Mary Magdalene, or Peter, or the Beloved Disciple—hurrying to the tomb of their Lord and stunned to find the body gone. And like them, he quickly formulates a rational and mundane explanation. Mary's was that the body had been only temporarily deposited in a convenient nearby tomb and it must have been moved elsewhere in the meantime. The thing to do was simply to find out where. To jump to the conclusion that God had resurrected the corpse would have been like finding your apartment a mess when you thought you had tidied it up and concluding that a flying saucer alien must have ransacked the place while you were out.

But let's turn it around another way: Lawrence had moved the body, creating an empty tomb scenario, in order to keep hostile parties from stealing the corpse, committing some mischief with it, and thus to keep the resurrection faith intact. This is just what motivates Judas to sneak in and rebury the body in the medieval Jewish gospel parody, *Toledoth Jeschu*: he fears the disciples will steal it, point to the empty tomb, and launch the hoax that Jesus has arisen. He wants to gain control of the crucial item of evidence before the hooligan disciples do. But Judas' strategy first backfires: the absence of the body gives rise to the very error he feared! So he reveals his deeds and recovers the body, nipping the resurrection faith in the bud. That is a danger that the Gospel of Matthew has the members of the Sanhedrin seeming to recognize; instead of taking the body in hand themselves, they attempt to secure the body by posting guards at the tomb to prevent anyone from taking it away.

The gratuitousness of a resurrection hypothesis to explain the absence of the body in *Earthly Remains* implies the same in the case of the gospels' empty tomb scenario. But just suppose for a moment that Paul Davoren had drawn a different inference from the missing body there in a rural Mississippi mausoleum. Suppose it had struck him intuitively not only that the body had indeed been that of Jesus, but that after all these centuries he actually *had* been raised from the dead! Suppose the second coming was near at hand as the risen Jesus made his way among mankind again. What a sequel that would make!

18 But I'm Not Dead Yet!
Daniel Easterman, *Brotherhood of the Tomb*

WHEN IRISH EYES ARE MISSING

THIS VERY FINE SUSPENSE novel[1] by Daniel Easterman (pseudonym of Professor Denis McEoin, professor at University of Newcastle-upon-Tyne, an ex-Baha'i) opens with the chance discovery of a tomb within a tomb, cleverly sealed up to avoid detection. Having made our way this far through the Lost Gospel genre, we do not really need to be informed that it is the tomb of Jesus Christ, mistakenly rumored to have been raised gloriously from the dead. One Bishop Migliou, learned amateur archaeologist, is along for the ride, and, paradoxically, rejoices to recognize the identity of the once-messianic corpse! Spouting a tirade of anti-Semitic gibberish at his Israeli guide, he shoves him to his death amid the sharp-edged stones, reseals the tomb and leaves, waiting off stage until needed again later in the story.

Switching scenes quickly, we meet two young students at Trinity College, Dublin. One is Patrick Carnavan, student of Semitic languages, the other Francesca Contarini, daughter of an ancient Venetian aristocratic line. The two become lovers, savoring their joy until her untimely death, in 1968. Patrick's life having been shattered, he takes his talents (and his anger) to the CIA whom he serves well until the consequent bruises to his conscience become too many and too painful and, like Patrick McGoohan in *The Prisoner*, he resigns. We meet him again with the discovery of the bloody, near-corpse of an old friend and mentor with whom he had once studied Aramaic. He finds the old priest gushing blood from stabbed-out eye sockets at the altar of his dilapidated church

---

1. All page references are to the HarperCollins edition.

in depressed Dublin, and the rasping voice's last word, like Charles Foster Kane's "Rosebud," was the enigmatic "Passover."

Ex-agent Carnavan undertakes to bring what scant clues he possesses to the Vatican to see who might know anything he could use to solve the case and bring his friend's killer to justice. This turns out to be a bad idea, as the Vatican bureaucrat he meets belongs to the very conspiracy Carnavan seeks to discover and expose. He escapes with his life and with a new ally, an Ethiopian priest and Vatican flunky named Assefa (after the biblical Asaph) Makonnen. The young priest intuitively grasps something of what is going on and deserts his superiors, taking a sheaf of strategic papers with him. Much more happens that we need not summarize here. Suffice it to say that Carnavan eventually comes to suspect that his beloved Francesca is still alive, and probably not far away. Her apparent death would have been a deception engineered by the same powerful secret society that had his old friend killed: the Brotherhood of the Tomb. And here is where we zero in on our particular interest in the novel.

YOU'RE NOT FOOLIN' ANYONE!

It comes out that Francesca's family had been implicated in the doings of the Brotherhood since the thirteenth century, when an ancestor had made connections with them in Egypt. But who was the mysterious order? There was an inner circle of seven, stemming from seven of the disciples of Jesus who believed they understood their Master's mission better than did the other disciples—or even Jesus himself! And they made it their business to make sure Jesus did not shirk his responsibility as they understood it. We read this in a fragment of an Aramaic *Gospel according to James* passed down secretly among the Brotherhood. James the Just, Jesus' brother, was one of the original Seven.

We have already seen our authors in this genre play with the Swoon Theory, the hypothesis that Jesus survived crucifixion without dying. It is not, despite all the predictable jeering by mainstream scholars, incredible by any means. But Easterman takes the whole business an astonishing step further. For him, the great secret—which a shadowy confraternity has exploited, presumably by blackmail, to gain vast wealth and power—is not that Jesus survived the cross and begat children with Mary Magdalene (as in *The Da Vinci Code*) or that he survived Golgotha to live on, preaching around the Mediterranean for more decades until a second crucifixion (as in *The Word*). Rather, the secret is that he survived the cross only to succumb to the fanatical designs of some of his disciples, who buried him alive.

> God's will had been thwarted, and His Sacrifice remained unfinished. Wherefore, we met together in Simon's house that is in the Street of the Water Gate and swore a solemn oath binding us to finish what had been left undone. That night, we came to a place outside the city, where Jesus had been hidden, and took him from there over the cries of the women that watched over him, and carried him to the place outside the city, where Joseph of Arimathea had given a tomb for his burial. And he was bound with cords and his mouth tied with cloth, lest he break free or the Romans hear his cries and send men to investigate. (pp. 372–73)

We are quite used to the idea, historical fact or not, that Judas betrayed his teacher, but the other disciples did, too? I have argued elsewhere,[2] at a length inappropriate to reproduce here, that the gospels feature various texts that might be read, by the methods of René Girard, as implying that the disciples as a group turned on Jesus and handed him over to death. Underlying the analysis is the Girardian concept of *mimetic rivalry*. In a dynamic repeated in both religious discipleship and fan celebrity worship, we behold a devotion that expresses itself in the form of the admirer (the "disciple") seeking to become like the model in every possible way until the follower's goal turns into the fanatical desire to *become* the model, to replace the model, and then, accordingly, to kill the model. This is why various celebrities (John Lennon, Selena, etc.) have been stalked and killed by their biggest fans, time after time. Sensing the uncomfortably close approach by an admirer, the model sometimes sets up road blocks or challenges to mark the distance between the follower and himself (see Mark 8:34; 10:35–40). The follower may rise to the occasion and outstrip the challenge, or he may take his model's distancing gesture as a disappointing failure to live up to (really, to embody) the ideal that inspired his imitators to emulate him in the beginning.

Such a case, apparently, occurs in the story of the anointing of Jesus at Bethany (Mark 14:3–11). An admirer anoints Jesus' head with oil (a standard gesture of hospitality; see Ps 23:5; Luke 7:44–46). It is admittedly a bit of extravagance, and one of the disciples (or, in Matt 26:8,

---

2. Price, *Deconstructing Jesus*, 169–211.

all of them) carps at the "waste." Why was the ointment not sold so the proceeds might be donated to the poor? That is Jesus' own command to those who would follow him, is it not? And now he sanctions this gesture—on his own behalf? Jesus has failed to live up to his own ideals, and this disappoints his disciples: the model they have hitherto sought to imitate has proven himself unworthy. They have imitated him in vain. Worse yet, his own failure tends to invalidate the ideal itself, not just the model, for if the model himself could not finally live up to it, no one can! Admittedly, such a reaction involves continuing to hold up the model as perfect even in his failure ("Even the perfect cannot attain perfection! Alas!"). Strange, but that is often the way the mind works.

So here is the perfect opportunity to supercede the model, to displace, and to *replace* him! Of course the next step in the gospel narrative is for Judas to go straight to the Sanhedrin and to contract with them to see to Jesus' arrest. The clay-footed idol must be toppled! And if, as Matthew has it, they were all disillusioned with Jesus on the occasion of the anointing, it is not difficult to penetrate the curtain of apostolic myth and to recognize the disciples as a whole as complicit in the betrayal.

The Brotherhood of the Tomb makes perfect Girardian sense. The disciples have grimly witnessed Jesus going to his death (not that they engineered it in Easterman's version), their grief somewhat ameliorated by their belief that Jesus' death would once and for all bring to a close God's ancient demand for atoning blood sacrifices. Jesus' own sacrifice should establish forgiveness of sins henceforward. But then Jesus does not really die on that cross! James, Andrew, Simon Zelotes, and others do not rejoice. For them, Jesus' rescue from the cross signals that the divine process of redemption has been short-circuited! And Jesus appears to be in no hurry to get things back on track. He has disappointed them and even ruined the plan of salvation. If his own determination to go the way of sacrifice has flagged, proving him to have been an unworthy model, theirs will not! They prove their own superiority by seeing to it that the task of Jesus' saving death is completed after all, despite his own cowardice. In so doing they have succeeded both in casting down the false idol Jesus has become and in taking his place for themselves.

The Girardian paradigm might lead us to predict exactly what subsequent events spring from this deed. The Brotherhood soon becomes convinced that the sacrifice of Jesus is not, after all, enough to appease the wrath of God. In a sort of devil's bargain with God, the secret cabal undertakes an ongoing practice of child sacrifice, playing the role of Abraham sacrificing his beloved Isaac, in order both to secure eternal salvation and to win worldly wealth and power. Imagine Tony Soprano embracing the Deuteronomic theology: disclaiming all efforts of his own and humbly acknowledging God as the sole source of his worldly successes! But what makes this Girardian? Such ongoing sacrifices prove necessary (in the theological imagination of the Brotherhood) precisely because the sacrifice of Jesus, once imagined as all-sufficient, has proven to be the offering up of an unworthy victim, a lamb with spot and stain, because Jesus had to be dragged, literally, to his fate after avoiding it the first time. His sacrifice is thus devalued and cannot serve to end all sacrifice, any more than the unsatisfying armistice concluding World War One would allow it to truly be "the war to end all wars."

What had happened to Francesca, though? Why her hoax-death and funeral? That follows from the unique passion narrative of the *Aramaic Gospel of James* in which Jesus is entombed alive. Making this into a pattern (again, a mimetic "*imitatio Christi*"), the sect selects certain of its children to be withdrawn from public life, with an official funeral to render them legally dead, and then has them trained as assassins. It's not what one might consider a proper role for women, but Francesca's brother was originally slated for the position, then unexpectedly died for real, and Francesca had to fill the family quota.

Well, Francesca eventually emerges from the shadows, joining Patrick and his allies in a last-ditch effort to stymie a fiendish ploy of the Brotherhood. Long an underground rival of the Catholic hierarchy, although deeply infiltrating it, the Brotherhood has decided that the time has come to seize power in the Vatican and replace the current pope with none other than the murderously anti-Semitic Bishop, now Cardinal, Migliou. He and the Brotherhood are licking their chops in anticipation of a return to bloody Crusades and Inquisitions. The current pope has arranged a Middle Eastern Peace Summit to enhance his legacy as an historical figure, and, as part of the event, he plans a photo-op with a hundred orphan children from the war-torn nations of the region. What he does not know is that the Brotherhood has a squadron of crack assassins ready to crash the party, guns blazing, and to kill the children (not to mention the old pope), whose shed blood should serve as a sacrifice to God to win the Brotherhood the power they covet.

The agents of the Brotherhood meet unexpected resistance from our heroes, and the relevant lives are saved. Patrick and Francesca are reunited, though the omniscient narrator tells us that she expects some mysterious development a couple of years yet in the future that will put their newly happy world in jeopardy again. Was there a sequel? I can't seem to find out.

19 | The Q Contender
J. G. Sandom, *Gospel Truths*

GONNA TRY NOW

No unknown *Gospel of Bif* or *Epistle of Chet*, no *Acts of Meg* or *Apocalypse of Milt* awaits us in this novel[1] of grizzled policemen and wonky architects, occasionally nude widows and backstabbing bishops. The lost gospels striving to make a *re*appearance are instead special (very early) copies of two gospels that were already known to scholars when Sandom wrote his *Gospel Truths*. They are *The Gospel of Thomas* and another dependent upon it, *The Book of Thomas the Contender*. The title of the latter denotes "Thomas the spiritual champion in training" as in 2 Timothy 2:5, "If anyone competes as an athlete, he does not win the prize unless he competes according to the rules." Similarly, 2 Timothy 4:7, "I have fought the good fight, I have finished the course, I have kept the faith." Again, "one thing I do: forgetting what lies behind and reaching forward to what lies ahead, I press on toward the goal for the prize of the upward call of God in Christ Jesus" (Phil 3:13–14). "Do you not know that those who run in a race all run, but only one receives the prize? Run in such a way that you may win. And everyone who competes in the games exercises self-control in all things. They then do it to receive a perishable wreath, but we an imperishable. Therefore I run in such a way, as not without aim; I box in such a way, as not beating the air; but I buffet my body and make it my slave, lest possibly, after I have preached to others, I myself should be disqualified" (1 Cor 9:24–27). That is precisely the sort of contender Thomas is.

The Book of Thomas the Contender purports to be a conversation between the resurrected Jesus and his twin brother Judas Thomas, taken down by Mathaias (the apostle Matthew?) as he walked with them short-

---

1. All page references are to the Bantam edition.

ly before Jesus ascended into heaven. The book's basic aim is to condemn of any sort of fleshly satisfaction. It looks like a later editor has added to this the theme of salvation by self-knowledge, an idea common to many ancient religions and philosophies, including Platonists and Gnostics. *Thomas the Contender* demonstrates the kind of thing that happened to early Christian texts: they kept getting rewritten and re-edited, adapted to fit the beliefs and practices of each new sect that copied them.

A recurring image in *Thomas the Contender* is that of "fire," referring both to the fire of bodily passions that vex the pious soul, and to the flames of hell that are reserved for those who indulge in the delights of the body. Even so, it contrasts the wise one who grasps the truth of the invisible with the fool who cannot see past the flickering illusions of the visible realm. All this is based on Plato's contrast between the visible world of appearances and the unseen world of reality. We can choose between wisdom (the soul taking wing to flee bodily appetites) and foolishness (being held hostage by one's own seductive physical passions). The deciding factor is faith in the savior, a messenger of light who opens one's eyes to see the reality beyond the veil of worldly illusion. The focus of the book is more ascetical than Gnostic, since the goal is more that of overcoming desire than the revelation of cosmic secrets, the latter being the distinguishing mark of Gnosticism.

It looks as if *Thomas the Contender* were originally a straightforward treatise on asceticism and self-conquest. But a subsequent Christian editor has cut up the text, making its assertions into replies by Jesus to interview questions posed by Thomas. This or another redactor has added a number of independent sayings credited to Jesus in the second half of the book. The resultant book is a kind of sequel to, as well as an elaboration of, *The Gospel of Thomas*. It repeats but exaggerates that gospel's ascetical teaching about wandering, nakedness, women, and the transitoriness of all things. It uses the same themes of seeking, finding, resting, and reigning that are found in *The Gospel of Thomas* and depends on the same metaphor of Judas Thomas as the twin (the equal) of Jesus. Mathaias plays no further role after his introduction as the recorder of the dialogue; he is important only as an additional guarantor of the authority of the work, a link between the reader and Judas Thomas. He plays the same role as the lengthy chains of transmitters tacked onto every story or saying of the Prophet Muhammad in Islamic tradition: "How do we *know* he said it? Who said so?"

The Q Contender

I COULDA BEEN A CONTENDER

We can usually find ample clues to tell us whom an author expected to be reading his book. Such clues in *Thomas the Contender* are the various beliefs and behaviors condemned by Jesus, which must be sidelong glances at certain types or groups of people whom the author wants the reader to avoid. Likewise, behaviors or beliefs endorsed by Jesus must represent the religious faction to whom the author belonged. In other words, the text is a dramatization of a controversy experienced by the author and his readers against some opponents. Judas Thomas stands for the author and his allies, "twins" of Jesus whose views (they are sure) exactly mirror those of Jesus. Mathaias is a name just as symbolic as "Thomas," the twin, since "Mathaias" is a natural pun for the Greek word *mathetes*, "disciple." Mathaias would be the counterpart inside the text of the actual author/redactor outside the text. Similarly, when Jesus derides the unwashed masses outside the community of disciples, he means, no doubt, the worldly crowd, the hypocrites or irreligious.

The *Thomas* text also seems to have an eye on some intermediate group of believers who know the truth, but who are too caught up in the concerns of daily life to get serious about strict Christian living. These are the "babes," the "apprentices," or the "elect." These are chosen out of humanity at large to have faith in Jesus, but they know only the Sunday School version of the truth. Compare that to the significance ascribe to spiritual wisdom in the canonical New Testament, where "feeding" with milk is accepted only with the goal of progressing to solid food (Heb 5:11-14; 1 Cor 3:1-2), where Apollos is instructed "more accurately" (Acts 18:24-26), where Jesus bids an eager scribe to press on to perfection (Mark 12:28-34) and promises deeper instruction from the Paraclete (John 16:12-13); and where "growth in respect to salvation" is aspired to (1 Pet 2:2-3). The Sunday school believers of *Thomas* are following in the path of Jesus and Judas Thomas, but at a distance. They are the "laity." If Thomas represents those who are "contenders" against sinful passions, the second group are spectators watching the fight and wondering if they might have what it takes to step into the ring themselves—someday. Such people would be fairly typical for radical ascetic movements like the Marcionites, the Manicheans, even the Buddhists: an outer circle who practice a kind of vicarious discipleship by supporting the holy ones who actually do live by the rules.

Lower down are the clueless herd of "miserable mortals" who muddle through an earthly existence they are fated never to transcend, all the while trying their pathetic best to live a generally moral life. Worse yet, there is another group, not even expected to be among the readers of the *Thomas* text; they are poor creatures utterly without hope, since they appear once to have belonged to either the second or third groups but got themselves in deeper trouble by turning against the ascetical lifestyle with smug ridicule. The whole four-fold ranking is cut from the same cloth as the Valentinian Gnostic separation of the human race into three groups, the spiritual ones (pneumatics), the merely soulish ones (psychics), and the wooden ones (hylics), i.e., "blockheads." The Thomas contenders may have begun with the same three-fold system, ranking people by their innate spiritual potential (or lack of it), and then added the fourth rubric in order to put scoffers and detractors in a special category of their own, one more serious, since they were not merely oblivious of the truth but actually antagonistic towards it.

"WHAT GOOD'S THAT HIGHER CRITICISM GONNA DO YA IN HELL?"[2]

The single surviving copy of *The Book of Thomas the Contender* is written in the Sahidic dialect of the Coptic language. The Coptic version was probably translated from a Greek original, now lost. Most scholars think *Thomas the Contender* was composed in the first half of the third century CE, after the *Gospel of Thomas* (composed in the first or second century CE) and the *Acts of Thomas*, (probably written about 225 CE). It makes unmistakable references to the *Gospel of Thomas* and so obviously must be later than it.

Like the *Gospel of Thomas* and the *Acts of Thomas*, the *Book of Thomas the Contender* comes from the ascetic Christianity of Eastern Syria. Here and eastward into Mesopotamia, Christianity of the third and fourth centuries took its most radically ascetical form, requiring all baptized Christians, even the married, to pledge themselves to total celibacy and to a life stripped of all civilized luxury. It is easy, then, to imagine the position of *Thomas the Contender*'s second group, who joined the community but could not bring themselves to go all the way.

---

2. R. W. Shambach in a radio sermon.

What is to become of all these types of people? Thomas first spells out the destiny of well-meaning people, including Christians, perhaps even some from the writer's own ascetically "perfect" group, who have reneged on their original commitment to ascetical perfection and are thus destined for reincarnation. Also included are the noble pagans, who, in spite of their knowledge of an invisible reality, never had the commitment to gospel asceticism; upon death, they either perish or dwell as shades in the realm of the dead. They lack even the distant hope of reentering and perhaps one day escaping the cycle of reincarnation.

As for the worldlings who merely laugh at the ascetical ideal and, worse yet, those blasphemers who dare to make fun of the ascetics themselves, the first are destined for a painful reincarnation, while the second are doomed to the flames of hell immediately upon death.

The first group includes those who are completely blinded by preoccupation with daily affairs as well as those who know better but excuse themselves as helpless victims of the evils of the flesh. Such individuals are so closely bound to the body as to be considered mere beasts. They will share the body's fate in the nethermost abyss into which they will be thrown, where their flesh will be literally flayed from their limbs. Their so-called wisdom, once so smugly professed, will be revealed all too clearly as the rankest insanity.

The souls of the scoffers, we are now gravely assured, shall be handed over to the Archon above, the ruler over all the celestial powers, who shall cast them down to the abyss for punishment, the miserable wretches being dipped screaming into the ubiquitous lakes of boiling magma. And from this nightmare there will be no awakening. But there is potentially one exit, over to the east. Pious study of *Thomas the Contender* would have forewarned and forearmed the sinner, but he no doubt has better things to do, studying his pornography or his racing form. Unfortunately, he will realize the truth only on the Day of Judgment, which *Thomas* locates not in some vague distant future, but immediately upon death, and then it will be too late.

Q AND A

What on earth, we might ask, could possibly give novelist Sandom or his character Monsignor Wovyetski the idea that *this* text might be the Grail of gospel source critics, the Q source, the list of sayings common to Matthew and Luke but not Mark (pp. 145–47)? Not much. The theory is really impossible, but it might have been suggested by the fact that *Thomas the Contender* does at least, like Q, contain sets of both formulaic woes and blessings. The Q woes (Luke 6:24–26) appear to have been formulated by the early Jesus movement as bitter retorts to the rude rejection of their once-naively enthusiastic preaching of the coming kingdom. So also in *Thomas the Contender*, the woes seem to echo the bitterness of a frustrated and failing missionary movement. These gloating doom-cries seem to serve only as a smug self-justification for a group of forlorn insiders, who reassure themselves that their sacrifices were indeed worthwhile despite the universal ridicule from the sinners outside their circle. Missionary appeals to those outside are a thing of the past; the frowning righteous speak now only to themselves.

The three beatitudes in *Thomas the Contender* also mimic the form of the Q beatitudes in Matthew and Luke. There is a close parallel in language between the second of the *Thomas* beatitudes and the one found in the "Q" source at Matthew 5:10–11 and Luke 6:22. Like the "Q" parallel, it reflects a persecuted missionary movement that has experienced the rejection of its message. But otherwise, the content of Q (Matthean/Lukan) beatitudes and woes and their counterparts in *Thomas the Contender* are utterly dissimilar. Neither can be derived from the other.

The link between Q and *Thomas the Contender* is weak and speculative. Sandom has a fictive twelfth-century monk, Thierry of Chartres, refer to "your Thomas the Contender which Papias, bless him, copied from the sayings of Maththaios" (p. 101). Papias was an early-to-mid second-century bishop of Hierapolis in Asia Minor who recorded a tradition (already too late for credence) that Matthew (or Maththaios/Mathaias, the same name ambiguity as in the case of *Thomas the Contender*'s scribe) was the first to record the "*logoi* [sayings] of the Lord." Many scholars have supposed Papias to have meant that the disciple Matthew thus compiled the Q source, not the narrative Gospel of Matthew, which he or another subsequently composed using the earlier Q, as well as Mark's gospel, as sources. Sandom has cleverly (but implausibly) identified the "Matthaios" sayings (and thus Q) with the *Book of Thomas the Contender* ostensibly copied down by someone named Matthaios (p. 144). In fact, any medieval knowledge or mention of a copy of *Thomas the Contender* is fanciful, part of the novelist's creative license. No extant ancient writer mentions the work. We first learned of it in 1945 with the unearthing of the Nag Hammadi manuscripts, which is what Sandom refers to when he notes: "There were already other copies in both Greek and Coptic" (p. 132). Not quite: the single Coptic text seems to be a translation from a Greek text, but we do not have a Greek language manuscript of the work. The important thing about Sandom's (imaginary) copy hidden away in Amiens Cathedral is its date: it comes from about 100 CE (pp. 139, 144), automatically pushing back Gnosticism (a Gnosticism ascribed to Jesus, no less) to the "magic" century of Christian origins.

But the real object of desire among Thomas's contenders in this novel is the earlier *Gospel of Thomas*, said by Thierry of Chartres to be buried someplace within the labyrinthine angles of the semiotic puzzle box of Chartres Cathedral. (One can see that Sandom's *Gospel Truths* was already *The Da Vinci Code* waiting to happen!) Again, the novelty is that the Chartres copy would be demonstrably older than the Nag Hammadi text discovered in 1945 (but rumored by ancient Church writers and attested by a few untitled Greek fragments dug up in Egyptian tombs). Monsignor Wovyetski explains:

> It was written in Aramaic, instead of Greek or Coptic, which was used later... And if that isn't enough, it bears a reference—which was "added later"—to the plot which Piso of Syria "launched against the Emperor." That's Nero, and the plot he's talking about happened in A.D. 65!... [This would make The Gospel of Thomas] perhaps the oldest set of Logoi in existence... The very words Christ spoke!... Think what it would mean if we had a historically valid collection of His sayings. And then think what would happen if those sayings happened to be Gnostic... if the ideas which Christ espoused were not at all the same as those the Church has come to stand for. Can you see the headlines now: Christ Found To Be A Heretic! It would mean anarchy... The New Testament would no longer be viewed as the Word of God, but only as one set of gospel truths out of many. Can you imagine? Who could possibly be a more powerful spokesman against Christianity than Jesus Christ Himself? (pp. 147–48)

What so disturbed the Church authorities in a Gnostic-leaning gospel like *Thomas*? Well, you don't need to be spoon fed catechism if you can find the truth deep inside you via meditation. And when you do, it doesn't have to match up with any official definition (pp. 128–29). So what is at stake in the novel, as all its characters seem to realize instinctively, is that—should the primitive character of the Thomas books be established—institutional church demands for orthodox obedience in belief will be become a thing of the past, at least on a large scale. It is a repeat of the heady days of the Protestant Reformation when the Bible itself, translated into the vernacular and propagated among the common people, crashed on the scene with the force of a newly discovered revelation. The same danger alarms the Vatican in the 1999 movie *Stigmata*: a dippy Catholic beautician (Patricia Arquette) becomes possessed by the wandering spirit of a priest who discovered a slightly fictionalized version of the *Gospel of Thomas*, only to see the Vatican suppress it—as it already had some hundred other noncanonical gospels! Haunting her, he strives to bring the subversive, anti-institutional text to light, let the chips fall where they may!

But Sandom needs to do his homework: already arguing that the *Gospel of Thomas* does date from the first century and is earlier than the canonical gospels, scholars including Steven L. Davies,[3] Stephen J. Patterson,[4] John Dominic Crossan,[5] and Helmut Koester[6] have tried to convey exactly the point that Sandom's characters do: the first and final fact of church history is the wildly diverse nature of early Christianity.[7] Catholic Orthodoxy prevailed only after using its institutional clout to bludgeon all rivals into submission. Burton L. Mack[8] has helped isolate and distill the Q source as the self-sufficient scripture of an implied Jesus movement who knew nothing of Jesus' death and resurrection. He is quite sure that establishment Christianity, in light of his revelations, will succumb to the bankruptcy of its theology and the flimsy character of its credentials. "It's over ... We've had enough apocalypses. We've had enough martyrs. Christianity has had a two-thousand-year run, and it's over."[9] But does anyone really notice? Are Mack and the others playing the role of Chicken Little? Or, to be more biblical, are they wasting their time like the prophet Balaam, trying to get his donkey to move by smacking her in the head with an unheeded two-by-four?

---

3. Davies, *The Gospel of Thomas and Christian Wisdom*.
4. Patterson, *The Gospel of Thomas and Jesus*.
5. Crossan, *Four Other Gospels*.
6. Koester, *Ancient Christian Gospels*.
7. Bauer, *Orthodoxy and Heresy in Earliest Christianity*.
8. Mack, *The Lost Gospel*.
9. Mack, quoted in Allen, "The Search for a No-Frills Jesus."

20 | Profane Pilgrim
Wilton Barnhardt, *Gospel*

A BIBLE OF A BOOK

This mammoth picaresque novel[1] quickly dispels our haunting dread that it might be just another attempt (we've seen plenty) to fatten up a basic skeleton of a premise by packing on the flab of fungible soap-operatic blubber, connecting the microdots with a mile-wide magic marker. Here we witness a gallery of genuine character studies, portraits of paper people whom we should much enjoy knowing if we could meet them in the flesh. The external events of the narrative happen *to the characters*, and it is their reactions to events that we witness and come to care about, just as it is our own lived experience of events that concerns us, not some textbook account of them at a clinical distance. H. P. Lovecraft, who by his own confession was no good at characterization (or dialogue), never tried to hone his skills in that area, since his goal was to convey an overwhelming mood or sensation, and for this his characters served merely as a frame. We find ourselves looking *through* them, *at* something else. It works quite well. But Wilton Barnhardt's leisurely yet empathetic characterizations work very well, too, and the effect is like a Viewmaster stereoscope: we see two layers simultaneously, the events and the characters' internalization of them, creating a seductive image of 3-D presence. We are there.

And who are Barnhardt's winsome and amusing characters? The most conspicuous is Dr. Patrick O'Hanrahan, sometime Professor of Church History (theology, broadly defined) at the University of Chicago. Having entered the Society of Jesus early on—as a way of answering the call, if not of God, then of his own intellectual curiosity—he soured on conventional faith after a stint as a battlefield chaplain in the Korean

---

1. All page references are to the St. Martin's Press hardcover edition.

War. Marrying a Catholic nurse from a field hospital, he took her off the nunnish path while exiting the Jesuit fold himself. But the more alienated he became toward God and the Roman Catholic faith, the more fascinated he became with the shadowed corners of its history and theology. Turning this grotesque chaff of morbid masochisms and martyrdoms into the gold of tall (but true) tales, he became a popular lecturer and a hedonistic mischief maker. He proved as poor a husband and father (baffled at a homosexual son) as he had a Jesuit. When his wife and son perished in a pair of linked accidents (a plane crash followed by a car crash), he wrote off his past failures and found he was having such fun both with hedonistic habits (of which booze was the worst) and religious lore that he never got around to any serious scholarly accomplishments, no books on the shelves or on the resume. Then came an opportunity to break the peculiar code of the newly recovered *Gospel of Matthias*, which reawakened his hopes of scholarly achievement and his *joi d' vivre*.

O'Hanrahan is a roaring dragon of a man, a fearsome curmudgeon into whose circle of acquaintance one might nonetheless enter if one could but endure the initiatory abuse. He reminds the reader of both Professor Kingsfield of *The Paper Chase* and Sheridan Whiteside in *The Man Who Came to Dinner*.

The anima to his animus is geekish grad student and liberalish Catholic Lucy Dantan, sent by the Theology Department to track down Dr. O'Hanrahan at Oxford, where he may or may not be seeking the *Matthias* gospel in their name. Such contempt has he for his employers (whom he feels have slighted him in the past) that he has refused every attempt at communication, spending most of his time in drunken theological debate with an ecumenical spectrum of convivial clergy and elite scholars in cold and foggy Oxford. Lucy bears with the old man's scorn and insults, gradually proving her indispensability to him as a troubleshooter and assistant. She lengthens her stay week by week, month by month, as she accompanies Dr. O'Hanrahan from England to Ireland to Italy to Jerusalem to Greece to Egypt to the Sudan to Ethiopia, and finally to a televangelist's headquarters in Louisiana. It turns out that many powerful interests are eager to wrest the gospel and its secrets, and this means O'Hanrahan and Lucy, sometimes accompanied by Rabbi Mordechai Hersch (agent of Hebrew University in Jerusalem from which the gospel has been stolen), must dodge bullets, evade kidnappers, outwit fanatics, and risk plagues, sandstorms and plane crashes. In the process of all this, Lucy's world of safe certainties and righteous reticence breaks open like an egg shell as, under Dr. O'Hanrahan's tutelage, she learns to embrace venturesome, worldly, hedonistic existence, all the while trying to reconcile such an awakening, really a new birth, with her life-long Catholic loyalties.

A fourth major character, who makes himself known only in literally parenthetical comments, one-liners, and mini-revelations, is God. He is a deity who does his best encouraging humans to redeem their world, who whispers and woos his creatures toward righteousness, and who generally resembles the limited God of Process theism. He is created by his believers, even as he has created them (in some sense), and when their lives are done, an immortality of influence awaits them, as God takes up into himself the good they have done. And yet, on top of this, there also appear to be both an indescribable heaven and hell. Sometimes the divine quips are aimed at the characters, who occasionally hear them, but usually they are rhetorical devices, signaling the reader of future narrative possibilities, or just plain editorializing. The deity pictured here has little interest in theological or ritual niceties, demands good works for others as the criterion for salvation, and is surprisingly forgiving when it comes to sins. Indeed, this post-Rogerian God is not especially offended by mortal actions, which means there are, strictly speaking, no "sins," no specifically religious infractions. There are only childish, misguided, even tragically unevolved actions and character flaws, and God's role is mostly that of a therapist.

REFLECTING POOL

Barnhardt's *Gospel* is, like almost all Lost Gospel novels, a tale of a quest: an intrepid scholar is hot on the trail of a potentially explosive account of Jesus and Christian origins. And in this case we are almost in danger (but you needn't worry) of getting lost in a hall of mirrors, for Barnhardt has the *Gospel of Matthias* (which was anciently mentioned by Eusebius and catalogued as heretical) run parallel to and imbricated with his tale of the scholar criss-crossing the world to find it. Matthias' book (Barnhardt's fictional version, the only one we have) turns out to be the narrative of its apostolic author's own quest to recover the simple truth about his old master of many decades before, the Teacher of Righteousness (who is plainly supposed to be Jesus Christ, though he is never actually named). As Matthias' chapters are inserted between the much longer chapters of

Professor O'Hanrahan's travels, there is no mistaking how the one man's quest for answers reflects (and interprets) the other's. One broad hint is the striking "coincidence" that, two millennia apart, both men utilize the services of shady antiquities dealers with similar names: Duldul ibn Waswasah in the first century, Mustafa al-Waswasah in the twentieth!

Just as Dr. O'Hanrahan seeks at last to redeem himself by making a significant contribution to scholarship, an effort requiring world travels, so does Matthias seek to rejuvenate his faith in the primitive "Nazirene"[2] faith, now corrupted and confused on every hand. He is "in search of the scattered fragments of the Nazirene Church I longed to recover" (p. 91). Both men, centuries apart, have come to question their place in the larger picture painted by the religion that they love, even if neither quite "believes" in it any more. Will a search for truth finally vindicate faith, or make it forever impossible for the thinking mind? Of course, this is the underlying theme of the whole novel.

Barnhardt depicts Matthias much as conservative scholars like to picture Luke, author of the Book of Acts. While critical scholars today tend to view Acts as edifying or propagandistic fiction with the merest residue of facts, conservatives like to think of Luke as compiling information from extensive interviews with the heroes of the early congregations, including apostles and elders and relatives of the departed Jesus. Barnhardt knows Acts is not the product of such researches, and so he poses the implicit question: what if we *did* have a late-first century account of a Christian scholar's research journeys? Even on a conservative reading of Acts, the work leaves out so much of the story of early Christian missions that any reader must admit it is selective to the point of distortion. Why do we learn nothing of the possible deeds of apostles other than Simon Peter and his silent sidekick John son of Zebedee? Why is Paul so prominent when he was not even one of the original Twelve? And why take the trouble of replacing the traitor Judas with Matthias (Acts 1:15–26), whom we never hear from again? Why nothing about the glorious pioneering of Christianity in Alexandria and Rome (where churches are already alive and well by the time we read of them in Acts)? And so on.

---

2. Usually spelled as either "Nazarene," i.e., deriving from Jesus of Nazareth, or "Nazorean," i.e., "Keeper" of the Torah; here traced to the ascetical Nazirite vows of Judaism.

Barnhardt uses his imagination to fill in several of these blanks. There is so little explicit or secure data about the early days of the Christian faith that, as far as we can tell, almost anything may have happened. For instance, the Gospel of Mark gives us two lists of authoritative names. First is the catalogue of the Twelve (Mark 3:13–19): Simon Peter, James and John, sons of Zebedee, Peter's brother Andrew, Philip, Bartholomew, Matthew, Thomas, James son (or brother) of Alphaeus, Thaddaeus, Simon the Zealot, and Judas Iscariot. Second is the list of the Brothers of the Lord (Mark 6:3): James, Joses, Judas, Simon. Occasionally one or another of these names occurs in the gospels, simply as the name-tag of Jesus' straight man, eliciting some dominical teaching or pronouncement. Clearly, this is an artificial, purely literary role. Peter assumes this role more than anyone else, but this only means he plays the role of Dr. Watson to Sherlock Holmes. None of this need be historical data about the associates of Jesus. Acts tells us next to nothing about any of these individuals, with the conspicuous exceptions of Peter and Paul (again, not even a gospel character!), each of whom stars in a series of stock miracle stories and artificial speeches created by the author of Acts, which we can also dismiss as any sort of genuine biographical data..

Given the supposed centrality of the Twelve (and to a lesser extent the Brethren of the Lord) according to later tradition (enshrined in patently legendary works like the Apocryphal Acts of the Apostles), it is downright astounding how little is said of them in the New Testament. In fact, they are so insignificant as to give rise to theories that they were never historical individuals at all, but symbols of the houses of the Zodiac, or of the twelve tribes of Israel. For our purposes here, it is worth noting that author Barnhardt fully exploits the freedom to speculate, to fill in the details, indeed, to create characters from whole cloth. He assumes there really were close disciples of an historical Jesus, and makes an interesting gallery of them, all embodying distinct religious types familiar from various later periods in church history.

THE USUAL GANG OF IDIOTS

Jude (identified as the "Thaddaeus" of Mark 3:18) turns out never to have converted anyone. When Jesus chose him as a disciple, apparently that's as far as it went. Jude had been an end in himself, not a cog in a planned evangelistic machine. Barnhardt thus counters the Ponzi-scam ideology of Reverend Rick Warren (author of *The Purpose-Driven Life*), who thinks every convert to Christ is little more than a new recruit in a pyramid scheme of evangelization.

Any preacher or teacher knows too well how one's hearers tend to hear something quite different from what one thought one was teaching. So with Jude:

> "I wonder [if] I have given out incorrect information because some of the old and infirm have heard fantasies, have heard fictions. Two days ago a woman with an issue of blood, clothed in stained bandages, her face pale as new cotton, came to this house. She had heard that Our Master said that any who have such an infirmity are sure to reach Heaven for they are already washed in blood. You see how she was confused?" From what I made out, Jude confirmed her mistaken notion of Our Master's teachings ... I confess here to a certain desperation with this laxity concerning Our Master's teachings. (p. 104)

Another one of Barnhardt's fleshed-out ancient characters is Thomas, a businessman who combines business with evangelism in occasional trips to India. Like Rick Nelson, he seems to have a girl in every port, including the eight wives he keeps at home. Thomas remains a doubter, suspecting even at this late date (many years after Jerusalem's destruction) that Jesus may not actually have died upon the cross. For all Thomas knows, Jesus might have passed out, thinking he was breathing his last, then awakened from an induced coma, sincerely believing he had died and returned to life (p. 98). It hardly matters, though, since it is the teaching of their master that abides. And Thomas has taken pains to expound it. He says to his old colleague Matthias: "If it's gospels you want, why not peruse some of mine!" (p. 100). Gospels, plural? I imagine Barnhardt is thinking of the numerous works starring Thomas or ascribed to him in Syrian Christianity: *The Gospel of Thomas*, the *Acts of Thomas*, the *Book of Thomas the Contender*, the *Apocalypse of Thomas*, and so on. (He mentions these in a note on page 101). Matthias does take a look and reports:

> I will quickly record that Thomas's ramblings were heterodox in the extreme. Not without a certain Aramaic flair, or without a certain honesty of spirit, but clearly too much from his travels has been stirred into the broth. I am the light that is darkness, the ice that is within fire, he that is first is last—this kind of Eastern tiresomeness. (p. 101)

Indeed, these sayings do sound reminiscent of our Greek-Coptic *Gospel of Thomas*, though there is no exact match.

It is Thomas who informs Matthias that his selection as Judas Iscariot's replacement had not been purely a matter of divine inspiration by the casting of lots (Acts 1:21–26). Rather, the Eleven had already chosen him because of his education and his family fortune—much the way church leaders are chosen today, one might add! Peter later shows Matthias the loaded dice they used in the election charade. (They had previously been used by the Roman soldiers dividing the garments of Jesus at the foot of the cross—a delightful midrash!)

James, son of Alphaeus, is even more prolific an author of apostolic traditions and texts than Thomas. "He produces martyrologies by the firkin, alternating with invitations to martyrdom, though ... he manages to live quite well and grow quite fat as the decades pass!" (p. 197). Matthias finds him in Ptolemais and discovers that James also does a brisk trade in bogus relics right out of the souvenir bins of the Middle Ages. "Worse than his relic-mongering, truly, is the misinformation in his accounts and gospels" (p. 204). "One cannot list all the preposterous accretions" (p. 205). He writes and collects gospels, including Infancy Gospels such as survive even today under the names of Matthew, Thomas—and James! Matthias sneers at summarizing the pious enormities contained in the *Book of James* (also called *The Protevangelion* or *Proto-gospel of James*), a collection of miracles associated with the child Jesus and the events of the Nativity, as well as the infancy of Mary. But many of the episodes of miracles and prophecy that Matthias disdains we now read in canonical Matthew! Yikes! To Matthias' shocked protestations, James replies that it is necessary thus to build up the mythic credentials of their savior so that he may not appear less spectacular than Mithras in the eyes of the Gentiles to whom the gospel must be preached (pp. 206–7). "What I do here," James protests, "is what all holy men do, just as Daniel and Elijah have tales woven around them ... It is by such tales we move the mob" (p. 208).

Matthias knows that poor human memory has left the vacuum that James and other yarn-spinners have supplied. "I had only but one long meeting with the Teacher of Righteousness and with a sixteen-year-old's confidence I depended upon my memory" (p. 208). One is reminded of David Friedrich Strauss's caveat: "Eye-witnesses in the more extended sense, who had only seen Jesus occasionally and not been his constant companions, must . . . have been strongly tempted to fill up their imperfect knowledge of his history with mythical representations."[3] Even the climactic event of the resurrection is not so secure; James bar Alphaeus confesses, "Those few hours in those strange days when He appeared again passed as in a dream. Just ask, Matthias, any of the Disciples. You will not hear the same story twice! No one can agree on what happened" (p. 209).

Barnhardt's notes show his awareness of the already ancient ambiguity attaching to the name and character John. Was the disciple John bar Zebedee the unnamed author of the Fourth Gospel? Was either to be identified with the Seer of Revelation (which Barnhardt and his characters all erroneously refer to as "Revelations")? As far back as Eusebius some have speculated that either the gospel or the apocalypse "of John" was the work of a "John the Elder" mentioned in one of Papias' fragments. Traditionally most popular readers have simply assumed the identity of all the Johannine writers with the disciple, in turn identified as "the disciple whom Jesus loved," mentioned several times in the gospel, e.g., "Now there was leaning on Jesus' bosom one of his disciples, whom Jesus loved" (John 13:23 KJV). William Tyndale rendered it more literally, "reclined on Jesus' bosom." Most translators, eager to avoid any hint, however inevitable, of a homosexual attachment between Jesus and his "beloved" disciple, hasten to inform readers that nothing more is implied here than that the thirteen men were not sitting in chairs (true enough) but rather lying on their sides, propped up on an elbow, around the low, circular table, each roughly parallel to his neighbors, so that the favored disciple was simply the one directly adjacent to Jesus, the next spoke on the wheel. Yes, that may be so, but still one cannot help wondering if something more is intended. And Barnhardt's keen eye certainly does not miss it.

Barnhardt's John the Evangelist is portrayed as a sexually ambiguous eunuch, sublimating his confused libido into a mystical spirituality bordering on paranoia.

> John, who from a distance seemed to be ever twenty-one, showed his half century upon closer inspection—I believe he used a dyed oil to blacken his hair, but I did not say anything because one who has made oneself a eunuch, for the Lord or otherwise, is less likely to age, having robbed his body of the corrupting manly fluids that make the rest of us elder and gray. (p. 451)

3. Strauss, *The Life of Jesus Critically Examined*, 74.

John had surrounded himself with scrawny, malnourished visionaries, the only type liable, in Matthias' opinion, to esteem "John's doggerel worthy of remembering as Holy Scripture" (p. 452). Theologically, John turns out to be a docetist, one who believed the divine Jesus had a purely spiritual "body" and was actually more of an angelic phantom than a flesh-and-blood person.

> "Our Lord's eating and drinking," said John to me softly, "was but illusion, my brother, for His Divine Body had no use for this carrion and leafage we call food of this world. He was fed by angels each night." John's eyes dazzled with potential tears. "The Cherubim fed him the sweetmeats of Heaven on beams of light, the Seraphim poured him celestial wine while borne by the lyre music of David. Foods of every imaginable spice and color, arrayed before him on garnet and agate, bathed in the bejeweled Light from that one unconsumed, ever-burning Source of Light . . ." (pp. 452–3)

John, as Barnhardt depicts him, is technically a notch removed from pure docetism, granting that, though Jesus was both divine and human, he partook "of different Essences at different moments" (p. 453). This sounds a bit like the subsequent doctrine of the *communicatio idiomatum*: Jesus possessed both natures, manifesting now the one, now the other. His divinity made him walk on water, his mortal nature making it possible for him to die on the cross. But no upholder of that doctrine ever went so far as Barnhardt's John. Though John 4:31–34 has Jesus reject physical food in favor of invisible, heavenly fare, Barnhardt's portrayal comes instead from the docetic *Acts of John*, stemming from a radically ascetical and Gnosticizing Johannine sect.

Matthias is openly skeptical of all this, and only grows more so when John begins to share some of his Patmos visions of universal horrors attendant upon the end of the world. We ought to remember Matthias and his distaste for things Johannine when we elsewhere find Dr. O'Hanrahan sharing the same theological dislike of both John's sophistry and his fanaticism. Nor does Barnhardt mind having still another disciple excoriate John's theology. Thomas lets his disdain be known: "What I think sours converts is John's talk of Eternal Sonship and whether the Word or the Holy Spirit came before the Father—as if Yahweh was a father like I am a father! Amazing that Yahweh does not strike us down for such an idea!" (p. 99). That the author of the Fourth Gospel should already be discussing Trinitarian Mechanics seems a bit anachronistic, but then again, as Arthur W. Wainwright[4] amply shows, John's Gospel was certainly the seedbed of all such Nicene deliberations.

But perhaps the strangest aspect of John's theology as Barnhardt speculatively expounds it has to do with soteriology: the doctrine of salvation through Jesus' death.

> Having assumed the sins of all generations unto this one, having assumed within his Divinity all error and abomination, He fell through the many Hells until the seventh beneath Abaddon, where for three days a worse ordeal than the Cross transpired. (p. 454)

Today this very point is fiercely debated in a neglected corner of Charismatic Pentecostalism. Basing his case on the Pauline writings, E. W. Kenyon[5] spawned the JDS ("Jesus Died Spiritually") movement which holds something very much like the terrible vision Barnhardt's John reveals to Matthias, and, like Matthias, Hobart E. Freeman[6] and others reject the view as blasphemous heresy. Matthias sums up why: "Do you honestly believe, I asked of him, that God hurled his Greatest Prophet into a lake of fire with the fallen angels and Lucifer, Nero, Herod, and the like?" (p. 454) Take note, however: this is exactly the stunned indignation Muslims feel upon learning that Christians believe God abandoned Jesus to crucifixion, period. To them, as to Peter in Matthew 16: 22, such a notion is equally blasphemous. On the other hand, the JDS doctrine would meet the objection of skeptics that—if Jesus' suffering amounted to no more than six hours on the cross, which killed most of its victims over several days—he got off pretty light! Far better that than consignment to Auschwitz, eh? Better to be Jesus than Elie Wiesel! But if there were much more to it than met the eye, well, things start making a bit more sense.

When Matthias presents himself at Philip's doorstep, he thinks at first to have found another like John, maintaining the illusion of prolonged youth. But then his host tells him he is not the original Philip, but rather his greatest disciple, carrying on his retired master's apostolic ministry by assuming his name. One wonders if Barnhardt means here

---

4. Wainwright, *The Trinity in the New Testament*, 191–95, 221–23.

5. Kenyon, *Identification: A Romance in Redemption* and *What Happened from the Cross to the Throne?*

6. Freeman, *Did Jesus Die Spiritually?*

to suggest a solution for the puzzle of there being a Philip who was a disciple and apostle, and also a Philip who was one of the seven Hellenists of Acts chapter 6, the so-called seven deacons. The two are hopelessly intertwined in all early Christian discussion and narration. Maybe one became the apostolic heir of the other, like Elisha taking over the similarly named Elijah's career as prophet and thaumaturge.

Though the notion of an apostle carrying on the "company name" established by his teacher may strike the reader as new and odd, remember that this is pretty much what critical scholars say happened in half of the so-called Pauline Epistles. Though they differ in style and doctrine from the principle Paulines, they still share a broad family resemblance and are therefore probably the work of a second-generation "Pauline School."

Mary Magdalene, aged and veiled to conceal her many ascetical self-mutilations, wrought so as to repel would-be Roman rapists, turns out to be the head of a convent of women who have found their culture's only possible autonomy for women, in a celibate sisterhood. We know of such "widows' houses" already in the second-century Pastoral Epistles (1 Tim 5:16), but they are more fully attested a few centuries later when wealthy celibate women like Mary of Egypt, Melania the Elder and Melania the Younger, Constantina, and others organized communes for consecrated women ("widows" and "virgins") in their own homes and on their own property.[7]

In this way Matthias has his eyes opened to the God-given abilities of Christian women and their aptitude for scholarly and ministerial tasks he had hitherto considered suited only to men. In fact, we eventually discover that it was a hidden, long-surviving order of consecrated women dedicated to St. Matthias that protected his text for so many centuries among their collection of apostolic writings. It seems that women are most sensitively attuned to the Divine Sophia, more or less to be identified with the Holy Spirit (as considered female, as in ancient Middle-Eastern Christianity, where *Ruach*, Spirit, is grammatically female).

With this reference to a convent of the Magdalene, we approach a discussion of the wild range of sects and cults with which Barnhardt

---

7. See Price, *The Widow-Traditions in Luke-Acts*, 8, 181; MacDonald, *The Legend and the Apostle*, 75, for evidence of the early ministry of such women's communes and the increasing opposition to them by the patriarchal church even within the later New Testament period.

populates his fictive early Christianity. But first we must sum up the most significant implication of all this talk of apostles in their dotage. We have seen how the aging apostles could no longer trust their youthful memories, and how they tried their best to safeguard Jesus' sayings only to find them distorted in the ears and repeating mouths of the crowds who heard what they wanted to hear. We have seen, too, how the apostles freely embellished the store of Jesus-traditions with fabrications that seemed to meet the needs of the moment.

Obviously, Wilton Barnhardt has no way of knowing what did or did not happen. The important thing is that he has shown, via plausible narrative, that any and all of these processes of embellishment and of distortion could very easily have taken place in the lifespan of the apostles and under their very noses. We can well imagine that some, like Matthias himself, would bemoan the rank growth of the tradition—without being able, really, to do a blessed thing about it! We can very easily picture well-meaning evangelists making the Jesus stories more colorful, borrowing from the beliefs, myths, and rituals of rival sects. Anthropologists know that such developments commonly occur in the early decades of new religions. It would be an amazing surprise if such had not occurred in the case of Christian origins. The only reason we have been slow to recognize it is the inherited dogma that the gospels are theologically infallible and historically inerrant. Apologists like to insist that the apostles "would have" wanted to govern the transmission of the Jesus material and "would have" been able to safeguard it effectively. But that is to make the early Christians into the mirror images of today's apologists, to ascribe to the ancients a modern apologetical agenda. By contrast, Barnhardt shows us in bold colors how easy it is to imagine things going a very different way. The only way to determine the accuracy of the gospel material is to make a close scrutiny of it, such as the Jesus Seminar undertook for eleven years.[8]

CREATIVE CHRISTIAN CHAOS

One thing that critical study of the New Testament has made clear is that the canon, the official list of authoritative books, is anything but a random sampler of early Christian thinking and writing. There is a

---

8. Hoover and the Jesus Seminar, *The Five Gospels*; Robert W. Funk and the Jesus Seminar, *The Acts of Jesus*; Price, *The Incredible Shrinking Son of Man*.

surprising amount of diversity on display there, but to see this much requires the interpreter to remove the dogmatic blinders of traditional orthodoxy. All of us come up through church education in which the "problem passages" and "apparent contradictions" in the Bible, where they are even acknowledged, have been long ago artificially harmonized by our tradition's apologists (or "legitimators").[9] But as critics, we must learn to recognize these loose ends, these seams and mismatches in the fabric. We will then recognize them as valuable keys to unlock the depths, the pre-history of the texts. We will learn, as F. C. Baur and the Tübingen School[10] did, to read the fossils and to reconstruct the long extinct theological and sectarian life forms that lie embedded in the canon. Ernst Käsemann rightly remarks

> that only fragments of the discussion within primitive Christianity have been preserved for us and that the variety of the primitive Christian *kerygma* [preaching] must have been very much greater than a consideration of the state of affairs as revealed in the canon would lead us to suppose.[11]

That much might strike the reader as obvious, but it really is not. Käsemann here repudiates the approach of Catholic Orthodoxy (including traditional Protestantism), which is to start with an officially produced book—our New Testament, put together and heavily rewritten by Polycarp,[12] a bowdlerized book intended to suppress evidence of an earlier, "heretical" diversity of belief and practice—and then to reason that, since we cannot say for sure what else than orthodoxy might have been going on back there in the dawn age of the faith, it is safe to assume that *nothing* unorthodox was going on. Absence of evidence becomes evidence of absence. But that is unsound. As Elisabeth Schüssler Fiorenza[13] says, we must and can learn to listen to the silences in the canon. And I want to suggest that Wilton Barnhardt has done this. He has approached the problem with more constructive imagination than

---

9. Berger and Luckmann, *The Social Construction of Reality*, 116–28.

10. Hodgson, *The Formation of Historical Theology*; Harris, *The Tübingen School*; Harris, *David Friedrich Strauss and his Theology*.

11. Käsemann, "The Canon of the New Testament and the Unity of the Church," 100.

12. Trobisch, *The First Edition of the New Testament* and "Who Published the New Testament?"

13. Fiorenza, *In Memory of Her*, 41.

many critical scholars would feel justified in using, but that is of course because he is writing an overt piece of fiction. Nonetheless, his lesson remains: *something* like the chaotic array of sects he depicts must have existed in early Christian times, just as Käsemann said. We will see that, in Matthias' fictive description of some of these groups, Barnhardt has borrowed some later Christian movements and retrojected them into the first century CE. The procedure is somewhat anachronistic, but on the other hand, every Christian sect has grown from some seed scattered here and there in the pages of the New Testament: odd bits about self-castration for the kingdom of heaven, baptism for the dead, snake-handling, and so on. Again, Käsemann:

> [I]n primitive Christianity a wealth of different confessions were already in existence, constantly replacing each other, combining with each other and undergoing mutual delimitation. It is thus quite comprehensible that the confessions which exist today all appeal to the New Testament canon. Fundamentally the exegete cannot dispute their methodological or their material right to do this. If the canon as such is binding in its totality, the various confessions may, with differing degrees of historical justification, claim as their own larger or smaller tracts of it, better or less known New Testament writers.[14]

Barnhardt is, as I read him, starting with striking New Testament passages cherished by sectarian movements known from later Christian history and then inferring that like must have produced like. He infers that the odd passages themselves attest similar currents in the New Testament period. He ventures that the Medieval sects got it right, rediscovering this or that "heresy" that left its mark in this or that odd corner of the canon. One obvious example from recent history would be 1 Corinthians 15:29, which speaks of vicarious baptism on behalf of the dead. The Latter-day Saints (Mormons) practice it today because Joseph Smith spotted the text and was not intimidated by its weirdness into pretending it meant something more tame. He had burned his bridges to conventional orthodoxy and had nothing to lose by recognizing an ancient sacrament, one attested for the Marcionites and others, and reproducing it in his own day. Barnhardt likewise sniffs the smoke rising from various obscure texts and tries to reignite a fire with the same kindling and fuel.

14. Käsemann, 104.

FAITH'S FREAK SHOW

"For one, there are the Children of Adam, who plague every decency by their insistence on nakedness. What commune of theirs has not been found to produce unmarried women-with-child by the score?" (pp. 91–92). Norman Cohn discusses various "Adam-cults" active in Western Europe in the fourteenth century, some attached to the antinomian Free Spirit movement. Some were orgiastic or at least went in for ritual nudity.[15] Another group of Adamites, this time in fifteenth-century Bohemia, reveled in nude liturgy and sacred orgies, too, but these also made serious trouble by taking up the God-ordained sword against outsiders. Many of these Adamites were burnt at the stake.[16]

Matthias next attacks what he calls the "Opheisians." These are Christians who learned a sort of *ahimsa* doctrine from Jesus when, in some unrecorded pronouncement story, he prevented Peter from callously killing a snake outside of his house in Bethany. Jesus pronounced serpents good, not evil as in Eden, and the Opheisians majored on this minor, adopting the ritual handling and passing around of snakes. In this way they were reintroducing the ancient heathen snake-handling of nearby Crete (p. 92). Well, whoever added to Mark chapter 16 the dominical pronouncement, "Those who believe in me . . . shall pick up serpents" was presumably trying to legitimate some such practice, the like of which we still behold in Appalachian churches today. But Matthias' Opheisians are to be distinguished from a known sect of antiquity, the Ophites, whose name is based on the Greek *ophos*, serpent. In Hebrew they were called the Naassenes, from the Hebrew *naas*, serpent. This was a syncretistic Gnostic group who esteemed the Edenic serpent as a Prometheus analogue, the bringer of enlightenment to mankind. The Ophites did not handle snakes as far as we know. But, as we shall see in a moment, the real Ophites do lie in the background of Barnhardt's gallery of sects.

Next in the heresiological spot light are the Heliogenesians, known for rewriting Jesus into a sun god modeled upon the popular deity Mithras. We know of no specific, organized sect who did this, but many scholars have strongly suspected heavy influence from the older faith

---

15. Cohn, *The Pursuit of the Millennium*, 176–86.
16. Cohn, 219–22.

of Mithraism on the newer Christian religion. As Richard Reitzenstein[17] pointed out, it is obvious that between an older and a newer sect, the traffic is naturally going to flow from the former to the latter as many are eager for something new. And it is human nature to take along what one found to be of value in the old—why not have the best of both worlds?

Another of Matthias' detested sects was an unnamed group of Nazirenes and Jews in Philistine Ashkelon who assimilated Jesus to the ancient dying and rising god Attis. They regarded the late-comer Jesus as the second advent of Attis. Matthias regrets that these have adopted "the atrocious rites of Attis" (p. 93). The actual, historical Attis initiates castrated themselves, but Matthias saves that for another group, referring here instead to the Passion Play ritual in which Attis' devotees would strip a pine trunk and affix an effigy of their god upon it and then hide it for three days, to be retrieved upon the third to dramatize their Lord's resurrection. That is what they really did. Only, in order to aim a jibe at the pagan roots of Christmas, Barnhardt instead describes the custom as if each household placed an intact pine tree in its house, laden with gifts and surrounded by candles. That is something that would be more at home in the ancient Baal cult, though there certainly were Christian syncretists who identified Jesus with Attis. They were the second-century Naassene Ophites, who recorded this belief in the fragmentary *Naassene Hymn*.

Matthias does get to "the castration cults" (p. 93), one of whom he dubs the Celepheans, who dwell in caves in the Negev desert. Well, organized sect or not, there certainly were self-castrators in the New Testament period. One of them appealed to a hadith of Jesus for their warrant: "There are eunuchs who were born that way, and others made eunuchs by others, and there are eunuchs who have made themselves eunuchs for the sake of attaining the kingdom of heaven. Whoever is able to accept this, he must do so" (Matt 19:12).[18] The Alexandrian theologian Origen is said to have removed fleshly temptation in this manner, and he was not the only one we know of. Much later there was an avid sect of castrators amid the sectarian ferment in Czarist Russia. These were the genital choppers of the Skoptsy sect. Repeated attempts

---

17. Reitzenstein, *Hellenistic Mystery Religions*, 149.
18. Price, *The Pre-Nicene New Testament*, 153.

by the state authorities to stamp them out proved ineffective, and they still exist today.[19]

Yes, there are various New Testament intimations of the range of sects with which Barnhardt peoples his early Christian landscape. Those texts are the merest slivers and fragments, but, as Käsemann reminds us, that is all we may expect, given that the canon is the product of an attempt to make Christian origins appear a certain way in order to legitimate the emergent Catholic/Orthodox church. We get a better look at some of this fantastic, now-vanished theological diversity in the Nag Hammadi Gnostic collection. It is literally what was excluded from the New Testament (though not all of it), since the cache of "heretical books" were proscribed by St. Athanasius in his Easter encyclical of 367 CE. All books not on his approved list would be incinerated. To forestall that, the monks of Saint Pachomias' monastery hid their "extra" books away in caves for the future to retrieve. If one wants to know what material was shut out of the canon, we have a good sample of it. And it attests sects for whom Jesus Christ was the returned Shem or Seth or Melchizedek or Zoroaster! Based on this, one may say that something very much like what Barnhardt describes was indeed going on in the earliest Christian period.

I admit that our author has taken the liberty to borrow certain historic sects from their proper place in the time-line and placed them in the store window of the first century. But even here one must remind oneself that the same sauce is equally for the goose and the gander: are we not used to Christian apologists and historical theologians desperately trying to retroject mainstream Christianity of their own favorite types into the earliest period? They try to make Jesus and Paul into Lutheran preachers, pious Methodists, Liberation theologians, and Vatican 2 Catholics. And in so doing, they take the same liberty Barnhardt did, only they will not admit they are indulging in fiction.

THE DANGER AND THE DESTINY

The intrigue surrounding the elusive *Gospel of Matthias* is that, as in so many other novels of this type, it might contain some revelation inimical to the faith of millions. It is not merely that many reading it would be disappointed by the news, but that war and rioting might break out.

---

19. Larson, *Strange Sects and Cults*, 139–47.

Sniffing this possibility, various interests want to get their hands on the *Gospel of Matthias*, wanting either to avert or actually to foment violence. Some see it as a final piece in the puzzle of Armageddon, and they are eager to see the game begin. Others would sooner destroy it than have the faith destroyed. Well, does Matthias pack such a punch?

To keep the reader interested over nearly eight hundred pages, the novel must employ an effective element of *deferral*. The author must lead his readers on a merry chase. We must several times seem to be on the verge of satisfaction only to have it yanked away, so both our curiosity and our frustration will keep us going. Do we at length (and I do mean "length") find the fox? Yes and no. While the various characters have been engaged in the search, we lucky readers have been privy to the *Matthias* text all along, reading large chapters of it interspersed every hundred pages or so. We are perusing it before Dr. O'Hanrahan gets it translated, before he even knows how to decode the text. In fact, we never see him finish translating it. The chase continues within the gospel text itself. Here's how. Matthias, intrepid researcher that he is, picks up a tip that Jesus never rose from the dead but that Joseph of Arimathea disposed of the body, sending it far away in the care of servants. Furthermore, Matthias learns where the dangerous mummified relic now resides, down deep in Ethiopia. He decides it is worth the trip, even should his faith be destroyed. But at the last minute he cannot stand to unwrap the facial bandages. Better not to know! Faith before truth! Besides, perhaps faith is best understood as faithfulness to one's vision and values, something that cannot be verified by a miracle or debunked by the lack of one.

Patrick O'Hanrahan eventually grows beyond the need to establish his scholarly reputation and turns over to Lucy the job of shepherding the text into a published and annotated translation. But we are finally given only glimpses into the future. It looks as if Lucy plans to turn down the privilege in order to go back to Ethiopia and do some hands-on relief work with the legions of impoverished humanity she saw there during the multi-continent quest for Matthias. But *some*one must get around to putting the text into shape since we have been reading it all along, and with scholarly footnotes. One of these, you will find if you are reading attentively, implies that it is Dr. O'Hanrahan's work we have been reading. But even then he has not come to a satisfying end, for he comes to learn that scholars in Iran have identified yet another ancient treasure: the Q Document! Like a hardy Indiana Jones, O'Hanrahan will be off after that one next.

If one were to draw some theological lesson from this vast and sprawling book, it would likely be that spiritual enlightenment may come, not from "satisfying" answers, which put the satiated knower to sleep like a Thanksgiving dinner being slowly digested, but rather from a steady diet of question and quest. Only the hunger keeps one going, which is good, seeing that the road itself is the real destination.

21 | The Hidden and the Revealed
Paul L. Maier, *A Skeleton in God's Closet*

Paul L. Maier is a Harvard-educated historian, an Evangelical Christian, and the author of apologetics volumes including *First Easter*, *First Christmas*, and *First Christians*. He has the distinction of having studied with both Karl Barth and Oscar Cullmann in Basel, and this makes him surely the most sophisticated of the Lost Gospel novelists. His handsome protagonist in *A Skeleton in God's Closet*, Harvard Professor Jonathan Weber, is more than a little reminiscent of Dan Brown's scholarly sleuth in *The Da Vinci Code*, but there can be no question of borrowing (not that borrowing, otherwise known as "inspiration," would be a bad thing); Maier's book preceded Brown's onto the shelves by about a decade. It is simply that the subject matter requires that kind of hero if the book is to be a mystery adventure rather than a scholarly treatise. Maier's book is certainly scholarly, though. He devotes several brisk pages here and there to the science of dating archaeological finds, something he does not want the reader to have to take for granted.

The novel features characters that are rounder, more lifelike and detailed, than we might have required, but neither do we know them overly well. Maier gets the balance right, making his characters as colorful as they need to be for us to tell them apart, even though, structurally, many of them reduce to the same actant, the same narrative function. One of them sports a phony Irish brogue of the kind I frequently irritate friends and family with; another is a proper Britisher, another a voluptuous Israeli. The inevitable romantic element is well handled and persuasively written, substituting for the near pornographic sex scenes in some of our other Lost Gospel novels. Yet the narrative voice is of a writer who is at home equally in the church and in the world, and with a sprightly sense of humor, often on loan to his characters. Maier certainly knows how to write a page-turner and let the suspense mount. And he paints the reader into a corner in the finest mystery style.

Here is the story in a nut shell. At first a team of archaeologists believe themselves to have unearthed the tomb of Joseph of Arimathea in modern Rama, one of the possible sites for Joseph's famous home town. This implies that, after sacrificing his Jerusalem tomb for the burial of Jesus, Joseph abandoned his early plan to be buried in Jerusalem and decided to be interred back home, a little farther from the holiest part of the Holy Land. The identity of a skeleton found in the tomb is seemingly confirmed by the surprise discovery of a rolled-up papyrus, which turns out to be the tri-lingual *titulus* fastened to the cross and announcing (in Latin, Greek, and Hebrew) that Jesus was being executed as a Jewish royal pretender. But wait a minute...!

Suppose *this* was the tomb that Joseph had given over to the slain Jesus? Could the bones be those of Jesus? It sure looks that way, especially when still another scroll is discovered in the barrow, a letter from Joseph to Nicodemus:

> Joseph, son of Asher, to Nicodemus, son of Shimeon, peace! ... Do you remember the rabbi Yeshua whom we buried in my tomb a score and seven years ago during the governance of Pontius Pilate?... I feared that the noble rabbi, a man of much suffering, would not have the rest that should come to him after his pain. My servants heard rumors in the city that the priests had a plot regarding his body. Not many hours before cock crow, my servant Eleazar and I went to the sepulcher. We removed the body of Jesus and returned the stone to its place. We put the body onto a donkey cart ... and returned to my house in Jerusalem. The evening after Shabbat we drove the cart to Rama, where we reinterred the rabbi in the sarcophagus I had ordered for myself, but not taken to Jerusalem. Only later did I learn of the excitement over the empty tomb. Before my Lord, I do not know why the priests did not examine the tomb before they sealed and guarded it. It was empty on the first day of the week because it was empty already the day before.

Nicodemus had saved the letter and written a note at the bottom:

> I am burying this letter next to the tomb of Jesus. The truth is now in the hands of El-Shaddai. If He wills, the truth will come

to light. If not, then it may be His will that The Way survive, for it is a teaching of hope. Amen. (pp. 91–92)

Well, that about tears it! Subsequent batteries of dating tests of every conceivable type seem only to reinforce the verdict: the skeleton of Jesus has been found, and Christianity is never going to be the same again! The inner circle of scholars working on the find are at least nominal Christians, but it is more for the faith of the about-to-be-disillusioned masses that they fear. Besides our hero Weber, these include his one-time mentor Austin Balfour Jennings and the latter's beautiful daughter Shannon. It is, of course, she with whom young Weber falls desperately in love, filling the gap in his affections left by the death of his wife in an avalanche while skiing a few years before.

This cabal of researchers make the most valiant attempts to keep the discovery under their sun helmets till they can eliminate all doubt one way or the other. They want to be able to announce a genuine find or to wash their hands of a clever hoax, whether an ancient or a modern one. Why subject the religious public to the agony of uncertainty? As the various scientific tests secure the proper antiquity of all the discovered materials (except the ink that they dare not scrape off to test), our scholars seek to verify fine points of the letter of Joseph. Though they themselves boast considerable expertise in ancient Aramaic, they take the pains of traveling to various colorful climes to consult various specialists, some of whom appear to be pretty eccentric. The only really sane one is the great Frank Moore Cross. (The book mixes actual personalities such as Cross, Billy Graham, and Martin E. Marty with fictive analogues of various TV evangelists and caricature theologians. When Maier wrote, John Paul II was still with us, so Maier sets his tale in the pontificate of his imagined successor: Pope Benedict XVI! A lucky guess, unless then-Cardinal Ratzinger was a fan of this novel, which seems about as likely as him being a lesbian!)

The other Aramaic specialists are, shall we say, a bit too close to their subject. A spry old Coptic Archimandrite invites the researchers up Mount Sinai (he belongs to Saint Catherine's Monastery there) to see the sunrise—and promptly pushes them over the edge! Better the sin of murder now than to allow Christian faith to be destroyed by their discovery! Of course they survive, but the mischief isn't over. Another zealot, a French Dominican in Jerusalem, surreptitiously snips a piece off the edge of the blasphemous papyrus so he can later produce it as fake evidence that he himself had forged the thing years ago! He hadn't—he was, however, willing to take the rap in order to discredit "the terrible parchment."[1] (And, remember, in *The Q Document* and *The Word* which we reviewed in chapters 4 and 6, respectively, the hoaxers *do* keep back puzzle-piece fragments against the day they may find it expedient to explode their own hoaxes.)

The discovery leaks to the press, and most seem to accept the genuineness of the find, though Weber, Jennings, and the rest warn them to wait till all conceivable tests have been run, even though by this point the reader knows, as the public does, that such doubt is Cartesian. Let's face it, the verdict is in: no resurrection. It is the reaction to this news that chiefly concerns us, as we are interested in isolating just what it is that each novelist believes would be at stake in such discoveries. For instance, if the find would "blow the lid off" Christianity, precisely what element of the religion would have to be discredited? Suppose, as Father Guido Sarducci once said, he had obtained the papyrus restaurant check for the Last Brunch, and it turned out one of the apostles had stiffed the rest. How much would that matter? Suppose we discovered Jesus rose on the fourth day, not the third. Or would the truth of Christianity survive, as Tillich is said to have remarked, even if it could be shown no such person as an historical Jesus ever existed?[2]

Of all the novels we have yet considered, Maier, once a student of Barth and Cullmann (both fairly conservative, if Neo-Orthodox), is by far the most sophisticated in his treatment of the issue. He depicts a Christmas Day TV special in which representatives of various Christian churches seek to deal with the seeming debunking of the resurrection. Fundamentalists and charismatics embrace fideistic know-nothingism. They don't want to be bothered with any evidence. They *know* Christ is raised because they talked to him (probably in tongues) this morning. Billy Graham and a Roman Catholic archbishop agree that the find will ultimately prove to be a fake and warn against diluting Christian faith down to some non-supernatural moralism.[3] Liberal and radical Protestants, on

---

1. Wellman, "The Terrible Parchment."

2. Adele McCollum passed this hadith on to me. In his published writings, however, Tillich maintained that the truth of Christianity does require an historical founder, a first case of someone experiencing the New Being under the conditions of finitude and ambiguity, even if somehow it should turn out that his name was not Jesus. Tillich, *Systematic Theology II: Existence and the Christ*, 114–15.

3. I suppose what C. S. Lewis used to call "Christianity-and-water," a metaphor lost on teetotaling fans of his. Lewis, *Mere Christianity*, 46.

the other hand, express satisfaction that their Bultmannian skepticism has been thus vindicated. Study of the texts ever since Renan and Strauss had long since convinced them that the resurrection was a myth, albeit a transforming and edifying one. Maier shows various serious Christians, hitherto committed to a bodily resurrection, seriously chewing over the alternatives, considering whether to switch over to the liberal view that Jesus was raised in spirit but not in body.

It seems a very bitter pill. On one level, why should it? Either way, is the liberal view not a belief that Jesus defeated death and opened the way for us to do the same? Well, theoretically, yes . . . but how many people in the pews are likely to view it that way? How much difference is there between saying that "Jesus surely rose again, but he did so in the minds and hearts of his followers" (p. 189) and saying, "his followers imagined he rose, though in fact he didn't, and their delusion is what energized them"?[4] Theologians might find a non-physical version of "resurrection" palatable, since they embraced it in the first place as the last vestige of a largely defunct faith, some last piece of driftwood to hold onto and still say they were Christians. But wouldn't most folks, burdened with common sense, see the sophistry?[5]

The book shows church attendance shrinking, seminaries going out of business, frequent suicides among the devout, a retrenching of the most conservative sects, and a measure of opportunistic gloating by representatives of atheism, Marxism, and Islam. (Here Maier goofs: Muslims reject belief in the divinity of Jesus, as he says, and they do not believe he rose from the dead. But they would be equally aghast at the discovery of his remains, since the Koran has him raptured into heaven before his enemies can arrest and execute him.) Jews, by contrast, realize their best

---

4. Gordon Kaufman freely admits the resurrection visions of the disciples were hallucinations, but that their historical effects make them enough of an "event" for Christians to justify speaking of "an historical resurrection." Kaufman, *Systematic Theology*, 422–23.

5. Once at the Jesus Seminar, Gerd Lüdemann and I insisted that we vote on the New Testament assertion (in Acts 2:31) that Jesus' body did not decompose. The majority voted that the assertion was untrue: Jesus had rotted. The next day, John Dominic Crossan suggested we vote for his proposal that the earlier vote need not be taken to mean Jesus did not also rise from the dead in some sense. Crossan speaks of "damage control" as a giveaway sign of the inauthenticity of some gospel passages (e.g., Matthew 3:14 with Mark 1:9; Matthew 19:16–17 with Mark 10:17–18; John 12:27–28 with Mark 14:34–36; John 19:17 with Mark 15:21; Luke 23:46 with Mark 15:34). That day Crossan was indulging in some damage control himself.

course of action is to commiserate with the disappointed children of a sister faith, to welcome any theological refugees who might come knocking, but by no means to rejoice, lest they rouse the ire of anti-Semitic Christians eager to take their wrath out on somebody, anybody.

What Maier wisely does not depict or suppose is that the debunking of Christianity would plunge civilization into nihilistic chaos, as happened in *When It Was Dark*. This is because Maier can see that we now live in a culture that is in many ways post-Christian, one which is so pluralistic that no single faith, even a numerically predominant one, can any longer provide the "sacred canopy" legitimizing all values and laws for a whole society. One cannot bemoan the accomplished secularization of American society and at the same time propose that the discovery of Jesus' skeleton would bring society down like a house of cards. If, like Francis A. Schaeffer, you gripe about secularization, you pretty much figure the cards are already lying flat. Your goal, like that of the one-time fundamentalist political juggernaut the Moral Majority, is to rebuild the house.

Maier has so thickly piled on the evidence for the Rama discovery of Jesus' bones that the reader finds himself sharing the skepticism of various characters. It does seem ridiculous to hold out hope in the face of the seemingly irrefutable data. So well does Maier gull us that it comes as a genuine surprise when the whole thing turns out to be a fake after all! And this even though, given the Evangelical publisher, you knew the author simply was not at liberty to leave the resurrection debunked! Who dunnit? Well, well, well: what do you know? It was a member of the inner circle itself, Professor Jennings! Weber at length notices an odd but "probably" irrelevant detail or two, then manages to uncover a secret tale of Jennings's lifelong abuse by Christians and Christian institutions, upon whom (like Robert Le Brun, the forger in *The Word*, or like Morton Smith) he sought to gain everlasting revenge. I was reminded of the *National Geographic* TV special unveiling the newly discovered *Gospel of Judas*. In one scene the assembled scholarly elite are answering questions about the new text: could anyone have fabricated the thing? An embarrassed pause, "Well, one of *us* would have had the know-how!" (Or some equivalent words.) Some of us suspect one particular member of that team *did* in fact forge the supposed *Gospel of Judas*. But that is certainly what happens here in *A Skeleton in God's Closet*, and it is pretty effective.

This novel is an expression of the position taken by Billy Graham and others within the story: faith assures the believer that no such debunking will ever occur. Theoretically, of course, anything might happen. But believers have come to trust their experience, and that of so many others, and for them the issue is much like the crazy hypothetical, "What if your spouse were a foreign spy assigned to report on you, and your whole married life is a sham?" Well, it *could* possibly be so, but is there any reason to think so? Even if some nut urged it upon you as a fact? I understand the difficulty of this, but, as an historian early dedicated to pursuing the truth about the Bible and Christian origins, I have found that such emotional comforts are simply irrelevant when it comes to one's scrutiny of ancient texts, evidence, and facts, and one's weighing of them.

But then it comes as all the more pleasant and striking a surprise that the single dominant note resounding through Paul Maier's novel is that the true scholar must never suppress discovered truth, no matter what. Several times, characters urge Professor Weber to have mercy on the millions of believers, to save Christianity the ordeal, even the doom, that his discovery, if known, must cause. No skeptic, but no zealot either, Weber consistently and indignantly rejects the option. The truth is the only thing that counts. To think so is not to deem human welfare secondary but precisely to recognize that human well-being depends on how we deal with the tests the discovery of the truth sets forth for us. The pretended compassion for the flock that would lead us to hide the truth from them for their own good is really just the soporific over-protection practiced by the Grand Inquisitor.

22 | Book of Betrayal
Daniel Easterman, *The Judas Testament*

IN OUR CONSIDERATION OF Daniel Easterman's previous Lost Gospel novel, *The Brotherhood of the Tomb* in Chapter 18, I observed that the author seemed to be hinting at a sequel, though I did not know of one. Well, if he did get around to writing a sequel to the earlier book, this isn't it. Both the conception of Jesus and his implied fate are quite different between the two novels, impossible to harmonize. Both are great fun, and that is of course all our author intended to offer us.

As always, we want to take a look at the controversial text of the newly recovered gospel, which in this case (despite the novel's title) has nothing at all to do with Judas Iscariot, the betrayer of Jesus. The title seems instead to come from the theme of the novel, the rationale for most of its action: you cannot trust anyone. Even your loved ones harbor secrets, withholding them for your own good. Even allies who save your life probably had ulterior motives, and you may yet need to be rescued from *them*. The "testament of Judas" seems to be a not-too-oblique expression for "the legacy of betrayal." Throughout the novel, the discovered gospel text is called "the Jesus Scroll." One wonders, then, why Easterman did not call his book *The Jesus Scroll*.

My guess would be that he did not want to risk confusion with a 1972 book called *The Jesus Scroll* by Donovan Joyce. Nor would the title have been all that the two books had in common. Both posit a dangerous new scroll revealing Jesus as a nationalistic Jewish Zealot. Joyce claimed that a man arranged to meet him in a men's room in Tel Aviv to sell him a scroll written by Jesus himself. It had become too hot to handle, so he was eager to pass it on to someone else. But just as he was about to remove the papyrus from his satchel and show it to Joyce, he heard the approaching footsteps of some thug in search of him and the scroll—so he split the scene, leaving Joyce holding the bag, an empty one.[1] Joyce

---

1. Oddly, the fanciful men's room scene in *The Jesus Scroll* is painfully close to real-

spends the rest of the book speculating on what *might* have been in the vanished text. And the upshot is a picture of Jesus as a Torah-zealot who escaped the cross only to die decades later at Masada, at vengeful Roman hands, as the last Hasmonean king of the Jews. We might have included Joyce's *The Jesus Scroll* as a separate Lost Gospel novel in its own right except that the fictive, narrative element extends only so far as its (tongue-in-cheek) introduction. The bulk of the book is devoted to fanciful "historical" speculation like that of Baigent, Lincoln, and Leigh in *Holy Blood, Holy Grail*. Joyce's is a great deal more plausible, though, and is a very fascinating, albeit 100% speculative, book.

In Easterman's admitted fiction, the Jesus text is a letter of Jesus to Caiaphas. "To his excellency the High Priest, the Nasri, Lord of the Sanhedrin, Joseph [Caiaphas], may the Lord guide him and cause him to be brought close to the Law" (p. 119). *Nasri* is an Arabic name (not a title) meaning "victory." It is derived from an Egyptian town name, Nasr. I am guessing Easterman means it to be related to the Hebrew *Nozrim*, meaning "keepers" or "guardians" of the Torah. In the letter, Jesus continues,

> What the prophet has said: "The priest and the prophet have erred with strong drink." Your letter came to me today by the hand of your cousin Simon, my wife's brother, who is welcome in my house. A righteous man who dwells this night with the Perfect of the Way and tomorrow departs once more for Jerusalem, in accordance with the instructions of the procurator [Valerius Gratus]. (p. 119)

Wait a second ... Jesus was *married*? How little an impact that notion makes in this novel! Compare it to the universal hubbub attending the same "revelation" in Dan Brown's *The Da Vinci Code,* where that fact alone is said to be enough to sink Christianity! But Brown shows himself to be a poor researcher; he vainly supposes all pre-Nicene Christians to have been *docetists*, believers in a purely divine, phantom Jesus who had no fleshly body and thus could not have mated with a mortal female. (Though the angelic Sons of God appear to have had little trouble with

---

ity: the brilliant Gnosticism scholar Ioan P. Couliano (author of, e.g., *The Tree of Gnosis*, 1990) was murdered in 1991 with a single shot to the back of the head, in the men's room of the University of Chicago Divinity School. He was apparently rubbed out by an agent of the Romanian Iron Guard, a neo-Fascist ally of the fallen regime of Ceausescu! It all sounds eerily like Easterman's *Judas Testament*, only for real!

the stunt in Genesis 6:1–4, perhaps the inventors of some sort of metaphysical Viagra?)

In *The Judas Testament*, we see again the notorious (though not implausible) theory of Jesus having been a Qumran monk, an Essene sectarian. This scholarly position was at least superficially strengthened by the discovery in 1947 of the Dead Sea Scrolls, many of which employ characteristic New Testament terminology and attest organizational similarities with the early Jerusalem church in the Book of Acts.

Easterman tantalizes us with this identification of the High Priest Joseph Caiaphas as Jesus' cousin (p. 120). He lets it drop, but one wonders what he might have done with the possibility that suddenly suggests itself: what if Joseph Caiaphas and Joseph of Arimathea (a member of the Sanhedrin, too!) were originally the same person? The Grail legends made Joseph of Arimathea Jesus' uncle, that link itself suggesting a prior mutation of a hypothetical earlier version of the story in which "Joseph of Arimathea" had been none other than Joseph the carpenter, Jesus' father. As Dennis R. MacDonald points out, Joseph of Arimathea begging the body of the slain Jesus from the Roman hegemon Pontius Pilate suggests a parallel with Homer's *Iliad* in which King Priam of Troy comes hat in hand to Achilles, begging the body of his slain son Hector.[2] Robert Eisenman[3] shows a pattern in early Christian documents whereby figures once said to have been immediate relatives of Jesus (his brothers, parents) are distanced by one remove (as cousins, uncles and aunts) in order to distance Jesus (or Mary) from any hint of flesh-and-blood relations, an implicitly docetist theological tendency that is preserved in the doctrines of the Immaculate Conception and Perpetual Virginity of Mary. Joseph the carpenter becomes Joseph of Arimathea. John the Baptist, originally one of the brothers of Jesus, becomes instead his cousin (Luke's nativity story in Luke 1–2). As in Roman Catholic doctrine, the brothers and sisters of Jesus (Mark 6:3) become his cousins,[4] his mother Mary cloned as her own sister, also named Mary(!), with "her" sons becoming Jesus' cousins (Mark 15:47–16:1; Luke 24:10).

The letter continues:

---

2. MacDonald, *The Homeric Epics and the Gospel of Mark*, 154–55.
3. Eisenman, *James the Brother of Jesus*, 8–9 and frequently thereafter.
4. McHugh, "The Brothers of Jesus," 223–33.

> In your gracious letter you ask me to explain all that is fit to be known about myself. Who I consider myself to be and how I came to be known here as the Teacher of Righteousness. (p. 120)

Here see John 1:19–25,

> And this was the witness of John when the Jews sent to him from Jerusalem priests and Levites to ask him, "You are ... who?" And he confessed and did not deny, and he confessed, "It is not I who am the Christ." And they asked, "Then what? Are you Elijah returned?" And he says, "I am not." "Are you the Prophet like Moses?" And he answered, "No." Therefore they said to him, "Who are you? That we may give some answer to those who sent us! What do you say about yourself?" He said, "I am 'a voice of one crying out in the desert: "Straighten out the road of Adonai"', as Isaiah the prophet said." And some of those sent belonged to the Pharisee sect. And they asked him and said to him, "Then what is the point of your baptism, if you are neither the Christ nor Elijah nor the Prophet?"[5]

In Easterman's version of events, Jesus goes on to oblige us with a brief resume: "Of my family you are well informed," which of course means he is spilling the beans for our sake, not Caiaphas.' "You knew my uncle Judas" (p. 121). As Easterman tells us, this must be Judas the Galilean who led an armed revolt against Roman taxation in 6 CE, ending in the crucifixion of the man and his followers—a Jewish Spartacus. He will prove to be more than a mere physical forebear of Jesus. Just as the famous hero Judah Maccabee (Judas Maccabeus) gave rise to a succession—first of his brothers, then their heirs—in the struggle against the pagan Seleucids, so Judas the Galilean (or the Gaulonite) established a kind of informal "dynasty" of revolutionaries and rebel kings, including the would-be messiah Menahem. They were called "Zealots," and Josephus calls them "the fourth philosophy" alongside Pharisees, Sadducees, and Essenes. There was some overlap between Zealots, Essenes, even with early "Jewish Christians" like the Nazarenes, as Eisenman argues,[6] and Easterman presupposes that overlap here. His Jesus was a "zealot for the Torah" (Acts 21:20; cf. Matt 5:17–19). Piously biding his time till the great shift of the ages, Jesus would have only been awaiting the proper moment to take up the sword to banish the enemies

---

5. Price, *The Pre-Nicene New Testament*, 670.
6. Eisenman, "Maccabees, Zadokites, Christians and Qumran," 3–110.

of God and Israel, precisely as envisioned in the Dead Sea Scroll *The War of the Sons of Light against the Sons of Darkness*. Easterman naturally anticipates that such a picture of Jesus would scandalize the Christian faithful of today, who are used to stained glass depictions of Jesus as a gentle shepherd and posters of Jesus helping little kids with their softball bats and paper airplanes. But should the image of a sword-swinging, ass-kicking Jesus surprise anyone who has read Revelation 19:11–16?

> Next I saw the sky opened, and behold! A white stallion! And its rider was called the Faithful One and the True One, and he both judges and wages war righteously. And his eyes glow like coals of fire, and on his head are many concentric diadems, with a name inscribed there unknown to any but himself. And he was wearing a garment soaked in blood, and his name has been called The Word of God. And the celestial armies followed him on white chargers, dressed in fine linen, white and clean. And a sharp sword emerges from his mouth to cut down the armies of the nations. These he will shepherd with a crook of iron! And he tramples the grapes in the winepress of the raging fury of God the Omnipotent. And he has, embroidered on his robe and branded on his thigh, a name: "King of Kings and Lord of Lords."[7]

Easterman makes Jesus no mere Essene, but the Teacher of Righteousness himself. This is the title of the "New Moses" figure whose leadership of the sect set it on a new path of mystical scriptural exegesis. Traditionally, scholars had placed this figure (whose personal name was never vouchsafed in any Qumran text) in the first century BCE, but there have always been alternative datings[8] and guesses nominating John the Baptist or James the Just as the Teacher of Righteousness, and a very few have suggested Jesus as the secret identity of the Teacher. It is obvious which theory Easterman prefers (at least in terms of literary potential).

As to theme, the letter of Jesus to Caiaphas urges reconciliation between the priestly establishment and the legalistic fundamentalism of Jesus, an Essene sectarian. Together they could form an irresistible phalanx against the pagan Romans (p. 124). Obviously, in hindsight, it did not work. Caiaphas must not have been persuaded. He must have reluctantly "dealt with" Jesus, following the disastrous "cleansing of the temple," so as to reassure Rome of official Jewish loyalty. Forty

---

7. Price, 780–81.
8. E.g., Thiering, *Redating the Teacher of Righteousness*.

years later, popular revolutionaries would turn on the corrupt and collaborating priestly aristocracy and put them to the sword, precipitating the Jewish War with Rome in 68–73 CE, issuing in more crosses, more echoes of Judas the Galilean, history repeating itself. The implied intrigue among the various Jewish factions in Jesus' day foreshadows protagonist Jack Gould bouncing back and forth like a ping pong ball through the course of the novel, falling into the sincere yet brutal hands of one party after another.

The red-hot Jesus text had been discovered among the manuscript treasures of persecuted Jews during World War II and shipped, by hook and by crook, to the Lenin Museum in Russia. Its value as a trump card had always been obvious to the very few who knew of its existence. Now the opportune time seemed to have arrived, and various interests have taken a hand in securing or else destroying the Letter of Jesus. One can imagine, as Easterman does, the position of the Roman Catholic establishment. In a clandestine meeting of his top-level brethren, Cardinal Pierluigi Sabbatucci (of the Sacred Congregation for the Doctrine of the Faith, aka the Holy Office, aka the Inquisition) warns:

> It will serve only to give succor to the Judaizers who seek to make sacred history a battleground for their sordid disputes. I refer, of course, to those scholars,—and, I regret to say, there are not a few of them within the church—who maintain that our Savior was nothing more than a Jewish teacher, a Galilean rabbi, a political extremist, an Essene—whatever strikes their fancy. (p. 387)

The Prefect of the Sacred Congregation (remember, his predecessors would have held the title Grand Inquisitor) is Cardinal Vicenzo Bottecchiari, and it is he who called the meeting at which these opinions are shared. Incidentally, in order to gauge this character's great power, Easterman notes that Cardinal Bottecchiari is universally considered the best bet to replace the ailing Pope John Paul. Bottecchiari is, of course, Easterman's fictive analog to Cardinal Joseph Ratzinger, who was at the time of writing the head of the Sacred Congregation/Inquisition, and who did in fact succeed John Paul II some years later!

Who are the Trojan Horsemen within the Catholic Church whose wild-eyed books on Jesus so scandalize these conservative prelates? Surely in view is ex-priest John Dominic Crossan.[9] Easterman specifi-

---

9. Crossan, *The Historical Jesus*.

cally names Hans Küng[10] and Edward Schillebeeckx,[11] and Leonardo Boff,[12] a Brazilian pioneer of Latin American Liberation Theology and anti-Western fanatic. Easterman errs when he informs us that the whole movement derived its name from an early book by Boff which advocated the spreading of a Marxism-informed gospel among the poor of Peru. He is thinking of Gustavo Gutierrez,[13] a Peruvian priest and theologian whose book *A Theology of Liberation* (1971) may be said to have set the whole bonfire ablaze.

The tirade of the fictive Cardinal Sabbatucci (minus the suggestion to destroy the scroll!) reminds one of the party-line defensive posture of Luke Timothy Johnson[14] and even more of the harrumphing C. S. Lewis, in a snit at the effrontery of biblical critics who might dare to shoulder aside, a la Sisyphus, the burden of "received" opinion on the historical Jesus. Under Lewis's fictive persona of the devilish Uncle Screwtape, he writes:

> You will find that a good many Christian-political writers think that Christianity began going wrong, and departing from the doctrine of its Founder, at a very early stage. Now, this idea must be used by us [i.e., the demons of hell] to encourage once again the conception of a "historical Jesus" to be found by clearing away later "accretions and perversions"... In the last generation we promoted the construction of such a "historical Jesus" along liberal and humanitarian lines; we are now putting forward a new "historical Jesus" on Marxian, catastrophic, and revolutionary lines. [But in fact] each "historical Jesus" is unhistorical. The documents say what they say and cannot be added to; each new "historical Jesus" therefore has to be got out of them by suppression at one point and exaggeration at another, and by that sort of guessing (*brilliant* is the adjective we teach humans to apply to it) on which no one would risk ten shillings in ordinary life.[15]

Despite his reputation as the archetypical Oxford don, C. S. Lewis reveals himself in his writings to possess not the least inkling (if you'll

10. Küng, *On Being a Christian*.
11. Schillebeeckx, *Jesus: An Experiment in Christology* and *Christ: The Experience of Jesus as Lord*.
12. Boff, *Jesus Christ Liberator*.
13. Gutiérrez, *A Theology of Liberation*.
14. Johnson, *The Real Jesus*.
15. Lewis, *The Screwtape Letters*, 106–7.

pardon the expression) of what historical method is. The critical historian (of the gospels or anything else) does not merely parrot what his "authorities" tell him, harmonizing contradictions between them when he must. Rather, the critical historian regards his documents as "sources" of data which may or may not reflect what actually happened.[16] The historian knows that the reports of the ancients (and moderns! And postmoderns!) tend already to have suffered suppression, exaggeration, and fabrication.[17] It is never easy to reconstruct what actually happened in the past, nor to attain anything like certainty, as laughable as the absurdity of it may seem to a smug clubman like Lewis.

And yet, if something like the *Judas Testament*, the *Jesus Scroll*, were to come to light, would the damage to the Church, to traditional Christianity, really be so great? We are, after all, talking about an institution with two thousand years of experience in damage control. Listen to how Easterman's Jack Gould puts it: "Whatever the scroll says, the churches will make their own Jesus, a whole tribe of him to suit their own prejudices. They'll find ways of twisting everything he ever said to fit what they already believe" (p. 462). So it cuts both ways. Traditionalists insist that revisionists are merely writing up Jesus-figments from their own corrupt imaginations, trying to obscure what ought to be clear: the gospel truth. But revisionists, i.e., critical historians, understand the Church to be equally capable of fictionalizing evidence, spinning it toward a desired end. Assembling the story told by various biblical references (citations to which I have provided in brackets), Jack reflects upon why it is that the Jesus letter rings true, despite its seeming contradiction of any familiar version of the Christian story:

> If the letter was indeed genuine, . . . it would confirm the theories of many historians[18] and explain much that was otherwise inexplicable in the Gospels. How, other than by the use of force, could the meek and mild Jesus and a mere handful of followers have entered the Temple, expelled the money-changers [Mark 11:15–19], whose operations amounted to those of a national bank [Mark 12:13–17], remained in the building for several days

16. Collingwood, *The Idea of History*.

17. Lewis, *History: Remembered, Recovered, Invented*.

18. For example, Eisler, *The Messiah Jesus and John the Baptist*; Brandon, *The Fall of Jerusalem and the Christian Church*; Brandon, *Jesus and the Zealots*; Maccoby, *Revolution in Judea*; Segundo, *The Historical Jesus of the Synoptics*; Eisenman, *James the Brother of Jesus*.

[Luke 19:47–48], and then left unharmed? The Temple had been a vast complex with a staff of twenty thousand, protected by its own police guard [Luke 22:52–53] and the nearby Roman garrison of Jerusalem of five hundred to six hundred men. Why Jesus numbered at least one Zealot—Simon [Mark 3:18, *ton kananaion*, from the Hebrew *qana*, "the zealous"]—among his close followers; why had he told them to sell their cloaks to buy swords [Luke 22:36], and declared that he had come not to bring peace but to bring a sword [Matt. 10:34]; why had Peter and, it appeared, the rest of the disciples gathered in the Garden of Gethsemane been armed [Luke 22:49; Mark 14:47]; and above all, why had Jesus been put to death not on a charge of blasphemy but for sedition against the imperial power of Rome [Luke 23:2; Mark 15:9, 12, 18, 26]? (pp. 124–25)

When Cardinal Sabbatucci speaks of "Judaizers" within and without the Church, he may have reference to two schools of thought. Nowadays, in order to heal the terrible breach between Judaism and Christianity, occasioned by long centuries of Christian persecution, many Christian theologians are eager to reconstruct a "historical Jesus" who was a Jew, not a Christian. Such a picture of a yarmulke-sporting Jesus poses no real threat even to conservative Christian theology. One can always claim that the Christian dispensation, with its laying aside of the Torah stipulations, began only as of Easter or Pentecost, after the death of Jesus to atone for humanity's failure to live up to Moses' requirements. Jesus would then be seen, a la Bultmann, even by traditionalists, as a presupposition for New Testament theology, not one of the voices within it.[19]

But the Cardinal more likely means to hiss at people like Robert Eisenman who takes a strictly historical approach rather than an apologetical-theological one. Eisenman measures the chasm between genuine Judaism as we know it from the New Testament period and the ostensible "messianism" on display in the Christian gospels, and the gap is wide indeed. Imagine, Eisenman bids us, a Jewish messiah who welcomes Jewish quisling tax collectors and Roman centurions, who counsels obedience to Rome and placid payment of Roman taxes, one indifferent to kosher laws and the niceties of Torah observance! One who is totally irrelevant politically and warns against the "error" of taking up the sword against the pagan oppressor. Is this not a thoroughly domesticated, Romanized piece of propaganda, having utterly subverted an originally zealous mes-

---

19. Bultmann, *Theology of the New Testament*, Vol. 1, 3.

sianic Revitalization movement? It surely looks like the product of efforts to bury the movement's revolutionary past, to render the Jesus figure a harmless "personal savior," and to re-channel the whole thing into one more half-pagan mystery cult, like that of Sabazius. Christianity has busied itself with turning into the very Hellenistic syncretism that Judah Maccabee died fighting against. When Pauline Christianity triumphed, so did Antiochus Epiphanes. To reveal this is the danger of the Jesus Scroll. No wonder old-school Catholics want to suppress the thing.

To the right of the establishment Catholics is a secret power-elite called the Crux Orientalis, surviving from the 1940s, made of German, Croat, Austrian, Polish, and other Catholics of a Mesozoic coloring. They are anti-Semites once allied with Hitler's Reich and now eager to stamp out modern, liberal decadence (and Communism) in a new Catholic pan-European confederation, a new Holy Roman Empire. While the contents of the Jesus Scroll would seem to hold little of value to them, the threat it poses to Catholic dogma (presumably including their own!) makes the scroll useful to the Crux Orientalis as a weapon with which to intimidate the Vatican into backing their program. Disclaiming any of the old anti-Semitism (with fingers "cruxed" behind their backs), they look back with wistful longing to the days of *der Führer*, himself a Catholic, and whom they believe literally smiles down upon their efforts from Himmel (or Himmler) above. But would these Paleolithic papists really be so indifferent to a gospel revealing Jesus as "that Jew," as Adolf referred to him? It implies a radical "Christ of faith versus Jesus of history" dichotomy where the facts just don't matter. Worse yet, Easterman has them planning a shrine to be built around the Jesus letter in John Paul's native Poland, where the faithful might flock, seeking healing and renewal. And this implies a similar disjunction: the mere fact of Jesus Christ as author would drown out the actual content of the letter.

But then there is a third faction of gospel-toting gunmen, the Maximilian Kolbe Society. Named for a priest who died trying to save Jews in the Holocaust, this is a group of liberal priests open to Liberation Theology and willing to use the weapons of the world against it. Our hero Jack Gould is finally reluctant to trust them either. Sure, they are self-styled champions of the poor, but then who appointed them? It wouldn't be the first time that the vanguard of the proletariat turned out to be the car-jackers of the proletariat. The Kolbe Society wants to make the new gospel public; it will present a radical Jesus more in agreement with their own instincts. But why? They certainly do not mean to support radical Jewish nationalism a la Maier Kahane? There is a gross inconsistency here, but it is not necessarily author Easterman's doing. Remember Leonardo Boff, champion of Liberation Theology? How odd to hear him defending the Islamo-fascist savages of 9-11 as precursors of a new humanism!

> For me the terrorist attack of September 11 represents the shift towards a new humanitarian and world model. The targeted buildings sent a message: a new world civilization cannot be built with the kind of dominating economy (symbolized by the World Trade Center), with the kind of death machine set up (the Pentagon) and with the kind of arrogant politics and producer of many exclusions (...) For me the system and culture of capital began to collapse. They are too destructive.[20]

Apparently, for some radicals, political power emerges, like the sword of his mouth (Rev 19:15), from the barrel of a gun, and it doesn't much matter what the politics are, as long as they do come from that gun.

Dr. Gould is more of a reactive than a proactive character, but he is pretty clever, as clever as the narrative needs him to be as a source of timely surprises for the reader. In the end, once the plots of international schemers are knocked off course, the lovers are reunited, and the major villains are safely in their graves, Gould takes the Jesus papyrus, stashes it in a period-piece clay jar, and reburies it at Qumran, where he plans to "discover" it a year or so later on a legitimate archaeological dig. Then, presumably, he can offer it to the public with no strings attached. So, once again, as in so many of these Lost Gospel novels, the climactic explosion is deferred, and we are left guessing how great the impact of public revelation might be. But that's a good thing, from one vantage point at least: it throws the ball back into the reader's court. It leaves the reader to ask and answer the question, at least for himself.

---

20. Boff interviewed on the site "Comunità Italiana" in November 2001.

23 | Messiah's Memoir
Alan Gold, *The Last Testament*

"A MANUSCRIPT IN THE HANDWRITING OF JESUS!"[1]

THIS NOVEL[2] BEARS A few notable but incidental similarities to Daniel Easterman's *The Judas Testament*, but as soon as we locate the matching coordinates, we find ourselves moving in different directions from them. For instance, Easterman's bookish anti-hero Jack Gould was half-Jewish, half-Catholic, with neither side of his heritage defining him. Alan Gold's protagonist, Michael Farber, is also an expert on ancient Semitic manuscripts. He is a Jew turned Catholic, with both faiths struggling within him, neither a perfect fit. Both men come to learn of a newly discovered document, the *Jesus Testament* (a better title for Easterman's manuscript than the one he uses for it, if you ask me). Both reveal the historical Jesus to have been an Essene monk, though for Easterman Jesus was the Teacher of Righteousness himself, whereas for Gold he is a humble brother who receives visions from his Father to leave the order to spread their word (at least a basic ethical version of it, no doubt dropping all the in-house monastic strictures). Easterman cast the Essene Jesus as a rebel against Rome, biding his time against the day he and his brethren should join the descending angels to slay Romans and Jewish apostates. Not so Gold's Essene Jesus, who thinks the militant Essenes quite mistaken. He sees in history the futile treadmill of one

---

1. Mundy, *Ramsden* (or *The Devil's Guard*), 25. The adventurer James Schuyler Grim ("Jimgrim") leads his amazing crew on an expedition to forbidden Shambhala, where many hidden wonders, including this Jesus text, are rumored to lie deposited. He probably got the idea from Nicholas Notovitch's *The Unknown Life of Christ* (1894) in which Russian spy Notovitch claimed to have gained entry into the Tibetan monastery at Himis, where he found a manuscript recording Jesus' sojourn in Tibet, all an elaborate hoax. See Goodspeed, *Famous Biblical Hoaxes*, 3–14. Actually, that is the last we hear, in Mundy's novel, of the Jesus manuscript. No one so much as mentions it again.

2. All page references are to the 1996 edition.

empire replacing its predecessor on the chessboard, then in the dustbin. Only words of righteousness and peace can change men's hearts, and only changed hearts can improve the world. So his Father has told him (p. 87).

> I, Jesus, son of Joseph, of the generations of David and Aaron, born of Beit Lehem and who grew to manhood among the desert People of the Book, have looked with sadness through the eyes of my Father, Yahweh, into the land of the world to come, and I have seen and understood many things. (p. 86)

Interestingly, both books posit that Matthew's Wise Men ("Magi") who greeted Jesus' birth with exotic gifts were from much closer to home. For Gold (at least for his Michael Farber character), the Wise Men were not Parthian astrologers (as most scholars think), but Essene monks, albeit ultimately stemming from India (whatever that means: Indian Essenes, Essenes as descended from Hindus?) (p. 32). For Easterman, as we have seen, they were agents of the High Priest Caiaphas.

How did there come to be a *Testament of Jesus*? For Easterman, it was a letter by Jesus explaining his "no cooperation" policy with the Romans and urging preparation for an armed revolt. In writing such a testament, Easterman's Jesus was, of course, signing his own death warrant. The situation is quite different in Gold's book. He invents the idea that the Qumran monks each were allowed a kind of "vision quest," a day off from monastic duties to go into the surrounding desert and collect one's thoughts. These were to be written down on a scroll, then brought to a supervisor (that's what "bishop" means) and placed in a holding file. After its message had been read and considered for many years, it might make it to the next stage, being stored among the testaments of those considered luminaries with enough to say to merit the trouble of copying and passing down to future generations. Jesus shows up and hands in his scroll as if it were an exam booklet, insisting that it be immediately placed among the "greatest hits" section. Affronted at the seeming audacity, the Essene elder is unwilling to accede. Jesus leaves the matter to him and turns around to begin his mission to a wider world (a la Barbara Thiering's *Jesus the Man*[3] or Nikos Kazantzakis's *The Last Temptation of Christ*). Left holding the scroll, the puzzled Qumran elder, in a moment

---

3. Thiering, *Jesus the Man*.

of inexplicable inspiration, leap-frogs much farther than Jesus had suggested, placing his testament among the scriptures themselves!

Barbara Thiering can be glimpsed behind Gold's character Meg Thornton, a departmental rival of Michael's, a friendly nemesis whose theories are even more unconventional than Michael's own. Thornton tells him she is sure the *Jesus Testament*, once brought to light, will vindicate her pet hypotheses. But Michael does not agree: "It's historical proof of His existence. But not proof that He was married. And certainly not that He spent the rest of His life after His trial disguised as St Paul, dying by crucifixion in Rome" (p. 15). This reads like a summary of a few of Thiering's signal points, though she does not identify Paul with Jesus, something Lena Einhorn does in her *The Jesus Mystery: Astonishing Clues to the True Identities of Jesus and Paul*.[4] Thiering employed esoteric Essene exegesis techniques to formulate her theories; nothing is said of the fictive Meg Thornton using such methods, but Michael Farber is described as a practitioner. Gold speaks of "his interpretation of a secret code which he had discovered in one of the Dead Sea Scroll fragments" (p. 32). Thus the two effectively divide the Barbara Thiering role between them. Keep in mind, too, that Dr. Thiering lives and works in Australia, just like her imaginary colleagues Farber and Thornton. This novel was first published there, so we need not doubt author Gold expected his readers to know whom he was talking (joking) about.

There are other editorial or satirical pokes in the novel. Cardinal Ratzinger (now Pope Benedict XVI) appears as Cardinal Kitzinger, as if to combine Ratzinger with the diplomatic seniority and savvy of Henry Kissinger. He is the embodiment of old-school institutional inertia. Kitzinger tries his best to dissuade the "young" (a bit over 60) American Pope Innocent not to go ahead with his planned "Crusade" (my, how jittery that word makes everybody but Billy Graham!)[5] to find and publish

---

4. Einhorn, *The Jesus Mystery*.

5. I once had a couple of well-meaning ignoramuses urge me not to call a discussion group "The Grail" for fear of offending theoretical Muslims (a major bogeyman these days, even more prevalent than real, living Muslims). Huh? These ladies also believed the Great Pyramid was an air traffic control tower for incoming flying saucers. One of them was a reporter for the upper crust town newspaper. They thought the Arthurian Grail legend had something to do with the medieval Crusades and figured others would be just as ill-informed. Too bad, I said (though not in so many words), and I still say it. If it comes to the point where, so as not to confuse the general readership, we have to adopt their pathetic standard of discourse, well, then, to hell with it.

the *Testament of Jesus*. Even though everyone is excited, the text itself remains missing. What has come to light is a mere listing of its title in an ancient document.

At this point Gold permits himself a bit of conspiracy theorizing. In his narrative universe, the Dead Sea Scrolls were carefully "safeguarded" by an all-Catholic committee of scholars who deemed the world not yet ready for the full message of the Scrolls. In fact, Ratzinger—er, I mean, Kitzinger—tells Pope Innocent (innocent, till this point, of such matters, much like the clueless U.S. President in *Independence Day* who is in for a big surprise once he gets to Area 51):

> [B]efore the International Team publishes anything, it discusses what is about to be published with the Congregation [for the Doctrine of the Faith—which the real Cardinal Ratzinger headed up before he became Pope] to determine how the publication of the Dead Sea Scrolls and the other documents found at Qumran and Masada accord with the orthodoxy of the Catholic faith. (p. 209)

The pope is stunned. "Outraged" might be the better word. How dare they? Why not simply take the risk of faith and assume that new "revelations" will only confirm a true faith? And since all of these men supposedly do believe that Catholic Christianity *is* the truth, what is there to be afraid of? Underlying the pope's courage is the implicit admission that, if the *Testament* somehow debunks Christianity, it would be better to know it, and to be done with the whole thing. "Christians believe implicitly in the accuracy of the . . . Gospels. But if we discover His Testament and it proves them wrong, if it denies the Gospels' claims to His status as Messiah, then where will Christianity be?" (p. 113).

Implicit in the opposition by Kitzinger and his brethren is a cynical indifference: Christianity to them is not a truth claim but merely institutional policy that they are committed to uphold, come hell or high water, and they're hell-bent that the gates of hell shall not prevail against it.

Gold was writing when the International Committee stranglehold on the Scrolls had just been broken by Robert Eisenman and others, a bit of history we were introduced to when reviewing Peter Hernon's *Earthly Remains*. For decades, the International Team, all Catholics, yet initially appointed by Israeli authorities, had sat on fully a quarter of the catalogued material, like the proverbial dog in the manger, neither publishing anything nor allowing anyone else to publish—or even to glimpse—the rest of the documents. As time dragged on, the elite did recruit favorite grad students, each bequeathing his share of the Scrolls to his successor. This counts as a conspiracy of some kind; it is only a question of motive. Though it had been ecumenically impolite to say so, it had been by no means extravagant to wonder if the Catholic authorities had in fact been trying to suppress something very inconvenient to them.[6] But, as it turned out, the trouble had all along been the worst kind of "professionalism." The scholars placed in charge of the Scrolls had at a single blow become the world experts on some very intriguing material, and they wanted to keep it that way. Mirroring the pre-Vatican II attitude toward the Bible, the Scrolls team seemed to feel that no one else could be trusted to read the texts rightly.

As I pointed out in the *Earthly Remains* review of chapter 17, the team wanted to keep the material under wraps so they might say the last word on the subject before anybody else had the chance to say his first, but the publication of little-known photocopies of the Scrolls in the Huntington Library in Santa Barbara[7] made the secrecy moot. And it showed that there had been nothing especially startling in the last batch of Scrolls. Yet with the opening of the Scrolls to wider scholarly scrutiny, some old interpretations of them began to reemerge in a distinctly non-Catholic direction. Barbara Thiering revived the old notion of Jesus as an Essene. Robert Eisenman mounted an elaborate case that the Dead Sea Scrolls were the writings of the Jerusalem Christians of James the Just, a view suggested decades earlier by Jacob L. Teicher.[8] According to Thiering, the mysterious Teacher of Righteousness must have been John the Baptist. Eisenman opted for James the Just in the role. These theories (especially Eisenman's, to my way of thinking) are very powerful readings of the evidence, challenging the conventional interpretations given the Scrolls by the Catholic-dominated Committee, the International Team.

---

6. Baigent and Leigh, *The Dead Sea Scrolls Deception*.

7. "The biblical community is baying for the blood of the International Team, and since the publications by the Huntingdon [sic] Library in California, there's intense speculation about what else you have hidden up your sleeves." So quips Kitzinger, but in fact the Huntington copies exhausted the secret stash of the International Team and put an end to the speculation.

8. He wrote a series of articles, sadly never compiled as a book, in the *Journal of Jewish Studies*; see the list in Price, *Deconstructing Jesus*, 72 n. 24.

Father Roland de Veaux (appearing as Father Romain de la Tour in the novel) and company interpreted the Scrolls in a manner compatible with a traditional orthodox reading of the New Testament and then pivoted about to claim, unsurprisingly, that the Scrolls only showed how authentically Jewish the gospels were. Thus one could discard those critical theories that derived early Christianity from exotic entities like Gnosticism and the Hellenistic Mystery Religions and hero cults. That is, the Scrolls were interpreted in a Catholic-friendly manner, much as Gold suggests, though it is perhaps going too far to say that the actual translations were manipulated. Even outright manipulation would not really matter, given the heavily symbolic, cipher quality of the texts. It is a question of decoding them in any case. The question becomes: which interpretation seems most effective in fitting the Scrolls into any known religio-historical context?

It remains humorous today to read mainstream Dead Sea Scroll scholars, both Catholic and Protestant, selectively welcoming similarities between the Scrolls and books of the New Testament canon. They welcome the similarity of phraseology between the Gospel of John and the Qumran *Hymns*, as if this proved that John had a Jewish, not a Gnostic, provenance. But they turn on their heels when it comes to the similarities between the depiction of the Jerusalem Church in Acts and the communal monasticism of the Scrolls, which has suggested to so many that the two movements were one and the same. "Oh, no!" says the judicious voice of orthodoxy: "Thus far and no further!" It's like the Cherub whipping his sword about to guard the Tree of Life. Alan Gold is basically right, then: the "official" Scrolls Magisterium (not coincidentally, all Roman Catholics) did succeed in locking into place a reading of the Qumran texts that would domesticate them for Christian apologetics. Only recently has that glacier showed signs of melting.

IS THE GOSPEL THAT JESUS EXISTED AT ALL?

Let us recap where we are in Gold's tale: in the twentieth century, the existence of the *Jesus Testament* has become known far in advance of anyone getting a look at it. What surfaces first is a Dead Sea Scroll, modeled on the famous *Copper Scroll*, which was a list of buried treasures with enigmatic directions where to find them. Only these were paper treasures rather than the silver and gold (never found) of the *Copper Scroll*. One of these titles proves to be "the Testament of Jeshua the Nazarene."

Even without anyone setting eyes on the *Testament* itself, the very existence of such a scroll is enough to excite millions: even such a one-liner revelation as this, if nothing more were to come to light, would seem to be enough to secure the existence of Jesus as an historical figure.

And that poses an especially interesting aspect of many Lost Gospel novels. Today's neo-traditionalist "mainstream" biblical scholars smugly dismiss the Christ Myth theory as a discredited piece of lunatic fringe thought alongside Holocaust Denial and skepticism about the Apollo moon landings. An earlier generation of scholars admitted there was at least a serious point to debate, and it seems that a lingering doubt has never vanished among the general public, who hear all their lives of both Santa Claus and Jesus Christ, one of whom visits every child's home, world wide, in a single night, and the other (equally invisible to prying mortal eyes) who interacts with his millions of clients simultaneously in a "personal relationship" with each one. These novels reckon with that continuing (because inevitable) popular skepticism.

Gold's character Ari Wallenstein puts it in acutely revealing terms: the vindication of Christian faith would be the confirmation of the mere existence of Jesus—as if that is all Christian faith is supposed to be! But that may be what it has necessarily become after two millennia have passed, with so much water under the bridge that one can no longer simply take for granted the historical existence of the savior. New Testament faith is necessarily distorted by the historical position of Christians today. The issue of Jesus' historical existence has, in Bultmann's terms, become a false stumbling block to modern man's acceptance of the gospel.[9] In plain terms: that wasn't supposed to be the issue. As long as everyone could assume there was a historical Jesus (whether there had been one or not), one had to face the existential decision: what do I *do* with Jesus Christ?

It had very nearly come to this in Bultmann's day, from the 1940s up to his death in 1974. Bultmann observed that modern persons, imbued with science, cannot consistently live as though they really believed in the supernatural. It is such modernization and secularization through science and technology that militant Islam fears, the other side of the same coin. Only instead of turning back the cognitive clock, as Islamists want to do, Bultmann pressed for a consistently modern Christianity that would slough off belief in miracles. Moderns, when asked to consider

---

9. Bultmann, *Jesus Christ and Mythology*, 36.

the Christian gospel and the challenge it issues to selfish complacency (the real issue, taking up the cross of Jesus), will never even get that far if they believe an intellectual sacrifice is the price of admission. It shouldn't be. Miracles and the supernatural have become a false stumbling block, needlessly keeping people from the gospel.

And if one pauses at the prior question, "Did this Jesus even *exist*?" one is automatically placed at a much farther distance from the real, existential question. The less certain the prospect of an historical Jesus, the farther from the existential issue one gets. Put it this way: what would the proof that Jesus had lived get you? How far would it take you? Suppose the standard picture is basically right: Jesus existed and was a controversial figure. It is clear that mere temporal and spatial proximity did not guarantee faith. "The demons believe, too—and shudder!" (Jas 2:19).[10] Caiaphas, Pilate, and Judas harbored no doubt that Jesus existed—but this did not make them Christians. Ari says Christian faith would be vindicated with proof that Jesus had merely existed. Well, maybe not. But it might be the first step back. It might accomplish what Francis A. Schaeffer called "pre-evangelism," making it possible for one's culture to believe again.

But our boy Michael is considerably more optimistic than that. The likely results of the discovery? He envisions "the end of religious uncertainty, the ultimate fusion of Judaism with Catholicism, the end to the heresy of England and the Protestant experiment. All these things could now happen if Christ's Testament were found" (pp. 16–17). Down boy! Others imagine that the discovery would usher in the Second Coming of Christ. "Lead[ing] writers extolled the unearthing of the Testament as a precursor to the end of the second thousand Christian years" (p. 110). "Many were saying that it was a precursor to the Parousia, a herald to Christ's reappearance on earth" (p. 144).

We are forced to ask if the mere listing of a Dead Sea Scroll called "*The Testament of Jesus*" would be sufficient to anchor his historical existence. The title marks such a text as a member of a universally pseudepigraphical (pseudonymous) genre. We possess from Qumran and other similar venues plenty of these "Testaments," one and all of them fakes and forgeries, their authors hiding behind the authoritative names of ancient seers and saints in order to secure the clout that such a writing, circulating under the actual author's name, would likely not

---

10. Price, *The Pre-Nicene New Testament*, 879.

deserve. That is why we have *The Testaments the Twelve Patriarchs*, *The Testament of Moses*, *The Testament of Job*, *The Testament of Jacob*, *The Testament of Solomon*, etc. A self-titled "*Testament of Jesus*" would almost automatically be ruled out as a fake. And that would mean that the eponymous "Jesus the Nazarene" must have been an earlier, much renowned character already in the period of the Dead Sea Scrolls. Such a strange fact would comport best with the Christ Myth theory, implying that Jesus was a mythical, a symbolic, or a literary character who kept getting moved up into more and more recent history. An example of that is the mythic Canaanite sage Dan'el, who is still referred to as an ancient figure in the Exilic Book of Ezekiel (14:14, 20; 28:3) but is later updated to become a young Hebrew hero and younger contemporary of Ezekiel! To his credit, Cardinal Kitzinger is astute enough to realize this, warning an over-enthusiastic colleague: "How do we know that the Testament was written by Christ Himself? It may be a pseudepigraph, or palimpsest" (p. 331).[11]

Gold briefly raises the profound question we discussed in connection with one of the first of our fictions, *The Lost Gospel* by Arthur Train, and Robert F. Luccock's sermon upon it. Doesn't the eagerness for a new gospel reflect rather badly on the value of the familiar ones? Gold's Cardinal Daniel Rhymer asks the pope, "Aren't Matthew, Mark, Luke and John enough any more? Is that why you want to find Christ's Testament?" (p. 215). Pope Innocent's answer: "To bring them back, to reestablish their faith, we have to give them something new. New hope, new certainties" (Ibid.). "Here was a Testament which would cement the connective tissue between [modern Christians] themselves and their Messiah previously only found in the observations of Matthew, Mark, Luke and John" (p. 21). But there is a simpler answer: if four gospels are very, very good, a fifth gospel can only be that much better.

MAPPING EARLY CHRISTIANITY

It is always interesting to examine the picture each Lost Gospel novel traces of early Christianity. We have seen how several of our novels flirt with the old but still quite viable Tübingen model of an early ri-

---

11. Actually, a palimpsest is just a manuscript with a second text written over a first text that was washed off so the sheet could be reused. Sometimes the underlying text is still discernible, especially with today's technology. It is not clear what difference this would make. But it sounds pretty impressive.

valry between Jewish Torah-Christianity and Gentile/Hellenistic-Jewish Christianity. Alan Gold does not go in that direction, at least neither explicitly nor in detail. He makes Paul/Saul of Tarsus into a member of the Jewish Christian Nazarene sect, though in reality he must be counted on the other side of the great chasm, the leader of Torah-free Christianity. The author of the Acts of the Apostles does the same thing with Paul. The Acts author wants to paper over the early division. In Acts 24:5 Paul is called "a ringleader of the sect of the Nazarenes." But then Gold gives us a significant glimpse of the ultimate outcome of the Nazarene-Pauline schism F. C. Baur and his Tübingen colleagues discussed. Pauline Christianity blossomed into Marcionism, the doctrine that the Old and the New Testament deities were not the same. The Hebrew God was the Creator and law-giver, the Lord of his people Israel. But Jesus was the Son of a hitherto-unknown God, one who had not created humanity but took pity upon them and made a bargain with the stern Creator. Jesus' Father would freely adopt all who were willing to jump ship and come over to him. For Marcion, the inane and inept twelve disciples under Peter's clueless leadership could not keep the two religions, Judaism and Christianity, straight. They hopelessly mixed them up, Catholicism being the grotesque result. This is why the resurrected Christ bypassed the original disciples and chose Paul to proclaim the true, Torah-free (i.e., Old Testament-free) gospel instead.

As I say, Gold does not spell out such a theology. But he shows it germinating. Nazarene believer Raphael ben Eliezer asks John of Syracuse (a Gentile who converted him to the Jewish Christian faith—huh?), "But why do we also save the sacred writings of the old Temple? What is this to us? These scrolls are of the Jews. Not of the Nazarenes" (p. 105). John answers:

> "It is on the advice of Timothy of Brindisi. Timothy says that to know where one is going, one must also know whence one has come. Although Jesus Our Lord is the New Way, Timothy says that our converts will be from the Old Way. Your own family, before your baptism, followed the Old Way. In synagogue, you still read and venerate the Testament of Moses. [See Acts 15:21; 16:3.] Those Jews who see the light and come across to us will find comfort in the ancient books of the Temple" (pp. 105–6). Sarah adds, "I will pray to the God of the Jews *Adonai* and to the God of the Christians, Jesus. Between them, they may save you" (p. 107).

ELUSIVE REVELATION

Much of the rather large novel is occupied with a converging set of quests to unearth the *Testament*. Michael and his lover get a lead that the text awaits them among the remaining Falasha Jews in Ethiopia, and they do eventually find it there, but they leave it, deciding to wait until the international and interfaith communities can decide what to do with it. This turns out to be a big mistake, for the pope, who wants to find and publish it, is betrayed by lieutenants working for Cardinal Kitzinger. He winds up with the *Testament* in his possession and decides to keep it where the sun will never shine on it.[12] So in the end we are spared the effects (and author Gold is spared the work of imagining them) entailed upon the publication of a manuscript in Jesus' own handwriting. But this isn't necessarily bad. Why?

Though I cannot imagine that author Alan Gold gave any thought to this point (and no one can blame him), one may nonetheless point out how his plot, finally disappointing the reader's expectation of the publication of a Testament eagerly awaited by a religious world, provides an excellent parable of Jacques Derrida's[13] doctrine of the *continual deferral of the Parousia of the Word*. These New Testament terms historically referred to the long-anticipated arrival on the clouds of the living Word or Logos (Jesus Christ in his Second Coming). Remember, Gold says that some regard the discovery of the *Testament of Jesus* to be the precursor, practically the arrival, of the Parousia of Christ. At that time, we are told, all secrets are to be disclosed, all hitherto-baffling truths finally known and understood. "For now we know but fragments, we prophesy but hints. But whenever the perfect version of a thing appears, the imperfect intimations are cast aside... As yet, we still see the truth distorted, spoken in riddles; then we will see it as Moses did: face to face. For now, my gnosis is but partial; then I shall know as fully as God knows me" (1 Cor 13:9–12).[14] But the Second Advent, the Parousia of Christ, the Word of God, was deferred and deferred again. Dates were set and reset until the prospect faded off into the distant mists of "some day." The Blessed Hope

---

12. A major portion of the novel concerns itself with a wild caricature of a TV preacher who is also on the trail of the document but never gets hold of it because the cops catch up to him for beating his wife to a pulp and castrating her lover—all in good Christian fun. But it is a pointless red herring the size of the fish that swallowed Jonah.

13. Derrida, *Of Grammatology*, 154–55, 158.

14. Price, 357.

faded into a "doctrine of eschatology," and believers began to make the most of the fragments of truth they had: the Bible. They made an idol of it and became duty-bound to pretend it already revealed all the truth one might ask. Yet even then, when occasionally stumped by this or that "difficulty" in scripture, devout believers would defer their desired answer "till we get to heaven." Derrida notes how, in the same way, the very nature of language as uncontrollably indeterminate requires the eternal deferral of the arrival of clear and definitive truth. Each signifier points, not to the Thing Signified, but only to another signifier, then to another, never breaching the great impassible gulf (cf. Luke 16:26!) between signifier and Transcendental Signified (which is to admit that language is always *differential*, ricocheting between synonyms, opposites, parallels, etc., and never simply *referential*, as if one might use words to tag mute objects that require a label. Finally one despairs like Pontius Pilate, muttering ironically, "What is truth?" and turning away to other issues one is likely to have better chances of solving. And this endless, necessary deferral is all we are left with at the end of *The Lost Testament*: it *remains* lost, and the pope and his fans are left impotently praying for it to appear after all, some day, just as Christians have been doing unsuccessfully for two millennia.

24 | The Mother Lode
Barbara Wood, *The Prophetess*

This is our second Lost Gospel novel[1] by Barbara Wood (who is, of course, an accomplished mystery writer). Her first was *The Magdalene Scrolls*, published more than two decades before this one. Not only is this genre, which one might expect to be pretty obscure, seemingly irresistible to some writers, but now it looks as if even those who have once written a Lost Gospel mystery cannot help returning to the scene of the crime! This time out, the protagonist is one Catherine Alexander, a sun-bronzed beauty (what a surprise!) of an archaeologist. She is a woman with a mission, excavating on the eastern shore of the Sinai Peninsula, in hot competition with the bulldozers of a development corporation seeking to terraform the land into a string of resort hotels. Dr. Alexander is on the trail of a half-legendary Well of Miriam of which she has read in a medieval Arab pilgrim's diary.

She has a hunch that Miriam, Moses' sister, was a charismatic prophetess in her own right, exercising equal leadership with her brother. (This novel was written just before the rise of Old Testament minimalism,[2] which made it clear that there was no Moses, no Miriam, no Exodus.) Finding the old well is important to her because of the off chance that it might contain some sort of evidence vindicating that theory. And at length she seems perhaps to have found it and a tunnel connecting it, in ancient times, to its water source. "If I find the well, and proof that Miriam was who I think she was, then there will be an era of fresh, new empowerment from a book that some people are beginning to consider outdated—the Bible" (p. 9). Actually, such a case is already familiar among Old Testament scholars, expressed in the book *Has the Lord*

---

1. All page references are to the Warner Books edition.
2. Thompson, *The Mythic Past*; Coote, *Early Israel*; Lemche, *The Israelites in History and Tradition*; Davies, *In Search of 'Ancient Israel'*; Garbini, *History and Ideology in Ancient Israel*.

Spoken Only through Miriam? A Study of the Biblical Portrait of Miriam by Rita J. Burns.[3]

Like many of the novelists whose works we have already reviewed, Barbara Wood seems to overestimate the degree to which scholarly research would affect popular belief. History has many times proven that such a spark in the darkness is not likely to stir many people from the depths of their dogmatic slumbers. On the other hand, Christian feminists (already true believers in their cause) have derived great inspiration from exactly the sort of "engaged scholarship" that the Catherine Alexander protagonist convincingly represents. "I want to find a way to empower women...[I]n Scripture, women had power in the days of the patriarchs and kings, they were prophetesses and priestesses and wise women. But all that has gotten lost through time and I intend to restore it" (p. 81).

Her original object is soon rendered moot by the discovery, in the tunnel, of a basket full of six amazingly well preserved papyrus scrolls. A missing seventh is said to contain the secret of eternal life in the flesh. The old Arab account that guided Dr. Alexander to the find was apparently authored by a satisfied customer, claiming to have been over 120 years old at the time of writing! Oh yes, and the scroll promises to vouchsafe the secret of the date of the end of the world, a topic much on the minds of everyone in this Millennium-eve novel.

The first word on the first scroll is the name "Jesus." It soon develops that the ancient author of these scrolls was a first-century Christian deacon named Sabina Fabianus. This fact by itself is enough to galvanize Dr. Alexander, since she is chiefly motivated by the desire to vindicate her late mother's theories (for which she had suffered excommunication from the Catholic Church) that, as Mary Magdalene was the first to behold the risen Jesus, it was she, and not the latecomer Simon Peter, who should have served as Jesus' vicar on earth, the first in the line of popes. "Then the entire authority structure of the Catholic Church and the papacy would be blown out of the water! Cath, this is hot!" (p. 57).

The new discovery seems helpful to the feminist cause because, like Romans 16:1, it uses the masculine term *diakonos*, not the later, feminine derivative, to refer to a woman as a deacon ("servant," "minister"), implying that this document will be a window into that early

---

3. Burns, *Has the Lord Spoken Only through Miriam?*

period of a Christian "discipleship of equals" that Elisabeth Schüssler Fiorenza has explored.[4]

The notion of a dawn-age period of male-female equality in the early house-church communities is no hare-brained speculation. Most scholars accept it today. But what happened to that equality? It comes as no surprise that the same process took its toll on the early Christian community as overtakes all sectarian groups. Such groups begin with a break from mainstream society and its mores, its systems of rank and privilege, and declare everyone equal. But when the second generation comes up, and members are faced with the standard child-rearing decisions (e.g., doesn't one require a mundane job in order to feed one's family?), the movement begins to assimilate back into conformity with the norms of the society it once rejected. In precisely the same way, many who were hippies and campus radicals in the 1960s later found themselves taking the same mainstream jobs they had once scorned their fathers for taking. The Roman Catholic Church, being the most organized and institutional, curtailed the role of women in leadership quickest and most severely, so that women's leadership in church became a function only of "heretical" groups like the Marcionites and the Montanists. Disenfranchised Catholic women may have taken refuge in these alternative communities, or it may be simply that these "heretical" women are the only remaining women in ministry for history to have recorded.

Realizing at once that, should the authorities gain possession of this find, she would never see it again, Dr. Alexander decides to smuggle the scrolls out of the country. She succeeds in this attempt, but the news of the discovery spreads, and soon a fanatical collector of antiquities (who, it is strongly hinted, may be demon-possessed!) sends thugs and assassins to intercept and kill her and appropriate the scrolls. Much of the excitement in the narrative comes from this scenario of the fugitive heretical archaeologist on the run from the gangsters. The rest of it comes from the stubbornly blossoming romance between church-hating Dr. Alexander and a handsome priest, Michael Garibaldi, who takes her under his protection. Conveniently, he, a martial artist full of rage and guilt, is on the point of throwing over his priestly orders anyway. This is sheer soap opera: "Their pulses raced but their bodies moved slowly, seeking answers, and finding them at last in each other" (p. 419). "Michael had

---

4. Fiorenza, *In Memory of Her*; Price, *The Widow Traditions in Luke-Acts*.

held her and whispered in her ear, and when he had been able to go no further, Catherine had then whispered to him until they had spun a vision together that only they could see, their shared dream" (p. 422).

When the bare essentials of the discovery are made known, the Catholic hierarchy is seriously worried, though at first we do not know exactly why. Fundamentalists denounce Catherine Alexander as the Antichrist, sensing that new evidence regarding the life of Jesus can only threaten their cherished concept of a "personal savior." One of them asks, "Had Sabina met Jesus? And had she learned something from him that did not appear in the New Testament or in any of the Apocrypha? Something that was going to alter the face of Christianity forever?" (p. 72). Even the liberal Jesus Seminar comes in for depiction (as it must). The actual Seminar, founded in 1982 by radical liberal Protestant Robert W. Funk and radical Roman Catholic ex-priest John Dominic Crossan (both great New Testament scholars), was meant to publicize the hitherto-well-guarded findings of critical Bible scholarship, to let the cat out of the bag so that lay Christians might catch up with scholars. Many of their readers recoiled at what they perceived as blasphemy, while others rejoiced at the prospects of new ways of understanding Jesus and Christian faith. Barbara Wood thinly disguises Bob Funk as Dr. Raymond Pearson, "founder of the Historical Jesus Society." Characteristic of the late Bob Funk, Pearson says, "Rather than feeling threatened by these scrolls..., today's established churches should embrace what these scrolls can tell us about the beginnings of Christianity. The final result could be liberating" (p. 213).

Pearson goes on to outline a basic critical understanding of early Christian history:

> We know there was a power struggle after Jesus died.... This is clearly documented in Acts. And in the first hundred years there were many different Christian sects all over the Roman Empire, each with different beliefs, rules, and so forth, and everyone arguing over which was the True Faith. There were many gospels and letters being circulated; some groups clung to Peter's teachings, others to Paul's. Remember, Peter insisted that new converts be circumcised, Paul disagreed. These disputes continued for another two hundred years, with splinter groups breaking away and setting up their own churches, each saying that theirs was the True Faith, but each with different rituals and prayers and visions of who Jesus was and what He said. In the fourth century, the

most powerful "camp" won out and put together what they called the New Testament, choosing only four gospels from the many that people were reading at the time, declaring all others to be heretical. (p. 214)

Pearson says he hopes the new scrolls will provide a glimpse of the real, historical Jesus as he was before all the sectarian strife with its distortion began. That was, in short, the goal of the Jesus Seminar and Bob Funk. Some of us, however, suspect that this assumption, however critical and controversial it may seem to the traditionalist, does not go nearly far enough. As Burton L. Mack[5] has suggested, the buck does not stop at the historical Jesus. It may go back to some earlier point. The proper goal of Christian Origins studies is not to figure out how a single historical individual, Jesus of Nazareth, gave rise to so many various interpretations and beliefs, but rather how various figures, ideas, and pre-existing mythemes eventually combined to create the canonical "Jesus Christ." The whole notion of Jesus and his ostensible Easter Resurrection as the "Big Bang" that started Christianity may itself be simply a myth generated by one kind of proto-Christianity among several, albeit the one that became central once its competitors were eliminated. The diversity among early Christians is our primary datum; it is not some obscuring layer of detritus separating us from the original foundation. Dr. Alexander comes near to sensing the implications when she muses: "What *I* think would be amazing ... is if the scrolls offer proof that a man named Jesus really existed" (p. 139).

Actually, the scrolls turn out to disclose just that, supplying the single puzzle piece historians would need to settle the question of a single historical Jesus: a first-person, incidental reference to someone having met Jesus and heard him speak, and, for the sake of the story, this is what Sabina provides. Such passing mentions in ancient accounts anchor the historical existence of both Proteus Peregrinus, the Cynic-Christian martyr, and Apollonius of Tyana, the first-century Neo-Pythagorean sage, though much legend has grown around both figures.

But it is not long until further revelations from the stolen scrolls take our story in an altogether different direction. For Sabina tells her addressee Perpetua (a name borrowed from a famous second-century martyr) how she heard rumors that the risen Jesus had been spotted

---

5. Mack, *A Myth of Innocence*. I presume to carry Mack's analysis further in my *Deconstructing Jesus*.

continuing his ministry of teaching and healing elsewhere in the Roman Empire. Usually this theory (as in the cases of Robert Graves,[6] Barbara Thiering,[7] and the Ahmadiyya apologists)[8] entails the notion that Jesus did not die on the cross but survived it and then left Palestine for less dangerous climes. But Sabina believes Jesus did die and rise, just that he did not ascend to the convenient invisibility of heaven. She decides she has not heard enough of the word of her Lord, so she joins the company of a Stoic magician named Cornelius Severus (probably intended to remind the "in the know" reader of magician Cornelius Agrippa) who is pledged to the same quest, hoping thereby to rediscover the lost secret of eternal life in the body. In a sequence reminiscent of Levi Dowling's *The Aquarian Gospel of Jesus the Christ*, Cornelius and Sabina, first thinking to have found Jesus, come to realize that there have been many saviors whose sacred legends tell of miraculous births, adoration by shepherds, healing miracles, twelve disciples, undeserved executions, resurrections after three days, appearances, and ascensions into the sky. Each time, Sabina thinks she has run across groups gathered by Jesus in his latest theatre of ministry, only to have them tell her that their Redeemer lived many centuries before. The implication is that, either Jesus had incarnated upon earth many times, like an avatar of Vishnu, or that his gospel, clothed again and again with symbolic legends, forms part of the Perennial Philosophy.

And in this case that philosophy has a curiously modern ring (pp. 182, 395). We soon begin to recognize the rudiments of New Thought teaching, the kind of thing on display in Rhonda Byrne's *The Secret*.[9] In short, it becomes apparent that we are dealing with Barbara Wood's version of James Redfield's *The Celestine Prophecy*,[10] in which characters journey in search of an ancient manuscript containing New Age psychobabble "revelations." Redfield "discovers" Nine Insights (with a tenth in the sequel), while Wood condenses them into Seven Truths. Just as the Redfield novel predicts a marked increase in instances of Jungian synchronicity as the New Age draws near, so does Wood's novel: "This is

6. Graves, *King Jesus*.
7. Thiering, *Jesus the Man*.
8. Faruqui, *The Crumbling of the Cross*.
9. The reader might want to consult my critical analysis of this book and these ideas in my *Top Secret: The Truth behind Today's Pop Mysticisms*.
10. Again, see my analysis of this book in *Top Secret*.

the beginning of the End of Things... Synchronicity is real. How many of us are noticing more and more coincidences? It's an indication that things are coming together" (p. 242).

Wood leads us a merry chase. All the characterization, dialogue, and excitement make us forget that we are in search of the next fortune cookie, unlike Redfield's miserable book, which has all the narrative filling of a piece of pornography. As Dr. Alexander slowly translates the six scrolls, hoping for a clue to the whereabouts of the missing seventh scroll, we are reminded pretty strongly of the suspense element of her earlier *The Magdalene Scrolls*, where the scholars are frustrated by the slow progress of unearthing and passing on a similarly long autobiographical manuscript.

When, after various vicissitudes, Dr. Alexander and her boy-toy priest Father Michael find the elusive Seventh Scroll, the final revelation to Sabina turns out to be a vision of Jesus on Sabina's death bed in which he confirms that he is the same entity who has visited mankind as Odin, Tammuz, Osiris, Krishna, Hercules, etc. And whatever anyone believes is true. People will even enter into whatever afterlife they expect.

The fiendish Catholic Church, ever ready to squelch any spark of the truth, is desperate to prevent this revelation from coming to light, though in the end they fail to do so, and the truth is unleashed upon the world. We are not told how the world of faith is affected by the Sabina scrolls, for the book ends with it still being too early to tell. But if we exit the narrative universe of the book, we can see that the Catholic Church would have nothing to worry about. It would be quite interesting to have a genuine first-century account by someone who had once seen Jesus and heard him speak, and this much would at least dispel the Christ Myth theory, which traditional Christians laugh off anyway. But to find that such a person had traveled widely and been initiated into every type of pagan mystery cult available? So what? And to learn that she had claimed a vision of Jesus telling her such ecumenism was the wave of the future? People have visions all the time. The mere claim convinces few people.

But the whole business is confused. Let me get this straight: not only was there an historical Jesus, but there was an historical Odin, too? An historical Hercules? Tammuz really lived? Krishna? Osiris? No, the real issue entailed in placing Jesus on the level with all the other dying and rising redeemer gods is that Jesus, too, is implicitly rendered equally fictitious. Wood has turned this insight inside out.

25 | Sexy Swashbuckler
Donald Nassr, *The Scroll*

OUR AUTHOR IS IN a good position to explain to us why we enjoy thriller novels like the one he has written: Dr. Nassr is the Director of Psychiatry at the Medical Center in Bowling Green, Kentucky. A Roman Catholic, he is unafraid to use the possible truth of heretical notions as fear-fodder for readers with conventional beliefs. After all, if the enemy poses no threat, he isn't much of an enemy. Some religious novelists, like the authors of the famous *Left Behind* series, can never get to the point of scaring us with the depredations of the Antichrist because they dare not imply for a moment that the dedicated Christian might have reason to worry. With constant reassurances, even to the extent of depicting the Beast as a Keystone Nazi from *Hogan's Heroes*, LaHaye and Jenkins make real fear impossible.[1] Not so Nassr. No doubt the secrets of the eponymous "Scroll" would frighten him, shake his personal faith, and leave him reeling. But that's just the point. It's a piece of fiction, and he has to load the artistic gun with ammunition that can wound or kill—until the reader closes the book.

The Scroll is a thrill-a-minute pulp novel (no criticism implied, praise in fact), and Nassr has mastered the conceptual and stylistic conventions of the genre. He is not alone, but he is in the minority in placing at center stage a female operative, Juda Bonaparte—half Jew, half Austrian, sometime spy for the Israeli Mossad and for the Vatican, an assassin and an earned PhD. She seems destined to be portrayed on film by Angelina Jolie. Various Arab terrorists just cannot wait to get their meat-hooks on her comely form, to love her and to kill her, since she excites both passions in them. She is a woman, and what a woman! All the more exciting to men because of her masculinity that exceeds theirs. And since she is

---

1. See my critique of this book in my *The Paperback Apocalypse*.

always handing them their heads, or those of their wily subordinates, the bad guys smolder with both lust and shame that a "mere" woman has repeatedly humiliated, even killed, the best men that the macho villains can send against her. Juda is both a complex and a comic book heroine, an interesting protagonist to say the least.[2]

Who are the villains of the piece, and what have they to do with the controversial scroll? Some of the characters believe that a yet-untranslated Dead Sea Scroll contains a treasure map, like the *Copper Scroll* publicized by John Allegro, which turned out to be a list of buried treasures, with landmarks and directions. They somehow have come to believe that, because of a Templar connection, the scroll tells the way to a cavern containing the measureless riches of King Solomon, excavated by the Templar Knights back in Crusader times. It turns out they are half right. There are open chests of gold and jewels, but the real treasure is the secret of the burial of the body of Jesus, who survived crucifixion and went on to wed Mary Magdalene, move to Southern France, and found the Merovingian Dynasty, whose heirs hope to make a comeback today, founding a new worldwide religion based somehow on Manichaeism, a medieval form of which was practiced in Languedoc, the hotbed of Templarism as well. (Sorry for the long sentence, but it seemed the best way to convey the tortuous complexity of the novel's premise!) One of the main characters is a mad zealot trained from childhood (by members of a still-thriving Priory of Zion) in the Ninja-like arts of movie assassins and Black Ops agents. This novel shares with the 2003 bombshell *The Da Vinci Code* the whole nine yards of bogus modern Templar lore as popularized in the dreadful book *Holy Blood, Holy Grail* by Michael Baigent, Richard Leigh, and Henry Lincoln.[3] One wonders if perhaps Dan Brown borrowed a few ideas from Nassr's *The Scroll*.

What is this scroll? What secrets does it hold? We already know it will tell of Jesus' survival of crucifixion, his move to France, where he would never recognize the way they would pronounce his name ("*Cree?* Oh, you mean *me!*"), etc., but that's only half the fun. Much of the charm of these Lost Gospel novels lies in the pseudo-historical back story. Who wrote the scroll and why?

---

2. By the way, *The Scroll* is her second outing; she appeared first in Nassr's 1994 novel *In the Shadow of the Cross*.

3. Baigent, Leigh, and Lincoln, *Holy Blood, Holy Grail*.

It all starts with the infamous *Testimonium Flavianum*, that paragraph occurring in all our (very late) manuscript copies of Josephus' late first-century work *Antiquities of the Jews* 18.63–64. Here it is, in William Whiston's famous translation:

> Now there was about this time Jesus, a wise man, if it be lawful to call him a man; for he was a doer of wonderful works, a teacher of such men as receive the truth with pleasure. He drew over to him both many of the Jews and many of the Gentiles. He was [the] Christ. And when Pilate, at the suggestion of the principal men amongst us, had condemned him to the cross, those that loved him at the first did not forsake him; for he appeared to them alive again the third day; as the divine prophets had foretold these and ten thousand other wonderful things concerning him. And the tribe of Christians, so named from him, are not extinct at this day.

This passage appears first as a "quotation" in Eusebius' fourth-century *Ecclesiastical History*, and many scholars think Eusebius himself composed it and fathered it onto Josephus. In any case, it has long been recognized as a Christian interpolation. There is both internal and external evidence for this judgment. On the one hand, Origen of Alexandria, in the third century, commented upon Josephus, noting that the Jewish historian certainly did *not* believe Jesus to have been the Messiah. That is enough to prove his copy of *Antiquities of the Jews* cannot have read as ours does, since our copies have Josephus proclaim Jesus as the prophesied Christ in unambiguous terms. And that is also the internal evidence: Josephus, a Jew, is not likely to have confessed faith in the Christian Jesus! Especially since he owed his position in the Flavian court to his claim that the Emperor Vespasian was the predicted Messiah! Some scholars (apologists) still try to make bad evidence into good simply by trimming the bits of the passage that a Jew could not have written, on the outside chance that Christian scribes merely touched up an original, more neutral, Josephus passage on Jesus instead of concocting it out of whole cloth. But that is arbitrary.

Nassr pulls an interesting switcheroo at this point. For his fictional purposes, the passage in question is not an interpolation into Josephus' text, but it is still something of a foreign mass: it turns out to be Josephus' own quotation from an eye-witness report of Jesus by a Greek contemporary who, assigned to investigate radical Jewish movements of the day, became curious about the Nazarene and made it his task to follow him and report on his words and deeds. The result was none other than the Q Document, the source of Jesus-sayings shared by Matthew and Luke excluding the ones they took from Mark. On Nassr's conception, Q included quite a bit of narrative which we must picture Matthew and Luke omitting in the interest of Christian faith as it had already solidified in their day around the belief in the saving crucifixion and resurrection of Jesus. In other words, Matthew and Luke must have recognized the need to choose between Mark's version of the Jesus story, which concluded with the cross and the empty tomb, and the Q version, which would have had Jesus escape the cross alive and take refuge in Europe. That is just the sort of imaginative speculation that attracts many of us, not otherwise mystery fans, to books like this.

There remain a couple of problems with Nassr's clever reconstruction, however: he says that Josephus actually mentions the source from which he is quoting and describes the Q writer. There is nothing like that in any manuscript of Josephus. Just as bad, the content of the *Testimonium* passage ill comports with the rest of the (quite extensive) Q narrative as posited by Nassr, since the passage in Josephus is obviously a summary, encapsulating a wider sequence of events into a brief notice. Specifically, it appears to wrap up the story of Jesus precisely where Nassr says Q does *not* wrap it up: with the crucifixion and resurrection! Where is there any room, even implicitly, for the flight from Judea and into France? Oh, well.

Though it does not begin with her by any means, it is possible that Nassr picked up the idea of a surviving and traveling Jesus from the books of Australian scholar Barbara Thiering,[4] whom he mentions in passing as "Barbara Thierer." Nassr knows, too, of the great scholar of the Nag Hammadi texts, Henri-Charles Puech, but he becomes a character named "Emile Peush," not a typo but rather a wink to the reader.

Juda and others, including the murdering Templar Knight Rene Gervais (so reminiscent of Dan Brown's "the Albino"), finally locate the tomb of Jesus in a cave in France, and Gervais cannot resist the temptation to have a look: "If Christ is in there, then nothing matters, and I'm free!" (p. 358). He begins to tear the wooden planks from the sarcophagus, but Juda, who thinks nothing but trouble is to be gained by such knowledge, flips the switch on the explosives she had previously

---

4. Thiering, *Jesus and the Riddle of the Dead Sea Scrolls.*

wired the place with, and that's it for the earthly remains of Jesus, as well poor Templar assassin Gervais and the scroll he was carrying. The whole scene, so intended or not, is an interesting trope on the gospel Easter accounts of the disciples' visits to the empty tomb, only this time the tomb is anything but empty.

26 | Elementary, My Dear Mary!
Laurie R. King, *A Letter of Mary*

THIS NOVEL[1] IS PART of a series by the same author featuring the latter-day exploits of the Great Detective, Sherlock Holmes—and his wife, Mary Russell. A much younger woman, Mary came to Holmes to train as his apprentice, supplementing her skills as a scholar of the Hebrew Bible and ancient manuscripts with her guru's matchless techniques of forensic detection. The two eventually married, and the independent woman became Holmes's partner professionally, too, replacing the retired Dr. Watson.

Already a point is raised, at first seemingly irrelevant to gospel criticism, but in reality quite important. The function of the Dr. Watson figure sheds much light on the analogous role of Simon Peter in the gospels. Both are "straight men," fictional characters present in the narrative solely for the purpose of providing redactional commentary by the narrator, without breaking off from the narrative. The gospel writer has just had Jesus make some pronouncement and then realizes it may be too easily misconstrued. So he proceeds to have Peter (or, in John's gospel, the Jews) come back with some obtuse answer, anticipating the reader's possible confusion (and thus exactly equivalent to the Stoic diatribe found so often in the Epistle to the Romans, "But someone will say ..."), whereupon the evangelist supplies an explanation which he places in the mouth of Jesus. Arthur Conan Doyle, in the "canonical" Holmes stories, follows the same pattern (as do the Buddhist narratives in which it is the similarly thick-headed disciple Ananda whose misguided comments occasion further explanations from the Buddha): Dr. Watson, so slow to learn from his companion's brilliance, constantly displayed, asks, "I say, Holmes, how the deuce did you identify little Suzy as the Shropshire Slasher?" And of course this allows Holmes to explain what he would

---

1. Page references are to the Bantam edition.

otherwise have kept to himself: his elaborate chain of observation and inference.

But Mary Russell, Mrs. Holmes, is a good deal swifter than old Dr. Watson. She not only observes Holmes in action but also works with him, making her own significant contributions to the case, and thus she can explain things to the reader in her own narrative voice.

Holmes and Russell receive a visit from an old acquaintance, an elderly lady, an archaeologist working in British Palestine, who entrusts to them a papyrus which she believes to be an authentic letter from the gospel character Mary (Mariam) of Magdala. Oh, the experts to whom she has shown it have pooh-poohed it on the basis of no real evidence, just the "unthinkability" of it. She leaves the papyrus in their keeping, then goes offstage to get murdered.

The letter was to accompany Mary Magdalene's daughter Rachel as she sought asylum with Mary's sister Judith. The Romans are already besieging Jerusalem, and Mary fears for her life and that of her unnamed husband. But her intentions are left vague: do they plan to surrender to the Romans or to make a safe exit, at the eleventh hour? It begins: "From Mariam, an apostle of Jesus the Messiah, to my sister Judith in Magdala, may you be granted grace and peace" (p. 111). And what would be at stake if the letter were to be proven authentic and made widely known?

> The sure knowledge that one of Jesus' apostles was a woman would shake the Christian world to its foundation. Logically, there's no reason why it should, but realistically, I have no doubt that the emotional reaction would set off a bitter, bloody civil war, from one end of the church to the other. (pp. 87–88)

For one thing, it seems to me that, even if (as second- and third-century Gnostics believed) Mary Magdalene claimed the office of "apostle," she would scarcely have pulled rank like this in an entirely personal, private letter to her sister. This is not some epistle about church decorum or sacred dogmas. It contains no deliberation on matters of theological gravity. In such cases, one might expect the ancient author to supply her credentials, but here it implies a megalomania entirely out of harmony with the self-effacing character of the letter's author on display everywhere else in the text.

In fact, the self-reference to the authoress's apostleship appears solely to provide an ancient confirmation (for purposes of modern theological propaganda) of theories of female apostleship in the primitive church. And this element has importance in *A Letter of Mary* only in order to provide a red *ichthus* to throw the reader off the track. At first we are led to think the evidence points to one Colonel Edwards, an ecclesiastical arch-conservative who believes the Creator intended women to remain in the kitchen. Learning of the ancient document (we are led to suspect strongly), he would rather have the inconvenient secret perish with its discoverer. But he turns out to be innocent. The real murderer is the archaeologist's elderly sister, who had been lately made aware of her very minor role in her sister's Last Will and Testament.

But is there not perhaps more to it, even much more, than either Mary Magdalene, Mary Russell, or Laurie King lets on? Let us apply our own Sherlockian skills to arrive at the greater secret implicit in the letter. Ask yourself, why has Mary Magdalene mentioned her husband at all? The two allusions are utterly without significance, adding nothing to the information about Mary's witness to the fall of Jerusalem, the impending flight from the city, etc. Unless, of course, the two mentions of "my husband" are clues to something *else*. And then we notice that she does not mention her husband's name, leading the reader naturally to wonder what that name might be. I can only say, "Elementary, my dear Watson!" Her unnamed husband is surely one and the same with Jesus, her messiah and rabbi. This speculation is quite common, but to suggest it is more effective than blurting it out and offering an argument for it.

But I will offer one argument for the idea: it makes the large-scale parallel complete, the parallel between Mary Russell and Mary Magdalene. Both are hitherto-unknown female colleagues of the Great Hero, Sherlock Holmes in one case and Jesus Christ in the other. Mary Russell graduated from apprenticeship to Holmes to being Holmes' wife. And I have to infer that Laurie King intends that Mary Magdalene became the bride of Jesus Christ. More revelations follow from this: if Mary is about to skip the country with her husband, and if that spouse is none other than Jesus Christ, then we must infer that Jesus survived (or avoided) the cross, continuing to teach and finally departing for parts unknown. We are almost at the door of Dan Brown's *The Da Vinci Code*, to which, then, the present book ought to be regarded as an implicit prequel.

In the end, Mary Russell Holmes is not eager to witness the ecclesiastical furor that the publication of the letter will likely cause. She keeps it hidden in a vault with instructions that it be published ten years after her death, with faith in the readers of the twentieth century to know what to make of it. Having now made our way through this many Lost Gospel novels, we surely would.

27 | Nancy Drew versus Simon Magus
Chris Heimerdinger, *The Lost Scrolls*

This in-house adventure novel for young adults in the Church of Jesus Christ of Latter-day Saints (Mormons) is in many ways different from any and all the other Lost Gospel novels we are surveying here. Most of the others are adventure-espionage novels, but this one is a fantasy adventure. A couple of hardy, red-blooded Mormon kids find their way through a time portal hidden in a mountain cavern, and it takes them back to the vicinity of Jerusalem in 70 CE, during the terrible Roman siege of Jerusalem. There they meet various ancient characters known to us, in fragments and rumors, from the New Testament or early Christian apocrypha and tradition, including Simeon bar-Cleophas, the brother/cousin of Jesus, the Alexandrian preacher Apollos, and the Gnostic heresiarch Simon Magus. Heimerdinger depicts Simon Magus somewhat along the lines of his appearance in the movie *The Silver Chalice*, a nefarious cult leader who eventually seeks to facilitate the entrance of his hapless followers into the Divine Pleroma by means of downing a goblet of poison, a la Marshall Appelwhite (Heaven's Gate) and Jim Jones (People's Temple). For the record, Richard L. Tierney's[1] version of Simon Magus was inspired by *The Silver Chalice*, too, but mainly by Jack Palance's strikingly chiseled and planed features rather than his villainous character.

The writing is quite expert. Heimerdinger manages the feat of dividing the narration between the protagonists, our Mormon youngsters, soon separated. He places Meagan's narration in italics, Harry's in normal type. The story switches back and forth as the two accounts gradually draw closer together, finally rejoining at the close of the book. And the typeface is hardly all that distinguishes the two narrators. Heimerdinger

---

1. Tierney, *The Scroll of Thoth*.

makes Meagan sassy and cynical, a real spitfire, while the more mature Harry is courageous but less rash and cocksure because he sees the gravity of their challenges in more realistic terms. Their allies include a mighty warrior from Nephite times, who also found his way through the time portal, but from many centuries earlier than our Mormon young folks. He is the iron-thewed Giggidonihah, who manfully bears the burden of Joseph Smith's inability to coin plausible exotic-biblical names.[2] (One can be forgiven for substituting "Gibberishiah" whenever one runs across the name.)

What are the "Lost Scrolls" of the title? To answer that, we must borrow from the book to which this one is a sequel, *The Sacred Quest*, previously published with the unlikely title of *Tennis Shoes and the Seven Churches*. In that adventure our time-traveling heroes had sought to round up a set of testimonies of Jesus, his life and teachings, written, one each, by the twelve disciples. These would have justified the name Justin Martyr gave to the gospels: "memoirs of the apostles." And one of them turns out to be the autograph text of our familiar Gospel of Matthew. Here and elsewhere, author Heimerdinger shows an expected lack of acquaintance with critical scholarship, as if Matthew the evangelist were the same as Matthew the apostle (and it gets worse). Was our Gospel of John one of them? Presumably so. But imagine ten more gospels embodying eyewitness accounts of Jesus! Too bad the other ten were destroyed by the bad guys! That's the kind of thing that really makes the scholar cringe, as when we are told that the Arabs who stumbled upon the Nag Hammadi texts used some of them for kindling! Well, this time it's fictional, and it is a clever idea, accounting for the fact that we possess (as fundamentalists believe) two apostolic testimonies to Jesus Christ but no more.

But in *The Lost Scrolls* there is even bigger game afoot. Simon Magus captures our heroes and holds fifteen-year-old Meagan hostage while he sends Harry to find a rumored scroll said to be housed in the rubble of the burnt-out dwelling of James the Just (Jesus' brother, bishop in Jerusalem). It is called *The Scroll of Knowledge* and is purported to contain the secret teaching imparted by the risen Jesus to his disciples during the forty days before his ascension. This motif is an ancient Gnostic theme. Several of the Nag Hammadi texts claim to embody this

---

2. Too bad Smith could not have perused Lin Carter's chapter, "Of the Naming of Names" in his *Imaginary Worlds*.

teaching, as does the orthodox *Epistle of the Apostles*. The *Scroll* even sounds like the typical Nag Hammadi revelation: "The words of most sacred knowledge of Jesus the Resurrected Messiah to His holy apostles and written by Peter, James, and John" (p. 208).

Luke adopts the same device (Acts 1:1–6), only he conspicuously omits the contents of the secret teaching because he wants to leave a blank check to the second-century bishops for whom he writes, so that they may fill it in as they like, fathering onto the risen Jesus whatever doctrines they want to teach. "Well, of *course* you don't read any of this in the gospels, my man! Jesus said this in secret *afterward*!" And the real intent of this motif has not been lost on Heimerdinger, because, once *The Scroll of Knowledge* is opened, it is found to contain "the information that Joseph Smith taught repeatedly and relentlessly to his modern apostles in the months before the martyrdom . . . No secrets or formulas. Not complex rites, or recipes for splitting the atom, or distances to Kolob.[3] The simple, sacred covenants of eternal life. The ordinances of the temple" (p. 270). This is the stuff Joseph Smith claimed had been lost at the close of the apostolic age—until he himself restored it. You see what's going on here: the discovery of this material in 70 CE has no effect on the period in which it ostensibly occurs. One must suppose it is immediately lost again, or it would have been known in Joseph Smith's day; he would not have needed to restore it. So what *is* the importance of this "revelation"? It is to assure the reader not to worry: the seeming novelties of Joseph Smith would be familiar portions of the Bible had not someone fumbled the ball along the way. The ancient discovery simulated in this novel is an imaginary apologetic for the ancient authenticity of Smith's revelations. But they find other scrolls along with this, the most important one:

> "It's a veritable treasure trove of sacred scripture," he declared. He went down the line. "This one is the Epistle of James. This is another Epistle of James that we've never even heard of.[4] This one is Paul's [!] Epistle to the Hebrews. Here's a letter from Saint Jude. This is the Book of Isaiah, the Book of Ezekiel, the Book of Daniel. Here's a new and unknown letter from Saint Peter outlining the organization of the Church.[5] And this one—it's the testimony of

---

3. This is the far-off planet where God lives. In the Mormon-inspired series *Battlestar Galactica*, the name becomes Kobol, planet of the gods.

4. This makes sense: James might be expected to retain copies of letters he sent; they were found in his own house, remember.

5. Such "apostolic" church orders were numerous in the early centuries.

Saint Mark;" he read an inscription on the outside—'*Written for the Greeks from Alexandria for a blessing to the world.*'"..."Couple this with your Scroll of Matthew and we may have the only copies of half of the gospels in the entire New Testament." (p. 236)

We were promised, "This was incredible! I could potentially add ten new books to the Bible with a single pop!" (p. 207). But that's not going to happen. All this is meant only to tantalize: the discoverers do not manage to bring the various texts back with them when they return to modern times, so all we are left with is illusory confirmation of the traditional, pre-critical authorship of a number of disputed New Testament books.

The final irony lies in another tossed-off observation by Harry as he and his friends are striving to open the chamber where the scrolls are hidden. "I thought of Joseph Smith prying up that stone atop the Hill Cumorah. The treasures I might find inside seemed no less fantastic" (p. 207). And no less fictive.

28 | James M. Robinson in Strange Company
Ursula & Terry Loucks, *Burning Words*

*B*URNING WORDS IS, LIKE most of the novels we are surveying, quite well written, though one may feel the plot could have accommodated a few more labyrinth turnings, and that things move a bit too quickly toward the last in a mad rush to be over. There is a full quota of romance and adventure between young, good-looking and swashbuckling scholars. We might call that the Indiana Jones syndrome. But ultimately it is pretty clear that all such naturalistic fluff is mere sugar to make the medicine go down. Authors Ursula and Terry Loucks seek first and foremost to educate the reader. They pay some attention to the Dead Sea Scrolls (discovered in 1947) but hasten on to the Nag Hammadi discoveries (found two years earlier, but the object of much less media attention). They have a handful of lessons to teach, but where they impinge upon serious New Testament scholarship Loucks and Loucks are mainly concerned with the theories of James M. Robinson (personally known by the authors and appearing as a walking, talking character in the novel) and Burton L. Mack. Here the book does a real service to readers looking to learn something. It does so by painting ideas onto a larger, more colorful canvas than scholarly prose allows.

Early in the scheme of things we are brought to witness the disorientation that a young Harvard professor (protagonist Christina Sheridan) feels when a sudden, unsought encounter with modern critical scholarship threatens the once-pleasant certainties of her family's Roman Catholic faith. She is little relieved when her brother Ryan, a priest headed for his bishopric (in other words, a good corporate man), tells her to stop thinking in such heretical directions. Loucks and Loucks convey Christina's creative confusion with genuine insight and plausibility. One suspects this is because one or both of the authors have experienced the same sort of disillusionment/enlightenment and that the goal is to guide readers through the same intellectual metamorphosis.

As things progress, Christina finds she must put aside her childhood faith and keep searching for some viable alternative to replace it. The stakes are high. Apparently just keeping an open mind as one lives life each day is not enough. "If the creeds of the Church were not true, or at least were not based on historical events, then what was the meaning of life? . . . Was she just part of the green slime of organic life which covers this planet?" (p. 135).

Her alternative, however, turns out to be Deepak Chopra-style Hinduism hiding behind the (I think) misapplied insights of Quantum theory.[1] The formula seems to be that, once one gains a critical understanding of Christian origins, one has safely eliminated Christianity from contention and can henceforth move over into New Age Thought (or anything else) with a clear conscience. The initial promise that Christianity, having once been far broader and more diverse, might expand to fill out those more generous proportions again, soon gives way to a vague, private, personal religiosity masquerading as science.

In fact, the initial shock from which our heroine never really recovers is that of the *sheer diversity* of early Christianity, and the resulting factional strife, something she had imagined impossible given the harmonious "golden age" of the apostles she had learned about in Catholic catechism. Had it not been a simple matter of the Son of God catechizing his chosen disciples in his eternal truths, and the subsequent catechism by those disciples (the apostles) of their own successors, the bishops, and so on down the line to the pope? The work of nineteenth- and twentieth-century critical church historians (notably Ferdinand Christian Baur and Walter Bauer)[2] has exploded that propaganda picture. And of course it is the fundamental "Paul versus the Judaizers" schism (set forth by F. C. Baur) that first dismays Christina, as it does many theology students today. Apologists like W. Ward Gasque[3] have furiously sought for many years to discredit and refute Baur's thesis because they do not like its

---

1. See Price, "Karma Chameleon," 49–72.

2. Baur, *Paul, the Apostle of Jesus Christ*; Baur, *The Church History of the First Three Centuries*; Bauer, *Orthodoxy and Heresy in Earliest Christianity*.

3. Gasque, *A History of the Criticism of the Acts of the Apostles*; Harris, "The Tübingen School: An Evaluation," 249–62.

implications any more than does the pious Christina. Here Christina questions her colleague and future lover Riggs on the matter:

> The first schism in early Christianity was precipitated by Paul, who later became the chief adversary of James. He apparently had never even met Jesus. From the perspective of the Judean Christians, Paul became the first Christian heretic... As his mission expanded northward, however, and began to include more Greeks and Romans, he and others incorporated mythology from these cultures. The Greek mystery religions, for example, appear to have been an important source. (p. 95)

This sketch oversimplifies without necessarily misleading. And in it Loucks and Loucks supplement Baur with William Wrede's theory, still enormously popular today, of Paul being "the second founder of Christianity."[4] The notion of Paul and Hellenistic Christians blending the gospel with myths and rituals familiar to them from their former religions is also prevalent in critical New Testament scholarship. And it is paralleled in the modern expansion of traditional Western missionary Christianity when converts embellish their new faith with elements of their old faith, a kind of religious syncretism called "indigenization theology" by modern missions theorists.[5]

As James M. Robinson and the newly-discovered Nag Hammadi texts come further and further out on stage, Christina's knowledge of early Christian diversity expands again. The Nag Hammadi library contains various gospels, revelations, and acts that suggest their authors incorporated important elements of Platonism, Zoroastrianism, Hermeticism, and even of pre-Christian Jewish Gnosticism. This is the keenest insight I have discovered among the Lost Gospel novels, namely that the "shocking gospel discovery" that some relish and others fear *has already been made*. In all our Lost Gospel novels it is Loucks and Loucks who seem to get the point, and to have a character grasp it, too: the bewildering diversity of early Christianity implies there never was a divinely imparted charter of Christian teaching. If there had been, there could never have been such unbelievably wide and wild diversity of belief. Further, the subsequent unity, having been imposed essentially by one state-supported faction, is arbitrary and artificial, a barrier to discovering the original gospel, the original Christian faith. James M.

---

4. Wrede, *Paul*, 179. See also Davies, *The First Christian*.
5. Von Allmen, "The Birth of Theology," 37–52.

Robinson and Helmut Koester were two scholars who did recognize the real importance of the Nag Hammadi discovery, spelling much of it out in their groundbreaking essay collection *Trajectories through Early Christianity*.[6]

Burning Words is set long before the authors' own time, apparently back in the 1950s, so when they move on to flesh out the ideas of Burton L. Mack,[7] they leave his name out of it for fear of anachronism. This is a bit odd, since they do not seem to mind committing anachronisms elsewhere in their novel.

> Today in one of my classes the professor wrote down a quote from the philosopher Alan Watts, concerning the creative power of the present tense: "*The moment of the world's creation is seen to lie, not in some unthinkably remote past, but in the eternal now.*" (p. 126)

This scene is a flashback to 1927, but the maxim quoted there comes from Watts's section of the symposium *The Joyous Cosmology*,[8] which, er, ah, appeared in 1962!

Mack might be said to take up where Robinson and Koester left off, namely fleshing out several of the early Christianities (so diverse they deserve their own plural, rather than, say "types of Christianity") implied by the earlier scholars' work. Robinson and Koester had seen that the various basic genres behind our finished New Testament books must have stemmed from very different religious communities, since one has to assume that a community distils and expresses what is most important to it in the religious texts it produces. For example, the collections of proverbs attributed to Jesus referred to as "sayings gospels" imply an origin among people who viewed Jesus primarily as a teacher or guru. The Nag Hammadi *Gospel according to Thomas* is one of these, and the Q Document (which we have already encountered several times) would be another. Yet another would be the sayings document that al-Ghazali used in his *Revival of the Religious Sciences*, which set forth over a hundred sayings of Jesus preserved in Sufi tradition.[9] Conspicuous by their absence in sayings gospels are any explicit mentions of Jesus' miracle

---

6. Robinson and Koester, *Trajectories through Early Christianity*.

7. Mack, *A Myth of Innocence*; Mack, *The Lost Gospel*; Mack, *Who Wrote the New Testament?*

8. Watts, Leary, Alpert, *The Joyous Cosmology*.

9. Price, *The Pre-Nicene New Testament*, 47–62.

birth, miracles, crucifixion, or resurrection. If these texts were the product of what we would today regard as Catholic or Orthodox Christianity, it is very odd that such seemingly crucial items should be absent.

Mack likes to drive home the point that the very existence of such a "Christianity," if it even merited the name, would tend to debunk and discredit the whole present-day Christian edifice since it must imply that all the other familiar gospel materials (miracle stories, Passion narrative, resurrection) must be subsequent (and thus *spurious*) additions to the primitive Christian message, mere myths and legends that were either cobbled together out of the Old Testament or borrowed from the pagans whom one hoped to win to faith. In an interview with Roman Catholic journalist Charlotte Allen, Mack gleefully exclaimed, concerning Q: "It should bring an end to the myth, the history, the mentality of the Gospels!"[10] Here's how Christina sums it up, referring to "*Quelle*," the German word for "source" from which scholars take the abbreviation Q:

> First came the sayings of Jesus found in the sayings gospels of *Quelle* and Thomas. Later on, narratives were added about his life and crucifixion, relying heavily on oral tradition. Over time, miracle stories were added and Jesus was promoted to God by his enthusiastic followers. In the process some stories from Greek mythology and mystery religions, as well as the apocalyptic teachings of John the Baptist were added, eventually creating a bridge to the Apostle's [sic] creed. (pp. 223–24)

It might not be as simple as this makes it sound, but I believe Loucks and Loucks, speaking through Christina's mouth, are correctly grasping Mack's point. And the inference, though not inevitable, does square with good Higher-Critical logic: if the historian is faced with two rival accounts, one more spectacular, the other more mundane, he must choose the latter as closer to the truth. The assumption for doing so is that no one would have wanted to whittle down a spectacular set of facts, while anyone might inflate a less interesting story to make it more exciting. For Q to lack everything but sayings implies that the Christians whose beliefs are embodied in it knew of nothing else to be told. Mack's suggestions have met with a great deal of controversy, mostly among apologists for evangelical fundamentalism. More critical scholars tend to wonder what the big deal is, since they have already arrived at similar conclusions.

10. Allen, "The Search for a No-Frills Jesus."

Mack knows that, and aims his work at a popular (though sophisticated) audience. Like Robert W. Funk of the Jesus Seminar (of which Mack was an early Fellow), Mack's goal is to confront the laity with what scholars have long known (or surmised). The goal is not just idle mischief, to afflict the comfortable, but more important, to comfort those afflicted with the guilt of no longer being able to believe the impossibilities of an ancient, mythic worldview.

"Why wasn't *Quelle* included in our New Testament?" asks Christina, perfectly performing the role of Peter and other bemused interlocutors with Jesus in the gospels, i.e., giving the author a chance to explain at greater length. Her boyfriend/mentor continues: "It would have been excluded, and in fact banned, by those who followed Paul's Christianity. For the Roman Christians the teachings of Jesus were far less important than his miraculous life, as the Incarnate Son of God, who brought salvation to the world by his death and resurrection" (p. 149). The question and the answer alike suffer from a simple error: Q was not excluded from the canon. In fact, the reason we know of Q at all is that it appears to have been incorporated, virtually *en toto*, in Matthew and Luke. Remember what Q is: the set of sayings shared, with very little difference in wording, between Matthew and Luke but not Mark. On the almost universally accepted theory of Markan priority, what Matthew and Luke do share with Mark they got from Mark. What they share without Mark they got from Q. Just as almost all of Mark appears again somewhere or other in either Matthew, Luke, or both, we assume most of Q was used by either Matthew or Luke. Admittedly, Q does not survive alongside the later gospels which used it, as Mark does, but that is likely because Mark was written in Rome, and that gave it enough clout not to be dropped even when rendered superfluous.[11]

But why did the compiler(s) of the canon[12] not see what Burton Mack sees: that Q, with no miracles, death, or resurrection, gives the lie to the other accounts with their rampant supernaturalism? We cannot hold Paulinists responsible, as the Louckses do, for the simple reason that, while the Pauline epistles do not quote an historical Jesus (only occasionally citing pronouncements and oracles given in his name by

---

11. One dissenting voice concerning the existence of Q is Mark Goodacre with his *Case Against Q*.

12. Trobisch, *The First Edition of the New Testament*; Trobisch, "Who Published the New Testament?"

Christian prophets), neither do they once mention miracles performed by Jesus. A non-miraculous Q would have not offended Paulinists. We must also account for the fact that all four evangelists—belonging to varieties of Christianities which presumably made room for both teachings and miracles, not to mention death and resurrection—happily combined sayings with supernatural narratives, i.e., Matthew and Luke, using Q itself. This means that, by the time the canon was initially compiled in the late second century and finalized with the condemnation of all rival canons in the mid-fourth century, no one saw any incompatibility between any of these genres because all they knew of were the hybridized gospels that readers are stuck with today. It has taken a keen eye and an ocean of patience for modern source critics even to realize that there must have been discrete genres like sayings gospels and narrative gospels.

Finally, Loucks and Loucks, as revealed in these quotes, seem committed to a common-sense Christology in which the original, historical Jesus was a Gandhi-like mortal elevated only later by popular superstition to divine status. They would so like to find an earlier gospel featuring such a Jesus that they read *Thomas* through those lenses. Good luck with passages like saying 77, "I am the All! All things came forth from me!" Compared to Thomas' Jesus, even John's Jesus seems to have an inferiority complex.

From here things slide off into real fantasy scholarship so extravagant that it is liable to cast its garish light back over all the respectable scholarly speculation that we have examined up to now. You know there is going to be trouble as soon as the Turin Shroud gets trotted out. It has been definitively carbon-dated to the fourteenth century and should never be mentioned in connection with the historical Jesus again. Nor does it bear any traces of blood, only red ochre pigment.[13] Once again the much-abused linen portrait of Jesus is made to function as a two-dimensional ventriloquist dummy; this time the sindonological secret is that some of the blood on the linen sheet is fresher than the rest, implying that Jesus must have still been alive when taken down from the cross and buried. This fact comes in handy as making it easier for the characters (if not the reader) to believe that Jesus lived on for several years, exiting Judea for a Far East tour, finally expiring in and being interred in Kashmiri Srinagar, as the Ahmadiyya sect holds.[14]

---

13. Nickel, *Inquest on the Shroud of Turin*.
14. Faber-Kaiser, *Jesus Died in Kashmir*; Pappas, *Jesus' Tomb in India*.

Christina and Riggs make a journey to Srinagar in hopes of finding a first-century manuscript of Q, but once they arrive, they are told no such paper celebrity is to be found there. They must instead hop over to nearby Hemis, where Q is presently housed. Only it isn't. The Buddhist abbot there explains that, though they did once have a scroll about Jesus, it has since been moved to Dharmasala. But the Hemis librarian's description leads them to think the document in question cannot be Q, since there should not be anything in Q about Jesus traveling to India and Tibet. Of course, we are being teased with the old hoax about Nicholas Notovitch's "discovering" in the Hemis monastery a scroll called *The Life of Saint Issa*.[15]

At last our intrepid pair tracks Q down in Israel, where a liberal Catholic priest has charge of it, having found it in the Vatican Library misfiled among loose manuscript pages of Greek versions of the Old Testament Book of Proverbs. We find out that the Church, learning of this dangerous treasure, resolved to keep it under wraps, circulating instead a false Q that features (for all we read of it) a resurrection narrative modeled upon Luke's, but with an appearance to Peter, crowning him and his successors as popes in perpetuity. In a sudden tussle with an ecclesiastical goon squad, the priest drops the precious Q papyrus and one of the bad guys pours acid on it, contributing the title of the novel: *Burning Words*. Some few pages survive, though, and they send them to Professor Robinson to aid him in his computer-reconstructed edition of Q. (I'm betting Jim Robinson is hoping no one will take this apocryphal bit of biography too seriously).

The book ends many years later with Christina having become a convinced disciple of Chopraism and thinking fondly of Riggs, her lover, since killed (off-page) in a boating accident. Then she gets a call inviting her along on an archaeological dig to find the Z Document, a hypothetical *Grundschrift* (common source document) for both Thomas and Q. Perhaps the greatest contribution of *Burning Words* to popular religious understanding is not so much the specific theories espoused in its pages, but rather the depiction of the intellectual adventure of New Testament scholarship by means of the Indiana Jones metaphor.

---

15. Goodspeed, "The Unknown Life of Jesus Christ," 3–14; Beskow, "Jesus in India," 57–65; Fader, *The Issa Tale That Will not Die*.

29 | John's Gospel: The Sequel
Gary E. Parker, *The Ephesus Fragment*

THIS TIME THE FOCUS is off Jesus, giving him a well-deserved rest. Historical Jesus issues are not on the table in *The Ephesus Fragment*. No, the newly discovered manuscript in Gary E. Parker's fast-paced thriller is an account of the life of Jesus as told by his mother Mary to her care-giver in old age, the apostle John, son of Zebedee. Once it becomes known (though not yet translated), numerous parties embark on intrigues to secure the text for their own purposes. One of these is a cancer-stricken industrialist who thinks the Marian relic may possess power to heal (he is right). He hopes not to heal himself but his similarly stricken granddaughter.

At least two factions of Vatican conspirators send operatives to secure the text. There is a raging debate over whether the pope should go ahead and declare as an infallible dogma of the Church that Mary is Co-Redemptrix along with Jesus Christ (more on this presently). And scheming cardinals surmise that the new text might prove crucial in settling the debate, or at least in preventing a premature declaration. One cardinal sends a goon squad of bloodthirsty thugs, while another assigns the duty to his nephew, Father Michael Del Rio, a weight lifter and Notre Dame Professor of New Testament Studies. Father Michael, thus assembled by the author like a Dungeons & Dragons character, naturally turns out to be the hero of the story.

The book contains its share of action, adventure, psychodrama and soap opera, some of it too formulaic, most of it quite well crafted. But for us, as always, the real interest is in the brief sections of the novel that expound on biblical scholarship and speculate on the impact of possible manuscript discoveries. In one scene Father Michael and his uncle, Cardinal Roca, muse over the potential shock value of the document before they have seen it: "This discovery could make or break the entire

John's Gospel: The Sequel

Catholic system of belief about the Holy Mother! It could destroy or legitimize the idea of naming her Co-Redemptrix!" (p. 76).

What is this business about Mary as Co-Redemptrix? It is an unofficial doctrine, not an official dogma, and it denotes that Mary's cooperation with God's saving plan of incarnation and atonement, especially including her suffering over her son's misfortunes, made her, in a sense, a co-worker in the process of redemption. Protestants cannot help feeling that to use the epithet "Co-Redemptrix" betrays the real, deep-down belief of Catholics that Mary is a goddess, another Jesus, equally important, and that the official explanation is mere subterfuge intended for non-Catholic ears. And in Parker's novel, it is this Protestant distaste for the whole business that causes the pope finally to decide not to promulgate the Co-Redemptrix dogma, lest it deal a blow to ecumenism from which it could never recover.

Later, a villainous Arab speculates on the mischief to which the Marian gospel might be put. He thinks it stands to divide Christians and soften up the West for Islamic propaganda (p. 114). Actually, that seems a bit doubtful; any revelations about Jesus and Mary that offended Catholics would be an equal affront to Muslims, since the Koran, like the Gospels of Matthew and Luke, teaches the virginal conception of Jesus and accords great veneration to his mother. What Muslims do not believe is that the Virgin Birth makes Jesus God's son. For their faith, Allah can have no sons. But he can have great prophets, and Jesus is one of them.

Michael eventually gets the opportunity to translate the *Ephesus Fragment*, so named because it would have been written by John while Mary lived under his roof in Ephesus until her death, Jesus having committed her to his care when he noticed the two of them standing at the foot of the cross in John 19:26–27. Author Parker gives us but the merest glimpses of the Johannine-Marian memoir, and the most interesting thing he says about it is not a quote from it, but rather Michael's reactions: "Numerous stories untold by the other gospel writers flowed from the pen of the one who identified himself as John . . . If authentic, this book would turn Christianity on its head" (p. 202). Pretty tantalizing! But the quoted passages are less impressive.

Father Michael eventually decides the Ephesus gospel is authentic, neither an ancient nor a modern forgery. That is the way of things within the narrative universe of the novel. But in a broader sense, since the whole thing is fiction, the text *is* a "forgery" of Parker's making. Let us assess how well he did. Does it come across as a genuinely Johannine gospel text, as far as we can judge from the small portions he gives us?

The first passage (in logical order, not that of presentation in the book) reads, in part: "I, John, a follower of the Lord Jesus and witness to many signs and wonders that He did . . ." (p. 201). That self-reference emulates the introduction to the Revelation of John: "I, John, your brother and comrade in the affliction we must suffer if we are to enter the kingdom," etc. (Rev. 1:9). This already presents something of a problem because, as the author admits, it is not at all certain that Revelation was written by the same "Johannine" author as the Gospel or the Epistles of John. (The name is only traditional and is not given as that of the author within the text, as Paul is, for example, in his epistles.) But there does seem to be some connection, as if perhaps the various documents stemmed from different branches of a once-single movement, much like the variety of Plymouth Brethren sects descended from the original sect of John Nelson Darby. All share certain concerns and express themselves in similar, inherited vocabulary, despite the differences that fragment them. From what follows, it is evident that Parker wants his gospel author to sound more like the gospel writer John, not the barely grammatical Revelator. So here he seems to have the wrong John. Unlike the Ephesus author, the Fourth Gospel's author, again, does not identify himself with any name.

Parker's evangelist says he has seen "signs and wonders," but this is not quite the Johannine idiom. Jesus in John's gospel speaks frequently of "signs," referring to revelational miracles, but "signs and wonders" is an apocalyptic cliché (see, e.g., Mark 13:22) that does not appear in John's gospel.

Interestingly, Parker capitalizes "He" and "Him" when referring to Jesus in all gospel portions except the second one that depicts Jesus as an infant (p. 285). Was he not divine even as a child? Parker looks like a Nestorian, since Nestorius famously declared, "God is not a baby two or three months old!" If this capitalization represented the original Greek text, we might have a clue as to a Nestorian origin of the Ephesus gospel, but of course it does not. There was no such punctuation in the original Greek, where everything was either all caps ("uncials") or all lower case ("miniscules").

The third fragment (p. 202) makes the same dead-giveaway error as many ancient gospel apocrypha: combining elements from different earlier gospels. In this case, Parker has grafted Johannine language about the many mansions of the Father's house (John 14:2) onto a reference to the Matthean Nativity story (Matt 2:13–15, 19–23). The reference to Joseph's death is another typical mark of apocrypha: an attempt to satisfy long-standing Christian curiosity. The "darkness and light" language is characteristically Johannine, though a bit clumsy. Finally, the mention of Mary's cherishing these events in her heart comes directly from Luke's Nativity story (Luke 1:66; 2:19, 51). Parker here betrays a fundamentalist assumption that all the gospel stories are pieces of a puzzle, selections from a single, harmonious set of facts underlying the various gospels that draw on them. This makes it a matter of indifference what bits and pieces one pulls from what gospel: they all must reflect what happened, so why should not an independent writer reflect some events mentioned by one gospel and others mentioned in another gospel? The trouble is that the gospel stories, especially the Nativity stories, teem with irreconcilable contradictions, and this shows each is a self-sufficient fictive narrative rather than a selection of snapshots from a continuous underlying documentary.

The fourth and fifth passages betray their origins as merely ornamental narrative plugs, not portions of an original, longer narrative. Each makes a reference to the location of the event about to be narrated in a sequence already familiar to the reader and not to be narrated again. "On the night before His arrest in the Garden" and "On the day before His return to the Father after his resurrection" are just like the reference to the Passion Narrative in the didactic section 1 Corinthians 11:23, "the Lord Jesus on the night he was handed over," etc. In 1 Corinthians it is obvious the writer is, so to speak, finding his place in a narrative that he and his readers know, but which is open before neither of them. The time reference is a pointer to the place in the absent text of which he wishes to remind readers. In an actual Passion Narrative (such as Parker is ostensibly giving samples of), one would find no such phrase: the whole sequence would make the time reference clear by implication. Thus Parker's passages 4 and 5 never belonged in any larger narrative. (Of course we know they didn't; but Parker's job was to make it appear that they did in the fictional world he is creating for us.)

The fifth passage (pp. 202–3) is quite ingenious:

> "Fear not," Jesus said. "I am the resurrection, and death cannot hold the life. Forever you are my mother, and forever I am your son. I go from you now, but in the days to come you too shall be raised, and the sorrows of this life shall pass away. Be of good cheer, for I have accomplished the work the Father gave to me. I have taken away the sins of the world." Then Jesus ascended to the Father, and Mary told all that she had seen and heard to those who loved her and cared for her from that day until now. I, John, bear witness to her words.

Here Jesus simply appears to be predicting that Mary will, together with all the righteous, one day rise from the dead to greet the Kingdom of God. You might discern a reference to the Catholic dogma of the bodily assumption of Mary into heaven at the end of her earthly sojourn, if you were looking to spot it in that passage. But is the passage Johannine in style and theology? Parker does toss in an echo of Jesus' speech to Mary and Martha in John 11. There are other Johannine elements as well, directly lifted from famous passages of the Gospel of John. Not exactly subtle.

The Ephesus Fragment does not satisfy our curiosity about the public impact of a new gospel, partly because the text is by implication so orthodox and partly because the novel ends with Father Michael absconding with the text, intending to wait a while before publishing it, so as to let everyone cool down. The ending is a bit of a disappointment except that the stakes were not high enough to create much suspense. But at least it does what all good endings are supposed to do: it restores the initial equilibrium. The trouble is that equilibrium is dull.

30 | Discovering Faith and Flesh
Simon Mawer, *The Gospel of Judas*

REMEMBRANCE OF THINGS PAST

THIS WONDERFUL, WISTFUL, HAUNTING novel[1] perfectly interweaves the macrocosm of international events with the microcosmic impact these events have on individuals. The major world event is, naturally, the discovery near Qumran (where else?) an autograph text by Judas Iscariot that threatens to destroy and debunk all but the most liberal, reinterpreted version of Christianity. The translator of this shocking text knows what damage it will do and has already lost his own faith before he begins the task.

Leo Newman is a Catholic priest stationed in Rome, whose erudite gifts have come to dominate his ministry. He is engaged mainly in teaching New Testament studies and in interpreting ancient texts. One of his vestigial priestly duties places him in the shaded booth of the confessional, and one afternoon he speaks there with a uniquely vivacious and ironic woman whose piety is always giving way to her sense of humor and cynicism. She has little to confess, mainly occasional masturbation, and Father Leo patiently wonders why she bothers confessing such trivia. But he smells her perfume and is disarmed by her perkiness, which seems to contain an incongruous hint of despair. He recognizes the same clues to her identity the same night at a party where he meets her face to face. She is Madeleine Brewer, the wife of Jack Brewer, a British diplomat in Rome. Against his instincts, Leo cannot fight his fascination with this enigmatic, charismatic woman. He appears to be playing it safe by becoming a close friend of the whole family, accompanying them on day trips, dining with them, etc. The rest of them form a welcome buffer. But eventually, caught in the claustrophobic darkness of an ancient

---

1. All page references are to the 2000 hardcover edition.

catacomb when the lights go out, the pair embrace and realize they are in love, beautifully but illicitly.

Madeleine soon explains to Leo that she has lost her faith and was in fact on the verge of losing it the first time, when she went to confession as a last gasp gesture. And once the pair engage in admitted adultery, Leo, too, appears to lose his faith. It is as if his faith in Christ and Christianity was so deeply rooted in his identity as a priest and the discipline of his celibacy that to forsake these automatically makes him forfeit his Christianity. The denial of sex appears like impossible flat-earthism in the face of the undeniable force of sexuality. What can he do? Once his passion for this woman awakens, it seems to him a welcome and thrilling return of blood circulation to a body hitherto cold and restricted, a welcome burst of light ending his blindness. In retrospect, it seems almost self-evident that his faith was a too-snug cocoon from which the thrill of sex has liberated him. Madeleine has taken his hand and led him, not into sin, but into a long-delayed maturity. Even so, Leo knows it *counts* as sin. He has turned away from faith and vocation. He wanders in a No Man's Land, awaiting the next developments. And these are by no means slow in coming.

Leo has already gained international scholarly fame because of his deciphering of a few small papyrus fragments in Koine (New Testament) Greek that appear to date to the mid-to-late first century CE. Close scrutiny reveals that they must have belonged to a copy of Matthew's gospel, which therefore must date from much earlier than critical scholars were accustomed to date it. Leo reasons that the discovery pushes the texts back into the lifetime of actual eye-witnesses of Jesus, confirming the gospels' accuracy as reports of Jesus.

> "I suppose it's what I'd been hoping for all my life," he told Madeleine. "Concrete evidence that the gospels, at least the source of the gospels, predate the Jewish War, and that therefore they contain genuine eyewitness accounts." [What is at stake?] ... If the earliest manuscripts only come from the first century, if the gospels themselves were written that late – after Paul's ministry, let's say—then it's easy to make the kind of claim you hear often enough, that Christ was a construct of the early Church, a mythic figure given some kind of historical identity in order to help the simple people believe." (p. 28)

I suspect what Simon Mawer meant to say through Leo is that, if a whole century elapsed between Jesus (or Paul) and the writing of the gospels, it would be disturbing. But first-century manuscripts are just what he had been looking for and thinks finally to have found. It's a little confused. Or I am.

At one point Father Leo runs into a colleague with whom he has been engaged in debate. His rival had long been contending that one scrap of papyrus found at Qumran was from "an early gospel, a proto-Mark" (p. 124). That would refer to an earlier version of Mark, something often hypothesized. Its presence among the Dead Sea Scroll fragments is also a real theory, promoted by Catholic priest Jose O'Callaghan.[2] But that theory has never fared well. The postage stamp sized scrap has only some thirty-seven letters on several lines, a "doughnut hole" of manuscript, and, though the letters so arranged *could* come from a copy of Mark, given certain scribal parameters, it could just as easily be part of a manuscript of Exodus from the Greek Septuagint translation.

THIRTY PIECES MORE THAN HE BARGAINED FOR

With these achievements to his credit, Leo seems the obvious man for a new job; a new text, an intact scroll, has turned up in a Dead Sea cave. Can he come to Israel immediately to check it out? He does, and it turns out to be the testament of Judas Iscariot. The tale it tells rings the death knell for Christianity.

But the priest has become notorious for another reason: his closeness to Madeleine, which some in Rome are not slow to notice. Leo is called on the carpet by his bishop in London. Returning to his apartment in Rome, he is astonished to learn that Madeleine, who had let herself in with some flowers to spruce up the place, has fallen out the window and perished on the cobbled street below. Under judicial interrogation, Leo admits he was having an affair with Madeleine and is initially suspected of having murdered her to cover up the disgrace. When a suicide note turns up, followed by revelations from her husband that this was neither his late wife's first affair nor her first suicide attempt, Leo is off the hook, but not without major difficulties. As word of the contents of the Judas text leak out, he becomes Public Enemy of the Faith Number One as well as the laughingstock of tabloids the world over. Here, it seems, is

---

2. Herrero and White, *The First New Testament*.

an apostate (and that for the mere sake of sex) who is bound and determined to bring down his rejected faith with him. Imagine the hate mail, equally vitriolic, whether crude or cultured.

Father Leo finishes rendering the Greek into English. All fears are confirmed. He goes a little mad, though precisely how mad, even he does not know. First, he absconds with the last and most incriminating page of the Judas gospel, sneaking out of the "secure" facility housing it, and then ... someone, maybe Leo, plants explosives in the place. Leo is trapped in the explosion but survives, terribly burned. Through extensive skin grafts and rehabilitation he is finally able to resume his life in Rome, now officially excommunicated and taken up with one of his students, an East European immigrant named Magda. She is a waiflike but sensuous woman who dresses in black and says little. She is a painter but makes money by posing nude for low-budget porn magazines. Several of her paintings feature Father Leo in a shrine or at an altar, engulfed in flames. At first we read that as a prophecy of damnation for his apostasy, but this is because of the unique structure of the novel: three stories are progressing piecemeal, back and forth, each shedding more and more light on the events of the others as we go along. Accordingly, the flame paintings make sense only later, once we learn of the explosion.

One of the story threads, of course, deals with the traumatic events of Father Leo's seduction, the brief affair, his translation and loss of faith, and the aftermath of Madeleine's death. Another, a first-person account, takes up after the fire (though we don't realize that at first) when the disillusioned priest meets Magda and invites her to live with him. The third, perhaps surprisingly, is not a blow-by-blow account of Judas and Jesus, as we should expect, but rather a flashback to Leo's parents in wartime Rome. His mother Gretchen (a nickname for Margaret, thus reminiscent of Mary Magdalene) was a classical pianist, an Englishwoman, married to a German, a Nazi official connected to Mussolini's regime. Their young son is Leo, and Gretchen undertakes an affair with Francesco, a virile, young Italian hired to tutor Leo. When she can no longer deny her indiscretions, Gretchen agrees to lead her wrathful husband to Francesco's apartment, where the Nazi goons can arrest him for the crime of being a Jew (a secret her paramour made the mistake of confiding in Gretchen). She kisses the young man at his door, then moves aside for the thugs to rush in. She sees him in prison many months later and weeps, forever unable to forgive herself. And then we learn that her son Leo is not after all our protagonist, since the former Leo was killed in an Allied bombing raid. No, our Leo, a second Leo, is the bastard offspring of Gretchen and Francesco.

It becomes evident that the roles of Judas the betrayer and Mary Magdalene the temptress are shared like a borrowed hat between several of the protagonists, and this, more than the discovery of a literal testament of Judas, is what accounts for the title of the novel. The most obvious candidate for the Judas role is Father Leo himself, who has betrayed not only his own personal faith but the whole Christian religion. Though the majority simply refuse to believe the new revelations, they hate and vilify their discoverer. They strike at the messenger since they cannot gainsay the message. And it may have been these zealots who blew up the scroll repository. *Or* it may have been a (Judas-like) suicidal attempt by Leo to punish himself for the crime everyone charges him with. For even if Christianity is a lie, and it is good to expose a lie, one still takes a terrible step in destroying the faith of millions.

Leo's memory after awakening from the explosion is fragmentary. He cannot remember, when someone voices suspicions, whether he planted the bomb or not. But he doesn't rule it out. Months later, back in his apartment he finds an unremembered envelope in his own handwriting awaiting him. It is the final page of the Judas gospel that he had stolen. So it turns out that he had preserved the evidence and made sure he should still possess it if he survived the explosion. In the end, he gives the two thousand year-old papyrus sheet to Magda to paint over on one of her collage canvases.

Leo's mother Gretchen was as Judas-like as one can get when she betrayed her lover to the Nazis with a kiss. Madeleine betrayed Leo by seducing him with the dangerous truth of her flesh. And, again like Judas, she killed herself, "falling headlong" (Acts 1:18). Magda, a creature of almost feral, amoral sexuality, and Madeleine's successor in Leo's bed, almost counts as a resurrection of Madeleine, as Leo does for his slain older half-brother.

GLOSSING THE GOSPEL

Simon Mawer has a more secure grasp both of the New Testament background and of the sound and structure of ancient documents than some of the authors we have surveyed. And he has a strong dose of scholarly imagination. He uses the critical reconstructive imagination of the scholar but projects it farther, much farther, than scholars dare to in their attempts to interpret the ancient evidence. A fine example is the brilliant notion of making Jesus' mother Mary one of the numerous Herodian Mariams. And what a light the identification shines on the mythical tales of the Nativity in Matthew! Mawer supplies an entirely plausible rationale for Herod's murder of the children of Bethlehem: an embassy of Parthian Magi come to congratulate King Herod on the birth of an heir, but the paranoid king (who is well known to have eliminated several of his sons for fear of possible Absalom-like threats to his throne, almost a mortal version of the Titan Kronos) decides to destroy this royal heir. His grandson Jesus is taken secretly to Bethlehem because of its traditional Davidic-Messianic associations. But the king finds out and seeks to eliminate the threat.

The babe is entrusted to his uncle, Joseph of Arimathea, as a foster father. This device neatly explains the roles of the gospels' Joseph—Jesus' supposed father, though he is not the real father—and of Joseph of Arimathea: why was he so interested in salvaging the body of Jesus? Now we know! Tradition made Joseph of Arimathea Jesus' uncle anyway. Mawer has shrewdly tied many loose ends together. And yet his reconstruction does not count as a scholarly hypothesis (nor is it meant to be taken as one) because so much of it is speculation. There are dots to be connected, but the lines Mawer traces between them are too long for this to be anything but overt fiction. It is helpful to keep this in mind, to recognize the difference, for there are numerous cases (e.g., Baigent, Leigh, and Lincoln's *Holy Blood, Holy Grail*)[3] where the speculative reconstruction is novelistic in nature, like Mawer's, but the writer thinks he is writing history.

Mawer's gospel makes Jesus a Zealot revolutionist, refusing to brook pagan, human rule over the Chosen People in God's great garden. Jesus actually leads a raid on the temple and then sends men into combat against occupying forces. Mawer here follows in the footsteps of Hermann Samuel Reimarus,[4] and S. G. F. Brandon.[5] These scholars noted plenty of stray bits of evidence that Jesus was no pacifist prophet and must have taken up the sword like Judah Maccabee, Menachem, and Simon bar Giora in the periodic struggles against Rome. The Zealot

---

3. Baigent, Leigh, and Lincoln, *Holy Blood, Holy Grail*.
4. *Reimarus: Fragments*; Eisler, *The Messiah Jesus and John the Baptist*.
5. *Jesus and the Zealots*.

Hypothesis is a strong theory, perhaps the most persuasive, in my opinion, among all the would-be historical Jesus models. But this strength is at the same time a major weakness. One of Mawer's characters remarks that the scenario depicted in the new gospel in effect shows the events of the Roman siege of Jerusalem having a rehearsal forty years early. How is this a problem? If such a thing, on such a scale, really happened in the late 20s to early 30s of the first century—why is there no mention of it in Josephus' history of the period?[6]

Father Leo is astonished to discover that Saul of Tarsus, the Apostle Paul, had been one of Jesus' associates and sympathizers. He seems to infer that Saul had later, no doubt prompted by a vision, gone off in an unexpected direction, proclaiming the resurrection of a spiritualized, politically sanitized Jesus. We are left to suppose that it was the Pauline mission that led Judas to try to set the record straight: no resurrection, no heavenly salvation, just the memory of a courageous freedom fighter for his people.

---

6. Well, to be strictly accurate, there *is* if you count the Slavonic version of Josephus' *Jewish War* in which Jesus does mount an aborted revolution against Pilate, only to be crushed. But few think this version of Josephus is authentic. See the translation of the relevant portions in Josephus, *The Jewish War*, 398–99.

31 | The Q Conundrum
Jonathan Rabb, *The Book of Q*

THE PREMISE OF JONATHAN Rabb's fascinating and entertaining novel *The Book of Q* is the survival to the present day of an ancient world religion called Manicheeism (or Manichaeanism). It was founded by an intriguing prophet called Mani (or Manichaeus) who lived in the third century CE until his crucifixion at the hands of Persian authorities who did not care much for his new gospel. Mani signed himself "Mani, Apostle of Jesus Christ," but that just showed the extent of his humility. Though it might seem to betray a touch of megalomania to claim such a title, it was nothing compared to his full self-estimate, for he also deemed himself the Living Paraclete predicted by Jesus at the Last Supper (John 16:7). Not only that: he was also the latest embodiment of that Spirit who had previously touched down on earth as the Buddha, Zoroaster, and Jesus Christ. Mani was the only religious founder up to his time who understood himself to *be* the founder of a new religion (Muhammad would be another), not just a prophet or reformer within a traditional faith. He taught a distinctive form of Gnosticism in which the *gnosis* (secret knowledge) imparted to the initiates was a thorough-going dualism reminiscent of classical Zoroastrianism with its evenly-matched deities of good and evil, light and darkness.

But, whereas Zoroastrianism viewed the material world and its comforts as wholesome creations of the good deity Ahura Mazda, the Manichaeans turned this all around and, as Gnostics, prescribed a severe type of flesh-mortifying asceticism. The world of matter was the creation of an evil godling, the Platonic-Gnostic Demiurge. High up and exalted above the dark cosmos, the Unknown Father welcomed back to his kingdom of light all who would embrace the gnosis and renounce the flesh. Naturally, allowance was made for the common believers who were not yet ready for the compete renunciation, e.g., of sex and marriage. In this it was similar to Buddhism with its two-track system for monks on the one hand and the pious laity on the other.

Mani was known (from Manichaean scripture) to have grown up as the son of a priest in a baptizing sect, and for a long time scholars[1] (including our author; see p. 69 of *The Book of Q*) supposed it was the Aramaic-speaking Mandaean sect (still extant in Iraq today). But more recent discoveries revealed that his father had been a priest in the Elchasite sect,[2] a Jewish-Christian baptizing group with similar beliefs, including that their own founding prophet, Elchasai, had been a reincarnation of Adam, the True Prophet who had appeared many times among men.[3] Though the rest of Manichaean belief more closely parallels the complexities of Mandaeanism, the role of the founder is much closer to that of the Elchasites, since both claimed a near-contemporary prophet as founder, not a sacred figure of the past; Mandaeans claimed (probably correctly) to be the surviving sect of John the Baptist.

The Manichaean faith long outlived its apostle, enduring for an even millennium throughout Eurasia. It passed along the Silk Road into China, and we have some Chinese Manichaean documents as its relics. One sometimes reads of "Medieval Manicheeism,"[4] but it is more of a matter of analogy than identity. The reference is actually to a handful of once-influential "heresies" banned and suppressed by the Catholic and Orthodox churches of Europe, sects including (especially) the Cathari ("Pure Ones"), also known as the Albigensians, and the Bulgars and Bogomils. They were emphatic in piety and employed an imagination rich in mythology.[5] But these movements were not true descendants of Mani's Church. It is always possible that some few Manichaeans, once their churches were shut down by the authorities, continued their worship in secret, in which underground form it may possibly survive till the present day, though I know of no evidence of it.

In *The Book of Q*, Jonathan Rabb tells the tale of a conspiracy of still-thriving Manichaeans to gain the papal throne for one of their own and to use the Catholic Church as a vehicle for establishing the supremacy of

1. Widengren, *Mani and Manichaeism*, 25.
2. Rudolph, *Gnosis: The Nature and History of Gnosticism*, 329.
3. Schoeps, *Jewish Christianity*, 68–73; Andrae, *Mohammed: The Man and his Faith*, 101.
4. Runciman, *The Medieval Manichee*.
5. Eliade, *The Two and the One*, 83–88.

their own cult, soon no longer to be a secret. These sectarian schemers will try any base and villainous scheme to gain their ends, including kidnapping, assassination, torture, and terrorism. Given the temper of the times, it is frankly surprising to see the Manichaeans (on the fiction that they still thrive in secret—to the tune of some *ten million* members!) so thoroughly vilified. Contrast this with the treatment of the modern Gnostics (or whatever they are: fertility cultists? Religious nudists?) in Dan Brown's *The Da Vinci Code*, who are made veritable paragons of New Age enlightenment. But Rabb is safe: even if any Manichaeans do survive, they're not likely to blow their cover by publicly taking offense at his fictionalized characterizations of them!

The novel, like most of those we are surveying, is filled with viable and interesting characters, as well as labyrinthine plot twists. The ample writing skill of the author allows him to trace an intricate and inventive structure—modeled upon the central Gnostic/Manichaean motif of initiation—into deeper and deeper secrets. The protagonist is a young and scholarly Catholic priest named Ian Pearse who, like many counterparts in these books, experiences grave temptations to cast celibacy aside. The intrepid Father Ian finds himself swept up in a nightmare adventure in which he must secure a fabulous lost document. The Manichaeans will stop at nothing to seize it from him. Neither will the Catholics. And it is sometimes hard to tell which brand of thuggish zealot Ian must evade at any given time. And it's hard not just for the reader, for along one prong of the priest's long odyssey he experiences a series of revelations about those he first considered friends and allies. One by one they turn out to be part of the conspiracy that he is either opposing or serving (if he could only tell which!). This progress of betrayal and its revelation, closer and closer to home, is itself a graded process of initiation.

Simultaneously Father Ian is vouchsafed, or discovers, one secret document after another, each leading, by cryptical ciphers, to the next. He must learn to interpret the glossolalia in which each holy puzzle is framed before he can go on to the next. First he and his lover (eventually his wife) discover a set of symbol-inscribed Syriac parchment squares, all threaded together, and manage to shoot an unidentified goon who shows up looking for them and is on the point of gunning them down to get it. But then some highly suspicious agents, ostensibly from Vatican security, touch down in a helicopter to take charge of the odd patchwork manuscript. Some time later, in Rome, an old priest and old friend tells

Ian he has discovered a valuable scroll hidden behind some catacomb frescoes. His story doesn't quite compute, but it is apparent that people are getting rubbed out for having possession of the scroll, and the old priest palms it off on Ian, who is willing to assume the danger himself for the sake of his old friend.

Father Ian brings the scroll to a specialist, another old friend and mentor, and watches as she unfurls the scroll to discover that it is a series of epistles from writers writing under the names of the five great biblical prophets of Manichaeanism: Adam, Seth, Enosh, Shem, and Enoch. Here we think we have hit the jackpot, but the intrepid pair of scholarly puzzle-solvers at length breaks a subtle code hidden in the clever arrangement of the texts, and it tells where one may find the *real* manuscript treasure, which turns out to be on Mount Athos. After a brain-busting sequence of deductions from the clues in the Manichaean epistles, Father Ian discovers what at first appears to be the secret repository of a text called the *Hagia Hodoporia* (the Sacred Journey). But in fact what awaits him is a sixteenth-century manuscript by one who had found the secret book there and thought it best to rebury it elsewhere. After another leg of the journey, Ian finds the precious scroll carefully ensconced in the foundation of a village well in the Balkans. This time it is the real thing. And what is that? Well, the revelation is robbed of its thunder if you happen to remember the title of the book you are reading: *The Book of Q*.

Yes, it is a first-century manuscript of that long-lost source (German: *Quelle*) document used by Matthew and Luke in addition to Mark. (Well, it's *supposed* to be, though I'm not sure. Hold on.) It seems that both the conspirators and their Vatican opponents, none of whom knows the nature of the sought-after document, nonetheless feel pretty sure that it might contain some secret so explosive as to shake the foundations of Christianity, whether Orthodox, Catholic, or Protestant, as we know it.

> Could a scroll like that be seen as a threat—a single voice, Christ's teachings made plain at last? Could ... even the hint of it prompt someone in the church to suppress it—better to maintain the current structure than to upend it, no matter how true to Christ's own insights the source of that clarity might be? (pp. 56–57)

Of course, Catholics wouldn't relish the earthquake that would follow, but wouldn't Manichaeans be only too glad to see the ensuing ruckus? If traditional Christianity fell, why, here would be the golden opportunity for Manichaeans to pick up the pieces! Of course, poisoning the pope, rigging the papal election by threatening some of the cardinals' relatives, then killing all but a handful of the cardinals in a Vatican explosion wouldn't hurt either! The same schemers contrive to bomb thousands of churches and to lay the blame on Islamic fundamentalists, hoping by these expedients to cause the remnants of world Christianity to rally round the new (secretly Manichaean) pope. All this is, to put it mildly, so far distant from the Sermon on the Mount (the heart of Q) that one would think the evil Manichaeans would have more to fear from that text than the Catholics. But then, both religious bodies already have open access to the sayings of Jesus in Matthew and Luke, don't they? They have long since learned to ignore and interpret away the uncomfortable gospel sayings that condemn the worldly machinations used so nefariously by all parties to the struggle. If the Manichaeans knew that the ancient text they so covet was "merely" the Q source, one might expect them to continue to suppress it, not to reveal it, since the revelation would only highlight the failure of both sides to live up to its teachings.

What is Q as Jonathan Rabb conceives it? It was a "source contemporary with Christ, and thus unlike any of the four Gospels. Jesus' sayings, untouched, pure, written in His lifetime" (p. 331). And, Rabb continues,

> Q was half Gospel, half diary, one that traced twenty years in the life of a Cynic teacher named Menippus. . . . Menippus was a wanderer, no purse, no bag, no sandals. . . . Driven by a force he couldn't understand, Menippus had set off on his 'Hagia Hodoporia' from his home in Gadara . . . Along the way, he had lived in Sepphoris, not far from Nazareth, then spent several years with . . . the Essene community at Qumran.

In Nazareth Menippus met the young boy Jesus and recognized him as a vessel of great spiritual power. First Menippus tutored the lad, then became his "beloved disciple" and biographer. "Q was nothing less than a history of the lost years of Jesus' life, his development from ages twelve to thirty, all transcribed by the pen of a Cynic teacher" (p. 331).

In fact, the very notion of a "hidden period" already implies a dogmatic embellishment of the Jesus figure. It is only in the case of an incarnate deity that one feels pressed to "fill in" unknown years, since all of them must have been packed with divine significance.

Besides this, we have a gross anachronism here. The Cynic Menippus of Gadara was a real historical figure. The problem is that he was a contemporary of Mani in the third century, not of Jesus in the first. Rabb is using him as a focus for the current hypothesis that Jesus was a Galilean Cynic or at least heavily influenced by Cynics.[6] It is a viable theory with much evidence in its favor. A number of Jesus' sayings urge the hearer to renounce home, occupation, money, and family, and to go on the road preaching a gospel of simplicity, love, and non-resistance, which are all Cynic distinctives. Jesus is shown dismissing kosher laws with the mocking rationalization that all food will end up in the toilet anyway, so what's the difference (Mark 7:18–19)? When the pious accuse him of associating with sinners, he counters that no one blames the doctor for visiting the sick, just as Diogenes defended his visit to a brothel by reasoning that the rays of the sun are not polluted when they shine into a latrine. He tells his audience to learn to live care-free, like birds, flowers, and animals for whom God provides. As Greek-speaking Cynics proclaimed this "government of Zeus," i.e., living in accordance with nature by reason, so did Jesus speak of the Kingdom of God, perhaps meaning the same thing.

The trouble with the Cynic hypothesis is that the sayings about trusting God for provision need not imply, as they would for Cynics, that one ought to tempt fate by renouncing one's resources. Where Jesus does speak of "letting goods and kindred go," he may not mean voluntary poverty at all; he may rather be warning of persecution, which begins with the seizure of property (Heb 10:34). A martyrdom context is suggested, in fact, by the adjacent sayings about bearing one's cross, as in Luke 14:25–33.

But there is a considerably larger problem with Q as Jonathan Rabb envisions it. His Q is 845 verses in length (p. 331). The non-Markan material common to Matthew and Luke amounts to a mere 250 verses. Matthew and Luke would seem to have skipped the lion's share of Q. Rabb minimizes the implications:

> What was most clear from Q, however, was how strange the message had become in the hands of the writers of the Gospels and beyond. Not only had they inserted certain events—the Last Supper (and thus the Eucharist) was nowhere to be found in Q—but they had eliminated key sentiments that Pearse could only guess had run counter to the needs of the early church. The role of women as preachers (in keeping with the Cynic tradition),

---

6. Downing, *Cynics and Christian Origins*.

the constant emphasis on the individual's responsibility to maintain his or her own commitment, all disappeared once out of Q's hands. (p. 334)

But that's only the tip of the iceberg. It is not just that certain emphases have been redactionally omitted. For Rabb to call the larger entity Q is the tail wagging the dog:

> There are nonparable conversations with Jesus, transcriptions of early sermons He gave, a recounting of the two years he spent in Jaipur with a group of Buddhist monks. The eastern and Cynic influences are unmistakable. (p. 344)

Here we have the old Notovitch myth (see Nicholas Notovitch, *The Unknown Life of Jesus Christ*)[7] about the young man Jesus visiting India to learn Buddhism. It is plain to see that, while, as Rabb describes it, the Synoptic Q source must overlap the *Hagia Hodoporia*, the two cannot simply be identified. At least Father Ian ought not jump to such a conclusion. Why not theorize that the Pseudo-Menippus had access to a copy of the same Q collection that Matthew and Luke did, and that, like them, he built it into a larger whole, adding more material from other sources? As we will see in a moment, one of those sources is the *Gospel of Thomas*. Rabb has based several of his Q sayings (the ones that do not come from Matthew and Luke) on *Thomas*. And, again, the whole business about Jesus holding ecumenical dialogue with the Buddhists means we are dealing with a different kettle of fish altogether.

A brief examination of as much "Q" text as Rabb permits us to see will show what kind of job Rabb has done, how successful his attempts to pastiche New Testament gospel style have been.

> 1. *Blessed are those who have grown confident and have found faith for themselves.* (p. 333)

This saying seems implausibly redolent not just of modern terminology but of modern conceptuality as well. As with most of the sayings to follow, there is an entire absence of that distinctive ring we find in Jesus' sayings, whether actually his or the product of those who have mastered the form.

---

7. Fader, *The Issa Tale that Will not Die.*

> 2. *Do not worry, from morning to evening and from evening to morning, about what you will wear. Consider the ragged cloak to be a lion's skin.* (p. 333)

The second sentence is plausibly Cynical, since it alludes to Hercules donning the hide of the vanquished Nemean Lion. Hercules was a favorite exemplar for the Cynics. Hercules' strength, it is implied, lay in his will power, a special virtue for the philosophers.[8] But omit the second sentence, and what you have left is *Thomas*, saying 36.

> 3. *When you know yourselves, then you will be known, and will understand that you are children of the living Father. The task lies within you, the journey yours alone. Do not look to another to find a guide for yourself. He will not be there.* (p. 333)

The first sentence comes right out of *Thomas*, saying 3. The rest of it is absurd, asking you to heed a guide who tells you to heed no guides!

> 4. *When you make male and female into a single one, so that the male will not be male and the female will not be female, then you will enter the kingdom.* (p. 333)

This is simply *Thomas*, saying 22.

> 5. *And so with all instruction and teaching, men and women share equally in perfection. In me, there is neither male nor female.* (p. 333)

The first sentence looks and sounds as if it came straight from a church order document, not a collection of Jesus' sayings. It originated, as anyone can plainly tell, as a *written stipulation*, seeking to counter 1 Timothy 2:12, "I do not allow a woman to teach or exercise authority over a man." The second sentence is obviously a clumsy reworking of Galatians 3:28b, "There is neither male nor female, for you are all one in Christ Jesus."

> 6. *And how is it possible that a man who has nothing, who is naked, houseless, squalid, without a city, can pass a life in peace? See, God has sent you a man to show you that it is possible. Look at me. And what do I want? Am I not without sorrow? Am I not without fear? Am I not free?* (p. 334)

---

8. Malherbe, *Paul and the Popular Philosophers*, 8, 14, 57, 82–83, 168–69.

This is, word for word, a saying from the *Discourses* of the Stoic sage Epictetus.

> 7. And He said to them, "For what would you find through others that you cannot find in me alone? What walls exist that can house my power? And if they should try, I shall throw down this building, and no one will be able to build it." (p. 334)

The last sentence is from *Thomas*, saying 71. The first might be a paraphrase of Peter's words in John 6:68, "Lord, to whom shall we go? You have words of eternal life."

> 8. If God does not have a house, a stone set up as a temple, dumb and toothless, a bane which brings many woes to men, but one which is not possible to see from earth, nor to measure with mortal eyes, since it was not fashioned by mortal hands. (p. 334)

This is a clumsy and confusing paraphrase of the anti-temple ideology of Stephen's speech in Acts chapter 6, which equated temple buildings with heathen idols.

> 9. For those who name themselves bishop, and also deacon, as if they received their authority from God, are, in truth, waterless canals. (p. 335)

Granted, Jesus might be pictured as puncturing the pretensions of Qumran "overseers," but the coupling of "deacons" with "bishops" marks this saying as a gross anachronism: it is an anti-hierarchical condemnation of the Catholic Church, and therefore hardly a product of a young rebel who had no thought to build an institution that would much later evolve these offices. Jesus is presented as speaking across time to a church that hijacked his legacy.

> 10. And at that time, a great noise went up through Jerusalem, a wailing for the death of this Son of Man. And with it came word of a resurrection, His tomb laid empty, His being risen and returned. "But this will not be so," He had told me, "though some will try to say otherwise. It is but the folly of men to need such signs, their folly to place their faith in the body and not in the spirit." (p. 335)

Unless I miss my guess, this saying is based on a similar passage from the Apocryphal Acts of John, the portion known as The Preaching of John (section 101):

> So I have suffered none of the things they will say I suffered . . . You hear that I suffered, yet I did not suffer; that I did not suffer, yet I did suffer; that I was pierced, yet I was not struck; hanged, yet I was not hanged; that blood issued from me, and it did not issue forth. In sum, what they say about me did not happen to me, but what they do not say, that I did suffer![9]

Isn't it perfectly obvious that both are attempts, long after the fact, to correct an earlier, literalistic understanding of Jesus' crucifixion in the one case and his resurrection in the other? To have Jesus anticipating a false rumor of his resurrection is as artificial as the gospel passages (e.g., Mark 14:28) in which he is made to predict that resurrection.

Have I not gotten carried away, arguing that the *Hagia Hodoporia* is not an authentic set of Jesus sayings, when the whole thing is admittedly a fiction, just part of a novel? I don't think so, because my point is to apply to this novel the scholarly tools its author claims to have used in writing it. He acknowledges a great many contemporary scholars of the New Testament and of Gnosticism from whose books he has profited (p. 377), though he misspells a couple of their names. I am just suggesting he could have learned their lessons better and done a much better job trying to speak for Jesus. The tendency and effect of his attempt are to claim the authority of the pre-canonical authentic Q source for his pet opinions (East-West syncretism, feminism, egalitarianism, anti-institutionalism), and then to read them into the source by positing nearly two-thirds more of "original Q" that got cut out of it! That is a clumsy piece of sleight-of-hand. Why not just invent a new gospel? Well, really, that is what he has done.

In the end, once Rabb's version of Q is brought to light, the Manichaeans are off the scene, having over-reached themselves and pretty much rubbed each other out in a revenge orgy. Thus whatever use they might have made of the document to blackmail the Catholic Church is moot. The Catholics want to suppress it because of the denial of the resurrection, something that would supposedly give the lie to their authority, as if that were the main issue at stake in a denial of the resurrection.

> And that resurrection is a literal one, confirmed by Peter. Without that doctrine, without Peter standing there saying, "I was the first, I can vouch for His return. He gave me the keys and told me

---

9. Price, *The Pre-Nicene New Testament*, 728–29.

to tend to the sheep, and so forth and so on," there's no need to have a group of men—the leaders of the church—sustaining that confirmation. In other words, without the doctrine of bodily resurrection, there's no way to validate the apostolic succession of bishops. No way to lay claim to the papacy.[10] (p. 73)

The logic here is far from obvious. What does a resurrection have to do with it? Wouldn't the situation be the same if no one claimed Jesus rose from the dead? The disciples might still have succession disputes, just as sects, philosophical schools, and even monarchies have always had. But it is simple in principle for an unresurrected founder's companions and disciples to lay claim to primacy based on their association with him during his life and career. On the other hand, a claim for resurrection appearances as credentials of apostleship (1 Cor 9:1) settles nothing either, since rivals may all make the same claim, and who knows who, if anyone, is lying?

Our intrepid priest, Ian Pearse, bargains with the new pope. (The Manichaean usurper was quickly assassinated!) Ian agrees to trim Menippus' debunking of the resurrection if the new pope will publish the rest of the document and use it as a charter for the liberalization of the church. It is a disgusting spectacle, but it is one way to deal with our recurring question: would the making public of a newly-discovered gospel wreak havoc? Sometimes it appears too stiff a challenge for the novelist to try to depict such repercussions, so he or she has the gospel get lost again, to restore an easily-described status quo. That is the not-so-holy journey Rabb follows by having his hero bowdlerize the gospel in such a compromise.

Finally, we ought to ask how correctly Jonathan Rabb portrays Gnosticism. We can overlook one minor error: "Seth, Enoch [are] not part of Gnostic tradition" (p. 179). If this were so, we would not have all the Sethian revelations in the Nag Hammadi corpus. More importantly, Rabb gets a crucial point right that Dan Brown got egregiously wrong in *The Da Vinci Code*. Brown had the notion that Gnostics understood Jesus as modern Unitarians do: a simple, human moralist. The truth is just the opposite:

> "So Gnosticism humanizes Christ?" "No," Angeli shook her head.
> "It elevates human self-awareness to a deified status, and places

---

10. The argument comes direct from Pagels, "The Controversy over Christ's Resurrection," 3–27.

the responsibility to achieve that status on the individual's shoulders. Jesus remains elevated. It's just now, He might not be alone." (p. 74)

And perhaps the best thing about this novel's portrayal of Gnostic Manichaeanism, despite all the hyper-Machiavellian intrigue, is its depiction of the religion as a living, cherished faith. Too often scholars seem to look at Gnostic texts in the abstract, as mere collections of motifs, rather than as scriptures that enhanced and informed the lives of those who pored over them.

32 | The Q Conspiracy
Paul Nigro, Q

THE QUESTION OF THE QUEST

THE MORE CONTROVERSY THE Q hypothesis generates (or renews) among scholars, the more novelists there are who seem to see it as a good bandwagon to jump on—and why shouldn't they? I doubt if anyone enjoys such novels more than the scholars who are actively engaged with Q scholarship! Well, here's another one. Paul Nigro knows a bit about Q, but his main concern seems to be the extent to which one's acceptance of it as a reality would threaten the foundations of simplistic Sunday School faith. He stresses the urgency of the Q question by depicting the actual (albeit fictional) discovery of the text itself, which prevents the characters and the reader from dismissing it as a mere theory and hoping it will go away.

The perspective from which Nigro writes is plainly that of an easily threatened, simple faith. His main characters are students and faculty members at Southwestern Baptist Seminary in Fort Worth, and Southern Baptist pastors from the same city. That creates a microcosmic hothouse in which the issues look very different from their appearance in some of our other Q novels. That much is plausible, for the repercussions of the Q Document or the Q hypothesis surely ought to be felt there, too. But the focus is still too narrow. Too much of the action and intrigue takes place in Fort Worth, giving the novel the air of one of those soap operas in which *Time* magazine is published in the tiny hamlet of Port Charles and all national and international affairs are somehow focused there. Again, one is reminded of *Buffy the Vampire Slayer*, with a handful of local kids and their high school librarian battling against the forces of cosmic evil. It's the Scooby Gang versus the Higher Criticism.

The Q Document resides in the collection of a village atheist and local newspaper publisher named Daniel Withers who plans to use it as a weapon, Burton Mack style, to topple Christianity by showing that the earliest Christians lacked belief in Jesus as any more than a wise man and knew nothing of any farfetched resurrection doctrine. If the earliest gospel source knows nothing of miracles, Christology, or a resurrection, mustn't those things be secondary and thus spurious? This is, naturally, enough to make Withers a Snidely Whiplash of a villain in a born-again Christian mystery novel. But he is a shady character on other grounds, too. It turns out he has bought the Q manuscript from a thief. It was originally the property of a mysterious tweedy British clique called the Order of Saint Matthew, dedicated to hiding the existence and contents of Q from the public, for fear of shattering faith! Any reader whose sympathies lie with scholarship rather than dogmatism has to wonder who the real villain is! Withers's scholarly allies (who authenticate the Q manuscript as from the mid-first century) are similarly drawn caricatures: pompous stuffed shirts who care not a fig for faith or truth but are motivated only by professional jealousy and self-aggrandizement.[1]

LIBELING LIBERALS

Nigro casts the worst scholarly villain, a man named Lester B. Bothwell, as a Fellow of the fiendish Jesus Seminar and a nefarious former mentor of upstanding Southern Baptist Professor of New Testament Ashley Dunbarton (who, however, like author Nigro, does not seem to have the faintest idea of what "textual criticism" is, though he mentions it often enough). Of his venerated mentor Dunbarton has this to say: "He makes my blood boil—always has. My interest in textual criticism is based in part on a desire to prove him wrong" (p. 143). What dread blasphemies does Professor Bothwell spew?

> One should say that Q, being the earliest documentation of the sayings of Jesus (along with [the Gospel of] Thomas, naturally) places our true Christian heritage in focus, leaving the superstitions of our ancestors in tatters on the cutting-room floor . . . I do believe we have discovered the Teacher at long last and are no

---

1. Such stereotypes are so common they must have a basis in fact, but all I can say is that in my long involvement with the Jesus Seminar and the Jesus Project, I have rarely if ever met such a creature.

longer required to offer explanations for those traditions which are, quite frankly, indefensible. (pp. 142–43)

It's not that the expressed views of Bothwell (whose name, I suspect, is meant to remind one of Rudolf Bultmann) are depicted as a straw man. I doubt that Jesus Seminar founder, the late Robert W. Funk, would have had qualms about putting his own name under that quote. Where Nigro veers off into sectarian caricature is in the *motives* of Bothwell and his iterations, "the liberals." Listen to "your precious Ashley" wax righteously indignant:

> I'm saying that liberal scholars have already made their findings known. Since the discovery of the *Gospel of Thomas* at Nag Hammadi in 1945, which was simply a collection of sayings, the search for Q has become an obsession with people who are out to prove that Jesus was just a man who had some profound, witty sayings to his credit and that he later was mythologized by followers who sought their own agendas, not his. (pp. 143–44)

Accordingly, Bothwell does eventually become the most hay-fever-inducing of straw men, when he is hired by publisher Withers to write commentary on each saying and gloss (see below) in Q as he publishes the document piecemeal, week by week, in the newspaper. Every installment features ludicrous ranting vilifying Jesus as some kind of Reverend Ike or Charles Manson. It facilitates the dogmatic slumber of fundamentalists to believe that such psychotic vitriol motivates scholarly elites who disagree with them. It always has. It's a new way of saying the devil is inspiring their heresies.

Why do these modern Jesus-hating Pharisees spend their time undermining the beliefs of the faithful? To give cover to their unbelieving souls, of course. It is the universal assumption of fundamentalists that any intellectual dissent from fundamentalist dogma is a mere smokescreen pumped up by sinners who will generate any pretext to avoid repenting of their cherished sins. (To which one may respond, "What happened to the inerrancy of 'Judge not that ye be not judged'"?) Pardon me if I view "the liberals" a bit differently. I cannot help thinking of Albert Schweitzer, who believed Jesus was a failed, though heroic, would-be messiah from whom a stream of spiritual force floods forth to engage even the modern gospel-reader and call him or her to discipleship.[2] Schweitzer renounced

---

2. Schweitzer, *The Quest of the Historical Jesus*, 401, 403.

the wealth and prestige he enjoyed as part of the European intelligentsia to enter missionary service in French Equatorial Africa, where he built a hospital and introduced the wretched African nationals to their first taste of modern medicine. Not exactly self-serving or self-aggrandizing. And I think of Rudolf Bultmann, whom William Barclay described as the most evangelical preacher he had ever heard. Not one to discourage a decision for Christ.

When conservative biblical scholars (a euphemism for "apologists") take on "liberals" (a slur for biblical critics), there is a strange game going on in which the two teams are playing not only by different rules but for different goals. In my reading and meeting critical scholars (including Van A. Harvey, Bart Ehrman, Bob Funk, Dennis R. MacDonald), the impression I have gotten has been that their disillusionment with orthodox faith has been an unforeseen result—not a presupposition, and much less a motivation—of their studies. Their disappointment with faith has simply resulted from a poor fit of the data they found with the dogma they had held. Having once been "infected" with a zeal to understand the biblical text better, with every means at one's disposal, many avid Bible students finally reach the point where they recognize that the old dogmas like scriptural inerrancy serve to block the fuller understanding of the text, not to facilitate it.

One reaches a crossroads and sacrifices Sunday School faith for an adult, critical grasp of the text, and the honest scholar must perforce let the chips fall where they may. Having been warned that naïve Biblicism was the only bulwark against nihilistic unbelief, and with Biblicism out of the way, one may reject faith altogether as one was, in effect, coached to do by one's former co-religionists. Or one may realize that was a hollow threat and begin to search for a new, more viable faith stance. But, in the eyes of the fundamentalists from whose ranks one has departed, one is equally an apostate either way. Thus it is no surprise to behold, as in Paul Nigro's novel, the cards laid flat on the table: fundamentalists engage in a pretense of scholarship. Their goal is not to discover anything new about the Bible but precisely the opposite: to club to death any new discovery or theory that raises its head. It is like the paranoid King Herod who killed his own children lest they grow up and challenge him for the throne. Why does the fundamentalist oppose the notion that early Christians might have considered Jesus "only" a great sage? One of the Southern Baptist clergy in the novel answers us forthrightly.

> Jesus is a real person to me. He isn't merely a historical figure, a man who lived long ago. He isn't a cult leader, or an opportunist or an eccentric religious nut. He is the living God who became man and dwells in us through his abiding Spirit. I know this, because I know him. (p. 324)

I would love to know the details of this supposed knowledge! Has the good Reverend heard a voice in his head, Jesus telling him, "By the way, the Nicene Creed is true. I'm the Second Person in the Trinity"? I doubt it. How would telepathic contact with an Athanasian Jesus feel different from grokking an Arian or Semi-Arian Jesus? In fact, my experiences with born-again Christians, both as a member and then as an outsider, lead me to believe that none of them has ever had an experience that they could meaningfully dub "a personal relationship with Christ." It is all mere sloganeering. At most, pietistic Christians engage in psychological projection in which they imagine the Sunday School portrait of Jesus, or perhaps the stained glass version, listening to them and patting them on the head. I dare to suggest even that sophisticated, degree-bearing graduates of conservative institutions are no different. All their effort goes to keeping up a Sunday School account of gospel origins that will not disturb the dozing faithful (including themselves, as long as they can manage to hide from themselves the game they are playing). For instance, Nigro's scholars and seminarians all believe the four gospels were written by eyewitnesses of the ministry of Jesus (p. 376), though they also sometimes speak as if aware of the basic source criticism refuting that claim.

THE HISTORICAL Q

In the beginning of the book, Nigro introduces us to a scribe named Ezra who has heard Jesus preach and begun to make a written record of his sayings. He eventually applies for membership as a disciple, as his IRS agent brother Matthew has successfully done. Only Jesus will not have him, apparently skeptical that Ezra can brook the necessary sacrifices. (Later, though, Ezra joins the ultra-strict Essene monastery at Qumran, which made Jesus and his disciples look like the Delta House screwballs in the movie *Animal House* by comparison.) Ezra keeps showing up at Jesus' public appearances, but the Savior never gives him the nod to come join the after-party. Ezra had been a disciple of John the Baptist, but his water-logged mentor is now in jail. After Jesus is seized and executed,

Ezra publicly cat-calls Caiaphas, blaming him for the deed, and then he finds he must take it on the lam. This he does, entrusting his diary of Jesus' sayings to the hands of his sister Mara. He ends up at Qumran, where he gets a job copying Dead Sea Scrolls in the scriptorium. In his spare time, he rewrites Q, annotating it with comments on the *Sitz-im-Leben*, the circumstances that led to this or that saying of Jesus, including Matthew 8:19–20 ("And a certain scribe came and said to him, 'Teacher, I will follow you wherever you go.' And Jesus said to him, 'The foxes have holes, and birds of the air have nests, but the son of man has nowhere to lay his head.'"). It turns out that Ezra was that scribe. He does not fit so well into the Lukan counterpart in 9:57, where the would-be recruit is simply said to be "a man." Scholars with a bit more on the ball than Nigro or his characters realize that, since Matthew appears to have introduced "scribes" into various Q contexts from which they were originally absent, this is also no doubt a Matthean redactional addition. Luke has preserved the original, as usual.

So, in this novel, there were two editions of Q: the original, which contained nothing but the sayings of Jesus, recorded on the spot by a frustrated admirer, and a new edition with autobiographical annotations. The first remained in possession of Ezra's and Matthew's sister Mara until she pulled it out of a drawer and handed it to Matthew. It came in handy when he was writing up his gospel. One supposes Matthew had remembered the sayings of his master as best he could but welcomed an on-the-spot transcription. Once he was finished with it, he gave the copy to Paul, thinking it might come in handy in the latter's preaching missions. Paul, in turn, let his personal physician Luke use Q in writing his own gospel. But all this is impossible and illustrates the typical fundamentalist's poor grasp of New Testament scholarship. For one thing, the authors of the Pauline Epistle to the Galatians (1:6–9; 2:14–18; 4:10–11; 5:2–4) bitterly assails whoever advances the pro-Torah agenda of Matthew 5:17–19. That passage in turn attacks anyone preaching the Pauline doctrine that Gentiles need not observe the fine print of the Torah. There is no way these writers got along, or would have gotten along. Similarly, if anyone ever gave Paul a set of Jesus' sayings, he must have lined a birdcage with it, because he never uses any of them in any of his letters. Some imagine that 1 Corinthians 7:10–11 ("To the married I give instructions, not I, but the Lord, that the wife should not leave her husband … and that that the husband should not send his wife away") is supposed to be a Jesus quote. I think it is a prophetic word from the Risen One, which later passed on into the gospels misattributed to the historical Jesus.

THE DUNBARTON HYPOTHESIS

Why does Q contain nothing about the death or resurrection of Jesus? Not because Ezra represented a more primitive type of Christianity that knew nothing of these spurious, add-on doctrines, but simply because the Q author Ezra had de facto finished his work before the resurrection occurred. Not surprisingly, the intrepid Dr. Dunbarton is able to reconstruct enough of Nigro's history of Q to set forth "the Dunbarton Hypothesis."

> Having given the liberals their due, we cannot accept their explanation that the resurrection passages are not present in Q because it never happened.... [W]e believe the reason our scribe failed to document it is simply that he was long gone when it occurred ... So we can assume the scribe, whether he knew about the Cross or not, never knew that Jesus had risen again. (p. 376)

How ironic that much the same explanation of Q's lack of the resurrection has been advanced by one of the hated "liberals" themselves. Walter Schmithals suggested that the gospels combined Synoptic narrative material including the resurrection of Jesus (factual or not is beside the point) with the Q source, which came from Galilee where Jesus was known only as a sage from the days he lived and preached there. Schmithals did not share the Sunday School belief that the evangelists were reporters covering the Jesus beat, but he did recognize that early Christian documents, like Q, might have been compiled in ignorance, not rejection, of the resurrection doctrine. Schmithals conjectured that the gospels combined Q with the narrative material in order to attract the Q communities to join Christianity proper by getting them to accept the resurrection and messiahship of the One they had formerly revered merely as a "teacher of righteousness."

> In view of the fact that the Easter confession and, accordingly, a christology is foreign to this [Q] tradition, and that Jesus, like John, appeared on the scene as a prophet, who announced the imminent inbreaking of the reign of God, this Q-community must have persisted in the pre-Easter situation. It cannot be assumed that the confession that God raised Jesus from the

dead reached all the followers of Jesus, or, as the case may be, convinced them all.[3]

Burton L. Mack sees things similarly.

> By degrees scholars have been moving toward the view that the gospel was indeed Mark's creation, a narrative that brought together two distinctively different types of written material representative of two major types of early sectarian formation. One stream was that of movements in Palestine and southern Syria that cultivated the memory of Jesus as a founder-teacher. The other was that of congregations in northern Syria, Asia Minor and Greece wherein the death and resurrection of the Christ were regarded as the founding events.[4]

Strictly speaking, Mack (whose views about the explosive character of "Q without Easter" the fictional Bothwell's most closely resemble) does not say that Q's compilers knew of the resurrection doctrine and rejected it as a fanciful innovation. The Jewish-Christian Ebionites *did* know and reject the Virgin Birth doctrine. Mack's point is rather, if I read him right, that it is difficult to imagine an established Jesus Movement in Galilee chugging along quite satisfactorily for years or decades, hearing nothing of Jesus' resurrection *if it had actually occurred, and only two or three days following the crucifixion*. This is Nigro's assumption (via his Dunbarton character), too: if the resurrection had occurred, Q's compilers would have known of it right away. But it is circular to conclude, as Nigro/Dunbarton does, that this means the resurrection was scant days in the future as of Q's compilation. What separates this "hypothesis" from Mack's is the unstated assumption that the resurrection *must* have taken place, since the inerrant Bible says so. So the whole thing turns out to be one more lame, contrived harmonization stunt. No thanks.

Mack believes that different Jesus groups evolved myths reflecting their various needs, and this is why some early documents contained resurrection myths, others incarnation myths, others Virgin Birth legends, etc.

> Each of the several movements stemming from Jesus had worked out a rationalization for its distinctiveness in which Jesus played a founder's role by inaugurating just those features of the new social unit that set it apart.[5]

3. Schmithals, "The Parabolic Teachings in the Synoptic Tradition," 30–31.
4. Mack, *A Myth of Innocence*, 11.
5. Mack, 13.

For instance, those influenced by the sacramental initiation of the Mystery Cults required and developed myths of the saving death and resurrection of Jesus, modeled upon the earlier saviors of the religions of Attis, Osiris, etc. Non-sacramental Jesus sects had no need of a dying and rising Christ and therefore did not develop one. Eventually they were all amalgamated into the gospels and the canon of gospels that we have inherited, every one embracing everyone else's myths.

The story ends with the Baptist seminarians announcing the upcoming publication of the new material, but we don't get to see any real reaction to it. That would amount to another story in itself, one the author didn't feel like telling. But it is hard to deny the truth of Professor Dunbarton's cynical prediction, worthy of Ecclesiastes, made earlier in the tale: "And if [Q] does appear, what's going to happen? I'll tell you what—nothing! The conservatives will have explanations for the variants. The liberals will attack their positions. Same old story. Nothing will change" (p. 164).

33 | The Merovingian
Dan Brown, *The Da Vinci Code*

As we have seen, these books that claim to "blow the lid off Christianity" by means of new discoveries, real or imagined, find an avid public. Many of those readers might be called sophomoric skeptics: having learned proper suspicion toward their inherited Christian faith, they remain uncritical about the assertions of those who would substitute any other hypothesis, often equally wild. Despite their admirable curiosity, these seekers just do not know how to separate fact from fiction. Their imaginations have been much stirred by Dan Brown's best-selling novel, *The Da Vinci Code*. It is a fictional narrative, but its author claims it is based on fact. Alas, that too is part of the fiction.

A NOVEL IDEA

The Da Vinci Code is certainly a page-turner. Its brisk narrative is spangled with sudden twists, deft turns of phrase, sparkling metaphors, and resonating observations. Yet the book has grave shortcomings. First, there is no real protagonist. The ostensible hero is a Harvard professor. No Indiana Jones, our man is merely a passive intra-narrative incarnation of the reader, figuring out occasional puzzles simply because the narrative requires their solution before the action can continue. Too often, those solutions pop into the text in italics capped by exclamation points, cueing the reader in the manner of a sitcom laugh track to feel astonishment and a sense of (illusory) discovery.

Second, much of the resolution of the plot depends on a series of arbitrary mechanical reversals, where this or that character suddenly reveals unsuspected good or evil dimensions or hitherto-unhinted connections with other characters. The reader is jerked about by a chain of mere fiats on the part of the omnipotent author.

Third, Brown trips over himself in supplying a background of plausibility for the great secret that forms the prize that all his characters seek: the fanciful speculation that Jesus Christ and Mary Magdalene married and gave rise to the Merovingian dynasty of France with present-day heirs. Surely the whole premise of the book is that this supposed knowledge is a carefully guarded secret, in fact the secret of the ages. Yet as we shall see, this "secret" is well known to scholars—if only as a hoax. Apparently it is only the definitive proof, in the form of first-century documents salvaged from the ruins of the Jerusalem Temple, that awaits disclosure. What exactly is the secret? The truth or the proof? Brown seems to shift from one foot to the other and back again.

FALSE FACTS

Despite its shortcomings, *The Da Vinci Code* is astonishingly popular. We may hope that this betokens rising public suspicion that there is a deeper truth to Christian origins than what the churches teach. If readers hunger for the inside story, they aren't getting it in *The Da Vinci Code*. But Brown assures them that they are. Right up front he promises: "The Priory of Sion—a European secret society founded in 1099—is a real organization. In 1975 Paris's Bibliotheque Nationale discovered parchments known as *Les Dossiers Secrets*, identifying numerous members of the Priory of Sion, including Sir Isaac Newton, Botticelli, Victor Hugo, and Leonardo da Vinci" (p. 1). None of this is quite true.

Here are the inconvenient facts: While there was indeed a medieval monastic order called the Priory of Sion (Zion), it was absorbed by the Jesuits in 1617. The name was revived in 1956, appropriated by a far-right French political faction led by Pierre Plantard, an anti-Semite and Vichy sympathizer who fancied himself the rightful Merovingian heir to the throne of France. Plantard's group claimed connection with the original Priory for the same reason that Masonic Lodges claim (spuriously) to be descended from the Knights Templar.[1] This is like Ralph Kramden's Raccoon Lodge claiming the ancient secrets of Solomon. As for the *Secret Dossier*, also known as the *Priory Documents*, these have been exposed as modern fakes perpetrated by Plantard's political sect as

---

1. Richardson. "The Priory of Sion Hoax."

part of its attempt to fabricate a venerable pedigree.[2] Once these facts are known, Brown's whole house of cards collapses.

The Priory of Sion hoax (of which Dan Brown appears to be a victim, not an accomplice) was made popular thirty years ago through a tedious pseudo-documentary tome called *Holy Blood, Holy Grail*, by Michael Baigent, Richard Leigh, and Henry Lincoln.[3] (Brown's scholarly character Lee Teabing is a scrambled version of the names of Baigent and Leigh.) These gents argued that the Templar Knights were sent by the ultra-secret Priory of Sion on a top-secret mission to retrieve the legendary treasure of Solomon's Temple. They succeeded beyond their wildest dreams, discovering also a cache of documents telling the real story of the Holy Grail, which turned out not to be a chalice but rather the secret of the royal blood line of Jesus. Fortified by these riches and the highly volatile secret of Jesus and his queen Mary Magdalene, the Templars and the Priory of Sion bribed and blackmailed their way to centuries of prominence, all the while protecting the descendants of Jesus and Mary among the Merovingian dynasty. The Merovingian heirs, notably Crusader Godfrey de Bouillon, were mindful of the messianic destiny implied in their very DNA. Seeking to regain their lost glory, they finally established the short-lived Crusader Kingdom of Jerusalem.

Baigent, Leigh, and Lincoln were little encumbered by inductive historical method. Much as their disciple Dan Brown would do decades later, they constructed their hypotheses in novelistic fashion, linking odd bits of data from medieval chronicles by means of one speculation after another: "What if A were really B?" "What if B were really C?" "It is not impossible that . . . " "If so-and-so were the case, this would certainly explain that and that." Admittedly, *had* the Templars discovered proof that Jesus and the Magdalene were husband and wife, this might account for their considerable clout. But what are the chances of that being the explanation?

THE KNIGHTS WHO SAY . . .

Who were the Templar Knights? They were a monastic order, the Poor Knights of the Temple of Solomon, founded between 1110 and 1120.

---

2. As such, they are only the most recent in a long chain of Templar-related forgeries. See Partner, *The Murdered Magicians*, 103, 135, 140, 146, 161–63.

3. Baigent, Leigh, and Lincoln. *Holy Blood, Holy Grail.*

Their sworn duty was to protect Christian pilgrims on their way to and from Jerusalem. Over the years, they acquired considerable fortunes and power, laying the groundwork for modern banking as they used their vast funds to bail out the crowned heads of Europe. Finally, in 1308, Philip the Fair, King of France, subjected the Templars to a ruthless inquisition, stripping them of their moneys, the real object of his holy zeal. What was the pretext for the persecution? It is difficult to tell, as we can never know the degree to which tortured wretches eagerly signed any crazy-sounding confession shoved in front of them. The beleaguered Templar Knights "confessed" to blasphemies including the worship of a goat-headed demon statue called Baphomet and kissing its anus, as well as ritual homosexuality, trampling the cross, and eliciting oracles from a still-living severed head! Actually, "Baphomet" is, contra Baigent and company, almost surely an Old French spelling of "Mahomet" or "Muhammad."[4] This in turn means that the accusations against the Templars reflect not actual Gnosticism or even diabolism, but garbled French beliefs about Islam.

In any case, the Templars became lionized in later folklore as adepts who guarded heretical secret doctrines they had discovered, perhaps in the form of rediscovered manuscripts, during their years in Jerusalem. Baigent, Leigh, and Lincoln sketched fanciful links between the Templars and other arcane groups beloved by modern occultists, such as the French Cathars (or Albigensians) wiped out in the Albigensian Crusade in 1209. Twenty years later, Brown follows in the esoteric footsteps of Baigent, Leigh, and Lincoln, who sued him for using their research, despite the fact that he gave them ample credit. This supremely tasteless stunt only served to demonstrate, if further proof were needed, that the *Holy Blood, Holy Mackerel* authors were fiction writers, not scholars. Novelists are the ones inventing original plot ideas for which they might conceivably have a right to sue, whereas scholars are in the business of factual information and are generally delighted to see colleagues building upon their work.

SWEET DREAMS AND FLYING MACHINES IN PIECES ON THE GROUND

What on earth does the great name of Leonardo da Vinci have to do with the Templars, Mary Magdalene, etc.? Not much. Throughout *Holy Blood,*

---

4. Partner, 138.

Holy Grail, Baigent and company recounted their attempts to authenticate a sheaf of modern, privately printed documents, the *Secret Dossier* or *Priory Documents*. We have seen that these were the hoaxes planted by Pierre Plantard's sect. And *only* this false source lists Da Vinci as one of the Grand Masters of the secret order. Thus there is no Da Vinci connection at all.

What of Brown's claim that Mary Magdalene appears next to Jesus in da Vinci's Last Supper? There is nothing to it. The figure is surely intended as John, son of Zebedee. In view of church traditions which imagined John penning his gospel as an old man at the close of the first century, it was traditional to picture him as a callow youth among the disciples of Jesus. In Renaissance painting, this means he winds up looking effeminate, as Jesus himself would were he not sporting a beard.

O NEGATIVE

We have several times had to get ahead of ourselves by mentioning the tantalizing notion that Jesus Christ and Mary Magdalene were married, and that their union would have issued in the Merovingian dynasty beloved by the modern French Far Right. How does the Teabing hypothesis (if we may so dignify it, using the name of Brown's scholarly character to stand for Brown's recycling of the fanciful pseudo-scholarship of his unwilling mentors) make this connection? There are a number of individual issues tangled up here.

First, is it possible for Mary and Jesus to have been married or at least to have been romantically involved? Of course it is. As all discussions of this issue point out, the apocryphal *Gospel of Philip* says, "Now Mary was the favorite of the Savior, and he often used to kiss her on the lips." Indeed, if there is any historical basis to the gospel portrait of Jesus traveling with unattached women (Mark 15:40–41; Luke 8:1–3), we must even consider whether, a la the suspicions of husbands alienated from their wives who had left them to follow the Christian apostles in the Apocryphal Acts, Jesus had been using the group of women as his harem. And in view of parallel cases from the whole history of mystery religions and Utopian communities, we cannot dismiss the possibility.

Still, possibility is not probability, as it seems to have become for upholders of the Teabing hypothesis. Conservative apologists and New Age paperback writers alike have a sad way of leaping from possibility to unjustified belief. "If there might be space aliens, we can assume there are." "If the traditional view of gospel authorship cannot be definitively debunked, we can go right on assuming its truth." No, you can't. And though Jesus might have had sex with one or many women or men, the mere possibility is of no help. He might have been a space alien, too. Some think he was. But historians don't.

Second, would it be a theological scandal if Jesus could be shown to have mated with a woman? The Teabing hypothesis so asserts. One of the gross historical errors in *The Da Vinci Code* is the claim that, in the interests of imperial propaganda, Constantine and his vest-pocket bishops abruptly replaced the hitherto-prevailing understanding of Jesus as a simple mortal with their mythic view of Jesus as a god who only seemed to be human. As any seminary freshman knows, Constantinian/Nicene orthodoxy stipulated that the Word made flesh (John 1:14) shared the same divine nature as the Father, not that he was no longer to be considered human. In any event, it is in no way clear that for Jesus to have had sex or begotten children would have been incompatible with either his sinlessness or his divine character.

Third, what would any of this have to do with the actual fifth- to eighth-century Merovingian dynasty—Clovis and his storied heirs? Our authors appeal to fourth-century French legends that Mary Magdalene eventually arrived in a boat on the shores of Gaul. In later versions she arrives with the Holy Grail. We usually think of the Grail as the communion cup of the Last Supper, as in medieval epics where Joseph of Arimathea brings the Grail to Brittany, whence it is taken to England to figure into the Arthurian mythos. But in fact the Grail is variously described. Wolfram von Eschenbach pictured it as an engraved emerald tablet like those mentioned in the Hermetic documents, where such artifacts are the vehicles of esoteric revelations (eventually reflected by the Golden Plates of Joseph Smith, also influenced by Masonry).[5] The Teabing hypothesis echoes Baigent and company, supposing that the Holy Grail (*San Greal*) is really the Royal Bloodline (*Sang Real*), the dynasty of the Messiah, to which the Merovingians belonged.

Whence comes the legend of Mary Magdalene's advent in the south of France? It is possible that it stems from the activity of Carpocratian missionaries in the region (chronicled by Irenaeus, circa 180 CE: *Against Heresies* 1:25:1–3). They claimed to have received choice revelations from Mary Magdalene, as did many early Gnostics. But even if they

---

5. Brooke, *The Refiner's Fire*.

did, that does not imply Mary's own presence there. Another attractive possibility is the suggestion of Dr. Robert Eisenman that the legend of Mary Magdalene, bearer of a royal bloodline, taking refuge in Gaul, is a scrambled memory of the fact that the disgraced Herodian heirs, Herod Antipas, Herodias, and Herod Agrippa, were exiled to the same region.[6] These are royalty with New Testament associations, and it is easy to see how the confusion might have arisen.

HOAX OR HISTORY? YOU DECIDE...

If engagement with the sources and impostures of the Templar/Magdalene hoax teaches us anything, it may be that modern gospels cut from the cloth of sheer imagination are in principle not so different from the venerable four that we have long known. After all, the methods we have used here to account for the one text work pretty much the same way when we study the others. If a "gospel" fires our imagination, perhaps it has done its proper work. But some are better than others. One of Professor Teabing's revelations to Dan Brown's readers is that there were in the early church some eighty gospels to pick from. (He gets the number, I gather, from its occurrence in a medieval tract by Muslim savant Abd al Jabr.) That is not much of a stretch; casual scrutiny of the table of contents in J. K. Elliott's *Apocryphal New Testament* will yield at least some sixty-five texts that could reasonably be denominated as gospels. But not all gospels are on the same level. One only need read them, and one will find oneself making one's own "canonical" list! Brown's *Da Vinci Code*, I must admit, would not be on my list.

APPENDIX: BETTYE JOHNSON, *SECRETS OF THE MAGDALENE SCROLLS*

Imagine yourself reading *The Da Vinci Code* by moonlight some clear evening. Only it does not occur to you that it is the *full moon*! And now it is too late! Your copy of Dan Brown's epic begins to tremble, to shake, to mutate and to become a monstrous caricature of itself! It would have turned into *Secrets of the Magdalene Scrolls: The Forbidden Truth of the Life and Times of Mary Magdalene* by Bettye Johnson. This absolutely awful book descends, from the first of too many pages, to the sub-literary level and merits mention here only because, if it weren't mentioned,

---

6. Eisenman, e-mail to the present writer, November, 2003.

someone would complain that I had overlooked it—which, honestly, I would much rather do. The best one can say of the writing is that it is . . . not confusing. It does a passable job of conveying its shameful nonsense.

The book begins with a couple of divorcees, affluent spiritual seekers, taking a hike in the Pyrenees, whereupon one of them falls into a hidden cave where a row of ceramic amphorae are sitting plainly in view. They contain ancient scrolls. It's as simple and as pat as that. They decide to get a good look at the ancient writings before turning them over to the French authorities lest the scrolls turn out to be great revelations subversive to the Christian faith, in which case the authorities would surely suppress them. A renegade Catholic priest shortly congratulates them on their wisdom since, as he is in a position to know, the fiendish Church will stop at nothing, including murder, to hide damaging discoveries. And all this *before* any of them has read a single word of the scrolls! But don't worry: they are explosive stuff! Or maybe a better word would be "implosive." The reader is subjected to some *twenty-three* scrolls written by a widowed Mary Magdalene with too much time on her hands. The resulting revelation is a trash basket filled with every crackpot theory and hare-brained New Age fad-belief one can find on the bookshelf, from the Law of Attraction to Zechariah Sitchin's ancient Akkadian space aliens, from *Holy Blood, Holy Mackerel* to bogus quantum physics. Mary Magdalene, a black Ethiopian, turns out to be a Messiah in her own right, the incarnation of Divine Wisdom and the reincarnation of the Queen of Sheba. She is an Ethiopian princess and priestess of Isis. Eventually she and Jesus undergo a sacred wedding, taking the roles of Isis and Osiris. Both are healers, New Age teachers, and pagan polytheists. Mary's Ethiopian civilization possessed advanced knowledge inherited from space visitors at the dawn of time.[7] The whole thing is like *The Da Vinci Code* written with the literary ineptitude of James Redfield's pedantic *The Celestine Prophecy*. Endless speeches by Mary Magdalene and the modern characters (when their exploits do not emulate those of mildly pornographic women's romance novels) take every kooky bit

---

7. Much like Hawkman, an ancient Egyptian pharaoh who appropriated the "Nth Metal" technology of a crashed saucer from the planet Thanagar, gaining the power of flight. He, too, was many times reincarnated until his appearance in the twentieth century as a winged superhero.

of misinformation in Dan Brown's pseudo-historical novel and carry it ten times farther into the Nonsense Zone. The author's portrait photo adorns the back cover, and she looks exactly like you would expect, down to the purple feather boa. One is by no means surprised to learn from her bio that she has endured seventeen years at the Ramtha School of Enlightenment. What a shock that an ancient text from the hand of Mary Magdalene would perfectly match bubble-headed New Ageism of the late twentieth century, adding nothing to the insipid Mulligan Stew of it.

34 | Skeleton Lock and Key
Kathy Reichs, *Cross Bones*

MOST OF THE BIBLICAL speculation in Kathy Reichs's novel *Cross Bones*[1] comes from two sources. "Dr. James Tabor, Chair, Department of Religious Studies, University of North Carolina at Charlotte, lit the initial spark for *Cross Bones*" (p. ix). "Credit must be given to ... *The Jesus Scroll* by Donovan Joyce, Dial Press, 1973" (p. x). As our task is to analyze biblical scholarship as portrayed (sometimes fictively) in the Lost Gospel books, and Reichs admits her dependence upon these two writers, it is their work, more than Reichs's, that must concern us.

THE VIEW FROM MOUNT TABOR

James Tabor's *The Jesus Dynasty*[2] reads like *Holy Blood, Holy Grail* and *The Messianic Legacy* by Baigent, Lincoln, and Leigh, too much so for my liking. It chronicles the travels, researches, and thought processes of the author, trying to draw the reader along to the finish line of his conclusion. I prefer to have the case set forth in a vacuum, built up and defended on its own objective merits. As it is, Tabor's case is a chain of weak links soldered together by supposition, possibility, and "what ifs." Tabor often simply asserts, "I believe that ..." That is a matter of hunches, not evidence. What is his basic claim, and upon what evidence does it rest? He believes that Jesus was a would-be king with genuine Davidic credentials, which he inherited from his mother Mary. Jesus' legal father Joseph was of Davidic descent, too, but he descended through King Jeconiah, whose descendants Jeremiah the prophet (Jer 22:30) disqualified from ever taking the throne. (In the real world, would that have mattered?)

---

1. All page references are to the Pocket Star paperback edition.
2. Tabor, *The Jesus Dynasty*.

Jesus was actually the son of Mary and of Pandera, perhaps even a particular Tyrian Roman legionary named Adbes Pantera whose tombstone Tabor visited in Germany. Joseph fathered no children and died young. His brother Clophas (a harmonization of two gospel names, Cleopas from Luke 24:18 and Clopas from John 19:25) begat James, Joses, Judas, and Simon with Mary, then died or bowed out of the picture, transferred to Germany, where Tabor saw his monument. But they were all, as per the Levirate marriage custom, considered Joseph's sons and heirs.

Everything is wrong with this. Tabor is willing to take both gospel genealogies as true and historical. That they conspicuously fail to agree is grist for his mill, for like the sixteenth-century scholar Annius of Viterbo,[3] Tabor gratuitously makes the Lukan genealogy the family tree of *Mary*, even though it plainly says it is the line of Joseph (Luke 3:23), her husband. He decides that the Jewish jibe that Jesus was the bastard son of the Roman Pandera was true and not a pun on the virgin (*parthenos*) birth claim, just because Pandera was a common name for Roman soldiers. He ignores the fact that there would be no pun to begin with unless there were actually men named "Pandera." The hardly reliable Epiphanius (fourth-century bishop of Salamis) tried to co-opt the slur by saying that Pandera was part of the name of an ancestor of Jesus. And that's good enough for Tabor.

Tabor swallows the obvious Lukan fiction of John the Baptizer being Jesus' cousin as an historical fact. He gratuitously posits that "Nazareth" (which, as archaeology shows, was not inhabited during the ostensible lifetime of Jesus)[4] is named for being a settlement of many who belonged to the lineage of David, and hence stemmed from the "branch" (*netzer*) of David. This is fantasy. Another Lukan figment he accepts is the trial of Jesus before Herod Antipas (Luke 23:6–12), a redactional doublet of the Pilate trial. From Mark 6:17 he absorbs the error of making Herod Antipas woo away the wife of his half-brother Philip. Herodias was actually the wife of Antipas' brother Herod.

Tabor has an interesting discussion of the presence of three different Marys at the tomb, an improbable circumstance, he suggests, even though, as he acknowledges, "Mary" was the most common female

---

3. Brown, *The Birth of the Messiah*, 89, referring to the work of Heer, *Die Stammbäume Jesu nach Matthäus und Lukas* and Vogt, *Der Stammbaum bei den heiligen Evangelisten Matthäus*.

4. Salm, *The Myth of Nazareth*.

name among contemporary Jews. I have many times been in a room with two or three other Bobs, so pardon me if I don't see it as that odd. And the empty tomb narratives are hardly historical reporting anyway. Nonetheless, Tabor reasons that it is too much for one of the Marys to be Jesus' mother (John 19:25) and another to have sons named Joses and James (Mark 15:40), names also of Jesus' mother Mary's other sons (Mark 6:3). So maybe the other Mary is Mary the wife of Clopas (John 19:25). And maybe she is a fictive doublet of Mary, Jesus' mother, which would explain why "they both" have sons with identical names. This doubling would have resulted in a later attempt to suppress Mary's levirate marriage as somehow unseemly, or perhaps just as a mistake.

Tabor notes the fascinating fact that "Cleophas" (and its variant "Alphaeus") come from a root meaning "replacement, substitute." Tabor says that would fit with this man's having been Joseph's brother standing in for him to beget children for his name. But then are we to suppose that his parents named him because they foresaw his future task? "Cleophas" would be better understood as a subsequent epithet. But who would this man be a substitute *for*?

Tabor is building toward the venerable theory of Adolf Harnack and Ethelbert Stauffer,[5] though he fails to mention them in his book. They postulated that Jesus was a messianic king, and that in his absence, James, then Simeon his brother, took over as "caliphs" in Jesus' place, as Abu-bekr, Umr and Uthman did after Muhammad's passing. Tabor even points out how the name "Cleophas" comes from the very same root as "caliph," though he seems to think it is an English word. I have to think he means that "caliph" is the Anglicized version of the Arabic *khalifa*. So I should think Robert Eisenman's approach would make more sense of these intriguing bits. Eisenman realized that none of the narratives of the gospels, and hardly the Nativity stories, preserve any real sequences of events, but that all gospel narratives must be decoded, reflecting, at best, dim echoes and clues of what was really going on. And in this case, surely the "Cleophas/Alphaeus" business must denote that placing James the Just as the brother of Simeon bar Cleophas (and therefore another "son of Cleophas") barely conceals the fact that James and Simeon were both "Cleophas," the caliph, or stand-in, for Jesus.

Tabor makes James the Just the secret identity of the Beloved Disciple, but how can that be, since John, whose exclusive property the

---

5. Stauffer, "The Caliphate of James."

Beloved Disciple character is, makes clear that Jesus' brothers were derisive skeptics (John 7:3–5)? Tabor simply posits that the brothers of Jesus were among the twelve disciples, so he must discount this verse, as well as Mark 3:31–35. His refutation? Nothing more than to say that, if the brothers were among the twelve, then scholars have been misreading these passages. Presto!

Again, Eisenman saw the link but made more sense of it: the Twelve were indeed fictive doublets, by and large, of the Pillars, the ostensible "brothers of the Lord." For Eisenman,[6] these names are islands on the surface, emerging from a vaster, hidden mass below, the outlines of which can still be dimly discerned. But Tabor is handicapped by taking way too much of the narrative surface at face value.

Tabor makes Luke a Paulinist and imagines that he was not eager to uphold the leadership rights of the Heirs, the relatives of Jesus. But this is a bad misreading of Luke-Acts, where the implication is that the family of Jesus were disciples already before the resurrection (compare Luke 8:19–21 with Mark 3:20–21, 31–35, and see Acts 1:14).

Tabor recaps David Friedrich Strauss's theory[7] that John 3:22–24 attests an interim period in which Jesus acted as an apprentice of John, sharing his baptizing work. (Of course, the casual reader would never guess anyone before Tabor had come up with the theory.) You can decide if that is more plausible than the alternative scholarly guess that the scenario of Jesus baptizing represents simply an anachronistic retrojection of Christian baptism into the narrative so as to juxtapose the (later) competing baptisms of the two emerging sects and to have John give his blessing on the winners (John 3:25–30). If they were indeed colleagues in baptizing, they might have conspired together to become the dynamic duo of Qumran saviors, the Priestly and Royal Messiahs. So Tabor suggests. Yes, maybe so. Maybe not. In any case, it's another old theory. And maybe they derived their revolutionary timetable from Daniel's prophecy of the Seventy Weeks.[8] Could be. Who knows? I don't think Tabor does. He is winging it, merely speculating.

---

6. Tabor gives a friendly shout-out to Eisenman in his Acknowledgements, but he never once refers to Eisenman's work in the body of the book.

7. Strauss, *The Life of Jesus Critically Examined*, 233, 246, 287; Guignebert, *Jesus*, 162.

8. Silver, *A History of Messianic Speculation in Israel*, 8.

There is little or nothing new in Tabor's book. It is but a pale ghost of Eisenman's magisterial *James the Brother of Jesus*.[9] It is dedicated to Albert Schweitzer, which is no accident, since it basically recapitulates his theory[10] that Jesus expected he would usher in the apocalypse by his ministry of healing, preaching, and exorcism, but that John the Baptist's shocking death made him reconsider, making him realize for the first time that he might have to die, too, taking the Great Tribulation onto his own shoulders. To this add Hugh J. Schonfield's *The Passover Plot*,[11] which Tabor's book greatly resembles in its imaginative mind-reading of Jesus and how he *might have* (ergo *must have*) applied various scriptural prophecies to himself, then endeavored to fulfill them.

NO JACK IN THE BOX

In October 2002, several magazines and internet message boards were all aflutter at the announcement that the ossuary, or bone-casket, of James the Just, brother of Jesus Christ, had been discovered among the possessions of an amateur collector. The limestone box was of a type used by Jews in the Holy Land between 20 BCE and 70 CE and recognized by all authorities as sufficiently ancient to be the genuine article. But what made anyone identify its one-time resident as James the Just? Across the front stretched the inscription, "Yakub, son of Yusuf, brother of Yeshua" (i.e., James, son of Joseph, brother of Jesus). Archaeologist Andre Lemaire went public with the claim, reasoning that, given the attested frequency of these names, only about thirty men in the Jerusalem area where the box was discovered might have been both the son of the one man and the brother of the other. Subsequently, Kamil Fuchs of Tel Aviv University narrowed that figure down to a grand total of three. And it seemed even more of a clincher than that, since it was quite unusual for any dead man thus interred to be identified as someone's brother as well as someone's son. Only one other ossuary whose occupant was so identified has ever been discovered. Lemaire reasoned that the surprising occurrence implied that the brother was famous. And how many Jameses do we know from this period, in Jerusalem, who had well-known brothers named Jesus?

---

9. Eisenman, *James the Brother of Jesus*.

10. Schweitzer, *The Mystery of the Kingdom of God*; Schweitzer, "Thoroughgoing Scepticism and Thoroughgoing Eschatology," 330–97.

11. Schonfield, *The Passover Plot*.

On the other hand, archaeologist Kyle McCarter pointed out early in the discussion that the brother's name might have been included if he had simply paid for the burial or owned the tomb where the box would have been placed. But at this point, most of the occasional doubts that surfaced were based on the mysterious credentials, or lack of them, of the artifact. Initially, Lemaire refused to divulge so much as the name of the owner of the ossuary, though the owner soon revealed himself as one Oded Golan. Lemaire confessed that the history of the box was unknown. Such a circumstance, as with the now-discredited Shroud of Turin, immediately raises suspicions that it *had* no history until a recent hoaxer cooked it up. Golan eventually claimed that he had bought the ossuary a quarter century ago from some unofficial Arab antiquities dealer (he could not remember which one) in Old Jerusalem, who told him it had been dug up in the village of Silwan south of the Mount of Olives. That was still pretty iffy. But veteran New Testament scholar Joseph Fitzmyer went on record seconding Lemaire's assurance that the inscription was indeed in the proper ancient handwriting style, a fact at least consistent with an ancient origin for the inscription.

Evangelical apologist Ben Witherington III dashed out of the starting gate, claiming the ossuary as definitive proof of the historical Jesus, and clubbing Roman Catholics over the head for good measure: the box said "brother" of Jesus, not "cousin," so *there*! But even as he feasted like Belshazzar, doubts were beginning to undermine the fortress by creeping in like Cyrus' troops through the sewer tunnels. Kyle McCarter and Rochelle Altman independently claimed that close analysis clearly showed that "brother of Jesus" had been added to the original inscription by a later hand. McCarter admitted that the second inscriber might still be an ancient one, and might even have known whereof he wrote, but that in any case he wrote in cursive, whereas the original "James, son of Joseph" was in formal script. Making this James into "the brother of Jesus" is a redactional addition. In effect it's two different inscriptions! At this point I would say, pop goes the theory.

It remained for Daniel Elyon, a materials engineering professor at the University of Dayton, Ohio, to announce his own findings. Though the limestone box itself showed appropriate signs of aging, the inscription cut into the stone did not. On an inscription of equal antiquity with the box we should expect the edges of the cut letters to have become rounded, chipped, weathered, run through with occasional cracking.

But only three letters (all in the name "Jesus") evidenced anything of the kind. Elyon declared the inscription a fake. His guess was that someone had copied the parts of it from L.Y. Rahmani's *A Catalogue of Jewish Ossuaries in the Collection of the State of Israel* (1994).

Soon a committee of officials from Israel's Antiquities Authority unanimously declared that the inscription was a fake. Spokesman Shuka Dorfman, Director of the Authority, added that the box itself, while ancient, looked to have come from either Cyprus or Northern Syria, too far away to have been James', since Jerusalem limestone would have been ready to hand for the burial of the Just One's bones.

It is no surprise that Oded Golan, the box's owner, would be reluctant to surrender his claim of being a modern Joseph of Arimathea, host for the remains of the holy, and he roundly dismissed the findings of the Antiquities Authority. Not long after this, the authorities raided Golan's residence, where they found a virtual factory for faking artifacts. But none of this is enough to dissuade James Tabor, who continues to affirm the authenticity of the box and the biblical identity of its one-time inhabitant. But even this is not the end of Tabor's story.

A CROWDED BUT EMPTY TOMB

Tabor connects the James ossuary with a tomb whose discoverers claim is that of Jesus—and his family! The chamber housing several ossuaries was found in Talpiot, in Jerusalem, while engineers were working on new construction. They blundered into the unsuspected site. Upon close examination, the ossuaries bore scratched-in names including Jesus son of Joseph (the word "Jesus" is not even certain), Maria, Joseph, Judas, Matthew, and others from the New Testament period. Backed by professional statisticians, James Tabor argues that, given the estimated population of Israel at the time, the chances of finding all these names, though common in themselves, combined in a single family, are six hundred to one. This means, they say, the tomb is that of Jesus Christ, his parents, his brothers, and quite possibly, his wife Mary Magdalene and their son Judah. But here is an elementary error. One cannot select certain of the names, those echoed in the gospels, leaving out others from the same tomb inscriptions, then base a statistical argument, implicitly, on the chances of *just these names (i.e., and no others) appearing together.* Then you pivot around and say, if this group must represent the family of Jesus, then these *other* names appearing with them must be additional, hitherto unknown members of the same family. One argument undercuts the other. If you started with the whole set of names, the probability of their being identified with the family of Jesus disappears, since you no longer have a striking, exact match. It is a blatant selection fallacy.

One might guess that the disappointed fans of the James box would rejoice at this "new" find (again, it was actually made a few years earlier). But then (uh-oh!) this set of ossuaries would seem to prove too much. It would mean that, a la Dan Brown and *The Da Vinci Code*, Jesus survived or escaped crucifixion, got married, and fathered children—much as happens in Jesus' dream-escape from the cross in *The Last Temptation of Christ*. No saving death, no resurrection. Yikes.

The James ossuary and the vault full of bone boxes would seem to stand or fall together. Both identifications depend upon name and population statistics. Both sets of artifacts have the same physical characteristics (patina quality, etc.). Tabor points out that the James ossuary and the others very likely come from the same site. Without that common provenance, the set lacks the requisite name of James, a famous sibling. And at Talpiot, there were empty spaces set aside for three more ossuaries. Tabor proposes that someone snuck into the vault and absconded with the James box. His theory implies that the James box and the "new" ones are all genuine. And, again, Tabor is among the few still defending the authenticity of the James ossuary. But suppose he is right about the seeming connection, the James box looking like the missing piece of an incomplete puzzle set. Then the lifeboat must sink along with the ship. *All* of them would appear to be fakes. One thing's for sure: you have no business appealing to the James box as proof of a historical Jesus if you don't also accept a larger family unit including Mrs. Christ and Jesus, Junior.

PORTRAIT OF THE MESSIAH AS AN OLD MAN

The other foundation for the book we are ultimately concerned with here, Kathy Reichs's *Cross Bones*, is Donovan Joyce's book *The Jesus Scroll*. I had briefly considered reviewing *The Jesus Scroll* as a Lost Gospel novel in its own right but decided against that because it appears to sit astride the fence between novelistic fiction and a pseudo-documentary hoax. (I believe it does author Joyce no insult to read him as a hoaxer, since he anticipates readers may so judge him and defends himself, which, given the rules of the hoaxer's game, need be no more than defensive bluffing, maintaining a poker face. I am merely saying: I don't buy it, which Joyce is giving me the option to do. Besides, I love a good hoax!) *The Jesus Scroll* begins and ends with chunks of narrative relating reporter Joyce's attempt to visit the ancient mountain fortress of Masada to investigate archaeological findings there. He relates his efforts in prose much suggestive of fiction narration,[12] telling how archaeologist General Yigael Yadin and his wife stymied and ultimately frustrated his efforts *as if they had something to hide*. Encountering a shifty archaeologist going by the *nom de guerre* of Max Grosset, Joyce says he learned what it was: besides the trove of fourteen scrolls discovered there, Grosset, when no one else was looking, spotted a fifteenth scroll and snuck it off the site. Now he hoped to sneak it out of the country (since it was legally the property of Jordan, this all taking place before the Six Day War of 1967). When he meets Joyce again in the airport, heading for Joyce's native Australia, Grosset presses him to cooperate in a luggage switcheroo to prevent the customs officials discovering the forbidden scroll. The two men are conspiring in the airport men's room and Grosset is at the point of showing Joyce the scroll when the cops burst in and Grosset grabs the scroll and takes it on the lam. (One almost expected some stratagem whereby the scroll would be substituted for a roll of toilet paper.)

Joyce claims that all he got to see of the scroll, and all Grosset told him it said, was that it was the last testament of one Jesus of Genessaret (Galilee), self-styled last king of the Hasmonean (Maccabean) dynasty. It would have been written during the dark hours before dawn brought the final Roman assault on the doomed fortress, manned by die-hard Zealot commandos and besieged by Romans in April of 73 CE.

The rest of Joyce's book operates in a "what if?" mode reminiscent of Lincoln, Leigh, and Baigent's *Holy Blood, Holy Grail*. He looks at the gospels and Josephus (including the neglected Slavonic version of *The Jewish War*, which deals with Jesus in much greater detail than the more familiar Greek text), trying to connect the dots and fill in the blanks in such a way as to identify the throne-contender Jesus of Genessaret with our old friend Jesus of Nazareth. Not only that, but Joyce argues that a group of skeletons found at some distance from the Masada defenders were those of the Hasmonean royal house, the real object of defense in the stronghold. It is another of Joyce's inferences, though Josephus says nothing about the presence there of a Hasmonean pretender. One of

---

12. Hamburger, "The Fictional or Mimetic Genre," 55–193.

these skeletons was that of a seventy year old man, hence, Joyce infers, the king himself—Jesus, plus his queen Mary Magdalene. In truth, Yadin had been strangely cagey about the identification of these skeletons, but why? Joyce figures, anything fills a vacuum.

But, er, didn't Jesus die some forty years earlier, on a Roman cross? Joyce is able to show (and I think he is correct) that the gospels contain clear clues that Jesus was believed (at least by some) to have cheated death on the cross, having been sedated and taken down before death could claim him. Joyce concludes that Jesus lived on for a generation, giving his life at last during the siege of Masada.[13]

From there, Joyce speculates that archaeologist Grosset eventually lost the scroll to the Soviets, who were now using it to blackmail the Vatican. That is why Pope Paul VI blessed the Arab enemies of Israel while refusing to recognize Israel. Joyce thinks the Russkies might yet put their trump card on the table, debunking Christianity as we know it. In the meantime, he seems to be trying to prepare their way, to make their paths straight.

Joyce builds upon the earlier speculations of Hugh J. Schonfield (*The Passover Plot*) and Walter Phipps (*Was Jesus Married?*) and in fact shares with them a great ingenuity for spotting odd bits in the ancient sources and turning them to his theory's advantage. There is a cumulative effect, which seems to lend the emerging framework a sense of plausibility. But I dare say it is because of the cleverness of the result and the author's skill in manipulating the data like one of Uri Gellar's spoons. I would go further and suggest that the method that Joyce (like Schonfield, Tabor, and Lincoln, Leigh, and Baigent) employs to connect the dots, i.e., by a series of "What if's" and hunches, is less reminiscent of genuine historical reconstructive reasoning, and more like that of a novelist, like Kathy Reichs, to whom we will return in a moment. The novelist witnesses at-first disparate plot elements coming together in his head as he plots out his novel. I should say that Reichs has based *Cross Bones* on sub-narratives already worked out, albeit in ostensibly factual, documentary form, by Tabor and Joyce. Their books were implicitly novels, while hers is explicit.

---

13. For the record, I would claim only that one ancient version of the Jesus story had Jesus escape death on the cross, not that this is the way it actually happened, which we can never know.

AUTOPSY

In *Cross Bones*, Reichs gets a couple of biblical details wrong. "The New Testament indicates Mary and her children took up residence in Jerusalem following the crucifixion" (p. 302). I suppose she infers this from their presence there from Easter and Pentecost (Acts 1:14), but Luke 24:49 ("Stay in the city until you are filled with power from on high") seems to indicate this was but a temporary arrangement. "Matthew's gospel plainly states that, after Jesus was born, Joseph *knew* Mary" (p. 210). No, it does not. Reichs is thinking of Matthew 1:25: Joseph "knew her not until she had borne a son; and he called his name Jesus." The point of this is to rule out any possibility of Jesus being Joseph's biological son. It speaks of what did *not* happen before Jesus' birth, not of what *did* happen afterward, a question left completely open and consequently left in dispute between Catholics and Protestants to this day.

Ultimately *Cross Bones* peters out into a first-class disappointment. We are electrified again and again by the hushed assertions of this or that character that he knows the identity of a suspicious Masada skeleton—some specific major first-century figure, perhaps Jesus as per Donovan Joyce's theory, or (when that identification proves impossible) some other Big Shot. But finally the evidence is destroyed, the bones cannot be identified, and the intrepid investigators decide there was nothing all that important to begin with. There is even a second skeleton, this one actually discovered (in the novel) in the Talpiot tomb, but they lose this one, too. For a while they think that one or another pile of bones is Jesus, sought for by various extremists for use to their own nefarious ends. Muslim fanatics might want to use the bones to explode Christianity, for example. But they would hardly do that, since the same discovery would debunk the Muslim doctrine of the Rapture of Jesus into heaven before he could be crucified. Or maybe it is the usual suspects in the Vatican, hoping to prevent their bluff from being called and their authority from being discredited (as in *The Q Document* and *The Book of Q*). But in the end the whole thing turns out to be merely a sordid mess of adultery, theft, professional jealousies, and murder among mundane creeps. What a waste of time.

35 | The Loosely-Conceived Gospel
Paul Christopher, *The Lucifer Gospel*

PRINTER'S DEVIL

THIS ACTION-ADVENTURE MYSTERY HAS all the standard components of the model: a random collection of far-flung and exotic locales, a pair of virile and beautiful young protagonists, a cabal of ultra-wealthy conspirators with bizarre political or religious connections, and of course some ultimate Mystery Grail for which the heroes will dare anything and the villains will kill anyone. The conformity to genre is so absolute, so taken for granted, that author Paul Christopher makes—and has his characters make—occasional, overt comparisons to Indiana Jones movies and Dan Brown's *Da Vinci Code*. As if you weren't thinking it anyway, and that's the point. Genres evolve, Tzvetan Todorov[1] reminds us, by pushing and bending the conventional limits of the genre. But there is no effort to shake things up here. And by now the gimmick of the Lost Gospel is, as we have demonstrated, one of the old stand-bys for this "desperate quest and scheme" premise. In fact, it is so taken for granted in *The Lucifer Gospel* that the author does not bother relating the interesting specifics of his gospel to either the interests or the actions of any of the parties struggling with one another to gain possession of it.

It remains unclear (to me, at least) just why the Christo-Fascist villains want to get their Sieg-Heiling mitts on the hidden text, as it would seem to undermine their own religious legitimacy. We are talking about

> the so-called Lucifer Gospels [sic], written by Christ himself—after the Crucifixion. The gospels themselves [sic], sometimes known as Christ's Confession, told the story of how Christ's place was taken by his brother James in the Garden of Gethsemane and then "betrayed" by Judas to the Roman soldiers who came to

---

1. Todorov, "The Typology of Detective Fiction," 43.

> arrest him, the soldiers having no idea what Christ looked like. Christ, with the help of several recently converted Romans, was spirited away into the wilds of the Libyan Desert, where he lived a long life as a hermetic monk... [It seemed] the gospels [sic] had been transported by early Templars deep into the central United States [sic], perhaps along with the greatest treasure of all: the bones of Jesus Christ himself. (p. 209)

The editor should have spared a few minutes to eyeball this paragraph. For one thing, we read here of gospels, plural, which makes no sense even in the immediate context, as it refers to a single, autobiographical account. After this passage, Paul Christopher sticks to the singular "*Lucifer Gospel*" of the title. The second sentence here is grammatically confused, though the point seems to be that James was betrayed and arrested. "Betrayed" is placed in quote marks for some reason, presumably implying that it was all a set-up, with Judas a double agent on behalf of both the Sanhedrin (who did not know what was really going on) and Jesus (who did). The notion that the arresting party did not know what Jesus looked like seems odd, since the reason Jesus was being arrested on the sly, in the middle of the night and away from the crowds, was that he was so popular and well known, that a riot might ensue should the authorities seize him in public. Furthermore, the arresting party, according to the gospels, was composed of temple police and paid roustabouts. Roman troops had no place in this scene because the Sanhedrin had not yet approached the Roman procurator to take a hand in the case.

And what are we to make of Christopher's "recently converted Romans"? Converted to *what*? Judaism? There was no Christian religion yet for them to convert to! As for the Medieval Templar Knights sailing the ocean blue centuries later, getting to "the United States" (obviously he means North America and should have said so), we are getting too close to *The Da Vinci Code*, and later the author changes the story. It wasn't the Templars after all (according to these novels, they had a pretty busy schedule!), nor did the trans-Atlantic voyage (worthy of the proto-Mormon Lehi and his family) occur so long after Jesus. Later we read how

> Luciferus Africanus... was a legionary in Judea at the time of Jesus, that much is known. Some credit him as being the Roman who guarded Christ's tomb and witnessed the Resurrection [p. 134]. Luciferus Africanus had somehow traveled from the deserts

of Libya to the central United States, perhaps bringing the Lucifer Gospel with him on his journey. (p. 273)

And now we know why the hidden text is called the *Lucifer Gospel* and, more importantly, why the novel uses that for its title. Of course, the real reason for that choice of a title is its eye-catching appeal, leading us to believe that we will be reading something about the Antichrist, as in *The Doomsday Scroll*. But we will not. Nor is it clear why anyone within the novel's narrative universe would have dubbed the manuscript "the *Lucifer Gospel.*" Sticking with calling it "Christ's Confession," as in the passage from p. 209 quoted above, would have been quite sufficient and less misleading—but also less marketable, I suppose.

Paul Christopher seems not to be too clear even in his own mind why the text should be called the *Lucifer Gospel*. He cannot decide which of two ancient Roman Lucifers might have been its namesake. It has nothing to do with the devil, since "Lucifer" is simply the Latin name for the planet Venus, and all sorts of people, including a Christian bishop, bore the name with no evil associations. Did they call the text the *Lucifer Gospel* because of the man who carried it to safety in the Western Hemisphere ("the United States"), or did they name it for a much later figure? Paul Christopher mentions

> [t]he legends of the Luciferians and the Lucifer Gospel . . . The Luciferians were a schismatic group within the Catholic Church during the late fourth century. They followed the teachings of a man named Lucifer Calaritanus, who was a bishop in Sardinia. Lucifer had once been a follower of Arius, a quite important theologian who argued that Christ was not part of the godhead but only a mortal expression of it. Some people . . . thought that Luciferus Africanus was the namesake of Lucifer Calaritanus, the bishop. (p. 135)

Here the novel gets the date right but miscasts Bishop Lucifer as the opposite of what he actually was: a staunch opponent of Arianism and a great supporter of Athanasius, Arius' theological rival. Ambrose and Augustine bemoan Lucifer's involvement in sectarian strife, but we have no real evidence that there was ever a schismatic sect of Luciferians. His disputes with other bishops concerned issues of church discipline, not doctrine. In any case, what has this man got to do with a heretical gospel penned by Jesus himself over three centuries earlier? Would the *Lucifer Gospel* have vindicated this bishop's views? It is hard to see how, whether we are thinking about the historical Bishop Lucifer or Paul Chistopher's rewritten version of him.

SAVING THE SAVIOR'S SKIN

Where did our author get the idea of Jesus shamefully allowing someone else to take the rap while he himself slunk off to safety somewhere else? It goes way back to the second century, at least to the Gnostic Basilides, who read Mark 15:21–24 as asserting that it was Simon of Cyrene who was crucified, not Jesus. Note whose proper name is given before we run into a string of personal pronouns:

> And they commandeer a particular passer-by, *Simon*, a Cyrenian, coming in from the fields, the father of Alexander and of Rufus, that *he* should bear *his* cross. And they carry *him* to the place Golgotha, which is translated "Place of a Skull." And they offered *him* wine spiced with myrrh, but *he* did not accept it. And they crucify *him* and distribute his garments, casting lots for them to see what one might take.[2]

The same notion enters the scripture of a world religion in the fourth Sura of the Koran:

> They denied the truth and uttered a monstrous falsehood against Mary. They declared: "We have put to death the Messiah Jesus son of Mary, the Apostle of Allah." They did not kill him, nor did they crucify him, but he was made to resemble another for them. Those that disagreed about him were in doubt concerning his death, for what they knew about it was sheer conjecture; they were not sure they had slain him. Allah lifted him up to His presence. (4:156–8)[3]

I understand the passage to mean something like this:

> Instead of the truth they told Mary something terribly wrong. They told her they had executed her son, the Messiah, the Apostle of Allah. But in fact they had not killed him, even put him on the cross, for it was another, made to look like him. Those who erred in their report were not as sure as they thought, and what they took for knowledge was mere surmise. They were wrongly sure they had killed him. In fact, Allah had rescued him, taking him up into his presence.

---

2. Price, *The Pre-Nicene New Testament*, 108.
3. All passages are from the translation by N. J. Dawood.

The Koran elsewhere seems to assume that Jesus did die on the cross,[4] but this version was to prevail and became Islamic orthodoxy. How did this old Gnostic mytheme enter Islam? Muhammad's biographer (or legend collector) Ibn Ishaq relates the following:

> A man who was a Christian and became a Muslim told me that when God's message "I am going to raise you to Myself" came to Jesus he said, "O company of disciples, which of you would like to be my companion in paradise on the condition that he is made to resemble me to the people so that they will kill him instead of me?" Sergius said, "I would, O Spirit of God." He said, "Sit in my seat." So he sat in it and Jesus ... was raised. They burst in on [Sergius] and took him and crucified him. So he was the one they crucified and "a semblance was made to them" through him.[5]

It seems likely that the escape of Jesus had been brought over in the early decades of Islam from "heretical" Christianity, which survived outside the reach of Constantinian orthodoxy in the Arabian Peninsula. As such Christians came to embrace Islam, they brought some of their previous beliefs along with them, just as early Christians seem to have assimilated important elements from the pagan Mystery Religions they had formerly espoused.

Over the centuries, Muslim commentators have nominated many candidates for the honor of substituting for Jesus on the cross, including Pontius Pilate, Judas Iscariot, and even Satan! But, as far as I know, Paul Christopher is the first to suggest James the Just. I imagine the reason no one has made the suggestion before is that it would create another riddle: who was impersonating James during the three decades he served as bishop of the Jerusalem Church?

One wonders, on reflection, why Jesus would have penned a confession of his "Passover plot" if he had allowed his brother to sacrifice his life in order to preserve the illusion that Jesus had died on the cross. Wouldn't such a revelation render his brother's death in his place a futile gesture? And why would Jesus not simply have snuck out of danger, fleeing to Libya or Britain or Tibet? Why would *anyone* have to masquerade as Jesus and end up on the cross? The whole thing presupposes the gos-

---

4. "I was blessed on the day I was born, and blessed I shall be on the day of my death; and may peace be upon me on the day when I shall be raised to life" (19:33). "Jesus, I am about to cause you to die and lift you up to Me" (3:55).

5. Robinson, *Christ in Islam and Christianity*, 131.

pel story of salvation, as if *somebody* had to get crucified and kick-start the Jesus salvation religion; it was just a question of *who*.

That question calls to mind Michael Moorcock's novel *Behold the Man*. There, a time traveler, Karl Glogauer, goes back to witness the ministry and death of Jesus. But when he gets there, he sees that Jesus is a vicious idiot locked away in his parents' attic. So Karl decides the show must go on, and he will take the role of Jesus as set down in the gospel story. He knows in retrospect what "must" happen, because it "did" happen. Somehow things have gone awry, and it is up to him to set them right. But would Jesus have seen things this way, before the fact? He would have had no sense of the necessity of a gospel saga waiting to be written. Why not just flee Jerusalem as Aristotle fled Athens? Why did he think someone had to go to the cross? It is all an anachronism.

Worse yet for the premise of Paul Christopher's novel, we are left wondering for whose eyes did Jesus write this confession? Who did he think would see it? Maintaining his seclusion, he presumably meant to maintain his secret, so why write up a self-expose? Well, obviously "he" wrote it for the sake of the reader of this novel!

And apparently it was not that much of a secret, since somewhere along the line the truth must have leaked out. Otherwise, our intrepid protagonists and antagonists would not know of it. Christopher makes the same error Mark the evangelist did when he ended his gospel with the women disciples failing to tell anyone about the angel's proclamation of Jesus' resurrection. If they never told anyone, then how did *Mark* know about it, pray tell? Unless you subscribe to the fundamentalist belief that the gospel writers were mere stenographers for divine dictation, the unavoidable answer is that Mark made it up. So did Christopher; that's no surprise. But you'd think he would take a little more trouble, here and throughout, to cover his tracks.

In the end, our heroes do finally manage to get hold of the *Lucifer Gospel*. And what do they do with it? Figuring that it has caused just about enough trouble, they pitch it out into the sea. Yeah, that makes a lot of sense. One can be forgiven for having the same reaction to Paul Christopher's novel.

36 | Mary Maudlin
Kathleen McGowan, *The Expected One*

ANOTHER DESCENDANT OF DAN Brown's *The Da Vinci Code*, this book[1] bases itself on the sandy foundation of the same Merovingian/Templar Jesus hypothesis and proceeds to build from there. Alas, it falls into Brown's unforgivable error of palming off fantastic speculation as historical data. Early on, McGowan is careful to differentiate scholarly methodology from beliefs based upon paranormal experiences and fellow-feeling among mutually supportive sectarians. Her heroine is one Maureen Paschal, a journalist and feminist historian, whose name is eventually revealed as code tying her to the Passover/Paschal Lamb Jesus. The name also reminds us of Roman Catholic mathematician and mystic Blaise Pascal, who affirmed that the heart has certain reasons of which the mind knows nothing. Maureen begins with the mind's reasoning, as she resists the blandishments of her New Ager friend Tamara Wisdom. "You're in the business of revising history based on your personal beliefs. I am not. . . . Your standards for 'evidence' and mine are clearly not the same" (pp. 64–65). But Maureen will not be long in yielding up her "better" (scholarly) judgment.

She has long experienced jarring nightmares depicting Mary Magdalene's perspective on events in the life of Jesus. In this she is like Roman Catholic seeress and novelist Anna Katherina Emmerich, whose long novel *The Dolorous Passion of our Lord Jesus Christ* became the basis for Mel Gibson's *The Passion of the Christ*. She receives a mysterious invitation from Berenger Sinclair, a super-rich Magdalene sectarian (and associate of Tamara Wisdom) to visit him in Languedoc, to be a guest on his estate. Maureen goes, accompanied by her cousin Peter Healy, a Catholic priest and New Testament professor. Tamara joins them there.

---

1. All page references are to the 2007 hardcover.

The narrative is clearly on the side of Magdalene sectarianism. Tamara bears the same name as Jesus' and Mary's daughter Tamar, as any half-awake reader knows hundreds of pages before the fact dawns on a flabbergasted Maureen. And her last name "Wisdom" marks her as a "donor" figure who is reducible to her role of imparting wisdom to the heroine (as when Obi-wan Kenobi teaches Luke about the Force, and that's it for him in the plot). Likewise, Lord Sinclair's unimaginable wealth symbolically makes him a personification of the mystery-filled Languedoc region, which he pretty much owns. Thus we are led to regard him as an unimpeachable source of "inside" information. A son and the master of the region, he seems to speak of the ancient secrets of Mary Magdalene, Jesus, and the Cathars as if they were personal memories of his own. And in a sense they are. For the old rivalries, at first just hinted at, between the ancient factions of John the Baptist and Jesus still live here, as a Hatfield-McCoy style feud raging below the public surface.

Once, in an optician's office in a North Carolina Walmart, I met a modern-day member of the battling Earp clan (kin to Wyatt, Morgan, and Virgil). He told me his family had recently gotten together with the remnants of the Clanton gang for a nice supper to heal old wounds. But imagine if one or both groups of latter-day descendants still nursed the old grudges and intended to even the score! That's the game that is afoot in *The Expected One*.

It is obvious virtually from the first page that Maureen is going to turn out to be the reincarnation or avatar of Mary Magdalene. No one makes much of a secret of it, and soon she is initiated into the mystery of her preordained destiny: it is she who is to rediscover the *Arques Gospel of Mary Magdalene*, the late-in-life musings and recollections of Mary Magdalene in France. Before she finds it (and she does, with only a miracle or two to guide her), we are treated to numerous page-long selections from this gospel. Eventually we will have to sit through a third-person summary and novelization of the very long (106 pages!) scroll. The first-person excerpts keep making me think of Kathryn Hepburn sharing memories of her movie career and the great names she used to work with, taking a final opportunity to set the record straight about this or that misunderstood celebrity.

The frame narrative of Maureen ("Little Mary") and the imbedded narrative of Mary Magdalene reflect one another, and each is a girlish princess fantasy, almost a girl's version of the Harry Potter books. So when Maureen steps out of the pumpkin coach into the fairy land of Magdalenism, it is not the tale of a scholar joining a strange cult, as it would have been in a more mundane narrative world. Rather, it is the story of a born heroine leaving the ranks of the Muggles to enter a wonder-world. It is sobering and saddening to read in the novel's postscript that the whole novel, apparently minus elements of violent intrigue, is supposed to be autobiographical, based on visionary experiences of the author and her initiation into certain Magdalene circles in France, with hush-hush secret documents that author McGowan dare not reveal! So, like her protagonist, Kathleen McGowan is no longer a Muggle either.

Precisely where is Maureen's mission predicted? Not in the Bible, but in another secret, sacred book, one penned in ancient days by Sarah-Tamar, daughter of Jesus and Mary Magdalene. And there are yet more gospels.

> The Cathars were the custodians of the *Book of Love*, the one— the only—true gospel ... *The Book of Love* was the one true gospel because it was written entirely in the hand of Jesus Christ himself ... It was brought from the Holy Land by Mary Magdalene and passed down with extreme caution by her descendants. It's highly likely that the Book of Love was the true purpose behind the Crusades against the Cathars. The officials of the Church were desperate to get their hands on that book, but not to protect and treasure it, I can assure you ... What if that authenticated document disputed not only many of the tenets, but the very authority of the Church itself? (pp. 134–35)

The Cathars, or Cathari ("pure ones," also known as the Albigensians) were a sect of late-blooming (eleventh-thirteenth century) Gnostic Christians, often called medieval Manichees[2] because of a (probably fortuitous) recapitulation of the ascetical dualism of the third-century religion of the Apostle Mani.[3] They believed that history was the expression of a behind-the-scenes cosmic struggle between God/Christ and his opposite number, the Rex Mundi ("King of the World"), a god of materialism much like the Buddhist tempter Mara. The Cathars strove to disengage themselves as fully as possible from the material order, e.g., practicing celibacy (though a great many laity were second-class members, not yet ready to make that sacrifice) and eventually self-starvation

---

2. Runciman, *The Medieval Manichee*.
3. Widengren, *Mani and Manichaeism*.

(as in the Jainist faith of India). They were systematically stamped out in a series of genocidal massacres (the Albigensian Crusades) by the forces of the pope.

Just above I mentioned an ongoing sectarian rivalry between the Magdalenes and the John the Baptist sect. The basis for this feud is detailed in another (fictive) ancient screed, *The True Book of the Holy Grail*. McGowan describes it as a detailed passion narrative of the Baptizer, highlighting the scheming of Salome and Mary Magdalene that led to John's demise, all in an attempt to steal his royal prerogatives for Jesus (p. 209).

Here's what "actually" happened. In McGowan's fantasy version of the Roman world of the first century, Mary Magdalene is a Benjaminite princess betrothed from infancy to Yeshua (Jesus), the scion of the Davidic dynasty. They are to be crowned King and Queen of Israel, an implausible thing to have happen in Roman-occupied Palestine. And we don't know if first-century Jews even knew or claimed any particular tribal pedigree at that point. Nothing daunted, McGowan paints us a picture in which the High Priest and his colleagues first support Jesus as the messianic king but become disturbed by his welcoming of revolutionist Zealots into his following, whereupon they switch support to John the Baptist! Listen, if these old boys are having back-room, smoke-filled deliberations on whom to back as *king*, they *are* the Zealots!

It seems that John the Baptist is an intolerant fanatic and sometime Qumran Essene, while Jesus has fallen under the sway of the more Torah-liberal Nazarene sect. Both the temple priesthood and the Pharisees, not to mention John, detest the flexibility of the Nazarene party as heresy, so there is another strike against Jesus. But it is actually another strike against McGowan: the pre-Christian Nazarene (or Nazorean) sect seems, from what meager sources we have, to have been a strict-observance sect like the Essenes. In fact their name means "the Keepers," i.e., of the Torah.

No evidence suggests they were gender-egalitarian or that women served as "priestesses" in their ranks. Despite that, McGowan misinforms us that "Mary" was a special name reserved for Nazarene priestesses, which explains why there are so many around Jesus. In fact, the name Mary was even more common in that culture than in ours. Every other woman you met was named Mary, Miriam, Mariamme, etc.[4]

---

4. Corley, *Women & the Historical Jesus*, 32.

McGowan casts the Pharisees as temple loyalists when actually their sphere of influence was the local Judean synagogues. She portrays them as a powerful elite dominating the lives of the average Jews, but there is no evidence at all for this, as E. P. Sanders has shown in his criticisms of Joachim Jeremias on the point.[5]

Whence the long-standing enmity between the rival sects of John and Jesus? Once the power-brokers withdraw their support from Jesus and nominate John to take his place as king (again one asks, *of what?*), Jesus spinelessly agrees to give his beloved "dove" Mary Magdalene into the unwashed, bony hands of the flea-bitten desert hermit John as *his* queen. She suffers the Baptist's loathsome advances as seldom as possible, while still dutifully trying to supply an heir to carry on the dynasty. He is to be, as in the Seales and Crofts song, "King of Nothing."

John is also an abusive brute, pummeling his delicate bride for imagined infidelities. One of Mary's gal pals is Salome, stepdaughter of Herod Antipas. McGowan identifies the disciple Salome (Mark 15:40; 16:1) with the pole-dancing daughter of Herodias (Mark 6:22–29) who is named Salome in Josephus but not in the gospels. (Too bad Salome was the *other* most popular female name among Jews![6] It's not too likely these two Salomes were the same.) Salome is pretty steamed at John's rude treatment of Mary, so she contrives to gull Herod Antipas into granting her wish and imprisoning the Baptist, just to keep his hairy knuckles off Mary. She doesn't mean to have the poor bastard killed, though it soon enough comes to that, at the behest of a visiting Roman who intimidates Antipas into doing the deed.

This, by the way, is one of several examples where Mary Magdalene mitigates the evil reputations of shadowed characters including Judas, Pilate, Peter, etc.—just about everybody except Paul, who comes in for a few choice comments. It must be part and parcel of the forgiveness teaching of Jesus and Mary: "There is no place for blame, as blame brings only vengeance. When we forgive we are closest to God. That is what we are here to teach the children of Israel and the rest of the earth" (p. 376). It is a bit difficult to see what interest the dagger-wielding Zealots could have had in a touchy-feely "messiah" like this.

Anyway, when John's head goes for a permanent vacation from his body, his disciples suppose just what the gospel writers did: that Salome

---

5. Sanders, *Jesus and Judaism*, 192–93.
6. Corley, ibid.

herself asked for John's decapitation. And when Jesus goes on to ask the widow Mary to marry him on the rebound, well, naturally, the Johannites (as McGowan calls them—a better tag than scholars have given them) infer that the whole thing was a scheme by Jesus and his buddies to eliminate their rival John and to give the paper throne back to Jesus. (Were they playing some sort of Dungeons and Dragons charade? Sorry, I still don't get it.) From here on in they swear vengeance on the descendants of Jesus and the Magdalene. And, sure enough, Maureen just survives an attempt on her life from a modern-day Johannite spy within the ranks of the Magdalene sect.

It is worth mentioning that there is an actual John the Baptist sect surviving into our day, the Mandaeans of Iraq.[7] That name means "Gnostics," and indeed they are the sole surviving Gnostic sect from antiquity. Their scriptures are of great importance for understanding the Gospel of John.[8] They do in fact venerate John the Baptist as the true messiah and excoriate Jesus as the Antichrist! And they do believe John was married.[9] McGowan mentions them in passing but essentially casts them aside because, being swarthy Middle Easterners, they do not fit into her fantasy-medievalism with blond and red-head Celts and Franks. Or so I surmise. (Also, the Mandaeans call themselves "Nasoreans," which does not fit with McGowan making the "Nazarenes" the enemies of John's sect.)

There is some of the usual anxiety that the newly rediscovered scrolls might pose a danger to traditional Christianity because they add a new (feminist) dimension to the old, old story. And literalist fundamentalists, biblical inerrantists, would gripe because the story as we read it here takes liberties with the gospel details, mixing and matching them, filling in gaps of detail or motivation, just like Jesus movies and novels always perforce do. But on the other hand, here is an ostensible eyewitness account from one intimately close to Jesus, describing numerous miracles, healings, and even his resurrection! Who's likely to complain? The Catholic Church does eventually get hold of the *Arques Magdalene Gospel*, and it is not clear that they'll oppose or suppress it. After all, they're not inerrantists, as the annotations to any Roman Catholic study Bible will readily demonstrate.

7. Lupieri, *The Mandaeans*.
8. Bultmann, *The Gospel of John*.
9. See "The Book of John the Baptizer" in my *The Pre-Nicene New Testament*.

The real question is just the opposite: given the revelations of the Magdalene text, what is the big deal?

> The stars remind us every night that we have the opportunity to create heaven on earth. I believe that is what [Jesus Christ and Mary Magdalene] wanted to teach us. It was their ultimate gift to us, their message of love. (p. 177)
>
> Remember what I have given you, and that is an understanding that the kingdom of God lives within you, and no oppressor can ever take that away. (p. 367)
>
> I will be there for you … No matter what. (p. 387)

Is it a collection of vague, sentimental platitudes, all over-familiar from the canonical gospels (and religious chick-flicks), that has been so closely guarded all this time? Sheesh, what a disappointment. But there are worse anticlimaxes to come, as Jesus finally appears to Maureen again—as Doc Brown does to Marty McFly and his girlfriend at the end of *Back to the Future*—to recruit her for a new adventure in the sequel: *The Book of Love*. Remember? The gospel that Jesus wrote? That one remains hidden. But to save you the trouble, once they do find it at the end of the next book, it turns out to be written in glossolalia. Maureen is suddenly enabled to interpret the code with a flash of spiritual enlightenment, but we are not privy to whatever she reads there. That "revelation" is no doubt saved for a third volume, which I think I shall not be reading. Tell me how it comes out.

37 | Ecumenical Revelation
Paul Block & Robert Vaughan, *The Masada Scroll*

FORTRESS PRESS

Certain documents, including several biblical texts, were discovered in the mountaintop fortress of Masada in 1963–1965. In the aftermath of Dead Sea Scrolls hysteria, some of our novelists imagined that Masada might be a good place to discover a lost gospel, Qumran having been a bit over-farmed. Donovan Joyce had his *Jesus Scroll* discovered at Masada, and now Paul Blake and Robert Vaughan have discovered their own Masada Scroll, the *Gospel of Dismas*. Here is how it begins:

> The account of Dismas bar-Dismas. Recorded in his own hand in the 30th year from the Death and Resurrection of the Christ, set down in the city of Rome at the command of Paul the Apostle by a Servant and Witness. (p. 20)

The scroll author's association with Paul might make it understandable for him to ape Paul's salutation style in the next paragraph. Compare the following with 1 Corinthians 1:1, "Paul, called to be an apostle of Jesus Christ through the will of God . . ." (KJV).

> I, Dismas, son of Dismas of Galilee and messenger of Jesus Christ by the will of God the Father and commissioned by the Holy Spirit, do hereby set down a testament for believers and those who may come to believe, according to His will. (p. 20)

LIKE LUKE

On the other hand, it is obvious that Block and Vaughan have modeled the preamble of their gospel very closely upon the twin introductions

Ecumenical Revelation

to Luke and Acts. Compare the emphasized portions of text below to see the dependence. First, two paragraphs from pp. 20–21 of Block and Vaughan's novel:

> (*Dismas:*) The *witness* I have made *of all that Jesus did and said before His crucifixion* by order of Pontius Pilate, the Roman prefect of Judea, *was by the word passed from the mouths of the holy Apostles themselves to me*, but of His crucifixion I bear direct testimony and of the aftermath *until He ascended to Heaven* at the right hand of the Almighty Father. (pp. 20–21)
>
> These are the things which the believers hold to be true: that a child was born unto Mary of Nazareth, in whose womb the Lord Himself by the power of the Holy Spirit entrusted the Son to be King of the promised Kingdom of Heaven; that the child of Mary, wife of Joseph of the house of David, she without stain of sin and Mother of the Lord, was foretold by the prophets of Israel as the Savior and sign of God among us, His covenant people; that His name was called Jesus . . .

Now, two passages from Luke-Acts which our authors are using as a template:

> (Luke 1:1–4) In view of the fact that many took in hand to draw up a narrative concerning the matters which have been carried to completion among us, *just as handed on to us by those who from the start became eyewitnesses and attendants of the message*, it seemed proper that I, too, who have traced all things accurately from their source, should write to you, most excellent Theophilus, so you might know the reliability of those things in which you have been catechized.
>
> (Acts 1:1–8) The first account I composed covering *all the things*, O Theophilus, *that Jesus started to do and to teach up to that day on which he was taken up, having issued instructions through the Holy Spirit to the apostles whom he had chosen,* to whom also he displayed himself alive after his suffering by means of many proofs that could not fail to convince, being seen by them over a period of forty days and speaking of the details of the Kingdom of God; and as he was eating with them, he ordered them not to leave Jerusalem, but to wait for what the Father promised, what you and your household have heard of from me, because just as John baptized in water, you will be baptized in Holy Spirit not too many days from now. So then, once assembled, they questioned him, asking, "Lord, is this the moment you will restore sovereignty

to Israel?" He said to them, "It is no concern of yours what times and turning points the Father has scheduled by his sovereign will. All you need to know is that you will receive power when the Holy Spirit overtakes you, and *you will be my witnesses* both in Jerusalem and in the whole of Judea and Samaria and to the last reaches of the earth.[1]

The problem with Block and Vaughan's effort to use Luke-Acts in this way is that it is a much later work than the Pauline Epistles, standing as it does at the far end of "apostolic" tradition. A work of the kind that the Masada *Gospel of Dismas* is supposed to be ("This could well be the only recorded word of someone who actually saw the living Christ," pp. 21–22), is not going to sound like this. Nor can such a writer have had aught to do with Paul, who knew and cared nothing for the likes of the historical Jesus.

Worse yet, there are more marks of a late, post-apostolic milieu. Take another look at the the novel's paragraphs reproduced just above. "Holy apostles"? Mary being "without the stain of sin"? This is all the language of the second-third century and later. We are dealing here with anachronisms. It must look as if I am too used to evaluating real ancient documents and have forgotten we are concerned here with an admitted piece of fiction, but my point is that Block and Vaughan are making goofs vis-à-vis verisimilitude. That does detract from their fiction, because they are making it harder for the "tuned-in" reader to suspend disbelief for the sake of the story.

MASADA MIDRASH

Our authors are quite creative in filling out the contours of gospel characters of whom we are given only the sketchiest impressions in scripture. In the hands of Block and Vaughan, the complex of names clustering around Jesus' crucifixion—Simon of Cyrene, Barabbas, Demas (Dismas), and Gestas—have more of a connection than merely appearing momentarily in the same narrative. As in the third-century *Gospel of Nicodemus*, the two "thieves" (as in the New Testament gospels, *lestoi*, implying "rebels") crucified alongside Jesus are named Dismas (Demas) and Gestas, Galilean Zealots. Gestas, though, is a Roman name, less likely to have been borne even by a Hellenized Galilean Jew. Barabbas is their

---

1. Price, *The Pre-Nicene New Testament*, 563–64.

co-conspirator, and all three were rounded up in the same Roman raid. Had the crowd not pressed for the release of Barabbas, these three would have died together, hanging above Golgotha. (Again, all this is Block and Vaughan's fiction.)

Dismas Senior turns out to be the "good thief" who rebukes his condemned colleague for deriding Jesus and professes at least an ironic faith in an innocent Jesus in Luke 23:42. As history, this is fatally problematic: in the Markan original, still followed by Matthew at this point, both criminals ridicule the failed messiah. Not even Luke gives us the standard Sunday School version according to which both thieves mock Jesus at the start, after which one of them thinks better of it and reproves the other. No, for Luke, one mocks Jesus, the other doesn't. The "repentant thief" is a redactional creation by Luke. A time traveler would not have found him. Not only that, but we cannot imagine that a committed Zealot, dying for his nation and his cause, would "admit" he is only getting what he deserves, as the crucified man says in Luke 23:40–41!

Simon is an acquaintance of Dismas Junior, he who wrote the Masada gospel. As for his association with Paul, that comes from 2 Timothy 4:10. All pretty clever, except that the novel makes Simon a black African rather than a Diaspora Jew from Cyrene in Phoenician North Africa, as the canonical gospels seem to cast him. Of course Simon performs the duty the gospels assign him, carrying the cross for an exhausted Jesus (something John deemed unbecoming, so he dropped Simon and had Jesus himself carry the cross—John 19:17).

But that is not the end of it. After Jesus' death, a brooding Simon, so moved by his momentary connection with Jesus (he had been briefly introduced to him by Dismas Junior), is stunned to behold the risen Jesus in an Easter appearance mentioned in no gospel.

> He appeared after his resurrection, first to Simon, who was on the road to Cyrene, and to whom He gave the symbol, then to Cephas, then to the twelve, and after these to five hundred brethren at once. (p. 116)

This list is a take-off on 1 Corinthians 15:3–11, adding Simon and subtracting James, "all the apostles," and Paul. The Simon appearance is fully narrated later in the novel, which alternates action in the present day with the first-century adventures of Dismas and the rest. In a scene with heavy Roman Catholic overtones, Jesus reminds Simon how the latter swabbed the former's bloody face on the way to the cross (just like Saint Veronica) and tells him to take the blood-soaked cloth out of his bag. When he does, most of the blood liquefies and drains away, the remainder miraculously tracing the lines of the "Trevium Dei." Jesus even calls it that when he displays it to Simon—a neat trick, since presumably neither Jesus nor Simon of Cyrene would have known Latin! It is a symbol of "the three ways to God," a combination of the Jewish Star of David, the Latin Cross of Jesus, and the Muslim Crescent and Star. Jesus is pointing the way to the ecumenism of the future and even transports Simon all the way into the twenty-first century, where he virtually shakes hands with Father Flannery, one of the scholars scrutinizing the Masada gospel.

Here we have the most outrageous anachronism of all.[2] Such religion-blending syncretism is by nature a development arising after all the religions to be combined have arisen and been established. In a similar way, the third-century Apostle Mani proclaimed himself the vessel of the Paraclete, the Spirit who had previously visited mankind in the form of Gautama Buddha, the Prophet Zoroaster, and Jesus Christ. The nineteenth-century manifestation of God, Baha'ullah, founder of the Baha'i Faith, similarly claimed to be the Promised One of all religions. Such a claim makes no sense unless made by one who perceives himself to stand at the end of the series. Muhammad could say such a thing about Jesus and Christianity, but it makes no sense for Jesus to say it about Muhammad and Islam.

SEEK YE THE OLD PATHS

Whether by coincidence or by design, our novel has certain striking elements in common with second-century apocryphal Christian texts. The doctrine of docetism ("seem-ism") was widespread among Gnostics and many other Christians. According to this teaching, Jesus did not die upon the cross but was rescued at the last moment by the subterfuge of another taking his place at Golgotha, undetected. This belief is still current in the faith of Islam. Depending on which version of the story one reads, Jesus' substitute might have been a loyal martyr eager to die for his Lord, or it might have been some enemy (Judas,

---

2. Another candidate for this honor might be the naming of a first-century Jewish character as "Herschel," a Yiddish name that did not exist at the time and wouldn't for hundreds of years!

Satan, Pilate, etc.) transformed into Jesus' likeness. On the other hand, the strange element of uncertainty as to Jesus' identity in Gethsemane, requiring Judas to point him out to the arresting party, may originally have anticipated an outcome in which the wrong man was fingered and crucified in Jesus' place.

It is Jesus who was crucified in *The Masada Scroll*, but we do find the docetic crucifixion scenario later on in the novel. Two Christians, Dismas bar-Dismas and Marcus, a converted centurion, are due to be led into an Ephesian amphitheatre to be crucified, but the unconscious, bloodied men are soon identified as a pair of soldiers assigned to guard them. The not-quite-martyrs have escaped to preach another day, and the allies who sprang them bound their captors in their place. The Roman governor is so mad that, not wanting to disappoint the eager crowds (munching their otters' noses and wrens' livers), he has the guards crucified anyway! The show must go on!

Later still, two Roman soldiers are ordered to kill Simon of Cyrene, but he escapes through still another false death: suddenly he pitches forward appearing to be gushing blood from a chest wound—which they have not yet dealt him! Confused and thinking they must have blacked out while doing the deed, the spooked soldiers leave him for dead. But Simon is all right, his shirt without a stain! Too bad God did not so rescue all martyrs, huh?

There was another form of docetism, which, remember, meant "seemism." Some believed that Jesus only *seemed* to be a flesh-and-blood human. Like the deities of Greek mythology, he could appear in whatever form he chose, even in different forms simultaneously to different viewers. When Simon is introduced to Jesus in *The Masada Scroll*, Jesus appears, in Simon's eyes, to be a black African like Simon himself, but only for a moment. The novel does not follow up the larger implications of the docetism it borrows for this scene, namely that Jesus had no true form at all, being an insubstantial spirit.

Docetism and the multiform Jesus appear in a number of the Apocryphal Acts of the Apostles, especially the *Acts of John*. These Acts couple docetism, an anti-flesh Christology, with a severe asceticism according to which all sex, even within marriage, was considered sinful. And they all sooner or later devolve upon a sequence in which a pagan noblewoman chances to hear an apostle preaching the celibacy gospel and is spiritually smitten. Converting to ascetical Christianity, she renounces the affections of her fiancé or husband in order to follow Christ. The spurned lover repairs to the king or the Roman governor and complains about the wizard who has enchanted and seduced his wife away from him. His highly placed friend orders the apostle arrested and imprisoned. The newly converted noblewoman visits the apostle in prison. His eventual fate in the various tales is to escape or be executed, sometimes even being resurrected. The genre appears to owe much to the contemporary Hellenistic romance novels.[3] But instead of star-crossed lovers discovering one another, then being cruelly separated, then seeking out the other, resisting all temptations in the meantime, the Acts genre has the woman fall in love with the preached Christ and display devotion to his earthly representative, the apostle. Spiritual love has replaced romantic love, but the pattern is basically the same.

Block and Vaughan have recapitulated this plot element, restoring some of the original romance. Marcella, wife of the Roman governor of the province of Asia, Rufinus Tacitus, hears the preaching of Dismas. She is almost hypnotically drawn to Christ and seeks to rescue her preacher Dismas from Roman execution. But she falls in love with a mortal hero, too, Dismas' younger brother Tibro, "a man who held her gaze with unnerving power and passion. As she thought of Tibro, her body warmed and she felt a tingling sensation in her skin. She was a married woman, but never before had she experienced anything like this" (p. 159). She remains faithful to her husband, as one should expect of a Christian, despite his paganism and sometime cruelty.

At one point, Marcella reflects upon what exactly led her to convert to Christian faith with so solid a commitment that she is willing to die rather than renounce it. "The steady strength of Dismas and Marcus, the warmth and acceptance of Gaius and the others in the group, convinced her that this was not a false teaching but a true path to the one true God" (p. 158). Here as elsewhere, the novel's picture of early Christianity partakes about half from *The Robe* and *Demetrius and the Gladiators* and half from the conversionism of modern evangelical fundamentalism. Marcella's "reasoning" (if such it may be called) illustrates the danger of pious subjectivism. "How do I know that Jesus Christ is really the Son of God? Because the people in my church are so nice." And this is a safe enough bet to sacrifice your life for, if it should come to that?

---

3. Reardon, ed., *Collected Ancient Greek Novels*.

THE INEVITABLE QUESTION OF Q

One of the characters muses over the Masada text that "It may be the Q document" (p. 22). This is hardly the first time we have seen such speculation in these books. But do Block and Vaughan even know what Q is, or is supposed to be?

> Its existence had been postulated by theologians who discovered they were better able to reconstruct the development of the New Testament by assuming a written source that the authors of the three synoptic Gospels—Matthew, Mark, and Luke—had used in their own writings. The name came from the German word for source: *Quelle*. (p. 22)

This is not by any means a full explanation, but it's not bad. By now we know that Q is the implicit source that both Matthew and Luke must have used in addition to Mark. Thus at first glance it looks like a basic error to say, as Block and Vaughan do, that Mark also used Q. But actually, in a nuanced form, the claim is quite viable. As Harry T. Fleddermann[4] has pointed out, it would explain the occasional seeming overlaps between Mark and Q. Matthew and Luke will sometimes each include two versions of a saying or story, presumably Markan (e.g., Mark 8:34; Matt 16:24; Luke 9:23) and Q (e.g., Matt 10:38; Luke 14:27). Where did these parallels between Mark and Q come from? It makes you wonder if Mark's version is his redaction of Q. However, I doubt that Block and Vaughan had such niceties in mind.

JEWISH JONESTOWN

In the end it becomes obvious that the Masada scroll could not possibly have been Q for the simple reason that no one in the ancient world ever got the chance to read it! (Thus Matthew and Luke could not have used it.) For some reason never explained, Dismas, the author, refused all requests to let others make a copy and insisted that his brother Tibro, with Marcella, take the single autograph text to the apostles in Jerusalem. But soon the Jewish War is raging, and Marcella and Tibro find themselves stuck on the crest of Masada with the doomed Zealots who eventually killed each other rather than be captured by their Roman besiegers. Just before the end, the two of them place the gospel in a jar and bury it, then

---

4. Fleddermann, *Mark and Q: A Study of the Overlap Texts*.

step off the precipice into thin air. Hence the scroll being discovered at Masada two millennia later.

As we have seen, the novel shows us modern researchers busy studying the *Gospel of Dismas* in some detail, but eventually the actual text is lost again. It seems that Gaius, the disciple of Dismas, who had begged his master to allow him to make a copy of the book before sending it to Jerusalem, founded a secret order dedicated to getting its mitts on the elusive gospel by hook or by crook. The order survived throughout the whole history of the Catholic Church, engaging in Black Ops maneuvers whenever necessary to safeguard the "true" teaching of the church and, lately, to get the Dismas gospel. Alongside them, there continued a chain of Keepers of the Trevium Dei, the token of tri-religious unity drawn in blood on the cloth scrap Jesus had given to Simon after the resurrection. In the end, one of the archaeologists (I have skipped her adventures here) turns out to have been the latest Keeper all along. She knew where the Dismas gospel was hidden, and it was she who brought it to light. But because it has issued in so much bloodshed at the hands of the Gaius cult, she just hands the text over to them. And she tells Father Flannery that he is chosen as the latest Keeper of the Trevium Dei symbol and successor to Simon of Cyrene.

The upshot is anything but clear. What is more important? *The Gospel of Dismas*, of which no ancient corroboration survives? (Or are the computer scans enough?) Or is it the Trevium Dei, which is never made public anyway? If it were to become the symbol of a new ecumenical gospel, you'd still have a major obstacle of which Block and Vaughan remain seemingly unaware: the symbol was written in the blood of Jesus and delivered by him after his resurrection. And Muslims are supposed to sign onto this? This is the basis upon which Muslims are to accept that Christians (not to mention Jews) are equally blessed in the sight of God? That's a tough one, since Muslims don't believe Jesus was crucified in the first place, or that he rose from the dead. And Jews—they're suddenly going to accept that Jesus was after all the Son of God? They would have to accept that conclusion along with the Trevium Dei being the bequest of the risen Christ. Not likely. But these issues never come up, since the Trevium Dei remains a secret at book's end. So what was the point? Trevium or trivia?

38 Is it I, Lord?
Richard Ferdinand Heller & Rachel F. Heller, *The 13th Apostle*

Perhaps the strangest of the Dead Sea Scrolls is the *Copper Scroll*, which purports to be a catalog of treasures removed from the Jerusalem Temple shortly before its destruction in 70 CE. Ostensibly, like the Dead Sea Scrolls themselves, these treasures were scattered in various locations throughout Judea to await unearthing by devout Jews when all danger was past. What is strange about it is that no one has ever been able to find any of the caches of riches listed there. That might be because treasure hunters long ago beat modern archaeologists to them. But there is no evidence for that, no disturbed dig sites like those found at the many looted tombs of Egypt. Perhaps the stipulated directions are not quite clear enough. But *nothing*? *None* of it has been located? Some have been driven to wonder whether the *Copper Scroll* might have been some sort of elaborate joke, or the work of a madman, though neither hypothesis makes much sense. Could it have been intended as an allegory of spiritual treasures and their gradual discovery? That seems pretty strange, too. Richard and Rachel Heller (authors of some dozen books about carbohydrate diets) have taken advantage of this unsolved mystery and hang from it the premise of their Lost Gospel novel *The 13th Apostle*.

In it, someone discovers a medieval diary in which has been crammed a fragment of manuscript implying the existence of a hitherto-unknown twin to the *Copper Scroll*. Various eager, even greedy, parties get wind of this and decide to pursue the second *Copper Scroll* in hopes that it will provide the key to locating the ancient treasures cataloged in the first one. But the mere fact that it might be a writing from the time of Jesus is even more interesting to some. Might it contain revelations about the historical Jesus? Already one must say this is such a stretch as to be implausible. For one thing, the whole premise of the document, a matching piece to a list written on the eve of 70 CE, means that Jesus would have been safely off the scene, dead fully forty years previously. Plus, there is no reason to believe such a scroll would bear on Jesus or early Christianity, in any literal manner, any more than the rest of the Dead Sea Scrolls. True, as per Robert Eisenman[1] and Barbara Thiering,[2] the Scrolls may indeed bear witness to Jesus and the early Christians, but if so, they are so thickly symbolic. No one could expect a demonstrable "smoking gun" in a new Scroll. Besides, the whole idea of suppressed secrets in the Scrolls that would threaten to expose or undermine Christianity proceeds from Qumran conspiracy paranoia.

The authors join in this paranoia by mentioning an official academic cabal trying "to squelch any actions ... that might have allowed nearly all of the Dead Sea Scrolls to be put on public exhibition. The translations that would have followed would have most certainly challenged some of Christianity's most sacred writings" (p. 57), "to keep particularly provocative sections of the Dead Sea Scrolls under wraps" (p. 58). Such suspicions were once quite plausible. As we saw in Chapters 17 and 23, the Scrolls were for decades under the thumb of an International Committee composed almost entirely of Roman Catholics, and they did indeed promote an interpretation of the Scrolls that made them safe for orthodox views of Christian origins.[3] But all the Scrolls had been made public fifteen years before the Hellers wrote this novel, and, again, any Jesus connection is a matter of interpreting heavy symbolism, since there is no explicit mention of Jesus or early Christianity in any of the Scrolls.

Basically, this suspense novel offers us new versions of the usual suspects in a race to secure the mysterious ancient documents. One group is a caricature of Far Right Evangelical Christianity verging on Nazism. They hope to find vindication of the canonical gospel story of Jesus or, if the text should read otherwise, to destroy it. Then there are Islamic zealots who hope the scroll will debunk Christianity, a confused notion, since Muslims believe the gospel story is substantially true up until the crucifixion, which even the canonical gospels "get wrong" any-

---

1. Eisenman, *James the Brother of Jesus*.
2. Thiering, *Jesus and the Riddle of the Dead Sea Scrolls*.
3. See my review of Baigent and Leigh, *The Dead Sea Scrolls Deception*.

way, so what would be the big deal about another gospel giving similar "false" teaching? Against these stand our heroes, Gil Pearson, computer geek and specialist in "pattern recognition," and Sabra (usually referred to by the inane nickname of "Sabbie") Karaim, former Israeli soldier and biblical translator. They end up in bed together later rather than sooner, but it comes as no surprise when they do. Nor is it much of a shock when they manage to follow the *Da Vinci*-esque clues to obtain the much-sought scroll. It seems that Micah, the author of the new *Copper Scroll* (which they find in a secret chamber in a monastery, led by clues in an old tapestry, yada yada yada), was the eponymous "thirteenth apostle." He knew Jesus personally and set down his account of their relationship and his role in the events of the Passion week. He wrote *two* scrolls, the second copper treasure list that is supposedly the key to the one found at Qumran, and his own gospel.

But it was a bait and switch tactic. There were no treasures at all, as far as Micah knew. The second copper treasure scroll was intended to lead the merely greedy, the treasure hunters, on a wild goose chase, whereas worthy readers would catch the clues that there was a far more (spiritually) valuable scroll hidden elsewhere. As it turns out, Micah had a particular future reader in mind.

We eventually get to read Sabra's translation of the gospel, which we are to believe she rendered, at stupendous length, in the back seat of a moving car over the course of a few hours. The result is quite disappointing, though, as we will shortly see, it does finally pack a wallop. There is just no attempt at all to make it sound like an ancient text. The style and voice of the gospel narration are identical to that of the novel as a whole. Not only do our authors not seem to have the faintest idea of what an ancient author might have said, or how; Heller and Heller have quite confused ideas about the conventions of ancient writing. For instance, they imagine that even autobiographical accounts in the ancient world were written in the third person: "Two thousand yeas ago ... no one would have thought to describe his own life in 'I' terms. Everything was written as if it were a story about someone else. First-person wasn't even a known concept" (p. 214). That is nonsense. Not only do the Books of Nehemiah and Ecclesiastes (or Qoheleth) provide good examples of first-person narrative, but one need look no further than the Book of Acts, in its "We" sections (Acts 16:10–18; 20:5–15; 21:1–16; 27:1—28:16). Most apocalypses were written in the first person (e.g., Revelation 1:9).

Nor is this the only egregious goof. Heller and Heller seem to imagine that in Jesus' day it was no longer legal for a man whose wife could not supply an heir to take a second wife for that purpose (p. 210). Rabbinic sources tell us otherwise. Our authors have Micah mention in passing that he was a boyhood chum of "Flavius Josephus," the great Jewish historian who wrote for Jews at the end of the first century (p. 297). Not only would that place Josephus decades too early, but it imagines that "Flavius" was the name he was born with, when instead it was only bestowed upon him by the Emperor Vespasian after Josephus abandoned his countrymen's revolt against Rome and predicted Vespasian's rise to power. The Hellers have Jesus and the Twelve speak of the group of disciples as "the apostles," whereas they condescendingly refer to poor Micah the red nosed reindeer as a "disciple." One would not expect the authors to know it, but this, too, is a gross anachronism. The notion of the "twelve apostles" is a second-century invention by Luke the evangelist.[4] Other New Testament writers know of "the disciples," "the apostles," "the Twelve," "the Pillars," etc., but to have the Twelve pat themselves on the back as the college of apostles is like having Jesus sign a check as "Mr. Christ."

The Micah character turns out to be both the Gospel of John's "Beloved Disciple" ("the disciple whom Jesus loved," as in John 13:23; 18:15–16 [?]; 20:39; 21:20) and Mark's young man who fled Gethsemane wearing nothing but a linen sheet (Mark 14:51–52). Jesus meets him and immediately recognizes him as a kindred soul to whom he can relate much more easily than the cloddish fishermen he has chosen as disciples. He admires Micah, a once-prosperous jeweler and metal-worker, thinking Micah can teach him worldly sophistication. The character understood this way is unbelievable. Jesus Christ Superstar finds an equal much too easily. Heller and Heller have just shoe-horned their Micah character into the gospel narrative; he does not fill a natural gap there. Worse still, Micah seems simply to concretize their own authorial hindsight regarding history. Micah and Jesus speak as if they know that the future of a world religion rests on their shoulders, as if they know the whole story in advance. It is the same device used by writers of "predictive" apocalypses: the author would pose as an ancient seer (Daniel, Enoch, Moses, Baruch) who narrates accurately the history leading up to

---

4. Schmithals, *The Office of Apostle in the Early Church*, 71–72, 247–78; Klein, *Die Zwölf Apostel*.

the actual author's time (for he has lived it or knows the history), but he places the action in the future tense so as to make it look like an inspired prediction before the fact.

As in so many of the Lost Gospel novels, the big news is that such a document would be better than the canonical gospels because it would seem to give us unmediated access to the table talk of the Messiah, not some blurry fifth- or fiftieth-hand version: "the immensity of the discovery of Jesus' teachings, teachings dictated in His own words and recorded by one who lived at His side, was simply too great to imagine" (p. 207). "It could lay bare a whole new truth that no one had ever considered, one that could shake the very foundations of Christianity itself" (pp. 260–61). And it does. We finally learn that Jesus determined to embrace his fate with eyes wide open, refusing to flinch at his martyrdom, but Micah just couldn't let things go that way. He schemed with Joseph of Arimathea to drug Jesus on the cross, bringing about a simulated death, after which they would recoup the body and administer an antidote. He explains his plan to the Twelve, who appear eager to cooperate. But once he gets the potion to the crucified Jesus, Micah overhears the deliberations of the "apostles" who are not so sure they want Jesus back! Will he not just make further trouble for himself and—more to the point—for *them*? They came as close to their own crosses as they ever want to this time around.

They decide it would be better for their yellow hides if Jesus were to expire. In the end, they empty the vial of reagent on the ground, steal the body from the tomb and proclaim the resurrection, knowing it is a hoax and a lie—but a lucrative one! It is actually not unthinkable to imagine a scenario where the disciples are Jesus' betrayers and murderers, as we saw when reviewing Daniel Easterman's *Brotherhood of the Tomb* back in chapter 18. In his novel, he also had the disciples make darn sure Jesus really died.

Heller and Heller add to the Jesus story a fascinating bit of Rabbinic lore, namely the doctrine of the fifty righteous on whose account the world is spared divine judgment.[5] It is based on the story in Genesis 18 where God is about to obliterate sinful Sodom and Gomorrah and so informs his friend Abraham. Abraham's nephew Lot has recently relocated there, so Abe tries to argue God into being merciful: would a just God

---

5. Schechter, *Some Aspects of Rabbinic Theology*, 190. I connect the doctrine with Jesus in a very different way in my short story "The Righteous Rise," in *The Dead Walk!*

destroy the righteous (Lot) along with the wicked (everybody else!)? Sure, Sodom may be corrupt on the whole, but God must not commit the division fallacy, supposing every citizen of Sodom to be so wicked. Suppose fifty righteous could be found there? Would God please spare the whole place? God agrees. Of course Abe knows how corrupt Sodom is, so he begins to revise his estimate downwards, until God agrees to spare the whole place for the sake of a measly five—which in the event he cannot find! But the doctrine grew that what might have worked for Sodom should work in the bigger picture, too. The world as a whole is pretty sinful, ripe for judgment one might think. But as long as God can find fifty righteous (Heller and Heller make it thirty-six, following a variant tradition)[6] in the world he will spare the human race for their sakes. Heller and Heller imagine that God conducts such an inventory every thousand years or so, mind-melding with a "High Zaddik" through whom he may get an accurate diagnosis of humanity as a whole. And if the High Zaddik is prevented from carrying out his mission, he may name an immediate successor. You guessed it: Jesus was the High Zaddik of his age, and with the cross on the horizon, he conferred the office upon his beloved disciple Micah. We must suppose Micah did his thing and managed to turn in a glowing report.

Why did Micah write his gospel, which he himself arranged to hide rather than publish? He wanted the next High Zaddik to find it and through it to surmise his own destiny. In the late twentieth- to early-twenty-first century, the High Zaddik was one Professor Sarkami, an expert in Near Eastern relics and Sabra's mentor. But the hoods are on his trail, still hell-bent on grabbing that scroll, and they kill him when he refuses to cooperate. Gil turns out to be the new High Zaddik. He protests his unworthiness, but in their last conversation, Sarkami explains that the High Zaddik needn't be perfect or even particularly special. Anyone who is basically righteous will do. He just needs to summon God to his millennial uplink to see if the world is worth saving for another ten centuries.

No one but the two High Zaddiks (and their future successors) will get to read this hidden gospel of Micah. One supposes that the document somehow equips its reader for the role he is to assume. In the end, the authors drop the narrative and briefly sermonize to the reader that we are all the High Zaddik, the Thirteenth Apostle. Their "work on earth

---

6. Ibid.

must truly be our own." Such democratizing spirituality winds up exalting the mundane as the sacred instead of revealing the sacred as a hidden dimension of the ostensibly mundane. It is all anticlimactic, finally much ado about nothing.

39 | The Ultimate Relic
Michael Byrnes, *The Sacred Bones*

Personally, I have heard more—and more importantly, *read* more—than enough about the dratted Knights Templar, from the ludicrous claims of the Masonic Lodge being their descendants to the equally absurd attempt to connect them with Jesus Christ and the Merovingian Dynasty. Templars seem to be everywhere these days, at least in the realms of fringe speculation on Christian origins. This is not so much because of Dan Brown's mega-blockbuster *The Da Vinci Code*, for as we saw in Chapter 33, that book is actually riding a larger wave unleashed by Baigent, Lincoln, and Leigh in their pseudo-scholarly tome *Holy Blood, Holy Grail*. Religion shelves in mall bookstores offer many rehearsals of the same bogus data and crackpot theories (which I call "crackpot" because of their lack of sound methodology, not because of the extravagance of their conclusions, let me hasten to add). One can hardly tell which are supposed to be fact and which fiction, if indeed their authors even grasp the difference. Now we arrive at one of the latest crop of Lost Gospel novels bearing the Templar stamp, Michael Byrnes's *The Sacred Bones*. (There is, by the way, a sequel, *The Sacred Blood*, but as it moves on past the element of a rediscovered gospel, it does not concern us here.)

As periodic flashbacks throughout the novel tell us, the Templar Knights were fighting the Muslims in Jerusalem, joined by their spiritual brethren of the Christian Essene Order, who are still (or again) resident in Qumran. The Order fared very badly in the fighting, and their last surviving elder, one Zachariah, came to Templar chief Hugues de Payen with an amazing secret, a scroll written by Joseph of Arimathea concerning Jesus of Nazareth and his fate. The scroll also reveals the final resting place of the slain Jesus. Eventually the scroll was interred along with the bones of Jesus in an ossuary—a bone box in which the disassembled skeleton should be reburied once the flesh had rotted during the course of a year after death. The bone box was interred, along with nine others containing the dusty bones of Joseph and his family, in a crypt beneath the Jerusalem Temple where it waited through the centuries for Muslim excavators digging in the Temple Mount, beneath the Mosque of Omar, to discover it.

This is only the beginning of intricate intrigues, as various interests seek to analyze the relics, or to hide or even to destroy them because of their potentially explosive implications. Our concern here, contra the author's intention, is pretty narrow: we just want to see how he envisions his rediscovered gospel and what imaginative new scenario of Christian origins he has created. Vatican functionary Father Donovon explains the nature of the document:

> The entries in these pages chronicle many events specific to Christ's ministry. Eyewitness accounts of miracles, like his healing the lame and lepers. His teachings, his travels with the disciples— it's all referenced here. In fact, after reviewing the language, I'm convinced this book is "Q." (p. 260)

The Q document again! He explains it as the hypothetical common source behind the synoptic gospels, Matthew, Mark, and Luke. That is not quite right—or is it? Traditionally, we have understood the Q document to be the other source Matthew and Luke used *besides* Mark, which they both copied, too. So it works out that whatever is common to Matthew and Luke *but not to Mark* comes from Q. But it seems there is a tiny but significant overlap between Markan and Q material. Both Matthew and Luke, for instance, have the same story, in the same words, as Mark for the baptism of Jesus at the Jordan and the ensuing temptation in the wilderness, but Matthew and Luke have in common a longer version. They add the same material to the Markan original, which ought to mean they derived the extra verses from Q. But that means Q and Mark must have been very, very similar—virtually identical where they overlapped. And that is best explained by suggesting that Mark used Q, too—just not much of it.[1] The same analysis applies to the Beelzebul controversy: Mark's account (3:22–30) is shorter than Q's but practically verbatim the same as far as it goes. Did Mark (whoever he was) use Q there and edit it slightly differently from the way Matthew (12:22–32)

---

1. Fleddermann, *Mark and Q: A Study of the Overlap Texts*.

and Luke (11:14–23) did? That is an attractive hypothesis, and in that case, Father Donovan is right on the money.

> There's much more here, however ... The book describes events leading to Jesus' apprehension and crucifixion. Again, most of Joseph's account is in agreement with the synoptic Gospels ... with some minor discrepancies. According to Joseph of Arimathea, he himself secretly negotiated with Pontius Pilate to remove Christ from the cross, in exchange for a hefty sum .... Joseph of Arimathea describes Jesus' burial rituals in vivid detail. How the body was cleaned, wrapped in spices and linen, and then bound. Coins were placed over the eyes. ... It claims that the body was laid out in Joseph's tomb ... for twelve months. ... According to Joseph ... there never was a physical resurrection. (pp. 260–61)

Characters in the novel reflect on this point, suggesting that a rotting body of Jesus would not really debunk the resurrection, since we know some early Christians interpreted the resurrection of Jesus as a spiritual event. There is something of a conceptual problem with that, i.e., how is it different from simply saying he died and went to heaven? Why use resurrection terminology if what you believe in is survival of the soul? At any rate, author Byrnes is quite correct. Many in the early church did believe in a spiritual resurrection, the emergence of a spiritual body unfettered by the flesh, notably the authors of 1 Corinthians 15 and 1 Peter 3:18.[2] And such a resurrection need not entail a tomb empty of mortal remains. This is why 1 Corinthians 15 mentions the death and resurrection, but no empty tomb such as we find in the gospels. But it is interesting that what we read of the Joseph testament—over the shoulders of the characters, as it were—does not suggest any notion of a spiritual resurrection, but instead seems to anticipate that Jesus will rise in bodily, fleshly form at the end-time general resurrection.

> Having fulfilled God's will, I, Joseph of Arimathea and my beloved family wait here for the glorious day when our fallen Messiah shall return to reclaim God's testimony from beneath Abraham's altar, to restore the holy Tabernacle. (p. 159)

That is supposed to be the end of the document, but a couple of hundred pages later either Byrne or Joseph seems to have forgotten it and to have produced a longer, more explicit ending. Nero invites Joseph and his family to a farewell banquet with poisoned food. Joseph knows

---

2. Carrier, "The Spiritual Body of Christ and the Legend of the Empty Tomb."

this going in and has made arrangements for Simon Peter to inter his remains in the crypt beneath the Jerusalem temple (p. 359). I don't see anything here about a spiritual Easter Sunday resurrection. Nor is the lack of one supposed to have been a secret, since obviously Simon Peter knows all about it, too. So where, according to our story, did the element of an already-accomplished resurrection (whether spiritual or physical) come from? Investigator Graham Barton makes what I should consider a pretty cogent guess:

> Keep in mind that the target audience for the gospels were pagan converts. Those people believed in divine gods who died tragically and resurrected gloriously. Life, death, then rebirth was a theme common to many pagan gods including Osiris, Adonis, and Mithras. Early Christian leaders, particularly Paul of Tarsus—a Hellenistic, philosophical Jew—knew Jesus needed to fit these criteria. He was selling this new religion in a very competitive environment. We can't discount that he embellished the story. (p. 164)

Jesus practically does rise from the dead in the course of the super-scientific analysis that Dr. Charlotte Hennesey and her colleagues perform on the relics. The rudiments of the body are evident from reassembling the skeleton, but once they scrutinize the DNA, they are able to reconstruct everything about the dead man. The result is surprising: a kind of textbook generalization, or Platonic archetype, of a human being. It betrays no signs of specific ethnicity and even has features hinting at androgyny. Of course the idea is that this is the Son of Man, the Second Adam encompassing all humanity in himself (pp. 215, 297).

Also, they find no junk DNA, such as the rest of us posses, left over from our evolutionary ancestors. The man even had an extra pair of chromosomes. "Only a divine being could exhibit such a genetic profile" (p. 357). There are some interesting things going on here. First, it is plain that, combining as he does the elements of all ethnicities, Jesus (for they conclude it is he) was the Son of Man, the prototypical human being, a second Adam as the New Testament calls him, who belongs to no race exclusively but to all inclusively (Gal 3:28). Still, there is no complete escape from "the scandal of particularity," since Jesus is not both male and female. But Byrne is trying to nod in that direction, too ("a subtle androgyny").

Second, the implication of his "born yesterday" genetic footprint implies the Christology of Radical Reformation thinker Caspar Schwenkfeld. Though Jesus Christ's body was completely and genuinely human, it was newly created for the sake of the incarnation and was heavenly in origin. It would not have been derived from Joseph or even from Mary. This Martin Luther dismissed as heresy, a cousin of Docetism, the belief that the divine Christ took on an only apparently solid body of mortal flesh but was really made of airy, heavenly substance impervious to human touch. I think that comparison is unfair. Schwenkfeld's *de novo* Jesus, Jesus without a belly button, simply reflects his status and role as the second Adam.

But the extra chromosomes? (The ones he used to work miracles, I guess!) That's certainly heresy (not that I care, you understand). It is another version, or so it seems to me, of the Christology of Apollinarius in the fourth century, who held that Jesus lacked a human spirit, though he possessed a truly human flesh body and a genuinely human soul.[3] After all, he reasoned, you have to leave room to plug in the divine Word somewhere, right? If he has both a human spirit and a divine one, does that not make him some sort of two-headed monster? Apollinarius' theory was met by the Three Cappadocians—Gregory of Nyssa, Gregory of Nazianzen, and Basil of Caesarea—who argued, "What is not assumed is not redeemed." They meant that any aspect of the human organism the Savior did not take upon himself when he became incarnate he could not redeem, since saving divinity passes from him to us, which implies a square peg and a square hole. The plug has to fit the socket.

Apollinarius' version of Christ was mismatched, and so would be Byrne's. If the Redeemer is not at all points like us, how is he relevant? How can we look to him as a pattern for ideal human behavior? If his personal victory over sin stemmed from his superhuman capabilities, how can we emulate him? He is like an angel. We can admire him, but he is no use to us either as a savior or a pointer of the way. As Schleiermacher put it: "whatever is involved in the ideality of the contents of His personal spiritual life must also be compatible with this purely human conception of His historical existence."[4]

Would this revelation bother anyone but theologians? It coincides with an old seminary joke. A young Anglican priest, fresh out of theo-

3. Raven, *Apollinarianism*.
4. Schleiermacher, *The Christian Faith*, 382.

logical school, is delivering a sermon way above the heads of his parishioners, whom he naïvely supposes to have the same level of interest and competence in doctrine that he has. He stops and says, "I know what you're thinking! I know what you're thinking! Apollinarianism!" Byrne has various characters overestimate the shock value of the newly discovered bones of Jesus in various ways: "a discovery so profound that if it were true, history itself hung in the balance" (p. 108). This reaction envisions a wholesale religious disillusionment and a reeling into moral nihilism, pretty much what we saw happen in *The Mystery of Mar Saba*, back in chapter 3. Another character agrees: "Over two billion Christians depend on the Gospels of Jesus Christ. To disrupt their faith is to disrupt social order.... This isn't just a matter of theology" (p. 265). But one rather suspects that it is. Only theologians would feel the impact of the blow.

> "What do you think Christians would think if our findings were made public?" "They'd think what they want to think.... [T]he faithful would remain faithful, like they have through other controversies. Don't get me wrong, it would certainly be an enormous dilemma for Christianity. And a public relations nightmare once the press got hold of it." (pp. 229–30)

But it doesn't come to that. Maybe in the sequel.

40 | Constantine's Conspiracy
David Gibbins, *The Lost Tomb*

BIBLE AND SPADE

This book, like several others we have surveyed, belongs to the "archaeological adventure" subgenre. It displays the usual scenes of intrigue, threats from secret cabal members, reversals of who's got the gun on whom, etc., combined with huge chunks of scholarly trivia and travelogue. The author's choice of an early Christian relic or a lost gospel as the ever-deferred object of pursuit determines which areas of scholarly exposition and speculation he will pack onto the typical syntagmic skeleton. It's the same plot logic as any other dozen or hundred thriller novels, this time fleshed out with historical-religious lore instead of, e.g., World War Two or space exploration lore. Gibbins's choice of grails is a mystery gospel, in this case, "the written word of Jesus of Nazareth, in his own hand" (p. 174)—only it is not that after all. Rather, our intrepid characters are in search of what turns out to be a few pages of what Jesus had dictated, as the gist of his preaching, to his admirer Claudius Caesar, who rendered it on the spot into Koine Greek. There is surprisingly little interest in the actual content of the text. All we ever see of it follows:

> The Kingdom of Heaven is on earth.
> Men shall not stand in the way of the word of God.
> And the Kingdom of Heaven shall be the House of the Lord.
> There shall be no priests.
> And there shall be no temples ... (p. 481)

DIG IT

This novel is one of a series by the author featuring courageous archaeologists Jack Howard and Costas Kazantzakis, including *Atlantis* and *Crusader Gold*. Fresh from those adventures, Howard and Kazantzakis have set their sights on recovering the remains of the ship on which the Apostle Paul sailed to Rome to stand trial before Nero, a journey narrated in great detail in Acts 27. (The author erroneously refers to the biblical book as "The Acts of St. Paul" once [p. 26], then gets it straight in later references. There is an *Acts of Paul*, but it is a noncanonical document.)[1] The ship, as we read, broke up off the Isle of Malta, but all hands swam or drifted to shore safely. Jack thinks the ship actually crashed off the shore of Sicily, and so it turns out. Not too surprisingly, they find it, including a clay pot autographed by Paul (presumably like an office coffee cup with one's name on it). After this, they follow clues to the hushed-up tomb of Paul far beneath the streets of Rome. But at every turn they find themselves working against seemingly pointless bureaucratic roadblocks—as if someone were trying to keep them from a greater discovery still. And such suspicions would be justified.

At first we are led to believe it is the nasty old Vatican scheming behind the scenes: "And believe me, there's one very powerful body in Italy that would rather not have any more written records from the first century AD" (p. 44). But eventually we discover that the villains are a cabal of self-appointed defenders of the faith called the Concilium. It seems these masterminds belong to a secret order founded in the first century by a group of Paul's first Roman converts. The group voluntarily disbanded a couple of centuries later when it felt the need for its presence had passed. But the order was reconstituted by the Emperor Constantine (p. 338), the favorite ecclesiastical villain of Anabaptists and mystery writers alike. This time the Concilium was a good deal more ruthless, Inquisitors before the Inquisition.

Why does Gibbins posit such a hiccup in the history of the order? It is, I think, a way of getting Paul off the hook. Many liberal Christians and mystery writers seem to regard Paul as "Constantine Lite," i.e., not quite as much a fiend as the Antichrist emperor in sheep's clothing, but still a bit of a male chauvinist as well as the one who killed and stuffed the living gospel of Jesus Christ. It all goes back to Adolf Harnack and the early twentieth-century Liberal Protestants who dubbed Paul "the second founder of Christianity" and the one who transformed "the religion *of* Jesus" into "the religion *about* Jesus."[2] So Gibbins makes the Concilium

---

1. MacDonald, *The Legend and the Apostle*.

2. Von Harnack, *What Is Christianity?*; Wrede, *Paul*; Adolf Deissmann, *The Religion of Jesus and the Faith of Paul*; Bacon, *Jesus and Paul*.

analogous to the Priory of Zion of which we read in Lincoln, Leigh, and Baigent, *Holy Blood, Holy Grail* and, of course, in Dan Brown's *The Da Vinci Code*. There was an ancient monastic order called the Priory of Zion, but it was absorbed by the Jesuits in 1617, only to be "refounded" by French neo-monarchists in 1956. In other words, the later group was not a continuation of the earlier but merely appropriated its name for propaganda purposes.

THE PAST AS TICKING TIME BOMB

The Concilium—one of whose shadowy members, a Cardinal Ritter ("Knight" in German, suggesting Templar Knights), we eventually meet—has long known of this Jesus document, but the Concilium believed it had been destroyed in the eruption of Mount Vesuvius. When archaeological delving showed that Herculaneum, a city that was engulfed by the volcano along with Pompeii, had been miraculously preserved beneath the shell of lava (p. 342), the fanatics began to worry: what if the document had survived? Hence their subsequent attempts to stymie all efforts to dig there. They must have known there was something to be afraid of, though no one any longer knew what the text said. They feared some radical teaching that would undermine the authority of Mother Church.

> There are those who are fearful of the ancient past, who would do all they can to close it off. They fear anything that might shake the established order, the institutions they serve. Old ideas, ancient truths sometimes obscured by those very institutions which sprang up to protect them. (p. 45)

The Concilium schemers judged the text a heretical forgery put forth by a pagan emperor and falsely attributed to Jesus. What they are afraid of, in effect, is another *Acts of Pilate*. Apologists in the second century, including Justin Martyr and Tertullian, urged their readers to go and examine the court records of Jesus' trial before Pilate if they had any remaining doubt as to Jesus' innocence. But those writers simply assumed there must be such records. Taking advantage of these challenges, Roman officials under the persecutor Maximinus circulated what they claimed were these records, these *Acts of Pilate*, showing that Jesus indeed deserved his condemnation. Christians immediately decried these pejorative Acts as a forgery, which one assumes they were. But one can *only* assume, since Christians, once they rose to power, destroyed all copies of the anti-Christian *Acts of Pilate* and replaced it with their *own* forged version (also known as the *Gospel of Nicodemus*). As I am fond of saying about Christian apologists, "Oh what a tangled web we weave when first we practice to believe!"[3]

SALAD DAYS WITH THE SAVIOR

But what would Claudius have been doing with a private transcript of the words of Jesus, dictated by Jesus himself? Our heroes discover a manuscript of Pliny's *Natural History* in the author's own hand, and it contains a brief notice about Claudius and his old pal Herod Agrippa II (Marcus Julius Agrippa) visiting Jesus and relaxing on the shore of the Sea of Galilee. Eventually we learn that Herod (who was raised with Claudius in Rome) had learned of the young prophet and healer Jesus and suggested that Claudius accompany him to Galilee to ask Jesus to heal his lameness. This was all before Jesus had set aside his carpentry business to embark on a public ministry, and before Claudius had become Emperor or Herod Agrippa taken the Jewish throne. Though Jesus told Claudius (enigmatically) that he was not ailing and needed no healing, Claudius was taken with the charismatic young man and persuaded him to dictate the gist of his message for him to keep in his own private library. Think of when Ringo Starr gave Peter Sellers a tape of the Fab Four's rehearsals for the White Album.[4]

No one needs to be told that this imagined scenario is implausible. One can never predict or verify the occurrence of specific events by means of probability. The chances of Joe Blow getting murdered today are pretty low, and yet when the day is over he may have been murdered. Someone will. But there are serious problems with Jesus entertaining Herod Agrippa and Claudius. The scenario only works if these three figures are not yet embroiled in public life. And so Gibbins describes things. Yet Jesus could not have come to Herod's attention if he were not already known far and wide as the Jesus of the gospels: a preacher and healer. It is plain that he was already active in his ministry (a term Gibbins even has him use) at that point.

---

3. Apologies of my own to Sir Walter Scott, *Marmion*, Canto VI, Stanza 17.

4. Tracks 6 through 17 of the CD *The Beatles: Unsurpassed Masters*. Vol. 4 (1968) (Yellow Dog Records, 1990).

NOTHING HIDDEN BUT TO BE REVEALED

As the novel ends, the efforts of the Concilium to stop the gospel's coming to light have failed. It is on the fast track to international publication. And it will indeed damage the credibility of Catholicism since it is obviously anti-institutional. See the quoted passage above—those sayings are in fact pointedly anti-institutional, like the speech of Stephen in Acts 7, only they go farther. They are not historically implausible as words of Jesus. It is easy, based on the gospels, to see Jesus as anti-sacerdotal, hostile to the priesthood (look at the Good Samaritan parable in Luke 10:30–37!)[5] and the temple sacrifices. But really, one might ask, are these the words of "Jesus Christ," the incarnate savior? If this is all he had to say, a set of liberal platitudes ("Worship at the golf course of your choice"), how did a major religion arise from him and his ministry? This, one might expect, would be the reason for the Church's fear of the text being published.

Once I heard a discussion over claims made by enemies of the Masons that the Lodge was insidious and evil. When one reached the fabled thirty-second degree of initiation one was vouchsafed the ultra-secret news that Christ and Satan were the same being. Well, none present was in a position to know if this were true, but one of them said it *should* be; once you get through that many levels of initiation, there ought to be *something* big at the finish line! And so with a much-sought gospel according to Jesus. But what a let-down we have here, where the point is not positive but negative. There is no attempt here to portray Jesus as a teacher of profundities, merely to make Jesus give the lie to Christianity as we know it. He need not be a better alternative. Put it this way: if you're disillusioned with Catholicism, are you automatically going to find Wayne Dyer much of an improvement?

MAKING THE OBVIOUS ELOQUENT

Gibbins bids us imagine Jesus-fan Claudius bemoaning the rapid degeneration of Jesus' movement into an institutionalized religion. Among other bad signs, he notes: "There is already dissent, there are already factions. Some say Jesus said this, some that" (p. 63). Putting it so simply,

---

5. It is excruciatingly funny to picture the parable's depiction of the priest and the Levite, arms extended and bent upwards at right angles with hands open, like doctors before operating, to keep them sterile and ritually pure for their altar service at Jerusalem, as they carefully step around the bleeding near-corpse of the mugged traveler!

in a mere two sentences, Gibbins supplies the *Sitz-im-Leben* (setting in life) of what the form-critics (like Bultmann[6] and D. E. Nineham)[7] were describing: a rapid and ongoing production of competing and spurious Jesus-words, each to authorize one particular faction's viewpoint. Many students of the gospels have been reluctant to admit that this kind of thing could have happened, even *must* have happened. Why? Because they are motivated by Biblicism, or, as the bumper sticker has it: "The Bible says it! I believe it! That settles it!" If someone wants to abdicate moral and intellectual responsibility and make the Bible into a book that answers every question, one cannot afford to admit that it issues contradictory commands. Thus a scholar with these biases cannot admit (to himself) that Jesus is pulled in opposite directions by the early Christians who transmitted (and fabricated) his sayings. As soon as we cast these blinders aside, things look quite different, and it appears the most natural thing in the world that early Christians made poor Jesus the obedient mouthpiece for their own pet views. This is why we have Jesus saying his disciples no longer fast (Mark 2:21–22), *and* that, though they do not fast at present, soon they will take up the practice again (Mark 2:19–20), *also* that his disciples are to fast, just not like the hypocrites (Matthew 6:16–18), *and* that fasting is actually spiritually dangerous (Thomas, saying 14). This is how Jesus can say both to keep one's eyes peeled for the signs of the End (Mark 13:28–29) *and* that there will be no such signs (Luke 17:20–21). And so on. Well, of course, everyone wants to win an argument, and if it takes a word "from Jesus" to do it, then Jesus suddenly becomes a chatterbox after the fact. Gibbins makes eloquent what should be obvious.

---

6. Bultmann, *The History of the Synoptic Tradition.*
7. Nineham, "Eye-witness Testimony and the Gospel Tradition."

41 | Copts and Robbers
Gregg Loomis, *The Coptic Secret*

THIS NOVEL CONTAINS ELEMENTS of action, adventure, and intrigue. It opens with the kidnapping (and soon the murder) of a British philanthropist during a gala reception at which he was to have announced he was donating to the British Museum a hitherto lost Nag Hammadi Gnostic text. Someone does not want the revelations of this old gospel to become available to the public, a theme we have often met with. Right before the rub-out, one character explains to hero Lang Reilly (really to the reader) just what the Nag Hammadi collection[1] contains:

> Apparent copies of some of the original Gospels, including some not in the Bible, the Gospel of Judas, for instance. This particular work is known as "The Secret Gospel of James" because it supposedly contains secret revelations made to James by Jesus. There's also the Book of James, or protevangelium, which in many ways parallels the gospels of Luke and Matthew. (p. 9)

This is a pretty sloppy description, actually. Somebody didn't do his homework, I'm afraid. For instance, if the "original gospels" refers to the canonical four—Matthew, Mark, Luke and John—the assertion is wrong, for none of these appears among the Nag Hammadi codices, and this for the simple reason that it is a collection of banned books, hidden by ancient monks from match-wielding censors. Then the *Gospel of Judas* is named as an example, but that is really out of the question. The *Gospel of Judas*, much ballyhooed just recently,[2] was not discovered at Nag Hammadi, though it is supposedly a kindred Coptic Gnostic writing. There were a great many of these in Egypt; they needn't all have come from Nag Hammadi, any more than the long-known *Pistis Sophia*

---

1. Meyer, *The Nag Hammadi Scriptures*.
2. Kasser et al., *The Gospel of Judas from Codex Tchacos*.

did.³ Plus, any casual reading of *Judas* makes it clear that the text is a late work, hardly one of the "original" gospels. And there is doubt, as we have seen, that *Judas* is even a genuine ancient text. It may instead be a modern forgery.

The *"Protevangelium" of James* (a horrific scholarly retitling of a document simply known in manuscript as "*The Gospel of James*") is, as Loomis tells us, a synthesis of elements from the infancy stories of Matthew and Luke. But it is long known and was not found in the Nag Hammadi material. Loomis could have gotten more accurate information from a quick Google search. I am guessing that Loomis—using, as he notes, Ron Cameron's collection *The Other Gospels*⁴ for his basic text of the *Apocryphon of James*—noticed that the *Protevangelium* was featured there, too, and he erroneously inferred the *Protevangelium* must also have been a Nag Hammadi text.

"This particular work," presumably the one being donated, "is known as 'The Secret Gospel of James' because it supposedly contains secret revelations made to James by Jesus" (p. 9). This is a real Nag Hammadi book, *The Apocryphon* ("Secret Book") *of James*, and it does purport to be revelations vouchsafed James by the ascended Jesus. Eventually, despite the earlier hype, the "new" Nag Hammadi text is not one that had gone missing immediately after the documents' initial 1945 discovery.⁵ It turns out to be another copy of the now-familiar *Apocryphon of James*. The copy we have, like many of the books in the Nag Hammadi collection, has a few lacunae (holes) in it, though in general it is in pretty good shape, with a lot less text missing than many of the other books. The premise of *The Coptic Secret* is that these omissions did not originate as chance damage to the manuscript but represent clumsy censoring of it. The monks who hid the books must have possessed one bowdlerized copy and one intact. And it is the copy that had retained the otherwise censored material that winds up costing so many lives in the intrigues of *The Coptic Secret*. What did the *Apocryphon of James* originally say?

---

3. Mead, *Pistis Sophia*.
4. Cameron, *The Other Gospels*.
5. Now *that* would be a pretty interesting premise: suppose the tale was false that Bedouin women used some of the newly unearthed texts for kindling. Suppose that instead they sold them to someone before the rest were bought as history records!

> "It is time that James lead my church."
>
> And Peter protested, saying, "Lord, didst thou not say, 'Upon this rock I shall build my church,' meaning me? Hast thou not called my name as Cephus [sic: Cephas], the rock?"
>
> And the Savior answered unto him, 'Didst thou not thrice deny me as was prophesied? Would a master have a servant that denied him?"
>
> And Peter grew wroth, saying, "Lord, who would serve you better?"
>
> And the Savior answered, "James," whereupon Peter became even more angry, demeaning James as a coward and one who had not forsaken his family to follow the Savior as had Peter. (p. 246)

The book closes with an appendix in which the spurned and demoted Peter finds James piously praying in the Temple, pushes him from a height, accuses him of betraying Jesus, and eggs on a mob to stone him to death (pp. 246–47)! The martyrdom of James the Just by stoning or by being shoved from a height is related in a few ancient sources including Hegesippus and *2 Apocalypse of James*. Needless to say, the death is never ascribed to Peter. Paul, however, before his conversion, is sometimes made the villain.[6]

At length we learn that the sinister cabal trying to kill Lang Reilly and everyone else associated with the James text is none other than the Knights of Malta, an elite of Roman Catholics with Crusader origins. They fear that, were the unexpurgated text of the *Apocryphon of James* made public, it would undermine Petrine primacy, the foundation of papal authority. (We saw the same theme in Barbara Wood's *The Prophetess* and Kathleen McGowan's *The Expected One*.) Two things are not so much wrong as nonsensical about this scenario. For one, as author Loomis himself points out, the Knights of Malta are also known as the Order of St. James. Doesn't that imply they would *want* James's side of the story to come out, to the acute distress of the successors of the man they hold to be their patron's murderer? Second, it is just beyond credibility that the public, the echelon of New Testament scholars, or any hyper-Catholic fanatics could for a single second take seriously the theosophic ramblings of a Nag Hammadi text like the *Apocryphon of James*. That text, like all the Nag Hammadi books, is indeed important in helping us reconstruct the fantastic, unanticipated diversity of early "apostolic"

---

6. Eisenman, "The Death of James in its Historical Setting" and "The Attack by Paul on James and the Attack on Stephen," 466–552.

Christianity. But there is no longer any public, any readership, that would take the *Apocryphon of James* as speaking with scriptural authority. And Roman Catholics certainly wouldn't lose much sleep over anything it has to say when they don't worry about the denial of Protestants that Peter was the first pope or that he ever set sandal in Rome.

It is quite ingenious of Loomis to make his suppressed gospel text a mere snippet of an otherwise familiar document. I hate to point it out, but if both versions of the text were real, the passage he has supplied as the original missing piece would immediately be taken by scholars as a later, secondary interpolation that was written by a scribe guessing what might have been in the lost portion. Obviously such a scribe would have had one heck of a gripe against Peter! This bit of text simply does not belong where Loomis's fictive scribe has placed it. That is evident first from the fact that it clashes in every way with the surrounding material, which is all spiritual exhortation. And, second, the new portion fits stylistically and thematically with the appendix, which is overtly post-James, written by another hand, whereas the rest of the *Apocryphon of James* purports to be the work of James himself. Of course that means the earlier patch added to the text is not by the original "James" writer, either.

Besides, it is no new discovery that the early church was shaken by succession disputes and rival authority claims. This has been clear since the nineteenth century when F. C. Baur[7] delineated the competition between the factions of Peter and Paul, with the one pressing for strict Torah observance and the other proclaiming freedom from the Torah. Adolf Harnack[8] pointed out the implications of the composite character of the resurrection appearance list in 1 Corinthians 15:3–11. There "Cephas and the Twelve" is parallel to "James and all the apostles," reflecting that different factions made Peter or James the leader of the disciples, and that their descendants finally buried the hatchet, leaving the redundant mention of the twelve apostles as a fossil reminder of their old rivalry.

Gregg Loomis confesses his wise dependence upon Robert Eisenman, the great expert on James the Just and his pivotal role in the early church. But he makes errors (or fudges the facts for fictional purposes) as Eisenman never would when he gets to the Jewish/Roman historian Flavius Josephus. Josephus "tells us James was reputed to be so

---

7. Baur, *Paul*.
8. Harnack, "Die Verklärungsgeschichte Jesu," 62–80.

pious, to pray so much that his knees were like those of a camel" (p. 123). No, he doesn't. Loomis is confusing Josephus with Hegesippus, a second-century Jewish Christian historian quoted by Eusebius in the latter's own *Ecclesiastical History* (23.17).

According to Loomis, Josephus "also refers to James as 'the brother of him that was crucified, held by some to be the Messiah.' I believe this is the closest thing to a contemporary mention of Christ that exists" (p. 123). Loomis pads out what was originally probably a mention of a different pair of brothers, James and Jesus (Jacob and Jeshua), sons of Damneus and candidates for the high priesthood. The actual text of Josephus' *Jewish Antiquities*, Book 20, chapter 9, first paragraph, reads (with the pertinent identification emphasized):

> And now Caesar, upon hearing the death of Festus, sent Albinus into Judea, as procurator. But the king deprived Joseph of the high priesthood, and bestowed the succession to that dignity on the son of Ananus, who was also himself called Ananus. The report goes that this eldest Ananus proved a most fortunate man; for he had five sons who had all performed the office of a high priest to God, and who had himself enjoyed that dignity a long time formerly, which had never happened to any other of our high priests. But this younger Ananus, who, as we have told you already, took the high priesthood, was a bold man in his temper, and very insolent; he was also of the sect of the Sadducees,, who are very rigid in judging offenders, above all the rest of the Jews, as we have already observed; when, therefore, Ananus was of this disposition, he thought he had now a proper opportunity. Festus was now dead, and Albinus was but upon the road; so he assembled the Sanhedrin of judges, and brought before them *the brother of Jesus, who was called Christ*, whose name was James, and some others; and when he had formed an accusation against them as breakers of the law, he delivered them to be stoned: but as for those who seemed the most equitable of the citizens, and such as were the most uneasy at the breach of the laws, they disliked what was done; they also sent to the king, desiring him to send to Ananus that he should act so no more, for that what he had already done was not to be justified; nay, some of them went also to meet Albinus, as he was upon his journey from Alexandria, and informed him that it was not lawful for Ananus to assemble a sanhedrin without his consent. Whereupon Albinus complied with what they said, and wrote in anger to Ananus, and threatened that he would bring him to punishment for what he had

done; on which king Agrippa took the high priesthood from him, when he had ruled but three months, and made Jesus, the son of Damneus, high priest.

The idea was that James son of Damneus was slated to become high priest, but he had been framed and executed on false charges. Once this injustice had been avenged, the priestly office was given to James' surviving brother, Jesus son of Damneus.[9] The phrase "who was called Christ" may be an interpolation by some Christian scribe who misunderstood what was going on in the passage.[10] Or it may be original to the text but intended to mean "he who was afterward called to be the anointed," i.e., "anointed as high priest."

It is hard to imagine how a copy of an obscure Nag Hammadi document could rile the Knights of Malta into such a murderous frenzy as Loomis depicts in *The Coptic Secret*. But then again, in the real world of religious fanaticism it has taken less, as witness a certain batch of newspaper cartoons featuring the Prophet Muhammad.

---

9. Doherty, *Jesus: Neither God nor Man*, 572–75.
10. Wells, *The Jesus of the Early Christians*, 194.

Conclusion
Don't Look Now...

> His disciples say to him, "When will the repose of the dead
> begin? And when will the new world come?"
> He says to them, "What you look for has already come,
> but you fail to recognize it."
> —*Gospel of Thomas* saying 51

WE HAVE SURVEYED OVER forty Lost Gospel novels. It was no surprise to discover that all of them simplify questions of New Testament scholarship. We should expect nothing else from popular novels, and that is no reproach. Anything else would be ill-considered, even perverse. Ironically, this popular, not to say vulgar, character is what gives the novels a prime opportunity to educate readers in the matter of New Testament research, even if that is not their goal. Indeed, the books would probably diminish in entertainment value if they were intended as vehicles for educating the reader.

But one might at least hope their authors would do their homework and get the details right. That is especially important if the goal of one's book is to use established biblical scholarship as a platform from which to launch in a speculative new direction. For instance, the reader must be told what the hypothetical Q source is if he or she is to thrill to the possibility that it has been discovered. No one will ever write one of these novels in which scholars are excited about unearthing a copy of the M source. (Don't worry if you don't understand the example; you have made my point for me.)

We have found a pretty mixed bag among our novels when it comes to the details, even the broad outlines, of biblical research. Some of our authors really do not seem to have the first idea what they are talking about. Dan Brown signs off on the worst available pseudo-scholarship and blithely passes it on to the reader. His *The Da Vinci Code* has given rise to study groups for people who recognize the fictive character of his story but are excited about the supposedly factual background material about early Christianity. And he has, through carelessness, misled them. Robert Ludlum's premise, the hidden documents his characters seek and die for, is so vague, even incoherent and inconsistent, that one hardly knows what the hubbub is all about.

But the Lost Gospel writers are naïve—and write for a public that is naïve—about what it would take for a discovery to shake up or destroy Christianity. They are even more naïve in their apparent assumption that, short of some discovery such as they narrate, Christianity is at present secure and sitting pretty. By contrast, the informed student of biblical scholarship knows good and well that the termites are already at the woodwork. The *Titanic* is already tilting. The jig is up, or at least about to finish up. For what the protagonists of these novels fear will happen, a discovery threatening to destroy traditional faith, has already occurred on multiple levels. There have been shocking manuscript discoveries such as those that the Lost Gospel novels envision. The *Gospel of Thomas*, found with many others at Nag Hammadi, Egypt, is but one of these. Scholars have spent quite a bit of ink trying to explain the implications of this early sayings gospel both for our understanding of the historical Jesus and for the nature of early Christianity. A seminal essay collection by James M. Robinson and Helmut Koester, *Trajectories through Early Christianity* showed how the Nag Hammadi documents allow us to delineate the unsuspected building blocks, the variety of pre-gospel sources that were used to construct the canonical literature. This means our gospels are the end result, not the beginning, of the process of gospel writing.

Instead of depicting the raw footage of Christian origins, they turn out to be the finished products of a long and complex process, chronicling the evolution of early Christian thought. Once one recognizes, for example, that John's gospel incorporates in its Last Supper Discourse (chapters 13–16) what must originally have been a post-resurrection dialogue, a distinctly Gnostic genre, one comes to realize that Gnosticism lies behind and beside the New Testament, not beyond it. One realizes that traditional orthodox claims to represent the simple, original teaching of Jesus are false advertising. This does not necessarily mean that the Christian religion is false; it just draws aside the curtain and allows us to get a glimpse of the entirely human "wizard" broadcasting his ominous threats of thunder and lightning. One sees that Christianity grew from several different roots, haphazardly, and did not fall to earth full-blown from the hand of God. Some of our Lost Gospel novels assume that readers fear the possibility of such revelations, but in fact scholars have long known it is stale news.

Nor is it just that discoveries from Egyptian and Palestinian caves have already yielded insights disturbing to the faithful. For three centuries now, intrepid delvers into the text of the Bible have laid bare long-buried "artifacts" that many had feared to find. Already in 1875 with the publication of his *Paul the Apostle of Jesus Christ*, F. C. Baur delineated the factional disputes dividing the early church just by connecting the dots within the canonical writings. And in 1934, by reexamining the evidence of the Church Fathers and other old Christian literature, Walter Bauer[1] showed that earliest Christianity was a many-headed hydra (an image the Fathers used to describe Gnosticism in its many forms), that in various quarters of the ancient world "Christianity" really meant Marcionism, Encratism, or Gnosticism.

Would faith be upset to learn from some new document by Judas Iscariot or Simon Zelotes that the historical Jesus was a revolutionist? S. G. F. Brandon[2] already made a pretty convincing case for that on the basis of clues in the canonical gospels. Or what if some archaeologist stumbled upon a text that showed Jesus did not expire on the cross? Several of the Lost Gospel novels play with that shocker. But in fact, certain bits and pieces of our familiar gospel narratives have urged that possibility upon sharp-eyed readers, both Christian and Muslim, for the past couple of hundred years.

If anyone imagines that traditional Christian belief remains untroubled short of the nightmare of discoveries like the *Gospel According to James* or the Filioque denials or the *Testament of Judas* or the *Gospel of Dismas* or the *Sinai Bible*, he is sadly naïve. He is like a Babylonian sentry confidently looking down from the city walls undisturbed by the Mede and Persian camps outside on the plain of Shinar, when at that very moment the invaders are coming up through the drainage pipes and pouring into the city streets behind him. Of all our authors, it is only the two most polemical evangelicals, Guy Thorne and J. H. Hunter, who

---

1. Bauer, *Orthodoxy and Heresy in Earliest Christianity*.
2. Brandon, *The Fall of Jerusalem and the Christian Church*; Brandon, *Jesus and the Zealots*.

understood this. For them the Joseph of Arimathea inscription and the *Shred of Nicodemus*, though ostensibly new discoveries, simply symbolized the threat that the nefarious Higher Criticism had already introduced. They underlined this metaphor by making both faith-destroying discoveries turn out to be malevolent hoaxes sponsored by "unbelieving" biblical critics. That's all that these conservative authors believed biblical criticism was anyway.

Why have rank and file readers not seen this, that the threat is not to be scanned on the far horizon but is already present? Remember that several of our authors have noted in passing that people, not having adopted their belief for rational reasons, would continue to hold to it no matter what contrary "smoking gun" evidence might be produced. They were never concerned with the facts in the first place. "How do I know Jesus rose from the dead? Because the people in my church are so nice." Those people don't become less nice because of what some archaeologist discovered, or because some ivory tower academic says he has a compelling new theory. More's the pity. This is not to suggest people would be better off discarding their faith. No, but it would be better if people based their beliefs on facts rather than sentiment and peer pressure. No textual or archaeological discovery is needed to prove that, nor can any ever disprove it.

Bibliography

Ahmad, Hazrat Mirza Ghulam. *Jesus in India: Being an account of Jesus' escape from death on the cross and of his journey to India.* Translated by Qazi Abdul Hamid. Abwah: Ahmadiyya Muslim Foreign Missions Department, 1962.

Allegro, John M. *The Sacred Mushroom and the Cross: A Study of the Nature and Origins of Christianity within the Fertility Cults of the Ancient Near East.* New York: Bantam Books, 1971.

Allen, Charlotte. "The Search for a No-Frills Jesus." *Atlantic Monthly* Online, December 1996.

Allmen, Daniel von. "The Birth of Theology: Contextuallzation as the dynamic element in the Formation of New Testament Theology." *International Review of Missions* 64 (1975) 37–52.

Andrae, Tor. *Mohammed: The Man and his Faith.* Translated by Theophil Menzel. New York: Harper & Row Torchbooks / Cloister Library, 1960.

Arthur, Richard J. "The Gospel of Judas: Is It a Hoax?" *Journal of Unification Studies* 9 (2008) 35–47.

Bacon, Benjamin W. *Jesus and Paul:* Lectures given at Manchester College, Oxford, for the Winter Term, 1920. London: Hodder & Stoughton, 1920.

Baigent, Michael, and Richard Leigh. *The Dead Sea Scrolls Deception.* New York: Simon & Schuster, 1993.

———, and Henry Lincoln. *Holy Blood, Holy Grail.* New York: Dell Publishing, 1983.

———. *The Messianic Legacy.* New York: Dell Publishing, 1986.

Barnhardt, Wilton. *Gospel.* New York: St. Martin's Press, 1990. Reprinted 1995.

Bates, Ernest Sutherland. *The Gospel according to Judas Iscariot.* London: William Heinemann, 1929.

Bauer, Walter. *Orthodoxy and Heresy in Earliest Christianity.* Edited by Robert Kraft and Gerhard Krodel. Translated by Philadelphia Seminar on Christian Origins. Philadelphia: Fortress Press, 1971.

Baur, Christian Ferdinand. *The Church History of the First Three Centuries.* Translated by Allan Menzies. Edinburgh: Williams & Norgate, 1875.

———. *Paul, the Apostle of Jesus Christ: His Life and Works, His Epistles and Teaching.* Translated by W. Menzies. Edinburgh: Williams & Norgate, 1845, 1873. Reprinted Peabody: Hendrickson Publishers, 2003.

Berger, Peter L., and Thomas Luckmann. *The Social Construction of Reality: A Treatise in the Sociology of Knowledge.* Garden City: Doubleday Anchor, 1967.

Beskow, Per. "Pilate's Own Story." In *Strange Tales about Jesus*, 51–56. Minneapolis: Fortress Press, 1983.

———. "Jesus in India." In *Strange Tales about Jesus*, 57–65. Minneapolis: Fortress Press, 1983.

Black, Matthew. *An Aramaic Approach to the Gospels and Acts.* Oxford: Clarendon Press, 3rd ed., 1967.

Block, Paul, and Robert Vaughan. *The Masada Scroll.* New York: Tom Doherty Associates/ TOR Books, 2007.

Boff, Leonardo. *Jesus Christ Liberator: A Critical Christology for our Times.* Translated by Patrick Hughes. Maryknoll: Orbis Books, 1978.

Bolland, G. J. P. J. *De Evangelische Jozua: Een poging tot aanwijzing van den oorsprong des Christendoms.* Leiden: Hoogleerar der Wijsbegeerte te Leiden, 1907.

Brandon, S. G. F. *The Fall of Jerusalem and the Christian Church: A Study of the Effects of the Jewish Overthrow of A.D. 70 on Christianity.* London: SPCK, 1951.

———. *Jesus and the Zealots: A Study of the Political Factor in Primitive Christianity.* New York: Charles Scribner's Sons, 1967.

———. *The Trial of Jesus of Nazareth.* Historic Trials Series. New York: Stein and Day, 1968.

Brooke, John L. *The Refiner's Fire: The Making of Mormon Cosmology, 1644–1844.* Cambridge University Press, 1994.

Brown, Dan. *The DaVinci Code.* New York: Doubleday, 2003.

Brown, Raymond E. *The Birth of the Messiah: A Commentary on the Infancy Narratives in Matthew and Luke.* Garden City: Doubleday, 1977.

Bruce, F. F. *The New Testament Documents: Are They Reliable?* Grand Rapids: Eerdmans, 1960.

Bultmann, Rudolf. *The History of the Synoptic Tradition.* Rev. ed. Translated by John Marsh. New York: Harper & Row, 1972.

———. *The Gospel of John: A Commentary.* Translated by G. R. Beasley-Murray, R. W. N. Hoare, and J. K. Riches. Philadelphia: Westminster Press, 1971.

———. *Jesus Christ and Mythology.* New York: Charles Scribner's Sons, 1958.

———. "New Testament and Mythology." In *Kerygma and Myth: A Theological Debate*, 1–44. Edited by Hans Werner Bartsch. Translated by Reginald H. Fuller. New York: Harper & Row Torchbooks, 1961.

———. *Theology of the New Testament*, Vol. 1. Translated by Kendrick Groebel. New York: Scribners, 1951.

Burns, Rita J. *Has the Lord Spoken Only through Miriam? A Study of the Biblical Portrait of Miriam.* SBL Dissertation Series 84. Atlanta: Scholars Press, 1987.

Byrnes, Michael. *The Sacred Bones.* New York: HarperCollins, 2007.

Cameron, Ron, ed. *The Other Gospels: Non-Canonical Gospel Texts.* Philadelphia: Westminster Press, 1982.

Carrier, Richard C. "The Spiritual Body of Christ and the Legend of the Empty Tomb." In *The Empty Tomb: Jesus Beyond the Grave*, edited by Robert M. Price and Jeffery Jay Lowder, 105–232. Amherst: Prometheus Books, 2005.

Carter, Lin. *Imaginary Worlds.* Adult Fantasy Series. New York: Ballantine Books, 1973.

Christopher, Paul. *The Lucifer Gospel.* New York: New American Library / Onyx Books, 2006.

Cohn, Norman. *The Pursuit of the Millennium: Revolutionary Millenarians and Mystical Anarchists of the Middle Ages.* Rev. ed. New York: Oxford University Press, 1970.

Collingwood, R. G. *The Idea of History.* New York: Oxford University Press, 1946.

Conrad, Barnaby, and Nico Mastorakis. *Keepers of the Secret.* New York: Jove Books, 1983.

Coote, Robert B. *Early Israel: A New Horizon.* Minneapolis: Fortress Press, 1990.

Bibliography

Corley, Kathleen E. *Women & the Historical Jesus: Feminist Myths of Christian Origins*. Santa Rosa: Polebridge Press, 2002.

Crossan, John Dominic. *Four Other Gospels: Shadows on the Contours of the Canon*. New York: Harper & Row, 1985.

———. *The Historical Jesus: The Life of a Mediterranean Jewish Peasant*. San Francisco: HarperSanFrancisco, 1993.

Cupitt, Don. "The Christ of Christendom." In *The Myth of God Incarnate*, edited by John Hick, 133–47. Philadelphia: Westminster Press, 1977.

———. *Radicals and the Future of the Church*. London: SCM Press, 1989.

Davies, A. Powell. *The First Christian: A Study of St. Paul and Christian Origins*. New York: Farrar, Straus and Cudahy, 1957.

Davies, Philip R. *In Search of 'Ancient Israel'*. Journal for the Study of the Old Testament Supplement Series 148. Sheffield: Sheffield Academic Press, 1992.

Davies, Stephan L. *The Gospel of Thomas and Christian Wisdom*. New York: Seabury Press, 1983.

Dawood, N. J., trans. *The Koran*. London: Penguin Books, 1964.

De Conick, April D. *The Thirteenth Apostle: What the Gospel of Judas Really Says*. New York: Continuum, 2007.

Deissmann, Adolf. *The Religion of Jesus and the Faith of Paul*. The Selly Oak Lectures, 1923. Translated by William E. Wilson. London: Hodder & Stoughton, 1923.

Derrida, Jacques. *Of Grammatology*. Translated by Gayatri Chakravorty Spivak. Baltimore: Johns Hopkins University Press, 1976.

Doherty, Earl. *Jesus: Neither God nor Man: The Case for a Mythical Jesus*. Ottowa: Age of Reason Publications, 2009.

Downing, F. Gerald. *Cynics and Christian Origins*. Edinburgh: T&T Clark, 1992.

Easterman, Daniel. *Brotherhood of the Tomb*. New York: Doubleday, 1990. Reprinted SF: HarperCollins, 1991.

———. *The Judas Testament*. San Francisco: HarperCollins, 1994.

Einhorn, Lena. *The Jesus Mystery: Astonishing Clues to the True Identities of Jesus and Paul*. Lyons Press/Globe Pequot Press, 2007.

Eisenman, Robert. *The Dead Sea Scrolls and the First Christians: Essays and Translations*. Rockport: Element Books, 1996.

———. "The Death of James in its Historical Setting" and "The Attack by Paul on James and the Attack on Stephen." In *James the Brother of Jesus: The Key to Unlocking the Secrets of Early Christianity and the Dead Sea Scrolls*, 466–552. New York: Viking Press, 1997.

———. "Maccabees, Zadokites, Christians and Qumran: A New Hypothesis of Qumran Origins." In *The Dead Sea Scrolls and the First Christians*, 3–110. Rockport: Element Books, 1996.

Eisler, Robert. *The Messiah Jesus and John the Baptist*. Translated by Alexander Haggerty Krappe. New York: Dial Press, 1931.

Eliade, Mircea. *The Two and the One*. Translated by J. M. Cohen. New York: Harper & Row Torchbooks, 1969.

Elliot, J. K., trans. and ed. *The Apocryphal New Testament: A Collection of Apocryphal Christian Literature in an English Translation*. New York: Oxford University Press, 1993.

Enroth, Ronald M., and Gerald E. Jamison. *The Gay Church*. Grand Rapids: Eerdmans, 1974.

Faber-Kaiser, Andreas. *Jesus Died in Kashmir*. Translated by Gordon Cremonesi. London: Sphere/Abacus, 1978.

Fader, H. Louis. *The Issa Tale that Will not Die: Nicholas Notovitch and his Fraudulent Gospel*. New York: University Press of America, 2003.

Faruqui, Mumtaz Ahmad. *The Crumbling of the Cross*. Lahore: Ahmadiyya Anjuman Isha'at-i-Islam, 1973.

Fiorenza, Elisabeth Schüssler. *In Memory of Her: A Feminist Reconstruction of Christian Origins*. New York: Crossroad Publishing Company, 1984.

Fish, Stanley. *Is There a Text in this Class? The Authority of Interpretive Communities*. Cambridge: Harvard University Press, 1980.

Fleddermann, Harry T. *Mark and Q: A Study of the Overlap Texts*. Bibliotheca Ephemeridum Theologicarum Lovaniensium CXXII. Leuven: Leuven University Press/Uitgeverij Peeters, 1995.

Fosdick, Harry Emerson. *The Personality of Jesus—The Soul of Christianity*. A Sermon Preached at Temple Beth-El, New York, Sunday, April 13, 1930.

Freeman, Hobart E. *Did Jesus Die Spiritually?* Warsaw, IN: Faith Ministries & Publications, nd.

Funk, Robert W., and The Jesus Seminar. *The Acts of Jesus: What Did Jesus Really Do?* Santa Rosa: Polebridge Press, 1998.

Garbini, Giovanni. *History and Ideology in Ancient Israel*. Translated by John Bowden. New York: Crossroad, 1988.

Gärtner, Bertil. *Iscariot*. Translated by Victor I. Gruhn. Facet Books. Biblical Series—29. Philadelphia: Fortress Press, 1971.

Gasque, W. Ward. *A History of the Criticism of the Acts of the Apostles*. Grand Rapids: Eerdmans, 1975.

Gibbins, David. *The Lost Tomb*. New York: Bantam Dell / Random House, 2008.

Girard, René. *Violence and the Sacred*. Translated by Patrick Gregory. Baltimore: Johns Hopkins University Press, 1977.

Glover, Willis B., Jr. *Evangelical Nonconformists and Higher Criticism in the 19th Century*. London: Independent Press, 1954.

Golb, Norman. *Who Wrote the Dead Sea Scrolls: The Search for the Secret of Qumran*. New York: Scribner, 1995.

Gold, Alan. *The Lost Testament*. Australia: HarperCollins Publishers, 1994. Reprinted New York: HarperCollins Publishers, 1996.

Goodacre, Mark. *The Case Against Q: Studies in Markan Priority and the Synoptic Problem*. Harrisburg, PA: Trinity Press International, 2002.

Goodspeed, Edgar J. "The Unknown Life of Jesus Christ." In *Famous Biblical Hoaxes, or, Modern Apocrypha*, 3–14. Twin Brooks Series. Grand Rapids: Baker Book House, 1956.

———. "The Report of Pilate." In *Famous Biblical Hoaxes, or, Modern Apocrypha*, 28–44. Twin Brooks Series. Grand Rapids: Baker Book House, 1956.

Grant, Robert M. *Irenaeus of Lyons*. Early Church Fathers. New York: Routledge, 1997.

Graves, Robert. *King Jesus*. New York: Universal Publishing, 1956.

———, and Joshua Podro. *Jesus in Rome: A Historical Conjecture*. London: Cassell & Company, 1957.

———. *The Nazarene Gospel Restored*. Garden City: Doubleday, 1954.

Guignebert, Charles. *Jesus*. Translated by S. H. Hooke. New Hyde Park: University Books, 1956.

Guthrie, Kenneth Sylvan. *The Long-Lost Second Book of Acts: Setting forth the Blessed Mary's Teachings about Reincarnation*. New York: Theosophical Publishing Co., 1904.
Guy, Jeff. *The Heretic: A Study of the Life of John William Colenso 1814–1883*. Johannesburg: Ravan Press / Pietermaritzburg: University of Natal Press, 1983.
Guttierez, Gustavo. *A Theology of Liberation: History, Politics and Salvation*. Translated by Sister Caridad Inda and John Eagleson. Maryknoll: Orbis Books, 1973.
Hamburger, Käte. "The Fictional or Mimetic Genre." In *The Logic of Literature*, 55–193. Translated by Marilynn J. Rose. Indianapolis: Indiana University Press, 2nd rev. ed, 1993.
Harnack, Adolf von. "Die Verklärungsgeschichte Jesu, der Bericht des Paulus, I Kor 15, 3ff. und die beiden Christusvision des Petrus." *Sitzungsberichte der Berliner Academie der Wissenschaften*, Phil.-hist. Klasse, 1922, 62–80.
―――. *What Is Christianity?* Translated by Thomas Baily Saunders. New York: Harper & Row Torchbooks, 1957.
Harris, Horton. *David Friedrich Strauss and his Theology*. Monograph Supplements to the Scottish Journal of Theology. Cambridge at the University Press, 1973.
―――. "The Tübingen School: An Evaluation." In *The Tübingen School*, 249–62. New York: Oxford at the Clarendon Press, 1975.
Harvey, Van A. *The Historian and the Believer: The Morality of Historical Knowledge and Christian Belief*. New York: Macmillan, 1969.
Hedrick, Charles W. with Nikolaos Olympiou, "Secret Mark: New Photographs, New Witnesses." *The Fourth R*. 13/5 (September–October 2000) 3–11.
Heer, J. M. *Die Stammbäume Jesu nach Matthäus und Lukas*. Biblische Studien 15 1–2. Freiburg: Herder, 1910.
Heimerdinger, Chris. *The Lost Scrolls*. Tennis Shoes Adventure Series. American Fork, UT: Covenant Communications, 1998.
Heller, Richard, and Rachel. *The 13th Apostle*. New York: HarperCollins, 2007.
Hernon, Peter. *Earthly Remains*. New York: Birch Lane Press, 1989.
Herrero, David Estrada, and William White Jr. *The First New Testament*. Nashville: Thomas A. Nelson, 1978.
Herrmann, Wilhelm. *The Communion of the Christian with God, Described on the Basis of Luther's Statements*. Translated by J. Sandys Stanyon. Crown Theological Library. New York: G. P. Putnam's Sons, 1906.
Hodge, Archibald A., and Benjamin B. Warfield. *Inspiration*. Grand Rapids: Baker Book House, 1979.
Hodgson, Peter C. *The Formation of Historical Theology: A Study of Ferdinand Christian Baur*. Makers of Modern Theology. New York: Harper & Row, 1966.
Hoover, Roy W., and the Jesus Seminar. *The Five Gospels: What Did Jesus Really Say?* Santa Rosa: Polebridge Press, 1993.
Howard, George. *Hebrew Gospel of Matthew*. Macon: Mercer University Press, 1995.
Howard, Wilbert Francis. *The Romance of New Testament Scholarship*. Drew Lectures in Biography, 1947. London: Epworth Press, 1949.
Hunter, J. H. *The Mystery of Mar Saba*. New York: Evangelical Publishers, 1940.
Johnson, Bettye. *Secrets of the Magdalene Scrolls: The Forbidden Truth of the Life and Times of Mary Magdalene*. Rainier, WA: Living Free Press, 2004. Revised edition 2005.

Johnson, Luke Timothy. *The Real Jesus: The Misguided Quest for the Historical Jesus and the Truth of the Traditional Gospels*. San Francisco: HarperSanFrancisco, 1996.
Josephus, Flavius. *The Jewish War*. Translated by G. A. Williamson. Baltimore: Penguin Books, 1959.
Joyce, Donovan. *The Jesus Scroll*. New York: Dial Press, 1973.
Kähler, Martin. *The So-Called Historical Jesus and the Historic, Biblical Christ*. Translated by Carl E. Braaten. Seminar Editions. Philadelphia: Fortress Press, 1964.
Käsemann, Ernst. "The Canon of the New Testament and the Unity of the Church." In *Essays on New Testament Themes*. Studies in Biblical Theology No. 41. Translated by W. J. Montague, 95–107. London: SCM Press, 1964.
Kasser, Rodolphe, et al., eds. *The Gospel of Judas from Codex Tchacos*. Washington, DC: National Geographic Society, 2006.
———, and Francois Gaudard, eds. *The Gospel of Judas, Together with the Letter from Peter to Philip, James, and a Book of Allogenes from Codex Tchacos: Critical Edition*. Washington, DC: National Geographic Society, 2007.
Kaufman, Gordon. *Systematic Theology: A Historicist Perspective*. New York: Charles Scribner's Sons, 1968.
Kennerley, Mitchell. *The Love Letters of St. John*. New York: Mitchell Kennerley, 1917.
Kenyon, E. W. *Identification: A Romance in Redemption*. Seattle: Kenyon's Gospel Publishing Society, 1968.
———. *What Happened from the Cross to the Throne*. Seattle: Kenyon's Gospel Publishing Society, 1998.
Kermode, Frank. *The Genesis of Secrecy: On the Interpretation of Narrative*. The Charles Eliot Norton Lectures, 1977–1978. Cambridge: Harvard University Press, 1979.
Kiefer, Warren. *The Pontius Pilate Papers*. New York: Harper & Row, 1976. Reprinted, New York: Harcourt Brace Jovanovich / Jove Books, 1977.
King, Donald C. *The Manuscript*. Living Books / Tyndale House, 1984.
King, Laurie R. *A Letter of Mary*. New York: St. Martin's Press, 1997. Reprinted, New York: Bantam Books, 1998.
Klein, Günter. *Die Zwölf Apostel: Ursprung und Gehalt einer Jdee*. Göttingen: Vandenhoeck & Ruprecht, 1961.
Koester, Helmut. *Ancient Christian Gospels*. Philadelphia: Trinity Press International, 1992.
Küng, Hans. *On Being a Christian*. Translated by Edward Quinn. Garden City: Doubleday, 1977.
Lamsa, George M. *New Testament Origin*. Chicago: University of Chicago Press, 1947.
Larson, Egon. *Strange Sects and Cults: A Study of their Origins and Influence*. New York: Hart Publishing Company, 1971.
Lemche, Niels Peter. *The Israelites in History and Tradition*. Library of Ancient Israel. Louisville: Westminster/John Knox Press, 1998.
Levi-Strauss, Claude. *Structural Anthropology*. Translated by Claire Jacobson and Brooke Grundfest Schoepf. Garden City: Doubleday Anchor Books, 1967.
Lewis, Bernard. *History: Remembered, Recovered, Invented*. Princeton: Princeton University Press, 1975.
Lewis, C. S. *Mere Christianity*. New York: Macmillan, 1977.
———. *The Screwtape Letters & Screwtape Proposes a Toast*. New York: Macmillan, 1970.
Long, Frank Belknap. *The Hounds of Tindalos*. Sauk City: Arkham House, 1946.

Loomis, Gregg. *The Coptic Secret*. New York: Dorchester Publishing / Leisure Books, 2009.

Loucks, Ursula, and Terry. *Burning Words*. Np: InfoNovels, 1998.

Lovecraft, H. P. "The Dunwich Horror." *Weird Tales* (April 1929) 481–508.

Luccock, Robert F. *The Lost Gospel and Other Sermons Based on Short Stories*. London: Harper & Brothers, 1948.

Ludlum, Robert. *The Gemini Contenders*. New York: Dial Press, 1976. Reprinted, New York: Dell Books, 1977.

Lupieri, Edmondo. *The Mandaeans: The Last Gnostics*. Translated by Charles Hindley. Italian Texts & Studies on Religion & Society. Grand Rapids: Eerdmans, 2002.

Maccoby, Hyam. *Revolution in Judea*. New York: Taplinger Press, 1973.

MacDonald, Dennis Ronald. *The Homeric Epics and the Gospel of Mark*. New Haven: Yale University Press, 2000.

———. *The Legend and the Apostle: The Battle for Paul in Story and Canon*. Philadelphia: Fortress Press, 1983.

Mack, Burton L. *The Lost Gospel: The Book of Q and Christian Origins*. San Francisco: HarperSanFrancisco, 1993.

———. *A Myth of Innocence: Mark and Christian Origins*. Minneapolis: Fortress Press, 1991.

———. *Who Wrote the New Testament? The Making of the Christian Myth*. San Francisco: HarperSanFrancisco, 1995.

Maier, Paul L. *A Skeleton in God's Closet*. Nashville: Thomas Nelson Publishers, 1994.

Malherbe, Abraham J. *Paul and the Popular Philosophers*. Minneapolis: Fortress Press, 1989.

Mason, Steve. *Josephus and the New Testament*. Peabody: Hendrickson Publishers, 1992.

Massey, Gerald. *The Historical Jesus and the Mythical Christ*. Brooklyn: A & B Book Publishers, 1992, reprint.

Mawer, Simon. *The Gospel of Judas*. New York: Little, Brown and Company, 2000. Reprinted by Back Bay Books, 2002. Reprinted by Abacus, 2005.

McHugh, John. "The Brothers of Jesus (III): St Jerome's Theory." In *The Mother of Jesus in the New Testament*, 223–33. Garden City: Doubleday, 1975.

Mead, G. R. S., ed. and trans. *Pistis Sophia: A Gnostic Miscellany: Being for the Most Part Extracts from the Books of the Saviour, To Which Are Added Excerpts from a Cognate Literature*. London: John M. Watkins, 1963.

Metzger, Bruce M. *The Text of the New Testament: Its Transmission, Corruption and Restoration*. New York: Oxford University Press, 1964.

Meyer, Marvin, ed. *The Nag Hammadi Scriptures: The International Edition*. New York: HarperCollins, 2007.

Mundy, Talbot. *Ramsden*. New York: Ridgeway Company / Bobbs-Merrill Company, 1926. Reprinted as *The Devil's Guard*. New York: Avon Books, 1968.

Nassr, Donald. *The Scroll*. Rouses Point, New York. No publisher named, 1997.

Nickel, Joe. *Inquest on the Shroud of Turin: Latest Scientific Findings*. Amherst: Prometheus Books, 1998.

Nietzsche, Friedrich Wilhelm. *The Anti-Christ, Ecce Homo, Twilight of the Idols, and Other Writings*. Edited by Aaron Ridley and Judith Norman. Cambridge at the University Press, 2005.

Nineham, D. E. "Eye-witness Testimony and the Gospel Tradition." In *Explorations in Theology* 1, 24–60. London: SCM Press. 1977.

———. *A New Way of Looking at the Gospels: Four Broadcast Talks*. London: SPCK, 1962.

———. *Saint Mark*. Pelican New Testament Commentaries. Baltimore: Penguin Books, 1971.

Pagels, Elaine. *Beyond Belief: The Secret Gospel of Thomas*. New York: Random House, 2003.

———. "The Controversy over Christ's Resurrection: Historical Event or Symbol?" In *The Gnostic Gospels*, 3–27. New York: Random House, 1979.

Pappas, Paul C. *Jesus' Tomb in India: Debate on His Death and Resurrection*. Berkeley: Asian Humanities Press, 1991.

Parker, Gary E. *The Ephesus Fragment*. Minneapolis: Bethany House Publishers, 1999.

Partner, Richard. *The Murdered Magicians: The Templars and their Myth*. New York: Oxford University Press, 1982.

Patterson, Stephen J. *The Gospel of Thomas and Jesus*. Foundations & Facets Reference Series. Sonoma: Polebridge Press, 1993.

Pearson, Birger A. *Gnosticism, Judaism, and Egyptian Christianity*. Studies in Antiquity & Christianity. Minneapolis: Fortress Press, 1990.

Pervo, Richard I. *Dating Acts: Between the Evangelists and the Apologists*. Santa Rosa: Polebridge Press, 2006.

———. *Profit with Delight: The Literary Genre of the Acts of the Apostles*. Philadelphia: Fortress Press, 1987.

Peters, Elizabeth. *The Dead Sea Cipher*. New York: Dodd, Mead & Company, 1970. Reprinted, New York: Dell Books, 1971.

Phipps, William E. *Was Jesus Married? The Distortion of Sexuality in the Christian Tradition*. New York: Harper & Row, 1970.

Plato. *Plato's Phaedo, Literally Translated*. Translated by E. M. Cope (Cambridge, 1875).

Price, Robert M. "Apocryphal Apparitions: 1 Corinthians 15:3–11 as a Post-Pauline Interpolation." In *The Empty Tomb: Jesus beyond the Grave*. Edited by Robert M. Price and Jeffery Jay Lowder, 69–104. Amherst: Prometheus Books, 2005.

———. *Deconstructing Jesus*. Amherst: Prometheus Books, 2000.

———. "Karma Chameleon." In *Top Secret: The Truth behind Today's Pop Mysticisms*, 49–72. Amherst: Prometheus Books, 2008.

———. *The Incredible Shrinking Son of Man: How Reliable is the Gospel Tradition?* Amherst: Prometheus Books, 2003.

———. *The Paperback Apocalypse: How the Christian Church Was Left Behind*. Amherst: Prometheus Books, 2007.

———. *The Pre-Nicene New Testament: Fifty-Four Formative Texts*. Salt Lake City: Signature Books, 2006.

———. Review of Baigent and Leigh, *The Dead Sea Scrolls Deception* in *Journal of Higher Criticism* 2/2 (Fall 1995) 148–51.

———. "The Righteous Rise." Vincent Sneed, ed. *The Dead Walk! Weird Tales of Zombies, Revenants, and the Living Dead*. Baltimore: Die, Monster, Die Books, 2004, 92–106.

———. *The Widow-Traditions in Luke-Acts: A Feminist-Critical Scrutiny*. SBL Dissertation Series 155. Atlanta: Scholars Press, 1997.

Rabb, Jonathan. *The Book of Q*. New York: Random House, 2001. Reprinted, London: Halban Publishers, 2007.

Raven, C. E. *Apollinarianism*. Cambridge at the University Press, 1923.

Reardon, B. P., ed. *Collected Ancient Greek Novels*. Berkeley: University of California Press, 1989.
Reichs, Kathy. *Cross Bones*. New York: Scribner, 2005. Reprinted by Simon & Schuster / Pocket Star Books, 2006.
Reimarus, Hermann Samuel. *Reimarus: Fragments*. Edited by Charles H. Talbert. Philadelphia: Fortress Press, 1970.
Reitzenstein, Richard. *Hellenistic Mystery Religions: Their Basic Ideas and Significance*. Pittsburgh Theological Monograph Series 15. Translated by John E. Steely. Pittsburgh: Pickwick Press, 1978.
Richardson, Robert. "The Priory of Sion Hoax." *Alpheus: Site for Esoteric History*. No pages. Online: http://www.alpheus.org/html/articles/esoteric_history/richardson1.html.
Riley, Gregory J. *Resurrection Reconsidered: Thomas and John in Controversy*. Minneapolis: Fortress Press, 1995.
Roberts, John Hall. *The Q Document*. New York: William Morrow and Company, 1964. Reprinted Greenwich: Fawcett Crest, 1964.
Robinson, James M., and Helmut Koester. *Trajectories through Early Christianity*. Philadelphia: Fortress Press, 1971.
Robinson, Neal. *Christ in Islam and Christianity*. Albany: State University of New York Press, 1991.
Rogers, Barbara. *The Doomsday Scroll*. New York: Dodd, Mead & Company, 1979. Reprinted, New York: Dell Books, 1980.
Rogerson, John W. *The Bible and Criticism in Victorian Britain: Profiles of F. D. Maurice and William Robertson Smith*. Journal for the Study of the Old Testament Supplement Series 201. Sheffield: Sheffield Academic Press, 1995.
———. *Old Testament Criticism in the Nineteenth Century: England and Germany*. Philadelphia: Fortress Press, 1985.
Roth, Cecil. *The Dead Sea Scrolls: A New Historical Approach*. New York: Norton, 1966.
Rudolph, Kurt. *Gnosis: The Nature and History of Gnosticism*. Translated by P. W. Coxon, K. H. Kuhn, and Robert McLachlan Wilson. San Francisco: Harper & Row, 1983.
Rumscheidt, H. Martin. *Revelation and Theology: An Analysis of the Barth-Harnack Correspondence of 1923*. Monograph Supplements to the Scottish Journal of Theology. Cambridge at the University Press, 1972.
Runciman, Steven. *The Medieval Manichee: A Study of the Christian Dualist Heresy*. New York: Viking Press, 1961.
Rylands, L. Gordon. *The Evolution of Christianity*. London: Watts, 1927.
———. *The Beginnings of Gnostic Christianity*. London: Watts, 1940.
Salm, René. *The Myth of Nazareth: The Invented Town of Jesus*. Cranford, NJ: American Atheist Press, 2008.
Sanders, E. P. *Jesus and Judaism*. Philadelphia: Fortress Press, 1985.
Sandom, J. G. *Gospel Truths*. New York: Doubleday, 1992. Reprinted, New York: Bantam Books, 1993.
Sapir, Richard Ben. *The Body*. Doubleday, 1983. Reprinted, New York: Pinnacle, 1984.
Sartre, Jean-Paul. *Being and Nothingness: An Essay in Phenomenological Ontology*. Translated by Hazel E. Barnes. New York: Washington Square Press, 1966.
Schechter, Solomon. *Some Aspects of Rabbinic Theology*. New York: Macmillan, 1910.
Schillebeeckx, Edward. *Christ: The Experience of Jesus as Lord*. Translated by John Bowden. New York: Seabury Press, 1980.

———. *Jesus: An Experiment in Christology*. Translated by Hubert Hoskins. New York: Seabury Press, 1979.

Schleiermacher, Friedrich. *The Christian Faith*. Translated and edited by H. R. MacKintosh and J. S. Stewart. New York: Harper & Row Torchbooks, 1963.

Schmithals, Walter. *The Office of Apostle in the Early Church*. Translsted by John E. Steely. New York: Abingdon Press, 1969.

———. "The Parabolic Teachings in the Synoptic Tradition." Translated by Darrell J. Doughty. *Journal of Higher Criticism* 4/2 (Fall 1997) 3–32.

Schoeps, Hans-Joachim. *Jewish Christianity: Factional Disputes in the Early Church*. Translated by Douglas R. A. Hare. Philadelphia: Fortress Press, 1969.

Schonfield, Hugh J. *The Essene Odyssey: The Mystery of the True Teacher & the Essene Impact on the Shaping of Human Destiny*. Longmead: Element Books, 1984.

———. *The Passover Plot: New Light on the History of Jesus*. New York: Bantam Books, 1967.

Schweitzer, Albert. *The Mystery of the Kingdom of God: The Secret of Jesus' Messiahship and Passion*. Translated by Walter Lowrie. New York: Schocken Books, 1964.

———. "Thoroughgoing Scepticism and Thoroughgoing Eschatology." In *The Quest of the Historical Jesus: A Critical Study of its Progress from Reimarus to Wrede*, 330–97. Translated by W. Montgomery. New York: Macmillan, 1906. Reprinted, 1968.

Segundo, Juan Luis. *The Historical Jesus of the Synoptics*. Vol. 2 of *Jesus of Nazareth Yesterday and Today*. Translated by John Drury. Maryknoll: Orbis Books, 1982.

Silver, Abba Hillel. *A History of Messianic Speculation in Israel: From the First through the Seventeenth Centuries*. Boston: Beacon Press, 1959.

Smith, Morton. *Clement of Alexandria and a Secret Gospel of Mark*. Cambridge, MA: Harvard University Press, 1973.

———. *The Secret Gospel: The Discovery and Interpretation of the Secret Gospel According to Mark*. New York: 1973.

Sophocles, "Oedipus the King." In *Classical Gods and Heroes: Myths as Told by Ancient Authors*, edited and translated by Rhoda A. Hendricks, 109–52. New York: Morrow Quill Paperbacks, 1974.

Stauffer, Ethelbert. "The Caliphate of James." Translated by Darrell J. Doughty. *Journal of Higher Criticism* 4/2 (Fall 1997) 120–43.

Strauss, David Friedrich. *The Life of Jesus Critically Examined*. Lives of Jesus Series. Translated by George Eliot (Mary Anne Evans), 1892. Reprinted Philadelphia: Fortress Press, 1972.

Tabor, James D. *The Jesus Dynasty*. New York: Simon & Schuster, 2006.

Talbert, Charles H., ed. *Reimarus: Fragments*. Translated by Ralph S. Fraser. Lives of Jesus Series. Philadelphia: Fortress Press, 1970.

Teicher, Jacob L. "Jesus in the Habakkuk Scroll." *Journal of Jewish Studies* 3/2, 67–99.

Templeton, Charles. *Act of God*. New York: Little Brown, 1978. Reprinted, New York: Bantam Books, 1979.

Thiering, Barbara. *Jesus and the Riddle of the Dead Sea Scrolls: Unlocking the Secrets of his Life Story*. San Francisco: HarperCollins, 1992.

———. *Jesus the Man*. London: Transworld Publishers, 1993.

———. *Redating the Teacher of Righteousness*. Sydney: Theological Explorations, 1979.

Thompson, Thomas L. *The Mythic Past: Biblical Archaeology and the Myth of Israel*. London: Random House, 1999.

Thorne, Guy. *When It Was Dark: The Story of a Great Conspiracy*. London: Greening & Co., LTD, 1904.
Tierney, Richard L. *The Scroll of Thoth: Tales of Simon Magus and the Great Old Ones*. Oakland: Chaosium, 1997.
Tillich, Paul. *Dynamics of Faith*. World Perspectives Series Volume X. New York: Harper & Row Torchbooks, 1957.
———. *Systematic Theology II: Existence and the Christ*. Chicago: University of Chicago Press, 1957.
Todorov, Tzvetan. "The Typology of Detective Fiction." In *The Poetics of Prose*, translated by Richard Howard, 42–53. Ithaca: Cornell University Press, 1977.
Torrey, Charles Cutler. *Our Translated Gospels*. New York: Harper & Brothers, 1936.
Train, Arthur. *The Lost Gospel*. New York: Charles Scribner's Sons, 1925.
Trobisch, David. *The First Edition of the New Testament*. New York: Oxford University Press, 2000.
———. "Who Published the New Testament?" *Free Inquiry* 28/1 (Dec. 2007–Jan. 2008) 30–33.
Udny, E. Francis. "Introduction" to G. J. Ouseley, *The Gospel of the Holy Twelve*. London: Edson, new edition, 1923.
Vogt, P. *Der Stammbaum bei den heiligen Evangelisten Matthäus*. Biblische Studien 13/3. Freiburg: Herder, 1907.
Wainwright, Arthur W. *The Trinity in the New Testament*. London: SPCK, 1969.
Wallace, Irving. *The Word*. New York: Simon & Schuster, 1972. Reprinted Pocket Books, 1973.
Watts, Alan W., Timothy Leary, Richard Alpert (Ram Dass). *The Joyous Cosmology: Adventures in the Chemistry of Consciousness*. New York: Vintage, 1962.
Wellman, Manly Wade. "The Terrible Parchment." In *The Necronomicon: Selected Stories and Essays Concerning the Blasphemous Tome of the Mad Arab*, 4–10. 2nd ed. Edited by Robert M. Price. Cycle Horror Series. Oakland: Chaosium, 2002.
Wells, G. A. *The Jesus of the Early Christians: A Study in Christian Origins*. London: Pemberton Books, 1971.
Whittemore, Edward. *The Sinai Tapestry*. New York: Holt, Rinehart and Wilson, 1977. Reprinted, New York: Avon Books, 1978.
Widengren, Geo. *Mani and Manichaeism*. Translated by Charles Kessler. History of Religion Series. New York: Holt, Rinehart and Winston, 1965.
Wilken, Robert L. *The Myth of Christian Beginnings: History's Impact on Belief*. Garden City: Doubleday Anchor, 1972.
Wood, Barbara. *The Magdalene Scrolls*. New York: Doubleday, 1978. Reprinted, New York: Avon Books, 1978.
———. *The Prophetess*. New York: Little, Brown & Company, 1996. Reprinted, New York: Warner Books, 1997.
Wrede, Wilhelm. *Paul*. Translated by Edward Lummis. London: Philip Green, 1907.
Zindler, Frank. *The Jesus the Jews Never Knew: Sepher Toldoth Yeshu and the Quest of the Historical Jesus in Jewish Sources*. Cranford: American Atheist Press, 2003.

www.ingramcontent.com/pod-product-compliance
Lightning Source LLC
Chambersburg PA
CBHW052052300426
44117CB00012B/2085